Teaching Persons with Mental Retardation

Teaching Persons with Mental Retardation

A Model for Curriculum Development and Teaching

Richard B. Dever
Indiana University

Dennis R. Knapczyk
Indiana University

Brown & Benchmark
PUBLISHERS

Madison, WI Dubuque Guilford, CT Chicago Toronto London
Mexico City Caracas Buenos Aires Madrid Bogotá Sydney

Book Team

Executive Publisher *Edgar J. Laube*
Managing Editor *Sue Pulvermacher-Alt*
Developmental Editor *Suzanne M. Guinn*
Publishing Services Coordinator *Peggy Selle*
Proofreading Coordinator *Carrie Barker*
Photo Editor *Rose Deluhery*
Production Manager *Beth Kundert*
Design and New Media Development Manager *Linda Meehan Avenarius*
Production/Costing Manager *Sherry Padden*
Visuals/Design Freelance Specialist *Mary L. Christianson*
Marketing Manager *Amy Halloran*
Copywriter *Jennifer Smith*

Basal Text *10/12 Palatino*
Display Type *Helvetica Bold*
Typesetting System *Macintosh*™
    QuarkXPress™
Paper Stock *50# Restore Cote*
Production Services *Impressions Book and
    Journal Services, Inc.*

Executive Vice President and General Manager *Bob McLaughlin*
Vice President, Business Manager *Russ Domeyer*
Vice President of Production and New Media Development *Victoria Putman*
National Sales Manager *Phil Rudder*
National Telesales Director *John Finn*

 A Times Mirror Company

Cover design by Kay Fulton Design

Cover image © Diana Ong/SUPERSTOCK

Copyedited by Erin Falligant; Proofread by Francine Buda Banwarth

Library of Congress Catalog Card Number: 96–83803

ISBN 0–697–20559–2

Printed in the United States of America by Times Mirror Higher Education Group, Inc.,
2460 Kerper Boulevard, Dubuque, IA 52001

10 9 8 7 6 5 4 3 2 1

TABLE OF CONTENTS

INTRODUCTION TO PART I   5

5   Developing a Curriculum   113

INTRODUCTION TO PART III   153

---

6   Planning an Assessment of Curriculum Objectives   155

9 Providing Information 245

10 Monitoring Instructional Plans 283

11 Modifying Instruction 307

PREFACE

This book has been in progress for nearly a quarter of a century. In a very real sense, it is the result of an odyssey that began when we first teamed up to conduct a teacher training program in 1973 and realized that we did not know very much about the instruction of persons with mental retardation. Consequently, we had little to teach our students, and it worried us enough to make us begin the work that resulted in this book. In the intervening years, we have thought long and hard about how to provide high-quality instruction to persons with mental retardation, and our work has undergone many fits and starts and long pauses while we grouped and regrouped our ideas and experiences. After many false starts and many fights about which road to take, we now think that we finally have begun to understand the problem and how to address it. This book presents the solution we have developed. It has been a long time in coming, and we hope the reader finds the book to have been worth the time and effort.

We would like to thank the following individuals for their professional assistance in reviewing the manuscript. Their insights and suggestions greatly improved this work.

Reuben Altman
University of Missouri–
  Columbia

Richard W. Brimer
Southern Illinois University

Jim Burns
College of St. Rose

Mary Lynne Calhoun
The University of North
  Carolina–Charlotte

William G. Callahan
University of Nebraska–Omaha

John H. Hoover
The University of North Dakota

Greg Prater
Murray State University

Richard F. Rodriguez
Western New Mexico

Richard A. Shade
University of Wyoming–
  Laramie

Prologue

Special education and rehabilitation services have not lived up to their shared responsibility of preparing persons with mental retardation to participate effectively in the daily life of the community. Many studies demonstrate how persons with mental retardation make less than satisfactory adjustments to adult life. For example, students with mental retardation who complete school programs tend to obtain very low-level employment, or they do not become employed at all (Afflek, Edgar, Levine, and Kortering, 1990; Edgar, 1987; Frank, Sitlington, Cooper, and Cool, 1990; Hasazi, Gordon, and Roe, 1985; Hasazi, Gordon, Roe, Hull, Finck, and Salembier, 1985). In addition, the number of young people who drop out of school is appalling: Nationally, the estimates of the number of students with disabilities who drop out of school range from 25% to 50%, depending on how the data are gathered (*Education Daily*, 1990; Sinclair, Christianson, Thurlow, and Evelo, 1994). Increasingly, literature suggests that the instructional needs of individuals with mental retardation, especially those with mild mental retardation, are not being met by current programs, and that these programs are greatly in need of revision (Afflek et al., 1990; Edgar, 1987; Patton, Cronin, Polloway, Hutchinson, and Robinson, 1989).

Remedial instruction obviously has failed to prepare persons with mental retardation for adult life (Edgar, 1987). Inclusion programs have been touted as "the answer" to the question of how to improve the quality of public school programs (e.g., Fuchs and Fuchs, 1994; Kaufman, 1993; Will, 1986), and indeed, those of us who work with students and staff in the public schools have seen some astonishing changes in the learning patterns of many elementary-age students with mild disabilities. But many of these same students begin to experience inordinate difficulties as soon as they reach the middle or junior high level when they begin to encounter the more rigidly academic curriculum that is found at this level. There is little data available on the efficacy of inclusion programs in the public schools, but in our personal experience, the drop-out rate doesn't seem to be affected very much by participation in even the best inclusion programs; therefore, we are skeptical that the drop-out and employment statistics will improve as a result of inclusion.

One reason that inclusion programs may fail to meet the needs of students with mental retardation is that the curriculum used in general education focuses mostly on getting young people ready for college, even when it is "watered down" in courses like Pre-Algebra and General English. Simply stated, this focus seems to be completely inappropriate for the instruction of students with mental retardation and also of those who experience other difficulties in learning academics (Bursick and Epstein, 1986). This focus on academics is a likely source of the drop-out problem in special education because young people may fail to see the relevance of much of the instruction they receive in secondary schools (Gajar, Goodman, and McAfee, 1993). Consequently, they may leave school before they complete their programs (Edgar, 1987; Sinclair et al., 1994).

Clark (1984) points out that secondary and adult instruction for people with mental retardation needs to be different from that provided in elementary education and that instructors of adolescents and adults with mental retardation should develop instructional skills that are consonant with the needs of their learners. Clark, Falvey (1986), and others further point out that this instruction should be functional, age-specific, and geared to preparing the learners for life in the community. Although these ideas are eminently sensible, they have not gained general acceptance (Halpern and Benz, 1987).

Vocational instruction alone does not address all the problems that individuals with mental retardation face in adjusting to community life or in their social interactions in the community at large (Halpern, 1985). We believe that all service programs must be reconceptualized in terms of instructing people with mental retardation to take control over their own lives. A clear focus on instruction can address many of the adjustment problems they experience. By "instruction," we refer to the age-old idea that first, it is necessary to discover what we must teach (the instructional goals), and second, it is necessary to work out useful ways in which to teach (the instructional methodology). Instruction cannot be done in any other way.

Researchers and practitioners have long agreed that people with mental retardation need goal-driven instruction (e.g., Brown, Branston, Hamre-Nietupski, Johnson, Wilcox, and Gruenewald, 1979; Brown, Branston, Hamre-Nietupski, Pumpian, Certo, and Gruenewald, 1979; Guess et al., 1978; Orelove and Sobsey, 1987; Sailor and Guess, 1983; Snell, 1983; Wilcox and Bellamy, 1987). In fact, both PL 94-142 (the Education for all Handicapped Children Act) and PL 101-476 (the Individuals with Disabilities Education Act) and their subsequent federal and state regulations require statements of long-term and short-term goals as part of the program of instruction for every learner with disabilities. Thus, it is clear that there is general support for the concept of goal-driven instruction for persons with mental retardation. It is also clear, however, that there is not much agreement on what the goals of instruction for persons with mental retardation should be. In fact, very few workers in the field have even attempted to address the subject of goals in any organized manner (Brolin, 1993; Dever, 1988; Disability Research Systems, Inc., 1991, 1992a).

There is also little or no agreement on what a curriculum should contain. The concept of curriculum in special education and rehabilitative services is currently so broad that the term has no real meaning. For example, documents called "curricula" can include (1) student activity guides; (2) descriptions of teaching methodologies; (3) suggestions for developing individualized programs of instruction; (4) randomly sequenced lists of skills (sometimes analyzed in great detail); (5) statements of instructional foci or thrusts; and (6) instructional sequences leading to clearly stated behavioral goals (Knapczyk, 1988). The confusion surrounding curriculum development in the field of mental retardation is often manifested by a lack of coordinated instruction across instructors and across schools and other agencies (Wehman, Kregel, Barcus, and Schalock, 1986).

Thus, on the one hand, professionals seem to agree that people with mental retardation require instruction, and on the other, we don't seem to have a firm grasp on the fundamental concepts of instruction. We will try to resolve this dilemma in this book by setting forth a system of thought about instruction that has been used to good effect for many years. Our thesis is that our job is to try to teach people with mental retardation not to need us, and we present a way by which we can accomplish this goal. Thus, this book calls into question many of the current instructional practices and generates an entirely new approach that, paradoxically, is as old as humankind.

Introduction

In Part I, we focus on three questions:

1. What is instruction?
2. Who are people with mental retardation?
3. What is the content of instruction for people with mental retardation?

These questions are extremely important because the way in which we answer them largely determines the manner in which we are able to respond to people with mental retardation. If we, as instructors, can answer these questions, we will have an understanding of instruction, of who people with mental retardation are, and of who we want them to become. Given this understanding, we will be able to develop the instructional programs that will help our learners get ready to leave us.

In Chapter 1, we will start our explanation of how to develop instructional programs by explaining instruction. Actually, our version of this concept is very old and well established; that is, instruction begins with a description of what the learners will become when all instruction is complete. This description allows the instructors to establish the skills learners must acquire, and then, by working backward from those skills, to discover what to teach the learners when they first enter their instructional programs.

In Chapter 2, we focus on the questions of "Who are people with mental retardation?" and "What should they *become* as a result of their instruction?" The answers to these questions will help us establish what we must teach them to do and govern everything else that we must do to teach. Thus, the two chapters in Part I establish the framework for the systematic approach to organizing and delivering instruction that we present in the rest of the book.

CHAPTER 1

Overview

This book expresses our conviction that the job of those of us who work with people with mental retardation is to try to teach them how to control their own lives. The conviction that persons with mental retardation should not have to rely on the assistance of paid staff contains within it the belief that our primary task is to teach. The focus of their instruction is how not to need us.

Our view resonates with the perceptions of a number of professionals and paraprofessionals in the field, but until now, it has not found an expression that allows the necessary instructional programs to be generated. Unfortunately, our ideas also clash with the views of many professionals, paraprofessionals, and laypeople, and consequently, this book may prove somewhat controversial. Nevertheless, the techniques that we will present will help those who work with people with mental retardation generate programs of instruction that assist their learners in attaining the dignity of being able to do for themselves.

We do not for one moment believe that every person with mental retardation is capable of learning to take full control over his or her own life, but we do believe that our job is to try to get each one of them to come as close as possible to this ideal. The more that people with mental retardation can learn to do for themselves, the closer they will come to being fully franchised members of our society. The mechanism for helping them do it is instruction. Purely and simply, our job is to teach, and this book presents a set of techniques for teaching.

The tool we will use is the **Instructional Model** (Dever, 1988, 1989). This model states that instructional personnel must perform six actions (see Figure 1.1). While the steps in this model look simple at first glance, carrying out all of them will require many of the staff members who work with people with mental retardation to alter the way they think about people with mental retardation. Specifically, the shift is to stop thinking in terms of

6

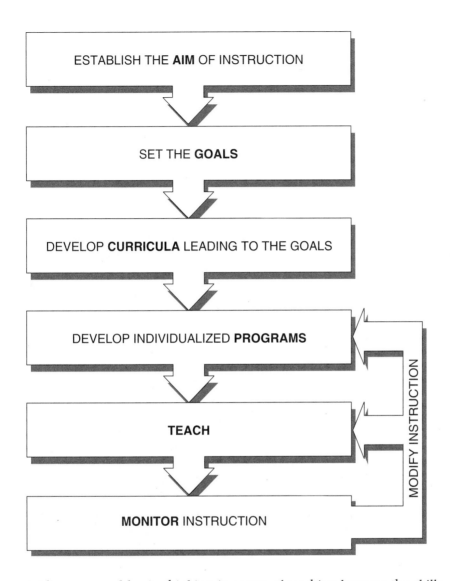

FIGURE 1.1
The Instructional Model.

ESTABLISH THE **AIM** OF INSTRUCTION

SET THE **GOALS**

DEVELOP **CURRICULA** LEADING TO THE GOALS

DEVELOP INDIVIDUALIZED **PROGRAMS**

TEACH

MONITOR INSTRUCTION

MODIFY INSTRUCTION

providing care and begin thinking in terms of teaching learners the skills that will reduce their dependency on staff assistance.

The good news is that the Instructional Model contains nothing new; that is, it represents exactly the way in which instruction has been conceived since humanity began, and millennia of use have shown that it is possible to develop good instructional programs for learners. We believe that it is possible to develop excellent instruction for people with mental retardation, as well, but typically, the steps required to do so have not been carried out for persons with mental retardation in the past. Therefore, beginning the process can be rather like entering uncharted waters for most workers in the field.

A View of Mental Retardation

Since perceptions are the only reality we know (Powers, 1973), there is no question that the way in which we perceive people determines how we act toward them. For example, if we perceive a person to be "good," "fun," or "pleasant to be with," we are more likely to interact with that person than if we believe him or her to be "odious," "tedious," or "repulsive." If everybody thinks the same way about an individual, then everybody will respond in approximately the same manner to that person.

How do we perceive people with mental retardation? Some laypeople (and even some professionals), due to persistent remnants of perceptions from times past, see people with mental retardation as "menaces to society" or "eternal children" (Wolfensberger, 1972). These views cause us to exclude people with mental retardation from society; indeed, in past years, we have locked them away in public residential facilities, kept them in special classes down by the boiler room, put them in sheltered workshops, and placed them behind closed doors in nursing homes, group homes, and other service facilities. All of these actions seem to serve the same function: to keep people with mental retardation out of society. However, we are convinced that our job is to accomplish just the opposite, that is, to help them become full members of society (Brolin, 1995; McGee, Menoloscino, Hobbs, and Menousek, 1987; Nirje, 1969; Wolfensberger, 1972). Instruction is the tool we can use to accomplish this goal.

Many people believe that people with mental retardation cannot learn to do very much, and as a consequence, do not try very hard to teach them. For example, in past years, we have seen entire curricula that focused on teaching little more than circles, squares, and triangles. However, after Marc Gold (1980a, 1980b) began to teach people with severe mental retardation to do industrial-type assembly work, professionals in the field finally began to believe that it is possible for people with mental retardation to learn to perform many vocational tasks. Since that time, the field has seen many new ideas develop (especially in the vocational area), and the idea that people with mental retardation can learn has taken hold in many places.

Unfortunately, the latest idea to come along is that we must provide people with mental retardation with "supports" (Luckasson, 1992). This concept seems to encourage the toleration of dependency because it does not focus on teaching people to gain control over their own lives. To those of us who believe that we must teach, the idea that we should support people as they are is anathema because it allows us to tolerate the status quo. That is, by supporting people with mental retardation as they are, we perpetuate their isolation and dependency. Frankly, we see little or no role for a teacher in the concept of supports. Our view is that we must try as hard as we can to teach people with mental retardation not to need us. Those whose vocation is teaching must help those who must learn, and our job is to help our learners develop the true dignity that comes from being contributing members of the community.

Teaching

In our minds, a teacher is someone who tries to help his or her learners become peers through the use of instruction. The very best thing that can happen to any teacher is to wave "good-bye" to his or her students, believing that they will return later to tell about all the good and wonderful things they have been able to do as a result of the instruction they received. Success in helping people to not need the teacher anymore is the highest good.

We believe that *everybody* who works directly with people with mental retardation must see themselves as teachers. In making this statement, we include the learner's parents because they have the greatest stake in ensuring that their child makes progress. In the final analysis, parents are the ones who must deal with the results of a lack of instruction, and other than the people with mental retardation themselves, parents are the ones who will have the most to gain when their children become functioning adults as a result of good instruction.

No matter what job titles professional and paraprofessional staff may have, they are teachers. This statement is true whether we work in infant and toddler programs, public schools, adult rehabilitation programs, residential facilities, or any other programs in which people with mental retardation are found. However, because there is a very strong cognitive association between the term *teacher* and the public schools, we will not use this word in the following chapters. Instead, we will use the more generic term *instructor* to designate both parents and the staff who work directly with people with mental retardation. Together, parents and staff should work toward the same end: to teach people with mental retardation to take their places in society and to behave in such a way that they seem to be typical community residents.

The Present Status of Instruction

Many current studies have demonstrated that persons with mental retardation make less than satisfactory adjustments to adult life. Nationally, estimates of the number of young people with mental retardation who drop out of secondary school prior to completing their educational programs range from 25% to 50%, and most of these dropouts have mild mental retardation (*Education Daily*, 1990; Sinclair et al., 1994). In addition, the students with mental retardation who do complete school generally obtain very low-level employment, or they do not become employed at all (Edgar, 1987; Frank et al., 1990; Hasazi, Gordon, and Roe, 1985). Increasingly, the literature suggests that the needs of individuals with mental retardation, especially those with mild mental retardation, are not being met by instructional programs currently found in schools and that these programs are greatly in need of revision (Afflek et al., 1990; Patton et al., 1989).

Much of the preparation of professionals who teach adolescents and adults with mental retardation tends to be inadequate. In the public schools, personnel preparation seems to be one-sided. That is, although elementary and secondary school programs should have very different instructional content, and possibly a different system of instructional delivery (Clark, 1984), only a few states separate elementary and secondary special education teacher certification. As could be predicted, the states that do separate them provide more training in secondary instruction (Bursick and Epstein, 1986). Unfortunately, however, because so few teacher education programs focus on preparing special education teachers to work at the secondary level, most preservice special educators learn to do the work of elementary teachers. The result is that those who teach in secondary schools tend to get mostly on-the-job training for the instructional role they must play. Even in states that certify elementary and secondary special education teachers separately, there tends to be a discrepancy between recommended and actual practice in that most of the instruction focuses on remedial academics rather than community preparation (Bursick and Epstein, 1986). This focus may shed light on the drop-out problem in secondary special education. If young people fail to see the relevance of much of the instruction they receive in the secondary schools, they may be more apt to leave school before completing their programs (Edgar, 1987; Sinclair et al., 1994).

The situation in adult rehabilitation programs seems even worse. Except for a few rehabilitation counselors and some vocational rehabilitation specialists who are trained to work in supported employment or sheltered work, most people who work with adults with mental retardation get very little training at all. Line staff who work in adult services, which include vocational programs, residential programs, and day programs, tend to have little or no training, and most have to "reinvent" the job when they get hired to work with people with mental retardation.

Clark (1984) points out that instruction at secondary and adult levels needs to be different from that provided at the elementary level, and that instructors of adolescents and adults need to develop teaching skills that are consonant with the needs of their learners. Clark, Falvey (1986), Wilcox and Bellamy (1987), and others further point out that this instruction should be functional and age-specific. Although these ideas are eminently sensible, they have not gained general acceptance (Halpern and Benz, 1987).

Edgar (1987) believes that the typical focus on remedial academic instruction has failed young people with mental retardation, and that radical curriculum changes are in order. These changes include the following: secondary curricula should become community-based (Falvey, 1986); secondary curricula should become functional in nature (Hamill and Dunlevy, 1993b); and remedial academics as the central program thrust should be reconsidered. Other authors agree with this assessment (e.g., Clark, 1984; Polloway, Patton, Smith, and Roderique, 1991). We would add that these same changes should occur at the adult level as well. If they should take place, they would cause a metamorphosis in the conduct of *all* instructional programs for people with mental retardation. That is, the changes made at the secondary and adult levels would reverberate throughout the system, right down through the preschool years.

Some of the needed changes have already begun to appear. Given the pioneering work of Gold (1980a, 1980b), Rusch, Sowers, Connis, and Thompson (1977), and Wehman and Hill (1980), vocational programming (especially for adolescents and adults with moderate and severe mental retardation) has improved enormously over what it was at the beginning of the 1980s, and the progress made in this area also may portend changes in other areas of instruction (Powell, Pancsofar, Steere, Butterworth, Itzkowitz, and Rainforth, 1991; Wehman, Moon, Everson, Wood, and Barcus, 1988). But vocational instruction alone does not address the problems that these individuals face in adjusting to community life or their need for social skills training (Halpern, 1985). Other changes must be made as well.

The reader will note that much of the previous discussion focuses on the secondary and adult levels. This focus was deliberate, because any changes that take place in the instruction of persons with mental retardation will have to begin at this point. The Instructional Model holds that all instruction begins at the end and works backward to determine what to teach at the beginning. To develop effective programs of instruction at the elementary and preschool levels, we must be able to look at the child and see the adult he or she will become. This book is concerned with instruction of persons with mental retardation at all ages, but if we do not begin at the secondary and adult levels, we will never truly find out what we must teach younger children.

Instruction and People with Mental Retardation

Instruction has been an important issue among people who work in mental retardation services ever since these services began in this country in the middle 1800s (Scheerenberger, 1981), and currently, a great deal of instruction takes place all across the country. In this section, we will focus on the system that generates this instruction and compare it to the system of instruction found in general education at all levels. The parallels and differences between the two systems will help us understand what we have to do to make instruction effective for people with mental retardation.

Instruction for People with Mental Retardation Compared with Instruction in General Education

It is clear that persons with mental retardation do not receive the same kind of organized instruction that people in general education get at all levels, from preschool through graduate school. The major exceptions to this statement are in the following instances:

- when young people with mental retardation are included in general education classes in the public schools (and therefore participate in the general education curriculum); and
- when people with mental retardation are placed in programs that teach specific skills, such as those taught in supported employment and other highly focused instructional programs.

Other than in these instances, instruction of persons with mental retardation tends not to be oriented toward obtaining clear results, perhaps because instruction in special education and rehabilitation services focuses on something quite different from instruction in general education. The differences between the two systems do not mean that one system is "good" and the other "bad." On the contrary, there is much good in both systems, and if the best could be taken from both, better instructional programs could be developed for learners with mental retardation.

Instruction in General Education

Traditionally, public school instruction has been organized around explicitly stated curriculum goals and objectives that lay out the content of instruction (Bloom, 1956). These goals and objectives focus primarily on academic areas, such as language arts, social studies, and mathematics, and for the most part, consist of the skills that learners need to have to enter college (except in a few peripheral subjects, such as art, physical education, and driver education).

As students go through the system, instruction builds grade-by-grade on the foundations laid by earlier instruction. For example, teachers in the third grade work to make students ready to go to fourth grade, and teachers in junior high school work to get their students ready to go to senior high school. By the culmination of their public school years, young people who have learned what they are supposed to learn and who have demonstrated their proficiency by earning good grades are allowed to go on to college. To view the continuity in the system, consider the connection between learning the letters of the alphabet in kindergarten, on the one hand, and reading textbooks for college courses on the other, and between learning the Arabic numeral system as children and mastering the material covered in college level math courses as young adults.

Note, too, that instruction in general education is similar at each grade level across geographical areas. That is, a student at any level who leaves his or her current public school and moves clear across the country will find little or no difference in the content of instruction in the old and new locations (although some may find themselves ahead of or behind their new classmates). In general, the content of instruction in all schools progresses in an orderly fashion toward college entrance, a fact that *requires* instruction to be consistent across schools, and even across instructors. This statement is true even when the subject matter has been "watered down" for slower learners. That is, academic work for those not going on to postsecondary education is usually a simpler version of the college preparatory work and appears in similar forms in schools all across the country.

Instruction in Special Education and Rehabilitation Services

Instruction in special education, residential services, and vocational rehabilitation generally stands in sharp contrast to the system found in general education because it is oriented toward the individual. The result is that what one instructor teaches is usually not connected with what another teaches, even when the two instructors teach the same learner in the same time period. Unlike general education, it is very difficult to predict what instructors will teach learners with mental retardation just by considering demographic factors such as age, disability, or functioning level (unless they are being included in general education settings). And, unlike students in general education, persons with mental retardation do not progress from one level to the next in an orderly fashion. In fact, most instructional experiences for people with mental retardation do not provide preparation for the next level.

Thus, the two systems appear to do very different things, and naturally, they have very different results. In order to clarify the task for those who must develop instructional programs for persons with mental retardation, let us examine the question of why these different conditions prevail.

Causes and Effects of the Different Systems

The differences between the two instructional systems seem to be rooted in the understanding of "instruction" held by those who work in each system. The concept is quite different for the two groups and requires very different actions on the part of the people who work in the two systems.

General Education Focuses on Content.   Most Americans would agree that instruction in general education attends first to the content of instruction and second to the needs of individuals who are learning the content. To illustrate this point, consider that regular education curricula are usually in place *before* students enter the classrooms because they are set by curriculum committees, school districts, state departments of education, or (perhaps most commonly) simply by the textbooks that teachers use. Thus, before children begin school, their course of study has already been established, and teachers at each grade level know exactly what they are supposed to teach before the students enter the classroom. These teachers plan instruction by assuming that their students have acquired certain skills before they enter the classroom and should have certain skills when they leave at the end of the school year. When students do not have those skills, they do not receive high grades and may even fail, in which case they are held back, sent to special education classrooms, or are passed on with the understanding that they will probably fail in later grades and eventually will drop out of school.

Traditionally, persons with mental retardation have fared very badly in this system (Franklin, 1994). At present, many schools with inclusion programs make accommodations for students who have difficulty while learning, and when these accommodations are made well, these students tend to do somewhat better. Nevertheless, even in these programs, the system remains basically the same and the emphasis is still on preparation for college.

Special Education and Rehabilitation Services Focus on the Individual.
The system for persons with mental retardation does not focus on instructional content, but rather, on individual differences and the problems that individuals encounter. As a result, instruction for persons with mental retardation is a kind of reverse image of that found in the general education system. That is, instructors of persons with mental retardation focus first on the problems experienced by individuals, and second on the content of instruction. This position nearly guarantees uncoordinated and discontinuous instruction because all decisions about instructional content are generated by the perceptions that instructors have of the needs of each individual learner. They are not based on commonly agreed-upon instructional goals.

Instructors of persons with mental retardation rarely perceive a clear end point of instruction for their learners; consequently, they have no external framework that will help them decide which skills to teach to their learners and in what sequence to teach them. Each instructor can (and often does) hold a different view of what learners with mental retardation should learn, and each naturally selects what to teach according to his or her own personal view. Consequently, each instructor may select very different things to teach to their learners. Interestingly, within the existing framework, each instructor can select appropriate skills to teach, even when the choices individual instructors make are very different from one another.

Needed: A Focus on Instructional Content

Since the beginning of the twentieth century, curriculum theorists have agreed that instruction must begin with a clear description of the aim and goals of instruction (e.g., Charters, 1923; Dewey, 1902; Tanner and Tanner, 1995). This traditional manner of developing instruction gives all instructors a view of the "big picture" and clarifies what instruction should accomplish. Curricula that lead toward clear end points give instructors a framework within which they can develop good individual programs of instruction. If instructors have good curricula, instruction can be progressive and lead learners in the direction of the goals regardless of their age or functional level. In other words, coherent, coordinated, and progressive instruction depends on the existence of clear end points toward which to teach. We believe that it is precisely the lack of clearly stated, commonly agreed-upon end points that has put instruction in mental retardation services into the position in which it finds itself today.

Impediments to Curriculum Development

Many professionals who work in mental retardation services believe that it simply is not possible to develop curricula for all persons with mental retardation since the learners present too much diversity in their skills and abilities. This perception is illustrated by the many writers who discuss the topic of developing instructional programs for individuals, but who do not address the process of constructing curricula that can guide the skill selection process (e.g., Certo, 1983; Falvey, 1986; Neel and Billingsley, 1989; Sailor and Guess, 1983; Snell and Browder, 1986; Wilcox and Bellamy, 1987).

The thesis of this book is that a type of traditional curriculum development for all persons with mental retardation is not only possible, but necessary before instruction truly can improve their chances of becoming independent. The idea that it is not possible to develop coherent, coordinated, and continuous curricula for persons with mental retardation simply is untrue. However, it *is* true that such curricula will require common agreement on the end points of instruction, and until such agreement is reached, curricula construction of the traditional type will be impossible.

Some of the new service delivery thrusts seem to be moving in this direction and attempting to combine the best of both systems of instruction. Many schools, residential settings, and rehabilitation units are beginning to focus on concepts such as inclusion, transition, and supported employment. Each of these thrusts is concerned with *both* the content of instruction and the needs of individuals. We believe that the successes being reported for these programs can be attributed to the merging of the two conceptual systems (Harris and Schutz, 1990; Villa, Thousand, Stainback, and Stainback, 1992). However, we also think that a greater focus on appropriate instructional content is required before adequate instruction is truly possible.

We are not suggesting that persons with mental retardation must go through the system of general education. The major problem with the inclusion of students with mental retardation in general education programs is that general education exists to prepare learners to go to college. The strength of this idea is indicated by the fact that to judge the quality of public schools, the general public turns to data from tests that try to predict how successful the students will be when they get to college (such as the SAT). Clearly, it is inappropriate to prepare persons with mental retardation to go to college, and thus, equally inappropriate to teach the content of general education to this group, even in its "watered down" form.

The data are not yet available to conclude whether the current concept of inclusion (CEC, 1993; Pugach, 1992; Will, 1986) is or is not a good thing, and for the moment, we must withhold judgment on it. However, in this book we *will* suggest that the entire instructional system for persons with mental retardation should be reconsidered from a different perspective. That is, we first should try to determine the end points of their instruction, and second, try to determine how instruction for individuals with mental retardation relates to these end points. These acts can bring together the best features of both systems: features of mental retardation services and features of general education. Once we understand how to bring the two systems together, it will become possible to make whatever changes will benefit the learners the most.

Functional Instruction

As a matter of public policy, instructional programs for persons with mental retardation have been offered in predominantly segregated settings, such as state hospitals, sheltered workshops, separate schools, or self-contained special education classrooms. In many of these settings, the instructional staff has tried valiantly to teach a wide variety of skills that increase the learners' level of independence in the community. For example, many school teachers who work in segregated special education classrooms have attempted to teach their learners basic skills in areas such as personal care, hygiene, social etiquette, and meal preparation. These instructional efforts, however, have had little or no success in preparing persons with mental retardation to interact effectively in their communities (e.g., Afflek et al., 1990; Edgar, 1987; Frank et al., 1990; Halpern, 1985; Hasazi, Gordon, and Roe, 1985; Hasazi, Gordon, Roe, Hull, Finck, and Salembier, 1985). A major reason these programs have failed is that the instruction has taken place out of context: that is, instruction is provided in settings other than those in which the learner's performance ultimately must occur. Because people with mental retardation tend not to transfer the skills taught in contrived settings to the appropriate community locations, such instruction has little or no effect on their community functioning.

During the last few years, workers in the field of mental retardation have looked closely at the provision of services in segregated settings and have generally concluded that such services have not furthered the involvement of persons with mental retardation in their communities. In many instances, these services actually have worked against this involvement (Brown, Ford, et al., 1983; Falvey, 1986; Frank et al., 1990). Parents and professionals have teamed together to advocate for functional instruction as an alternative to remedial academic instruction that takes place in segregated settings. In **functional instruction,** the content of instruction consists of the skills people normally need to live out their lives in the community. It often

TABLE 1.1 Advantages of Functional Instruction As a Strategy for Teaching Learners with Mental Retardation

Functional Instruction

- guides decisions on what to teach;
- can overcome the problems usually associated with transfer and generalization of behavior;
- provides models for appropriate behavior; and
- places realistic demands on learner behavior.

takes place in the community settings in which people normally interact and can be delivered in a variety of forms, including on-the-job vocational training, service learning, applied academics, and others.

Advantages of Functional Instruction

There is a growing body of research demonstrating that functional instruction can effectively prepare persons with mental retardation to be successful in their communities (Baker and Salon, 1986; Brickey, Campbell, and Browning, 1985; Halpern, 1985; Jacobs, 1978; Powell et al., 1991; Rhodes and Valenta, 1985; Wehman, Hill, Wood, and Parent, 1987). There are several compelling reasons to adopt functional instruction as a strategy in teaching learners to become independent (see Table 1.1).

Functional Instruction Guides Decisions on What to Teach

The content of instruction for people with mental retardation should be the skills that anyone needs to live, work, and play in the community in which they live. However, it is very difficult for instructors to teach or even to identify the necessary skills when they work with learners in segregated settings. We can gain a realistic picture of what people with mental retardation need to learn only when the community is used as the referent. Functional instruction allows us to identify the skills we need to teach. The arguments made by Wolfensberger for "normalization" (1972) and "social role valorization" (1983) support this statement, as does the work of a number of other researchers across the nation (e.g., Afflek et al., 1990; Browder and Snell, 1983; Brown et al., 1980; Brown, Ford, et al., 1983; Certo, 1983; Edgar, 1987; Falvey, 1986; Rusch and Mithaug, 1986; Sailor and Guess, 1983; Wehman and Kregel, 1985).

Functional Instruction Can Overcome the Problems Usually Associated with Transfer and Generalization of Behavior

Even when we know what skills people with mental retardation need to acquire, it is usually difficult, if not impossible, for them to use skills that they have learned out of context. Educators have traditionally assumed that the skills learned in classroom settings will transfer naturally to other settings, but research has shown that this assumption is inappropriate in the case of persons with mental retardation (Day and Horner, 1989; Hughes and Rusch, 1989; Park and Gaylord-Ross, 1989; Rusch and Hughes, 1989). Mental retardation can severely limit a person's ability to connect behavior learned under one set of conditions with the need to exhibit that behavior under another set of conditions. If we must teach skills to learners with mental retardation in segregated settings such as classrooms and sheltered workshops, we must also teach them to transfer and generalize these skills to the settings in which they would normally perform them.

Instruction carried out directly in the community can overcome many of the difficulties learners otherwise would experience when transferring skills to community settings. When instruction takes place directly in the community (a technique known as "community-based instruction"), everything to which the learners need to attend is already present, such as the behavioral cues upon which learners must focus when they actually use the skills and the outcomes that result from their use. To illustrate, trying to teach learners with mental retardation to carry an umbrella by using wall charts on a sunny day while the learners are in a classroom setting carries little or no meaning for many of them, but going outside when it is actually raining provides an important set of cues about when and why to carry an umbrella.

In a similar manner, it is very difficult to teach learners with mental retardation to perform skills in community settings that they have learned in segregated settings, because many of the variables related to performance are not present in the segregated settings (Brown, Ford, et al., 1983; Brown, Nisbet, et al., 1983; Falvey, 1986). In segregated settings, it is very difficult (and sometimes impossible) to duplicate the variables operating in natural settings. For example, a teacher who establishes a "store" in a classroom for the purpose of teaching purchasing skills will find it impossible to replicate many of the situations occurring naturally in stores. The customers waiting in line at a store's checkout counter are mostly adults who usually do not know each other, and the rules for interacting with strangers are in operation (Knapczyk, 1988). In contrast, all students in a classroom usually know each other quite well; therefore, the store setting is not duplicated. Many examples involving sheltered workshops, institutions, self-contained classes, and other segregated settings all point to the same problem: They are not community settings, and the rules that govern behavior in the community are not present, nor can they be. However, these problems usually can be overcome by providing instruction in the community.

Functional Instruction Provides Models for Appropriate Behavior

The behavioral models present in most community settings are usually quite appropriate to the setting and can be used to facilitate instruction. Since people in community settings are already doing the things that learners with mental retardation should do, their behavior can provide models of acceptable behavior, and the learners can be encouraged to imitate them. Recent studies have demonstrated, for example, that learners with mental retardation who have been behaving inappropriately in segregated settings will often begin to behave appropriately when they enter community settings (Baker and Salon, 1986; Berkman and Meyer, 1988). On the other hand, the behavioral models found in segregated settings are mostly those presented by other persons with mental retardation and do not illustrate what the learners are supposed to do (Brown, Ford, et al., 1983). When the behavioral models are inappropriate, many learners will begin to exhibit inappropriate behaviors.

Functional Instruction Places Realistic Demands on Learner Behavior

Learners in segregated settings often exhibit behavior that is quite different from the behavior exhibited by people in the community at large because segregated settings present different demands for generating behavior. In fact, segregated settings for persons with mental retardation usually seem to develop a culture of their own that is distinct in many ways from the culture of the world around them (Bercovici, 1981). This subculture, and the demands it places on learners, influences their perceptions and understanding of the world. Learners in segregated settings may, in fact, develop different perspectives on time, strategies for survival, information transfer, and other important matters. For example, they may become overly dependent on staff permission or respond only to tangible rewards. When such perspectives of the world are present, attempts to prepare the learners to interact successfully in the community may be futile because they may not be able to grasp the significance of the activities that are taking place around them.

Applied Academics: A Form of Functional Instruction

Applied academics (Hamill and Dunlevy, 1993b; Hamilton, 1980; Missouri LINC, 1989–90) is a form of functional instruction. For example, teaching math by having learners make purchases, build things, and fill out tax forms and teaching writing by having learners write "thank-you" letters for other persons or write reports on their job activities are all aspects of functional instruction. In fact, most academic subjects (English, mathematics, science, social studies, etc.) can be couched in terms of applied academics. We are very much in favor of teaching academics in this manner, especially to learners who have mild mental retardation and are capable of attaining a fair degree of academic success.

The advantages of functional instruction are great, and it is surprising that it has not been used more in instructional programs for persons with mental retardation. Under the definitions of mental retardation and independence presented in this book, however, there is no question that functional instruction must become a major focus of those working with persons with mental retardation.

Functional Instruction: A Useful Idea

Readers must not interpret our statements to mean that *all* instruction must take place in the community outside of schools, rehabilitation facilities, and residential units. On the contrary, we believe that elementary school children with mild mental retardation should be taught as many academic skills as possible because academic skills allow them to interact on a more equal footing with persons who do not have mental retardation. If they do learn such skills, they will be able to learn to do other things like fill out job applications, read the sports page in the local newspaper, and find out which stores have the best buys on food and clothing. In addition, children with mild, moderate, and severe mental retardation should learn to work and play with other children in a manner that will allow them to be accepted as peers in the society of children (Knapczyk, 1988).

However, functional instruction should take place in different locations at different ages. Instruction of preschool and elementary school children should occur in the locations in which other children are found, and for this group, functional instruction is instruction that takes place with children who do not have mental retardation. Certainly, this is not a new idea: Efforts to develop inclusion programs have focused on exactly this concept for some time (Harris and Schutz, 1990; Rotatori, Banbury, and Fox, 1987; Stevens, Blackhurst, and Magliocca, 1988). But as learners grow older, the focus of their instruction should shift from learning to do what other children do to learning to do what adults in our society do. Therefore, as the age of the learners increases, more and more instruction should take place in the community settings in which they live. By the time schoolchildren reach the secondary level, a great deal of their instruction should be taking place in the settings in which they will be expected to function when they leave the public school programs, and in adulthood, virtually all of the instruction of a person with mental retardation should take place in the community. Brolin (1993) similarly states that 90% of a learner's instruction during the elementary years should be academically oriented and 10% should be community based, and that the proportions should be reversed during the secondary years.

Overview of the Book

The flowchart illustrating the Instructional Model (see Figure 1.1) shows that the first step in planning instruction is to specify the aim of instruction, which indicates what the learners should *become* when all instruction has been completed. Once the aim has been established, it becomes possible to list clear instructional goals, the attainment of which will accomplish the aim. When the goals are available, the curriculum pathways that lead toward these goals can be laid out. Once the curriculum has been constructed, individual programs of instruction can be developed, and instruction can begin. If necessary, revisions can be made after instruction is under way.

This simple description of the Instructional Model is based on many years of curriculum theory and development (e.g., Charters, 1923; Dewey, 1902; Popham and Baker, 1970; Smith, Stanley, and Shores, 1957; Taba, 1962; Tanner and Tanner, 1995; Tyler, 1949). It seems natural to conceive of instruction in this fashion because it is pretty much the way it has been done for centuries. The Instructional Model focuses our attention on the most important aspects of instruction and forces us to approach it systematically. That is, if instruction is developed in the sequence suggested in the flowchart in Figure 1.1, it will be well-organized and deliberate, and it will maintain the conceptual checks and balances that keep instructors and other involved personnel on track. It will span the boundaries imposed by the characteristics of the learners and the different agencies that provide their instruction.

The following paragraphs give a brief description of each step in the Instructional Model. Each header refers to the corresponding box in the flowchart in Figure 1.1 and includes a notation on the chapter or chapters in which we will discuss each topic.

Establish the Aim of Instruction (Chapter 2)

The first step in applying the Instructional Model is to specify the aim of instruction, which states what the learner is supposed to *be* when instruction is complete. The statement of the instructional aim establishes the final outcome of instruction, and thus determines everything that will happen while developing instruction under the aegis of the aim. In a most fundamental way, specifying the aim of instruction clarifies the curricula that will be created to attain that aim. For example, if the aim of instruction is to prepare learners to be microbiologists, the curriculum will focus on training people to do the work that microbiologists do. If, on the other hand, the aim of instruction is to prepare learners to be carpenters, the curriculum must be structured to train people to do the work that carpenters do. Preparing carpenters to do the work that microbiologists do (or vice versa) would be inappropriate, but clearly stated aims for each of the instructional programs keep curricula development efforts for attaining those aims conceptually separate.

A clearly stated aim of instruction allows the instructional staff to develop clearly stated instructional goals because the aim establishes the parameters of instruction. If the aim of instruction is stated in a concise and understandable form, curriculum developers not only will be able to figure out appropriate instructional goals, they also will be able to identify any and all goals that are *not* focused on the aim. Thus, a curriculum designed to train carpenters probably wouldn't include the goal "identify bacterial organisms," whereas a curriculum designed to train microbiologists probably would.

When specifying the aim of instruction, it is necessary to recognize that a high-level aim does not obligate learners to accomplish that aim. It is a simple truth that instruction is not always successful because human beings have limitations in ability, interests, and/or endurance, and consequently, some learners may never reach the end of a curriculum. However, it is often the case that learners will benefit from instruction even if they do not complete a curriculum.

To use a personal example, consider that most mathematics curricula have the ultimate aim of producing research mathematicians. However, the authors of this text, like many other people, have been quite unsuccessful in learning higher math, and will probably never become research mathematicians. This is not to say that the mathematics curricula have been of no benefit to us, because we can balance our checkbooks, figure the number of board feet in a stack of lumber, and judge travel times and distances quite accurately. Thus, even though we have not reached the end of the mathematics curriculum, the parts that we have completed have increased our functional skills. This example illustrates that *learner progress* in a curriculum may sufficiently justify its creation. In the case of persons with mental retardation, as long as the aim is appropriate for the most proficient members of the group, it will benefit those who are less proficient and who will never progress all the way through curricula developed within its context.

Establish the Goals of Instruction (Chapters 3 and 4)

Instructional goals are statements of what learners are supposed to be able to *do* when all instruction is complete. Whereas the aim of instruction can be expressed with a noun ("The learner will be a *noun*"), goals refer to future learner behavior and must be expressed with verbs ("The learner will *verb*").

Instructional goals are important because it is necessary to understand the end of instruction before trying to find out what to teach learners who are just beginning. That is, the beginning steps in any instructional program cannot be specified until the end is known. Thus, instructional goals help curriculum developers construct curriculum pathways toward the goals.

Furthermore, once the goals of instruction are established, coordinated instruction across instructors and agencies becomes possible because everyone who teaches will understand what the learner must learn to do. All instructors can then focus their energies on helping the learners make progress toward the goals. Thus, as John Dewey (1902) observed, goals clarify the present direction in which the instruction should proceed and guide the ongoing thrust of instruction even if the end will not be reached for a long time.

This is not to say that goal specification is easy even if the aim is stated clearly. The process of constructing a statement of goals can be very difficult because although the first few goals may come easily, complete statements of goals require consideration of all possibilities. Establishing these statements can consume a lot of time and effort. In addition, once all the possibilities have been considered, all goals not within the parameters established by the aim must be deleted so that only the goals that are focused on the stated aim of instruction remain.

Develop Curricula (Chapter 5)

After the goals of instruction have been stated clearly, the next step in the Instructional Model is to develop a curriculum that helps learners attain those goals. A curriculum is a list of the skills that anyone would have to acquire to reach an instructional goal. It consists of pathways of sequenced objectives that lay out the content of instruction required to attain the goals. Furthermore, curricula can be used to devise assessment instruments that will help instructors discover what to teach a learner "next."

For persons with mental retardation, separate curricula must be developed by each service agency and by each separate program area within an agency. Each agency and program area has a different instructional mission and performs a different function: Elementary schools can teach some things while adult job-training programs must teach other things. Programs in group homes will probably focus on teaching homemaking and community-living skills while programs in rehabilitation centers will focus on teaching vocational skills. In addition, a functional curriculum must account for the unique characteristics of the community in which the learners live. Even when similar skills are required of all learners, these skills must be performed differently in different locations because no two settings are exactly the same.

It is important to note, however, that even though each service agency in a community will develop different goals and different curricula, all of their curricula should point toward the same aim and all should work in concert with one another. If they do, learners will move smoothly from program to program and from agency to agency with little or no disruption in their instructional programs.

Develop Individualized Programs of Instruction (Chapters 6 and 7)

The next step in the Instructional Model is to develop individualized programs of instruction for specific learners. This action is required by federal and state laws for preschools, public schools, and adult service agencies. To develop a good program, the instructional staff must consider the individual's circumstances, the thrust of the agency, and the different skills that might increase the individual's level of functioning in the community.

The most effective individualized instruction occurs when an agency has a well-constructed curriculum to follow. An agency that takes the time to develop appropriate curricula will encourage its staff to focus its instructional energies on the areas that will produce the greatest benefits to the learners.

Instructional programs that progress toward clear goals will also bring a business-like atmosphere to the learning environment. When all staff members know that their work is to teach learners to perform specific skills, the conceptual focus of the staff will be on those skills, and the focus of the students or clients will follow that of the staff. When both staff and learners agree that instruction is taking place, a sense of purpose develops that will foster the further development of good instruction. Very different behaviors will begin to emerge from both staff and clients when an agency's programs are structured in the context of the Instructional Model.

Teach (Chapters 8 and 9)

Instruction is basically an information transmission process. That is, the instructor has information that the learner does not have and the instructor's job is to see to it that the learner gets that information. Teaching is indeed both an art and a science: The science of instruction is in discovering what to teach (the information), and the art is in finding ways to get the learner to acquire new skills and to use them when they are needed (the methodology).

There are only a very few ways to transmit information during instruction: An instructor can (a) tell the learner what to do (verbal instruction); (b) indicate what the learner will do through gestures; (c) show the learner what to do (demonstration); (d) guide the learner's body through the motions (manual guidance); or (e) make the learner discover what to do (learner search). All instructional methodologies are variations on one or more of these five basic mechanisms. The art of teaching is the quest for the combination of mechanisms that is "just right" for each learner.

The instructor who knows what to teach can usually figure out a way to teach it. Personnel preparation programs that focus on specific instructional methodologies mislead their trainees because there is no such thing as "The Way" to teach anything. In fact, instructional methods that are very good for some learners invariably turn out to be not very good for others, and it is axiomatic that what works for John does not always work for Mary. In fact, what works for Mary this week may not work for her next week, or even tomorrow. Methodology must vary to account for the demands of the moment.

Monitor Instruction (Chapters 10 and 11)

Attempts to teach may or may not result in the desired change(s) in learner behavior. Therefore, it is necessary to monitor instruction to see if it is working. The late Marc Gold's famous dictum, "Train, don't test!" (1980a) referred to this fact. Clear goals enable instructors to develop clear performance criteria and sound monitoring techniques. If instructors track the learner's skill acquisition as it advances (or does not advance) toward the goals, they can make whatever adjustments are necessary to keep instruction moving forward. In this sense, revision becomes an integral part of instruction, and adjustments can be made in a systematic and timely manner.

Concluding Statement

Instruction of persons with mental retardation should not be the mystery some people believe it to be. Rather, what an instructor needs to do at every step of the way can be very clear-cut and deliberate. Under the Instructional Model, teaching is simple to the extreme: We must first find out what a learner needs to learn to do, and then find a way to teach him or her to do it. The Instructional Model lays out the steps for accomplishing both of these goals. It is based on the premise that learners are people who lack information, and instructors are people who find ways to supply them with the information they require.

The rest of this text will be devoted to explaining how to apply the model in developing programs of instruction for persons with mental retardation. The next chapter begins this task by explaining how to establish the aim of instruction.

CHAPTER 2

The Aim of Instruction

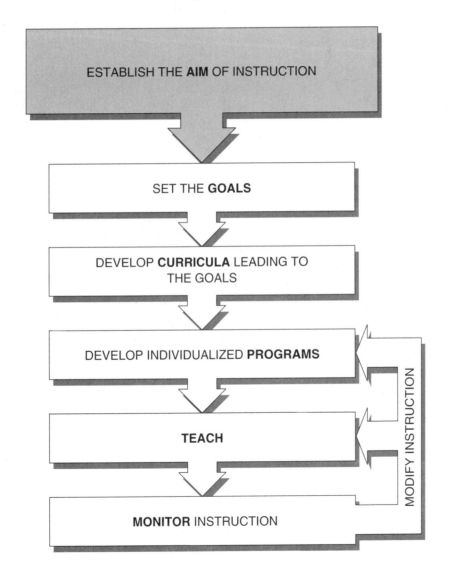

ESTABLISH THE **AIM** OF INSTRUCTION

SET THE **GOALS**

DEVELOP **CURRICULA** LEADING TO THE GOALS

DEVELOP INDIVIDUALIZED **PROGRAMS**

TEACH

MODIFY INSTRUCTION

MONITOR INSTRUCTION

In this chapter we will establish the aim (final outcome) of instruction for persons with mental retardation. This aim is in concert with the ideal expressed in Chapter 1 that our job is to teach people with mental retardation how not to need us. We will provide our rationale for this aim and explain its implications for planning instructional programs. However, the first thing we will do in this chapter is elaborate on our description of people with mental retardation, because this perception generates everything else we will say in this book.

An Instructional Definition of Mental Retardation

The definitions of mental retardation provided by groups such as the American Association on Mental Deficiency (Grossman, 1973, 1983; Heber, 1959, 1962; Luckasson, 1992) and others were all developed for administrative purposes. That is, they were developed to provide a framework for identification, classification, and placement activities, and for guiding many other administrative tasks that require categorization of people with mental retardation. However, they have not proven very useful to the people who must develop and deliver programs of instruction because their purpose is to discriminate those who have mental retardation from those who do not. A different definition of mental retardation could better help instructional personnel do their jobs by providing a set of clear-cut guidelines for planning and providing services.

The following definition provides a clear direction for service delivery. This definition, proposed by Dever (1989), reflects the perception that persons with mental retardation require instruction and provides a foundation for developing instructional programs.

> A person with **mental retardation** is someone who requires specific training in skills that most people acquire incidentally and which skills enable people to live in the mainstream of the community without supervision.

This definition presents people with mental retardation as individuals who require *instruction* in the skills that most of us learn incidentally. It states that this instruction should focus on the skills that will help people with mental retardation live, work, and recreate in their communities with no more support than that which would be required by any other person. That is, instruction should enable people with mental retardation to (1) make the same types of choices as anyone else would make about where to go and what to do and (2) act on these choices without undue reliance on either the direction or assistance of other people.

Although this definition describes what people with mental retardation are like, it is not an *administratively* useful definition because it cannot be used to discriminate all members of the class of "mentally retarded" from all nonmembers of the class. In fact, many individuals who do not have mental retardation could also benefit from instruction that helps them to live and work more independently in their communities. Therefore, this definition cannot be used either to classify people or to guide the allocation of funds and personnel. But it was not constructed to do these things. Rather, the definition highlights the types of services that we should provide to persons with mental retardation *after* they have been classified and declared eligible for services. It was developed to provide a formal set of guidelines for services and to serve as an adjunct to the definitions that focus on identification and classification.

The instructional definition of mental retardation was developed to guide the perceptions of staff who currently work with or who are in training to work with persons with mental retardation. It sets up expectations among those who provide services about the outcomes of the instructional programs. For this reason, the utility of the definition cannot be underestimated because, as we have stated previously, perceptions guide our behavior and ultimately affect the type of services we provide to persons with mental retardation. When they are guided by this definition, those who provide services to people with mental retardation will be well on their way to developing good instructional programs.

Corollaries to the Instructional Definition of Mental Retardation

Definitions often have corollaries that express the perceptions that flow from them. The corollaries that accompany the instructional definition of mental retardation (see Table 2.1) do three things:

1. clarify the concepts inherent in the definition;
2. state its implications for service delivery; and
3. show how the definition can be used to devise effective instructional programs for persons with mental retardation (Dever, 1989).

Corollary 1: Persons with Mental Retardation Can Learn

Perhaps the biggest deterrent to the instruction of persons with mental retardation has been a limited view held by many parents and professionals of their ability to learn. Corollary 1 states that these limitations are imposed by others and are not inherent in the persons themselves (Gold, 1980a). It may be true that persons with mental retardation learn more slowly than those without mental retardation and that some require instruction that is exceptional, but research shows that having mental retardation does not mean that a person is incapable of learning (Berkman and Meyer, 1988; Gold, 1980b; Rusch, 1983; Snell, 1983; Wehman, Hill, Hill, Brooke, and Pendleton, 1986). In fact, most people with mental retardation learn quite well when instruction is carried out appropriately. Recent research shows that even persons with moderate and severe retardation who require very intense forms of instruction can learn to perform jobs and many other complicated tasks required for living in the community (e.g., Brickey et al., 1985; Browder and Snell, 1983; Jacobs, 1978; Rhodes and Valenta, 1985; Wehman et al., 1987).

TABLE 2.1 Corollaries to the Instructional Definition of Mental Retardation

1. Persons with mental retardation can learn.
2. The need for instruction is central to mental retardation. All other responses are secondary.
3. The degree of retardation is a function of the amount and intensity of the instruction required to teach the person to live in the community without supervision.
4. A person with mental retardation who learns to live in the community without supervision can no longer be called "mentally retarded."
5. Some persons with mental retardation will never be able to acquire enough skills to enable them to live in the community without supervision.
6. The aim of instruction is identical for all persons with mental retardation despite the fact that some persons will never attain it.

Those who accept the above definition must also conclude that nobody knows how much persons with mental retardation are capable of learning. Thus, the lists of "ceiling skills," such as the one published by Sloan and Birch in 1955 and replicated in countless introductory texts (see Table 2.2), act as impediments to instruction. That is, statements of the upper levels of skill acquisition tend to place limits on what learners *should* be taught because if these skills are the most that people with mental retardation can learn, they are the end points of instruction. In reality, the place at which any individual will "top out" can never be known ahead of time.

Since persons with mental retardation can learn, and since they must be taught skills that others learn incidentally, it also follows that instruction can help learners move through the levels of retardation toward the status of "not retarded." That is, if retardation is indicated by a lack of skills for interacting effectively in communities, the greater the number of skills that persons with retardation acquire, the closer they will come to being "non-retarded." Thus, the degree of mental retardation can be described in terms of the amount and type of instruction needed by learners. If and when they progress to the point at which they can do what others can do or can learn through conventional means, we can no longer view them as mentally retarded (MacMillan, Siperstein, and Gresham, 1996).

Finally, if persons with mental retardation must be taught because they have difficulty acquiring information by themselves, this corollary implies that the amount and type of learning they experience (or do not experience) is the responsibility of those who provide the instruction. When instructional efforts are unsuccessful, the hypothesis must be entertained that the instruction has been inappropriate, and adjustments are necessary, either in what is being taught or how it is being presented to the learners. Persons with mental retardation cannot be blamed for not acquiring new skills, for those who carry out instruction have the responsibility for seeing to it that learning takes place as rapidly and efficiently as possible (McGee et al., 1987; Menoloscino and McGee, 1981).

TABLE 2.2 Sloan & Birch's Concept of Degrees of Mental Retardation

Level	Pre-School Age 0–5 Maturation and Development	School Age 6–21 Training and Education	Adult 21 Social and Vocational Adequacy
I	Gross retardation; minimal capacity for functioning in sensori-motor areas; needs nursing care	Some motor development present; cannot profit from training in self-help; needs total care	Some motor and speech development; totally incapable of self-maintenance; needs complete care and supervision
II	Poor motor development; speech is minimal; generally unable to profit from training in self-help; little or no communication skills	Can talk or learn to communicate; can be trained in elemental health habits; cannot learn functional academic skills; profits from systematic habit training ("Trainable")	Can contribute partially to self-support under complete supervision; can develop self-protection skills to a minimal useful level in controlled environment
III	Can talk or learn to communicate; poor social awareness; fair motor development; may profit from some training in self-help; can be managed with moderate supervision	Can learn functional academic skills to approximately 4th grade level by late teens if given special education ("Educable")	Capable of self-maintenance in unskilled or semi-skilled occupations; needs supervision and guidance when under mild social or economic stress
IV	Can develop social and communication skills; minimal retardation in sensori-motor areas; rarely distinguished from normal until later age	Can learn academic skills to approximately 6th grade level by late teens; cannot learn general high school subjects; needs special education, particularly at secondary school levels ("Educable")	Capable of social and vocational adequacy with proper education and training; frequently needs supervision and guidance under serious social or economic stress

Sloan, W., & Birch, J. (1955). A rationale for degrees of retardation. *American Journal of Mental Deficiency, 60*(2), 258–264. Used by permission.

Corollary 2: The Need for Instruction Is Central to Mental Retardation and All Other Responses Are Secondary

The second corollary states that the primary response to mental retardation must be instructional in nature. All other responses are made to conditions other than the mental retardation. While it is certainly true that persons with mental retardation require services other than those that are instructional in nature, they do not require these services because they have retardation, but rather, for some other reason. For example, if people with Down syndrome require medical attention, it is because they have colds, heart defects, or some other medical condition; it is not because they have mental retardation. While it is true that people with Down syndrome have a higher incidence of some medical problems than other persons, this fact has nothing to do with mental retardation. In a similar vein, some persons with mental retardation require greater levels of social or psychological services than most other persons. But, there are also many people who require these services who do not have mental retardation. In other words, these services have little or nothing to do with mental retardation itself. Rather, they are responses to human conditions that have to be made whether or not a person has mental retardation.

Corollary 3: The Degree of Retardation Is a Function of the Amount and Intensity of the Instruction Required to Teach the Person to Live in the Community Without Supervision

Some definitions contain classification systems that indicate various levels or degrees of retardation. The instructional definition of mental retardation does not address the issue of classification because it is not necessary to create levels or subgroups of persons with retardation in order to design effective instructional programs. Rather, the instructional definition of mental retardation considers degrees of mental retardation along a continuum of how much teaching would be required to enable persons who have mental retardation to live in their communities without supervision. Thus, the definition suggests that persons usually labeled "severely" or "profoundly mentally retarded" are individuals who require more exceptional instruction to enable them to assume control over their own lives than would be true of persons who are labeled "mildly retarded." That is, the instruction of very low-functioning persons must be more intense, precise, extensive, and systematic than the instruction of persons with mild retardation. Whatever a person's level of retardation, however, the only response we can make to mental retardation per se is instructional in nature, and it must be aimed at moving the person toward the status of "not retarded."

Corollary 4: A Person with Mental Retardation Who Learns to Live in the Community Without Supervision Can No Longer Be Called "Mentally Retarded"

The instructional definition of mental retardation, like all the definitions promulgated by the American Association on Mental Retardation since 1959, refers only to the current functioning level of individuals. It is logical to conclude that if persons with mental retardation need to be taught skills for living in the community without supervision, they can no longer be called "retarded" once they have learned these skills. Accordingly, successful instruction can cause people to be removed from the classification altogether, even if their IQ scores indicate that they would still be classified as "retarded" under other definitions (MacMillan et al., 1996). For example, if a person has an IQ score of 54 but learns to live in the community without supervision or extraordinary assistance, that person could no longer be called "mentally retarded." Thus, this corollary further clarifies the function of instructional programs by indicating the end place or stopping point of such programs, that is, when the person can live in the community without supervision.

Corollary 5: Some Persons with Mental Retardation Will Never Be Able to Acquire Enough Skills to Enable Them to Live in the Community Without Supervision

The instructional definition requires us to conclude that people with mental retardation must be taught until they no longer need instruction. Unfortunately, some persons with mental retardation have tremendous physical and intellectual disabilities and will never learn enough to be able to take complete control over their own lives. This fact does not change their need for instruction; it simply means that instruction for these people may never stop. Therefore, anyone who is classified as "retarded" will continue to need instruction that improves their ability to interact in their communities.

However, at some point during a person's life there may be a very good reason to decide to terminate instruction. For example, persons who have reached the age of retirement, or even middle age, may decide that their lives are going smoothly and that they are satisfied with their current lifestyle. These individuals may decide to opt out of instructional programs.

Another reason for discontinuing instruction is that an agency may have a severe shortage of funds and be forced to lessen or terminate instruction of some groups in order to provide it to others (the triage concept). In cases such as these in which the decisions that affect instruction can be made rationally and for reasons other than inability to learn, subsequent events may allow the decisions to be reversed. The basis for reversal should be inherent in the original decision to stop instruction.

Corollary 6: The Aim of Instruction Is Identical for All Persons with Mental Retardation Despite the Fact That Some Persons Will Never Attain It

The aim of instruction is the end point that defines the direction of movement for all the curricula constructed under the aegis of that aim (Dewey, 1902). This corollary guides the formulation of an aim of instruction for teaching persons with mental retardation. The importance of establishing a common aim for people with mental retardation is that it enables professionals to develop curricula that work in concert with one another, even if the instructional content and the means of delivery are different from the instruction usually provided to people who do not have mental retardation.

Knapczyk (1988) showed how curricula from the various community agencies that serve people with mental retardation can focus on the same end point and still teach skills that are quite distinct one from another. If such curricula existed, persons who receive instruction from one agency would be able to move into the services of another agency without experiencing disruption in their instruction. Furthermore, even though a person with mild retardation would have a different program of instruction from that of a person with severe or profound mental retardation, the programs for both should be derived from curricula that aim at achieving the same goals. That is, instruction should focus on trying to move all persons toward the status of "non-retarded."

The advantage of the definition of mental retardation presented previously is that it gives a clear and precise direction to the instruction of persons with mental retardation; that is, instruction must teach them to live, work, and interact in the mainstream of their communities. The definition expresses a very useful mindset for instructional personnel in carrying out their professional responsibilities.

The Aim of Instruction for Persons with Mental Retardation

Now that we have established our view of who people with mental retardation *are*, it is time to establish what we want them to *become* when instruction is complete. The aim states the final outcome of instruction and describes what learners will become if and when instruction is successful.

Instructional aims have been developed for a number of different groups of learners. Some examples of instructionally useful aim statements are as follows:

- "The learners will become skilled readers."
- "The learners will become concrete truck drivers."
- "The learners will become contemplative monks."
- "The learners will become competitive swimmers."

It is critical to make a statement of this sort because the aim establishes the point toward which all instructional energies will be directed and specifies when instruction will cease. A clearly stated aim expresses our ideals for learner outcomes (Charters, 1923) and establishes the parameters within which the instructional goals and the curriculum pathways that lead to those goals will be formulated. In a most fundamental way, a clearly stated aim of instruction sets the focus for curriculum development activities and prevents inappropriate curricula from being developed. For example, a curriculum for producing contemplative monks will be quite different from a curriculum for producing concrete truck drivers, and learners who are taught from each of these curricula will learn to behave in very different ways.

Once established, an aim is invariant until and unless a different aim is substituted for it. This invariance is important for planning long-range instruction for persons with mental retardation because many of these learners will need instruction that takes place over a period of many years. If the aim is stated appropriately, curricula can be constructed to span lifetimes. Thus, a clearly stated aim of instruction allows us to develop instructional programs that are coherent, continuous, and coordinated across the entire period of required instruction. It will help construct curricula that encompass the skills that all the learners will need no matter how young or how old they are, or how high or low their skill levels.

It is very important for those who share the responsibility for teaching persons with mental retardation to agree on an aim so that all instructional personnel can concentrate their efforts on helping the learners work toward the same end point. If all those who teach in the various agencies that serve persons with mental retardation have instructional programs that are directed toward the same aim, people with mental retardation will achieve a higher level of success than would otherwise be possible.

The aim of instruction for persons with mental retardation should emerge in answer to the following question: "What should learners with mental retardation become as a result of their instruction?" The answer to this question will express the ideals that we have for this group of learners.

The Ideal: Independence

Many workers in mental retardation express the ideal that persons with mental retardation should become independent, or, at least, more independent. These professionals say that achieving independence means that persons with mental retardation would become active, productive, and contributing members of their communities. At that point, they would overcome their dependence on other people, develop self-respect, and live their lives with dignity.

At first glance, independence as an aim seems to make a lot of sense. If we could help persons with mental retardation become independent, they would be able to take control over their own lives and would no longer need to rely on other people for assistance and support. They would truly be integrated into their communities and be accepted as part of society.

Unfortunately, from an instructional perspective, the concept of independence turns out to be slippery because none of us is truly independent: Everybody depends on other people, at least to some degree (Dever, 1988). For example, when you, the reader, awoke this morning, you may have turned on some lights, washed or bathed using hot water, and put on clothing. The lights, the water heater, and the material for the clothing were probably all made by other people, sold by other people, and delivered by other people. The energy required for the lights and hot water was provided by other people who used fuel and equipment that came from other places and that were obtained by other people. In fact, at any moment of the day, whether we are teaching, driving a car, sitting at a desk, eating a meal, or just relaxing, we find that other people have done something that allows us to do what we are doing. Clearly, few, if any, of us are truly independent.

Thus, from an instructional standpoint, the term *independence* presents a problem: On the one hand, it is common for professionals in the field of mental retardation to state that their job is to help people with mental retardation become independent, but on the other hand, nobody is truly independent. Because we have no behavioral referent for the term, it is useless from an instructional perspective and will remain so until we define it in terms of an instructional end point.

Instruction should focus on teaching people with mental retardation to go where other people go, do what they do there, and not look out of place when they do it.

Photo courtesy of Jean-Claude Lejeune.

A Definition of Independence

One way to look at the problem is to ask the question, "What do independent people do?" In response to this question, consider the following list of activities:

- Get jobs and earn a living
- Pay their bills
- Save a little money
- Maintain their health
- Travel throughout the community
- Shop and care for their clothing
- Buy, store, and prepare their food
- Use community facilities for leisure activities
- Chat with their neighbors
- Maintain the inside and outside of their living quarters so as to meet local standards

They also must do many other things that require them to move about the community, accomplish tasks, and interact with different people. And through all of this activity their behavior must meet certain standards to avoid attracting negative attention. Therefore, with this set of ideas in mind, we present the following definition of independence:

> **Independence** is exhibiting behavior patterns appropriate to the settings that are normally frequented by others of the individual's age and social status using only the assistance and supports used by the others while behaving in such a manner that the individual is not perceived as requiring assistance because of his or her behavior (adapted from Dever, 1988).

This definition expresses the ideal that people who are independent are those who live in the community, hold a job, have friends and acquaintances, and take care of their daily needs. They have living quarters that look like those of other people in the neighborhood, wear clothing seen as appropriate by other people, go to local stores for their food and personal items, and visit local places of entertainment for some of their leisure activities. They also seek assistance from the appropriate sources when they need it, see their dentist regularly, and use whatever transportation is normally used in the community. Furthermore, they can do all of these things without being perceived by others as requiring an extraordinary amount of help. That is, they do not appear to be any more inept or incompetent than anyone else, nor does their behavior attract any more attention than does anyone else's. In short, they are people who do what other people do to live their lives in the community.

Instructional Implications of the Definition of Independence

This definition of independence has three major implications for instructional programs for persons with mental retardation (see Table 2.3). Let us explore these implications, and in doing so, establish the parameters of instruction for this group.

Implication #1: People with Mental Retardation Must Be Able to Go out into Community Settings That Are Frequented by Other People.

The first major idea contained in the definition of independence is that, in order to be independent, people with mental retardation must be involved actively in a wide variety of community settings. By community settings we mean all the locations in the community in which activities take place and in which people interact, such as public school classrooms, municipal recreation sites, kitchens, grocery stores, public rest rooms, churches, bus stops, living rooms, meeting places, and shopping malls. Persons with mental retardation, just like everyone else, must be able to go into these and other community settings and participate successfully in the activities and interactions that take place in them in order to be seen as independent.

Fortunately, people with mental retardation do not have to be taught to go into every location in a community. Anyone could frequent a very large number of community settings, but the actual number of locations into which any individual actually goes on a regular basis is usually not large. Involvement in the community is limited by factors such as age, the neighborhood of residence, personal interests, social standing in the community, and preferences for one's friends and associates. For example, young children ordinarily go to their local schools, play in their neighborhoods, and visit friends who live close by. On the other hand, adults usually interact in a larger number of community settings than children, but the number of these settings is affected by such factors as their interests, their social standing in the community, and the ease with which they can gain access to various settings. However, even though most people frequent a somewhat limited number of

TABLE 2.3 Instructional Implications of the Definition of Independence

- People with mental retardation must be able to go out into the community settings that are frequented by other people.
- People with mental retardation must learn to act in ways that fit the demands of the settings that they frequent.
- People with mental retardation must learn to behave in a manner that allows them to be perceived as not requiring extraordinary assistance.

locations, everyone must be prepared to participate in a relatively wide array of settings in order to be seen as independent.

One problem with which professionals must deal is that many people with mental retardation usually do not get involved in their communities to the same degree as people who do not have mental retardation (McDonnell, Wilcox, and Hardman, 1991). Persons with mental retardation often do not go into many of the settings frequented by people their own age, and when they do, they often do not have the same opportunities for interactions that other people have. For example, young children with mental retardation who are in special education classes may not attend schools in their neighborhoods, and, if they do, they may not go into the same settings and engage in the same activities as their chronological peers. Similarly, adults with mental retardation may reside and work in segregated settings that do not give them many opportunities to establish normal relationships with other adults in the community. They often engage in work and leisure activities that are more in line with the preferences of the agency's staff rather than with their own preferences and personal interests (Bercovici, 1981). In other words, people with mental retardation often do not participate in their communities to the same degree as other persons either (1) because they are denied access to these settings by virtue of receiving "special" services or (2) because they have not been adequately prepared to interact with the people who are in these settings.

The definition of independence provides insight into the level of involvement that persons with mental retardation should attain in their communities: They should go where others of their age and social status go and they should do what others do there. This idea can help determine the type and number of settings on which all instructional programs should focus. For example, instructional personnel should ensure that elementary-age children with mental retardation attend the same schools as other children in the neighborhood attend; they should participate in the same classrooms and social settings as other children; and they should be involved in the activities and interactions that take place in these settings (Brown, Branston, Hamre-Nietupski, Johnson, et al., 1979; Brown, Branston, Hamre-Nietupski, Pumpian, et al., 1979; Brown, Ford, et al., 1983; Keogh, 1988; Reynolds, Wang, and Walberg, 1987; Skrtic, 1986). As they get older, attention should shift away from school and toward the community at large so that, by the time they are adults, they will be prepared to work at jobs that not only match their interests and talents, but that also allow them to contribute to the economy of the community (Powell et al., 1991; Wehman et al., 1987). In addition, they should live in community residences that are comparable to those of the people around them, and they should have easy access to community services and leisure facilities (Wolfensberger, 1972). To help people with mental retardation reach this level of involvement, instructional personnel must examine the settings in which other people interact and use them as referents for designing instructional programs.

Finally, persons with mental retardation must be afforded the experience and taught the skills that will enable them to discover where their interests and talents lie so they can learn to choose the settings into which they want to go. Making choices is a central feature of independence, but people cannot make choices if they lack information on the alternatives that are available. For example, adolescents will not be able to decide if they are interested in attending school dances or in going to the local pizza parlor with friends until they have the opportunity to find out what it means to do these things. Similarly, adults will not be able to decide what jobs they should seek until they have had the opportunity to find out what kinds of jobs exist. Therefore, instructional programs should focus on giving people with mental retardation the skills and information they need to interact in the various settings in a community in the same manner as everyone else.

Implication #2: People with Mental Retardation Must Learn to Act in Ways That Fit the Demands of the Settings They Frequent. The second major idea contained in the definition of independence is that anyone who is independent must be able to do what other people do during their interactions in community settings. That is, people in any setting have expectations for how other people should behave in those settings; thus, nobody can obtain the benefits of going into the community without knowing how to meet the expectations for behavior under those circumstances (Knapczyk and Rodes, 1996). For example, a person who goes to work is expected to perform the assigned work, and a person who participates in a sporting event is expected to follow the rules of the event. To be independent, people with mental retardation, like everyone else, must learn to do many things, such as hold conversations with peers and superiors, fix meals, and purchase clothing. And to do these things *successfully,* they must acquire the skills that enable them to meet the local expectations for performance (Rusch and Hughes, 1989).

To understand this implication, consider the following: Years ago, Roger Barker (1968) and his colleagues began pointing out that people usually behave in ways that are very similar to those of the other people in the locations in which they find themselves. In fact, they found that a person's behavior in any setting is more similar to that of the other people in that setting than it is to the person's own behavior under different circumstances. Barker also explained that there are definite limits to the behaviors people are allowed to exhibit in any situation and that these behaviors must conform to the demands and the circumstances that people will encounter in that setting. Those who meet these requirements will be able to participate in the interactions and activities that take place in the setting, but those who do not will attract negative attention and will be subject to sanctions, such as being excluded from the group or being denied access to the setting in the future.

Most of us rarely think about the behavioral limits that apply to a particular set of circumstances, but we act in very prescribed ways wherever we go. For example, when we go to a movie, we do what other people in the theater do: buy a ticket and maybe some refreshments, find a seat, sit and face the screen, watch the movie, and get up and leave when the movie is over. Similarly, when we go to a sporting event, we do what other people attending the event do: enter the stands, find a seat, watch the event, cheer, sing songs, stand and wave our arms, make loud comments, and do whatever else people do at sporting events. Note, however, that if we go to the movie theater and act the way we do at sporting events, we will attract immediate negative attention and probably be asked to leave the theater because we will not be doing what everyone is expected to do in that setting.

At all ages and in all social situations, it is necessary to meet the expectations of others. Just as is true of adults, young people must act in prescribed ways in every setting. For example, children in elementary school classrooms are expected to do certain things, but on playgrounds, they are expected to do other things. Children who act according to the demands of the settings get certain benefits: They receive praise, earn passing grades, have friends, and are generally considered part of the group. Children who do not meet these demands are reprimanded, receive failing grades, are excluded from activities, and are sometimes separated from their peer group and placed in "special" programs.

Readers should be able to generate many other examples showing that there are prescribed ways to behave for every location in the community, whether it be a supermarket, a swimming pool, a school lunchroom, a church, a grocery store, or a park bench. These examples will illustrate that people who are independent are those who can go to the places in which other people are doing things and behave in a manner similar to that of other people. That is, people who are independent act as they are expected to act in whatever location they find themselves.

A major problem facing people with mental retardation when they go into various settings is that they often do not know what they are supposed to do when they get there (Knapczyk and Rodes, 1996). Their behavior may be seen as "inappropriate," and consequently, either they are excluded from the activities that take place in such locations, or (more frequently) they are not even allowed to go into these locations. However, when people with mental retardation learn to do whatever other people do in community settings, they become accepted by others in those settings (Edgerton, 1967, 1975; McGee et al., 1987; Powell et al., 1991; Wehman, Hill, et al., 1986). They learn to behave the way everyone else behaves in the setting, and consequently, they seem to "fit in."

Thus, independence as the aim of instruction not only orients us toward the types of skills that persons with mental retardation must acquire, it also shows us how we can identify these skills. When we recognize that people with mental retardation must be taught to act like everyone else in school and community settings, our next task is to discover what other people in those settings actually do to be successful in their interactions. When this information is available, it will provide the foundation for deciding what to teach to individuals (Knapczyk and Rodes, 1996). The skills taught within this framework will help persons with mental retardation progress toward independence as we have defined it.

Implication #3: People with Mental Retardation Must Learn to Behave in a Manner That Allows Them to Be Perceived As Not Requiring Extraordinary Assistance. The third major idea expressed in the definition of independence is that the behavior of persons who are independent must not suggest that they require extraordinary assistance. The fact is that everyone requires at least some assistance while interacting in the community, but this assistance must be obtained within "acceptable" limits. For example, when we travel about the community, we must obtain assistance from the people whose job it is to provide information; the people who refine, deliver, and sell fuel; and the people who operate various vehicles, among others. But not many of us require paid staff to make decisions about where, when, and how to travel; with whom to speak; and when to begin an excursion. Those who require such assistance are not perceived as ordinary persons, but rather, as "different," and they are treated accordingly.

People with mental retardation must meet three criteria to avoid being seen as needing extraordinary assistance:

1. their behavior must be sufficiently proficient that other people do not perceive them as requiring assistance (i.e., they should not appear to be any more inept then anyone else);
2. their behavior should not attract negative attention by disrupting the activities of other people in the setting; and
3. their behavior must match their personal characteristics.

McFall (1982) pointed out that people judge the competence of others by evaluating the overall quality and adequacy of their behavior rather than their specific responses. Behavior need not be exceptionally "good" or even completely accurate, but it must at least be adequate and appropriate for the circumstances. Thus, there is a basic level of competence that behavior must reach in order for others to view the behavior as acceptable. If a person's behavior seems to fall below this level, others will perceive that person as incompetent (Knapczyk and Rodes, 1996). They will defer to the individual or will single him or her out for extra attention (which is often either patronizing or negative). Furthermore, because the individual stands apart from the group, other people will begin to react rather than interact with him or her.

The standards that people use to evaluate the behavior of a person and to judge whether or not he or she needs assistance are based, in large measure, on a combination of (1) the activities being performed; and (2) personal factors such as age, social status, and standing within the group.

The activities being performed. When behavior attracts attention for its ineptitude, people may try to provide assistance at first, but they will eventually either break contact or call for assistance from the "experts." For example, when two or more people talk to one another, the things they say and do should match the topic of the conversation and the flow of the discourse. If one person says or does things that are not in synchrony with the interaction, that behavior probably will attract negative attention and interrupt the interaction. For example, if a person interjects an outlandish comment into a conversation or laughs when he or she should look serious, the other person will wonder what is going on and may ask if the person understood what was being said. If the person's actions continue to be out-of-line with the conversation, the interaction will stop altogether and the other person will find someone else with whom to talk. The reader should be able to generate similar examples that show that behavior must follow strict guidelines defined by the location and the activity in which the people are involved.

Personal factors. People judge others as being competent if they behave in ways that are appropriate to their personal characteristics, such as chronological age, social status, and sex. For example, in most locations, adult behavior must meet different standards than adolescent or child behavior, men must meet different standards than women, and employers must meet different standards than employees. Therefore, successful preschoolers, adolescents, or employees must be able to recognize the standards that apply to their behavior and act according to these standards (Knapczyk and Rodes, 1996). If they do not, either they will attract negative attention or they will be perceived as requiring assistance. Thus, being independent not only means being able to do things, but also being able to do them in ways that are consonant with our personal characteristics.

The way we have defined independence can help identify standards of behavior that, if attained, will enable persons with mental retardation to act competently and to avoid being perceived by others as requiring assistance. We can observe how people who are successful in their interactions match their behavior to the circumstances, and we can find out what aspects of the social structure help them decide what behavior is appropriate for these circumstances. These performance levels represent standards of competence, and we can use them in designing instructional programs for persons with mental retardation. Our teaching can then be directed toward helping such persons attain these standards when they go out into community settings.

Clearly, the definition of independence makes it possible to plan instructional programs for people with mental retardation that actually will help them to be independent and to go where others go, do what others do, and not look as though they need assistance because of their behavior. In other words, this definition establishes a clear and precise aim for their instruction.

The Scope of Instructional Programs

To help clarify the concept of independence in terms of some of the current trends in special education, residential, and rehabilitation services, we will address two issues that pertain to the scope of instructional programs for persons with mental retardation:

1. vocational instruction vs. "total" instruction; and
2. services to persons with severe mental retardation vs. services to persons with mild retardation

Vocational Instruction vs. Full-Range Instruction

Perhaps because of the impetus provided by the federal government that came when Madeline Will, a former Director of the federal Office of Special Education and Rehabilitation Services, published *Bridges from School to Working Life* (Will, 1984), many secondary schools have begun to provide community-based programs in some form of transitional vocational training. These programs are designed to help high school students make an orderly transition from school to community employment by teaching a wide variety of job-related skills in community work settings. In addition, many adult rehabilitation centers have begun to provide vocational training in the form of supported employment in which persons are placed on competitive job sites in the community and are taught the skills for working in those sites.

Even though many of these efforts have been very successful, it is important to note that job training alone, regardless of its focus, is not sufficient to help learners become independent and fully integrated in their communities. As Halpern (1985) pointed out, in addition to vocational instruction, there are at least two other aspects of life in the community on which instructional programs should concentrate: (1) the residential environment and (2) social and interpersonal networks. Halpern's data indicated that success in one of these three areas is not related to success in either of the other two and that direct instruction in all three is required for successful adjustment to adult life. Therefore, we must view the aim of independence as pertaining to all aspects of community life and avoid emphasizing one aspect at the expense of the others. In other words, it is necessary to focus instruction on preparing persons with mental retardation to participate in a full range of community settings (Dever, 1988).

Services to Persons with Severe Mental Retardation vs. Services to Persons with Mild Retardation

The aim of independence and the other aspects of the Instructional Model can be used to develop instructional programs for persons at any level of mental retardation because the concept of independence applies equally to all persons with mental retardation regardless of their age and level of disability. Instruction toward independence should be based on the characteristics of individual learners rather than on some arbitrary classification system. Under the definitions of mental retardation and independence presented in this text, the actions of staff are determined by the relationship between a learner's current skill level and what that person must be able to do to live in the community without attracting negative attention or appearing to need assistance.

However, due to federal and state funding priorities, the funds for community-based research and demonstration programs have been allocated disproportionately toward children and adults with moderate and severe mental retardation and not toward programs for individuals with mild disabilities (MacMillan et al., 1996; Patton et al., 1989). There is no question that the programs that have been funded are important and that the resources have been put to very good use. However, the needs of young people with mild mental retardation are at least as great as those of lower-functioning students (Afflek et al., 1990; Edgar, 1987; Frank et al., 1990), and they truly seem to have been overlooked in the competition for federal, state, and local resources (Patton et al., 1989; Polloway et al., 1991).

The system of instruction that we propose in this book can be used across the full range of mental retardation, from mild through severe. The aim of all instructional programs for people with mental retardation should be independence, and the fact that people with mild mental retardation are more likely to attain that aim than are people with severe mental retardation does not alter the aim. Because the aim is the same for all persons with mental retardation, the goals must also be the same. The only thing that will be different for people with different levels of mental retardation will be the individual programs that are designed to help each learner progress toward the goals.

Beyond Independence

People with mental retardation who can live in their communities without extraordinary assistance will have come to the end of instructional programs designed with the aim of independence. When they attain independence, these same people may want or even require further instruction, but it would not be instruction that responds to their mental retardation. Rather, it would be whatever instruction is ordinarily provided to citizens of this country, such as instruction in job training, leisure activities, homemaking skills, or any one of the other thousands of things Americans decide to study. Whatever training an independent person would seek would be entirely a matter of choice on the person's part, just as it is for any ordinary citizen.

Concluding Statement

The aim of instruction conveys the ideals for the learners we teach and establishes the end point for their instruction. With the aim clearly in mind, we can begin to formulate instructional goals, outline curriculum pathways, assess learner performance, and complete the other tasks for planning and offering high-quality instructional programs.

The aim of independence, as we have defined it, communicates the ideals that parents and professionals have expressed for persons with mental retardation and gives instructional personnel an excellent starting place for planning instruction. Under the aegis of this aim, it becomes possible to identify the settings in which persons with mental retardation should be involved, list the skills they need to learn, and specify the level of competence their behavior must reach.

We must point out that groups of persons with disabilities other than mental retardation may require aims that are different, perhaps even radically so, from the one we have described for persons with mental retardation. For example, perhaps the aim of instruction for people with learning disabilities who have normal intelligence levels might be to complete the general education curriculum (Disability Research Systems, 1992b), and the aim of instruction for persons with visual disabilities might be to learn compensatory skills (e.g., in mobility, braille, etc.) that enable them to interact in regular education classrooms and in community settings with support. Each group of persons with disabilities presents unique instructional problems; therefore, we must respond to each group individually (Frey, Burke, and Lynch, 1990).

Goals and Curricula

Once we establish the aim of instruction, the Instructional Model requires us to define curriculum goals and then build the curricula that will be used to guide the development of individualized programs of instruction for specific learners. In the absence of a good curriculum, instructors have to develop all individualized programs of instruction by guesswork, but with a good curriculum, program objectives can be selected in a rational and straightforward manner.

The three chapters in Part II explain the process of curriculum development. Chapter 3 discusses the concepts of curriculum goals and curriculum objectives and shows how traditional views of a curriculum can apply to the instruction of persons with mental retardation. This chapter provides the conceptual foundation for curriculum development in public schools and rehabilitation agencies. Then, Chapters 4 and 5 describe the actual procedures for developing a curriculum: Chapter 4 explains how to formulate curriculum goals and Chapter 5 discusses how to establish curriculum objectives and organize them into curriculum pathways that lead to the goals. Thus, these three chapters explain the attributes of a useful curriculum for persons with mental retardation and show how schools and rehabilitation agencies can devise coherent, comprehensive, and coordinated curricula to guide the development of instructional programs for their learners.

CHAPTER 3

The Concepts of Curriculum and Curriculum Goals

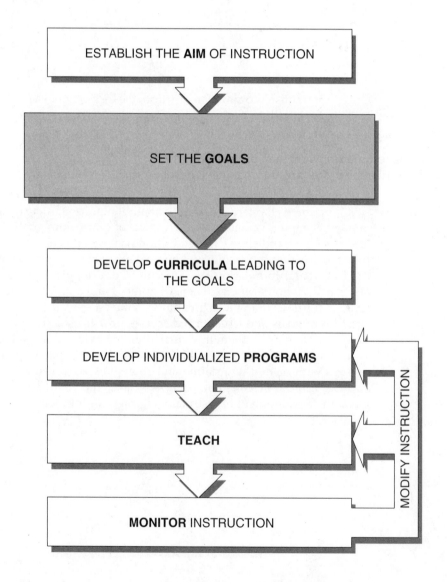

ESTABLISH THE **AIM** OF INSTRUCTION

SET THE **GOALS**

DEVELOP **CURRICULA** LEADING TO THE GOALS

DEVELOP INDIVIDUALIZED **PROGRAMS**

TEACH

MONITOR INSTRUCTION

MODIFY INSTRUCTION

In this chapter we will explain two fundamental concepts in the Instructional Model: (1) curriculum and (2) curriculum goals. We feel it is necessary to focus on these concepts in some detail because professionals in the field of mental retardation have used these terms in many ways. For example, various authors (e.g., Gaylord-Ross and Holvoet, 1985; Neel and Billingsley, 1989; Sailor and Guess, 1983; Snell, 1987; Wilcox and Bellamy, 1987) have stated that a curriculum should include such elements as component steps of task analyses, target responses for behavior management, descriptions of instructional activities, descriptions of teaching methodologies, and specification of learning aids.

In this book we will adopt a more traditional approach to curriculum development and use the term *curriculum* to refer only to the document that expresses the *content* of the instructional program that leads toward the goals established by a school or other agency. Our concept of curriculum does not include instructional technique, teaching tools, or any of the other elements included by other authors: For our purposes, it is simply a statement of the skills that learners must acquire to attain a goal or a set of goals. The reason for this narrow use of the term is that, under the Instructional Model, the curriculum should be in place *before* any individualized programs of instruction are developed for the learners. The instructional staff will make adjustments for individual differences and select the appropriate teaching techniques when they prepare to carry out teaching activities. We will describe the procedures for making such adjustments and choosing effective teaching techniques in later chapters of this book.

The Concept of Curriculum

We define the term *curriculum* as follows:

> A **curriculum** is a list of objectives leading to a set of curriculum goals that defines the content of instruction for a school or other mental retardation service agency. The objectives in a curriculum are organized into pathways that link each of the objectives to one or more of the goals.

There are two major terms in this definition that require clarification: *curriculum goals* and *pathways of objectives*. Briefly, these terms mean the following:

Curriculum goals are the behavioral end points of the curriculum. They state what the learner will be able to do when instruction in a curriculum pathway is complete. The goals make the aim operational in that, if a learner can perform *all* of the goal behaviors, he or she will have fulfilled the aim of the curriculum.

Pathways of objectives consist of sequenced lists of skills that progress toward a goal or a set of goals. They are formulated by working backward from the goals and describing the skills that learners must acquire to achieve the goals. Then the developers list these skills in a logical instructional sequence, which then becomes a "pathway" of curriculum objectives. As learners acquire the objectives, they proceed along the pathways toward the

FIGURE 3.1

The relationship between the instructional aim, curriculum goals, and curriculum objectives.

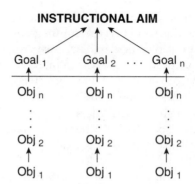

curriculum goals, and if they acquire all the objectives in a pathway, they will have attained the goal.

Figure 3.1 illustrates the relationship between an instructional aim, curriculum goals, and pathways of objectives. If the curriculum developers construct a curriculum logically and list objectives in appropriate instructional sequences, the pathways of objectives will be clear and progressive. That is, the skills that appear early in the curriculum will lay the foundation for skills that the learners will acquire later, and the learners' ability to acquire the skills listed near the end of the curriculum will relate to their ability to perform the skills listed earlier.

Note that a curriculum constructed in this manner provides an effective instructional assessment tool, as well. To conduct an assessment, the instructional staff compares the skills in the curriculum to the skill repertoires of the learners and lists the differences between what the learners actually can do and what the sequences in the curriculum suggest that they should be able to do. Such an analysis allows the instructor to make decisions about what to teach "next" to each individual learner (Provus, 1971). This type of assessment uncovers the skills that should go into the learners' individualized programs of instruction and focuses the attention of all instructional personnel on what instruction should accomplish for each individual learner.

Curriculum vs. Individualized Program of Instruction

To be able to use the term *curriculum* in a meaningful way, it is necessary to discriminate it from the term *individualized program of instruction*. Both of these terms refer to instructional content, and many workers in special education and rehabilitation services use them interchangeably. This fact is illustrated in the many texts and articles that discuss the development of individualized programs of instruction under the rubric of "curriculum" (e.g., Brown, Branston, Hamre-Nietupski, Pumpian, et al., 1979; Brown and York, 1974; Guess et al., 1978; Klein, Pasch, and Frew, 1979; Langone, 1990; Neel and Billingsley, 1989; Sailor and Guess, 1983; Vincent et al., 1980; Wambold and Salisbury, 1978; Wehman and McGlaughlin, 1981). But, under the Instructional Model, the concepts of curriculum and individualized program of instruction are very different. We believe that keeping them separate can help raise the quality of instruction by a considerable measure.

The distinction between curriculum and individualized program of instruction is as follows:

> A **curriculum** outlines the sequence of skills that *any* learner would have to acquire to attain a goal or a set of goals.
>
> An **individualized program of instruction** lists the skills that instructors will teach to a specific learner within a prescribed period of time (Dever, 1988).

Curriculum

The concept of curriculum is illustrated in the diagram of an instructional task presented in Figure 3.2. In this figure, the learner is shown as just entering an instructional program (contained within the box) conducted by a school or agency. At the end of this instructional program is a curriculum goal or a set of goals that establishes the end points of the instructional program in behavioral terms. When the learner reaches this goal, he or she will also have reached the end of the curriculum.

A curriculum always should be developed by starting at the end and working backward. The result will be a sequence of skills that lead directly to a goal or a set of goals. In Figure 3.2, the goal consists of a certain set of skills. However, before the learners can acquire that set of skills, they must acquire an earlier set of skills, and before that another set of skills, and so forth, right back to the beginning of the instruction that the agency or school provides. The staff has listed these skills in a logical sequence of instruction; therefore, the learners must have acquired the earlier skills before they can begin to work on the later skills. Because each of these sets of skills leads toward the goal, each is listed as an objective in the curriculum, and the sequence of objectives forms a pathway that leads learners directly to the goal.

To illustrate how sequencing works in a curriculum, consider the traditional mathematics curriculum for elementary and secondary public schools: At the earliest grade levels the learners concentrate just on learning numbers. Soon, however, they can begin to learn the basic mathematics operations of addition, subtraction, multiplication, and division. After learning these concepts, they can begin to learn fractions and decimals, and eventually move on to geometry, algebra, trigonometry, and perhaps, basic calculus. Each step builds on the previous step, and learners must master the concepts at the earlier stages before they can progress very far in the later stages.

Curriculum-Based Assessment.
A primary use of a curriculum is to conduct assessments, that is, to find out what to teach "next" to individual learners. To assess learners' skills, the instructional staff uses the following process: When learners enter the instructional program, the instructors must find out what skills in the instructional pathway the learners already have acquired. They compare the objectives listed in the pathway to the learners'

FIGURE 3.2

The concept of instruction.

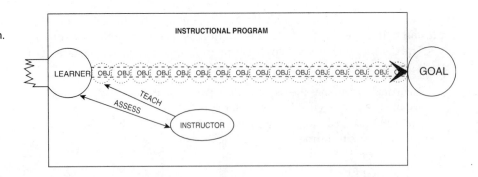

skill repertoires and place the learners somewhere in the curriculum pathway according to what they can do and what they have yet to learn. Once placed, the learners can begin to follow the pathway of curriculum objectives and work to acquire the skills that are required by the objectives they have not yet achieved. The skills the learners need to acquire first are the ones that are at the beginning of the pathway, and those they will acquire later are those that are later in the pathway. Each time the learners acquire a set of skills (i.e., "achieve an objective"), they can begin to work on the next set of skills, and so forth, until they complete the pathway. In this manner, learners follow a direct instructional route to the goal.

To illustrate how this process works, let us return to the example of the traditional mathematics curriculum. By assessing learner behavior, it is possible to tell how much the learner knows about numbers, or about using the basic mathematics operations, or geometry, or trigonometry, and so forth. Because the instructional staff knows the required skills in the mathematics curriculum, the assessment process can be quite straightforward and efficient. Once the staff discovers the skills the learner has, the next instructional steps are clear.

Thus, in the Instructional Model, a curriculum describes the skills that any learner would have to learn to attain a goal. A well-constructed curriculum contains pathways of objectives that lead to the curriculum goals and allows instructors to select specific objectives for individualized programs of instruction.

Characteristics of Curricula. Curricula have three major characteristics (see Table 3.1).

Group focus. Traditionally, the concept of curriculum does not attend to individual learner characteristics such as ability level or learning style. In fact, no individual learner should even be considered when curricula are being constructed. Rather, curricula are developed for groups of learners who have common characteristics. For example, curricula have been developed for apprentices in the building trades, military personnel, and salespersons. They have also been constructed for elementary students, secondary students, college freshmen, and doctoral students.

Curricula may be very large, or they may be relatively small. For example, the curricula in the system of general education are often organized into

TABLE 3.1 Characteristics of Curricula and Individualized Programs of Instruction

Curricula

- focus on the instructional needs of groups, not individuals;
- are different for different instructional units in schools and agencies; and
- have a long-term focus.

Individualized Programs

- focus on the immediate needs of an individual and indicate the procedures and resources that will be used to carry out instruction;
- clearly define instructional actions, how long the instruction will last, and how it will be monitored and evaluated; and
- have a relatively short-term focus.

successive levels and tend to focus on the same subject matter, such as mathematics and English, over long spans of years. Other curricula are focused more narrowly and have only a few pathways of objectives. For example, a curriculum for a vocational training program may contain a relatively small number of goals and only a few objectives, and learners may be able to complete it in a relatively short time span.

Curricula differ across instructional units.   Curricula are different in different agencies because the contents of a curriculum vary along four sets of variables:

1. the general characteristics of each group of students (such as their instructional histories, motor and sensory abilities, and current skill levels);
2. the subject matter selected for the curriculum (such as academic subjects, vocational skills, or personal maintenance skills);
3. the location of the program (such as what type of organization conducts the program and whether it is in a rural or urban setting); and
4. the settings in which the instruction takes place (such as in classrooms, playgrounds, community locations, or home environments).

As these variables change, the content of the curriculum changes accordingly. Therefore, curricula for persons with mental retardation must take these variables into account.

Long-term focus.   Finally, a curriculum usually has a long-term focus and lays out the sequences of skills that lead to distant goals. For example, school programs often construct their curricula to provide instruction over many years, and learners may take a long time to attain the goals. Some may never reach them at all, just as the authors of this book have not attained the goal of being able to conduct research in mathematics despite having had a fair amount of instruction in mathematics. The fact that some individuals never reach a goal does not necessarily mean that either the goal or the curriculum is inappropriate. Rather, the ability of a learner to make progress in a curriculum may be sufficient justification for carrying out instruction under its aegis.

Individualized Programs of Instruction

An individualized program of instruction is defined in the rules and regulations for PL 94-142 and other federal and state laws that provide guidelines for the instruction of persons with disabilities. It is called by different names in different service agencies, for example, "individualized educational plan" (IEPs), "individualized program plan" (IPPs), "individual habilitation plan" (IHPs), "individual rehabilitation plan" (IRPs), "individual transition plan" (ITPs), and several other terms. Because they all refer to essentially the same concept, we will use the term *individualized program of instruction* (IP) to refer to all of them. Whatever the term used by a school or service agency, an individualized program of instruction is very different from a curriculum because it focuses exclusively on the instructional needs of a specific learner. It is completely based on an individual learner's strengths and weaknesses, talents and disabilities, and unique circumstances.

Characteristics of Individualized Programs of Instruction.
An individualized program of instruction has three major characteristics (which also appear in Table 3.1) that sharply contrast with those of a curriculum.

Focus on individuals. IPs attend to the needs of individuals, not groups. They must attend to matters such as how to compensate for any physical and sensory disabilities that an individual may have, the learner's current skill level, and any unique circumstances that the individual may present, for example, in mobility, parental demands, medical needs, or the individual's choice of lifestyle. A curriculum ignores such matters, but an IP focuses on them directly because it must be designed to meet the needs of the individual.

Instructional actions are clearly defined. IPs are not open-ended. They are legally defined as plans and not contracts and must state a time frame within which the staff will try to teach the individual to acquire the skills that appear in the IP (generally 12 months or less). In contrast to curriculum goals and objectives, the objectives listed in an IP realistically must be obtainable within the specified time frame. That is, all objectives in an IP must be within the grasp of the learner and should be selected after the instructional staff conducts an assessment of what the learner can do now.

The appropriateness of individualized programs of instruction can be measured in terms of learner progress. That is, the measure of a good IP is whether or not the learner actually attains the program objectives that have been selected, and if he or she attains them, how quickly he or she does so. Unlike a curriculum, if the learner fails to acquire the skills outlined in the IP, the IP itself may require revision. Therefore, the IP must contain a plan not only for instruction, but also for monitoring the effects of the instruction. It should specify how the instructional staff will be able to judge the success or failure of the IP. These monitoring procedures should be based firmly in the objectives the staff selects for instruction and clearly state the criteria for concluding whether or not instruction has been successful.

Short-term focus.   Most IPs have a short-term focus and require periodic revision. Most state and federal agencies that oversee instruction require at least one revision each year. IPs should be revised more often if conditions change unexpectedly. For example, learners might acquire all the skills earlier than expected, they might develop additional problems in learning, or they might move to a new instructional program. A curriculum does not change rapidly, but IPs must be able to change according to the circumstances of the learner.

Thus, although the concepts of curriculum and individualized program are very different, they complement one another very nicely. A curriculum attends to the general content of instruction while the individualized program of instruction attends to the unique needs of the individual who should be learning that content. If curricula and individualized programs are constructed to complement one another, they will produce a very powerful approach to instruction that combines the best practices of two instructional worlds: the forward curriculum movement that is characteristic of general education and the individualized instructional planning process that is required of special education and rehabilitation services.

Curriculum Objectives

The curriculum pathways present the sequences of prerequisite and lead-in skills that learners must acquire to achieve the curriculum goals. The concept of skills requires an explanation. According to *Webster's New Collegiate Dictionary*, a *skill* is "a learned process of doing something competently; a developed aptitude or ability." Thus, teaching skills to learners means teaching them to perform competently in some way.

Unfortunately, this definition does not clarify the term sufficiently for instructional purposes because "a skill" for one person is not "a skill" for another. For example, it may require a major instructional effort for one learner to perform a simple pincer grasp, a skill that is a part of other skills, such as writing with a pen, opening a door with a key, adding a pinch of salt to a recipe, and assembling electronic equipment. Learners who can use the pincer grasp may be ready to acquire the higher-level skills. For these learners, then, a pincer grasp is no longer a skill that they have to learn. In other words, the concept of a skill changes with the needs of each individual learner.

Because the concept of a skill varies with individual learners, it must have a definition that allows it to be considered relative to each learner. Therefore, we will use the following definition of a skill:

> A **skill** is any learned process of doing something competently that an instructor would assess separately for an individual learner.

If an instructor finds it necessary to assess whether or not a specific learner can use the pincer grasp, the pincer grasp is a skill for that learner. If the instructor must assess whether or not a learner can assemble electronic equipment, then the assembly procedure is a skill for that learner. For each learner or group of learners, the instructor will have to determine the complexity of the sets of behaviors covered by the concept of a skill.

Restricted vs. Comprehensive Curricula

The number of prerequisite and lead-in skills that become curriculum objectives and the amount of detail used to express these skills can vary greatly in different curricula. In any curriculum, it is possible to list only the very few prerequisite and lead-in skills that are the most closely associated with advanced skills. But it is also possible to list the full range of skills leading back to the most basic body movements, such as crawling, grasping objects, or making utterances. Listing only the immediate few prerequisites and lead-in skills would result in a **restricted curriculum,** while listing a wide range of prerequisites and lead-in skills would result in a **comprehensive curriculum.** The characteristics of the learners and the mission of the agency for which we devise the curriculum will determine how comprehensive each curriculum should be. A small rehabilitation agency that conducts a day program for adults with severe and profound mental retardation probably would construct a restricted curriculum; a public school system with a number of different programs probably would construct a comprehensive curriculum.

An example of a restricted curriculum appears in Table 3.2. It is actually a microcurriculum that focuses only on the development of the motor

TABLE 3.2 Example of a Restricted Curriculum

Goal: The Learners Will Walk Unassisted

BALANCE				LOCOMOTION	
Head and Neck Control	*Trunk Control*	*Sitting*	*Standing*	*Prone*	*Vertical*
	Raises body to prone when suspended				
Lifts chin off ground when prone	Rolls partway to side from prone	Head bobs when sitting supported			
Lifts and holds head off floor when prone	Rolls side-to-side when prone	Holds head erect when sitting supported			
Supports weight on forearms	Lifts chest off floor when prone		Supports part of weight momentarily when held standing	Reaches for objects and falls forward	
Raises head and turns it side-to-side				Begins to creep on stomach	
	Rolls prone to supine; supine to prone	Assists in pulling to sitting position		Crawls one limb at-a-time	
		Sits unsupported briefly			
			Stands with considerable support		
	Draws knees to chest and kicks out when prone	Sits alone, forearms supporting			
			Pulls self to knees	Crawls contralateral	
		Sits erect for prolonged periods	Stands with object support		Walks touching stationary objects
			Pulls self to standing position		
			Stands unsupported, wide stance		Walks when led, wide stance
					Walks unsupported
			Stands, feet together		

skills that are required for a child to begin walking (Gallahue, Werner, and Luedke, 1975). This curriculum would be used to teach children who do not spontaneously acquire the motor skills listed in the pathways. Unlike a comprehensive curriculum, this curriculum can be completed in a relatively short period of time by children who are able to develop the necessary musculature and balance. Even though it is a microcurriculum, it has all the characteristics of any good curriculum: It has a clear set of end points, the skills (objectives) in the pathways are sequential, and the objectives can be used for assessment purposes.

When transforming prerequisites and lead-in skills into curriculum objectives, it is important to think about how easily instructors will be able to use the completed curriculum to plan instruction. The lists of objectives in the pathways must be properly detailed and presented so that the sequence suits the learners in the program. If the lists of objectives are too long or too complicated, it could prove difficult to use. Therefore, the curriculum objectives and pathways should be sufficiently detailed to carry out appropriate instruction, but the list should not be so extensive that instructors have difficulty selecting the items that individual learners must acquire. The instructional personnel who work in a school or other agency must think the curriculum through carefully so that the lists will, in fact, constitute an appropriate curriculum (Knapczyk, 1988).

Principles of Curriculum Development

We have taken eight principles from various sources to guide the process of constructing community-based curricula (see Table 3.3). These principles will guide the curriculum development activities of any school or adult agency and will help instructional personnel construct curricula that are community referenced and well suited to the capabilities of the schools and agencies in which they work. We will discuss each of them in this section.

A Curriculum Should Have Social Validity

Social validity refers to how well the goals and objectives of a curriculum express the behavioral demands of the community settings in which the learner will ultimately perform (Knapczyk and Rodes, 1996; Snell and Browder, 1986; Voeltz and Evans, 1983). The objectives in a curriculum should appear as clearly stated skills that learners must exhibit to meet the demands successfully. We can determine a curriculum's social validity by evaluating whether learners become functionally integrated in school and community settings following instruction.

A Curriculum Should Focus on Integration

In Chapter 2, we suggested that the definition of *integration* varies across a person's lifetime. In keeping with this view, we will now further suggest that there are four community referents that curriculum developers should use:

TABLE 3.3 The Eight Principles of Curriculum Development

A curriculum should:
1. have social validity;
2. focus on integration;
3. contain all required skills;
4. reflect the demands of both current and future environments;
5. have objectives and pathways that are broad enough to respond to the instructional needs of all learners in the program;
6. serve as a referent for monitoring instruction;
7. be seen as a local responsibility and define the purpose of the instructional program; and
8. promote coordination, collaboration, and continuity across instructional programs and agencies.

1. preschool and elementary curricula for children at all levels of mental retardation should be referenced to the world of other children and focus on integration in school and classroom environments;
2. in the intermediate grades, the curricula should begin to be referenced to the community at large but maintain a classroom and school base;
3. the curricula of secondary schools and adult agencies should focus primarily on the community at large, and nearly all the learners' instruction should be referenced to the community settings in which they will actually live, work, and recreate; and
4. when learners move out of school and into the community, the curricula should concentrate on helping them make further advances toward independence.

These statements mean that the curricula developed by schools and rehabilitation agencies should prepare learners not only to meet the demands of their current circumstances, but also to progress steadily toward more advanced and broader community circumstances. In addition, the curricula should help learners respond to the normal progression of any person's lifestyle that accompanies changes in age and maturation, and advance to whatever degree of independence they can achieve.

A Curriculum Should Contain All Required Skills

A curriculum for persons with mental retardation should reflect all of the behavioral demands placed on learners in community settings that can be taught within the scope of the instructional mission and goals of the school or agency (Ford et al., 1984). These demands include (1) the ability to perform the skills required to meet the demands; (2) the ability to use these skills when they are needed; and (3) the ability to put them together with other pertinent skills to form more complex performance routines (Knapczyk and Rodes, 1996). A curriculum must respond to these requirements because successful participation in most settings is not simply a matter of displaying discrete behaviors. Rather, it requires learners to produce a complex and integrated series of actions that indicate to other persons in the setting that the learners "belong." For example, proficiency in many school, vocational, and home living situations requires learners to perform the following routines:

- select an activity that people normally perform at a specific location and time;
- prepare for the activity;
- perform the activity itself; and
- make a transition to the next activity.

Overlooking any of these areas in the instructional program will result in learners who are unprepared to carry out the routines independently.

A Curriculum Should Reflect the Demands of Both Current and Future Environments

The degree of independence that persons with mental retardation attain will be determined by the age appropriateness of the settings in which they can participate effectively and by the types of opportunities of which they can take advantage (Falvey, 1986; Knapczyk, 1988; White, 1980). A curriculum should contain the skills that learners need (a) to interact competently in an ever-widening array of school and community settings and (b) to assume control over an increasing number of decisions that affect their daily lives. In other words, a curriculum developed by a school or agency should help prepare learners to function effectively, not only in the settings that are part of their current lifestyles, but also in the settings that will improve their lifestyles as they increase in age and status in their communities (Falvey, 1986; Ford et al., 1984). Thus, a curriculum for public school programs should prepare students to participate in a wide array of school settings and lay a foundation for learning to live, work, and recreate in the community. Similarly, a curriculum for an adult vocational training program should include both the skills required for obtaining entry-level jobs and the general skills (such as social skills) that are required to advance to higher levels of employment.

A Curriculum Should Have Objectives and Pathways Broad Enough to Respond to the Needs of All Learners in the Program

A curriculum should include sufficient detail to allow instructors to select curriculum objectives for *all* learners in the instructional unit regardless of their age, functioning level, talents, or preferences (Knapczyk, 1988). This guideline applies especially to circumstances in which the learners have diverse learning and performance characteristics. Under these conditions, (1) different learners may have a different set of school and/or community settings, and (2) each learner may work toward a different degree of participation in these settings (Neel and Billingsley, 1989). For example, learners with mild retardation might learn to use a full array of banking services, while learners with severe retardation might learn just to cash a check. In each curriculum, the starting and ending points in the curriculum pathways should provide a continuum of objectives for all of the learners in the instructional program regardless of their current status (Knapczyk, 1988).

A Curriculum Should Serve As a Referent for Monitoring Instruction

Instructional planning should be based on a sound assessment of the learners' skills (Brolin, 1993; Frey, Burke, and Lynch, 1990). In the context of the Instructional Model, assessment is basically a matter of finding out what skills the learners can perform now so we can decide what skills to teach next. When a curriculum of the sort that we are proposing is available, the assessment process involves comparing the skill repertoires of the learners to the objectives listed in the curriculum pathways. Discrepancies between what is in the curriculum and the skills the learners can exhibit will indicate what to teach next to each learner (Provus, 1971). Good observation procedures will ensure that we do not teach either skills the learners already can perform or skills for which the learners lack the proper foundation.

A curriculum can also provide an unbiased referent for judging the learners' rate and direction of progress toward the aim of instruction. Evaluation of progress requires the instructional staff to reassess the learners' skill repertoire periodically to find out which skills in the curriculum they have acquired and which they have not. This information will show the rate of new skill acquisition and will allow instructors to determine whether or not the learners are making satisfactory progress. These judgments will help to "fine-tune" the instructional program to accommodate learners with different needs and will ensure that instructional lessons and activities are indeed individualized.

A Curriculum Should Be Seen As a Local Responsibility and Define the Purpose of the Instructional Program

Curriculum development must be viewed as a local responsibility because each school and agency must teach different skills. The need to develop a curriculum that reflects local demands stems from the fact that communities in themselves are different, and the functions of schools and rehabilitation agencies in each community vary along with the ages and performance levels of the learners they serve. For example, preschools and public schools usually address more basic skill areas than do adult agencies, so the curricula for preschools and adult agencies must be quite different from each other. It is also true that two different adult rehabilitation agencies in a community that serve the same group of learners (or even two programs run by a single agency) can have very different functions in preparing persons with mental retardation for independence. For example, a vocational training program would concentrate on teaching learners to work in community job settings, and the curriculum for such a program would have curriculum goals and pathways that pertain to employment. But a residential program for the identical group of learners may concentrate on teaching skills that are required to live in the community outside of vocational settings, and its curriculum would focus on areas such as meal preparation, personal care, home maintenance, community travel, and other non-employment related instructional areas. Curricula, therefore, should reflect the purpose or charge that the service programs have for teaching persons with mental retardation and be developed by schools and agencies responsible for their implementation.

A Curriculum Should Promote Coordination, Collaboration, and Continuity Across Instructional Programs

The organization and format of a curriculum should guide not only the planning of instructional programs, but also the overall decision-making process of the school or agency (W. Frey, personal communication, 1992). Decisions regarding such administrative concerns as the allocation of resources, the scheduling of activities, staff assignments, and facility usage will naturally have an impact on the quality of instructional programs. Since the purpose of the curriculum is to make the instructional aim of the school or agency operational, it is imperative to base the decisions that affect planning and implementation of the individualized programs on (a) the priorities that have been set by the curriculum and (b) the amount and type of progress the learners are making toward the curriculum goals. Accordingly, a curriculum should provide instructors and administrators with continuous access to information on how well the learners are advancing toward the aim. A curriculum that creates a framework for obtaining this information will enhance the overall administration and coordination of instructional programs (Knapczyk, 1988).

It is also important to establish communication between every agency that provides instruction in a community because these connections will help the learners gain the maximum benefit from their instruction. Collaboration between schools and rehabilitation agencies in a community will provide appropriate ties across the various settings in which instruction will ultimately take place. The instructional connections that are inherent in community-wide curricula will encourage everyone who interacts with the learners to coordinate teaching efforts and will allow each agency to play to its instructional strengths. When a learner has acquired the skills that are the focus of one agency's programs, he or she should be prepared to move to the programs of another agency and continue to acquire the skills that lead toward independence. Good links across agencies will help prevent one agency from repeating or negating the instruction provided by another agency or program.

Schools and agencies also should construct their curricula to provide continuous instructional programming across the entire service network. This continuity will come about when the curricula used by schools and agencies complement one another and each instructional program carries out its specific role in helping learners progress toward independence in an orderly and systematic manner (Knapczyk, 1988). Preschools, public schools, and adult agencies can begin to meet this ideal by establishing and maintaining a close working relationship with one another during the curriculum development process. Thus, the ideal curriculum development process would be a collaborative effort that promotes continuity in instructional programming for all learners in the community.

The process of developing a curriculum should start with a dialogue between schools and adult agencies that establishes the aim of instruction for their learners. After reaching consensus on the aim, the staffs of these schools and agencies can define specific curriculum goals and objectives that reflect this aim within the context of the mission of each group. Such a dialogue should be community wide and include personnel from all the programs that provide instruction to persons with mental retardation, as well as parents, community officials, and, where applicable, the learners themselves. Devising curricula that are community referenced and well suited to the needs of the learners requires a major investment on the part of schools and agencies, but committing the time and resources to design high-quality curricula will produce many benefits for the learners.

Curriculum Goals

It is impossible to teach in the absence of instructional goals. To illustrate what we mean by this statement, consider the analogy of the traveler presented by Charters (1923):

When a traveler sets out on a journey and knows where to go, he or she will be able to find a way to get there. For example, a traveler who decides to go to Chicago will be able to plan a travel route, decide on conveyances, and do whatever else is necessary to get there, even when problems arise that require the traveler to make adjustments to the original plan of travel (such as when vehicles break down or routes get closed). Similarly, when an instructor sets out to teach and knows where to go, he or she will be able to find a way to get there. That is, instructors who have clear instructional goals not only will be able to develop instructional activities, teach appropriate skills, and do whatever else is necessary to help their learners reach the goals, they will be able to make adjustments if any problems arise. Thus, when the destination is clear, the activities of both the traveler and the instructor can be purposeful, but in the absence of clear end points, the behavior of both traveler and instructor will very likely be random and wandering.

The "destination" of instruction is defined by the curriculum goals that the instructional staff selects. When the curriculum goals are clear to all involved in instruction, the actions of the staff will be focused and the progress of instruction will be steady. Properly stated goals will do two things:

1. guide the rest of the curriculum development process; and
2. give direction to the total instructional program of the school or agency.

Therefore, when developing a curriculum, the most important thing an instructional staff can do (after establishing the aim) is to select the goals toward which instruction will proceed.

To illustrate the formulation of curriculum goals, imagine that we all work at a driver training school that has the aim of teaching learners to drive cars. In order to attain this aim, learners will have to become proficient in certain skill clusters, such as driving cars on highways, driving in cities, parking, planning travel routes, following the rules of the road, and following vehicle maintenance schedules. It would be necessary to teach all of these skill clusters in our driver training program because learners must acquire the skills in each of them to become adept at driving cars. If we stated these skill clusters as goals, they would guide the selection of the content of the instructional program because they would determine which skills to include in the curriculum and which ones to exclude.

After the curriculum goals have been formulated, we can construct the curriculum pathways that allow learners to make progress toward the goals. For example, a proficient driver must know how to drive in cities. If we consider "driving in cities" to be a goal, we can now identify the specific skills learners need to achieve that goal. We would identify some fairly basic skills, like starting a car's engine. But we also must identify other, more complicated skills, like making a left turn at a busy intersection during rush hour. These skills, along with all the other skills required to drive in cities, will become curriculum objectives, and each objective can be sequenced into a curriculum pathway. This pathway will then provide a logical order in which to teach the objectives that allow the learners to make progress toward the goal. Then, when the learners have progressed through the pathway and have acquired all the pertinent skills, they will, in fact, be able to drive cars in cities. In the same manner, it is possible to lay out pathways of objectives for driving cars on highways, for following vehicle maintenance schedules, and for all the other skill clusters that drivers must exhibit. When the learners have acquired all the skills in the pathways and have attained all the goals that serve as end points for the curriculum, they will, in fact, be proficient drivers of cars.

This example also illustrates that curriculum goals do more than just state end points: They also help establish what to include and what not to include in the curriculum pathways. That is, a curriculum goal clarifies not only the skills that learners must acquire, but also those they do not need in order to attain the goal. For example, the skills required to drive a car are very different from those required to read skillfully, to do analytical geometry, or to do the work of a grocery clerk; therefore, it clearly would be a waste of time and energy to include skills needed by readers, mathematicians, or grocery clerks in a driver training program. An instructional program for teaching learners to become skilled mathematicians or grocery clerks must work toward different end points and would contain different types of skills.

The Structure and Content of Curriculum Goals

Curriculum goals have both a structure and a content.

Structure

Anyone who accepts the definition of mental retardation presented in Chapter 2 must also agree that persons with mental retardation require direct instruction (Tarver, 1992). By definition, they are people who do not know how to do certain things, and their instruction must focus directly on teaching the behaviors that will allow them to progress toward being "not retarded" (MacMillan et al., 1996). Therefore, the curriculum goals that are most useful for their instruction will be those that most clearly state what the learners are supposed to be able to do at the end of instruction.

The following model can be used to specify useful goals in both a curriculum and an individualized program of instruction:

The learner will (*action verb*)

This behavioral orientation gives instruction a clarity that is impossible to obtain using any other format (Popham and Baker, 1970). By specifying the end points in terms of the behaviors that the learners must exhibit, instructors develop a precise description of what the learner must do to attain the goal, and instruction can be focused and purposeful. These statements are true even when the behaviors that are relevant to a goal are manifested differently in different places. For example, a goal may state that the learner will "travel from home to various points in the community." When instructors list various locations, such as the mall, the dentist's office, the learner's place of employment, and several restaurants, the skills the learner must acquire will start to become clear. Obviously, these skills will depend on the characteristics of the cities and towns in which the travel takes place, and the behavior pattern for going to the dentist will be different from the pattern for going to the grocery store. But because of the behavioral nature of the goal, the curriculum developers will have no difficulty identifying the required skills in each community.

Educators have used nonbehavioral terms to state instructional outcomes (Bloom, 1956; Frey et al., 1990). However, it is impossible to use these statements to establish curriculum sequences because they make it impossible to obtain agreement on what instruction is supposed to produce. To use the classic example, if the goal is stated as "The learner will increase appreciation for beauty," no two people will agree on what constitutes either "appreciation" or "beauty." Consequently, it is impossible to establish a set of curriculum objectives that lead to this or any other nonbehavioral goal. Note that it would be possible to provide a set of experiences that would allow *some* persons to attain this goal, but its attainment is open to neither instruction nor evaluation: We cannot teach it, nor can we tell when, or even if, it has been achieved. On the other hand, when goals are stated in behavioral terms, they will be both teachable and measurable. Table 3.4 gives examples of behavioral and nonbehavioral goal statements.

TABLE 3.4 Examples of Goals Stated in Behavioral and Nonbehavioral Terms

Behavioral

- Maintain cardiovascular fitness.
- Keep living quarters clean.
- Get and keep a job.
- Wear appropriate leisure clothing.
- Travel from Point A to Point B.

Nonbehavioral

- Enjoy physical fitness.
- Know the need for cleanliness.
- Understand vocational terms and concepts.
- Know effects of weather on leisure activities.
- Appreciate the need for transportation.

Content

Curriculum goals always state *what* learners should be able to do, but they never state the manner in which they should do it. There are two reasons why they should not:

1. curriculum goals are established for groups of learners, each of whom may have to perform the required skills in a different manner; and
2. different learners often must perform the goal skills in different locations, each of which will change the specifics of how they perform the skills.

For example, a goal for children in a preschool program may be "The learners will dress themselves." Clearly, males and females would perform many of the relevant skills differently, and someone who has moderate spasticity would perform them differently from someone who has full range of motion. Similarly, a goal in a residential program might be "The learners will shop for food." The skills for this goal would be performed differently in one food store than in another because all food stores are somewhat different from one another.

Since goals are established to guide the instruction of different learners with varying characteristics who may have to perform in a number of locations, goals must focus only on the "what" of instruction. Specifics such as the "how," "where," and "when" of instruction must be left for the time when instructors develop curriculum objectives and individualized programs of instruction. At that point, it becomes possible to deal with the vagaries of the environment and the challenges posed by groups of learners and individuals. We will address this process later in the chapters on curriculum development, individualized programming, and teaching procedures.

TABLE 3.5 The Functions of Curriculum Goals

Curriculum Goals

- clarify the perceptions of those who work with persons with mental retardation;
- show the direction(s) in which instruction should proceed;
- guide the selection of instructional items for the curriculum;
- help instruction to build over time;
- help curricula maintain internal consistency; and
- help instructors make judgments on the utility and appropriateness of existing curricula.

The Functions of Curriculum Goals

Curriculum goals serve six functions that can be filled by no other mechanism in the Instructional Model. These functions are found in Table 3.5.

Curriculum Goals Clarify the Perceptions of Those Who Work with Persons with Mental Retardation

Curriculum goals restate the aim and make it operational by presenting a clear behavioral vision of what learners with mental retardation must do to attain the aim. When goals are clearly stated, they provide a firm and unbiased view of the behavioral effects of instruction and thus guide the perceptions of instructors, administrators, parents, and other people in the community as to what the instructional programs should try to accomplish.

If all the staff in a school or agency agree upon the curriculum goals, they will develop a shared perception of possibilities. In a most fundamental way, mutually agreed-upon curriculum goals have the potential to modify the entire focus of a school or community agency program. As we explained before, many estimates of the ability of persons with mental retardation to learn have been limited by the perceptions people have about how far persons with mental retardation can progress. Clearly stated goals do the opposite: Rather than set limits, they encourage instructional personnel to think in terms of how much instruction learners need in order to move toward being "not retarded." Thus, by establishing an end point and a direction, goals can motivate the instructional staff to teach learners to achieve at higher levels.

Curriculum Goals Show the Direction(s) in Which Instruction Should Proceed

It is axiomatic that instruction cannot take place if instructors do not know what learners are supposed to learn. John Dewey (1902) once said that the reason curriculum goals are important is not simply because they state the ends of instruction, but because, even when they are far away, they clarify the present direction of movement for instruction. Even when good curricula are not available, instructors who focus on the end points of instruction usually can figure out appropriate skills to teach to their learners. For example, a curriculum goal for elementary-age children with mental retardation may be "The learners will play the same age-appropriate games as other children in the school." Most elementary teachers will not be able to find a curriculum that describes the games elementary school children play at any particular age level and the skills they need in order to play them. However, teachers who have a curriculum goal involving "game playing with peers" will be able to discover both what games their students should play and what skills they need to play them simply by observing the other schoolchildren at play (Knapczyk and Rodes, 1996).

In addition, instructional personnel, like everyone else, sometimes make mistakes, lose their concentration, and go off on unproductive tangents. Inevitably, instruction proceeds down the wrong road, and sooner or later every instructor must regroup. Those who know where instruction is supposed to go will be very much aware of when they lose their direction and will be able to identify the source of the problem quickly. They also will be able to see how to get instruction back on track. In this sense, curriculum goals are very much like beacons in the night: Even when they are far away, it is easy to see in what direction one must go to reach them. In the same vein, clearly stated curriculum goals help instruction remain consistent and on course.

Curriculum Goals Guide the Selection of Curriculum Objectives

Curriculum goals not only provide stable referents for choosing the "things to teach," they also set the boundaries for what to include in a curriculum and what to exclude from it. This function is especially important in developing curricula for persons with mental retardation because it is often very difficult to choose from the wide array of skills that instructors might teach. Curriculum goals give us a basis for determining which of these skills are needed to reach the aim of instruction and which are not. For example, "clapping hands in time to music" has been a popular item in programs for persons with profound retardation; "identifies circles, squares, and triangles" has been a popular item in programs for persons with moderate retardation; and "labeling the parts of speech" has been a popular item in programs for persons with mild retardation. Although instruction in these and many other "nonfunctional" skills is widespread in programs for persons with mental retardation, it is difficult to provide a strong rationale for including them in a curriculum that has the aim of helping learners become independent. However, as long as the goals of instruction are not stated clearly, these and similar instructional objectives will appear in individualized programs.

Curriculum Goals Help Instruction to Build over Time

Current instruction should build on past instruction and allow learners to make orderly and continuous progress in skill development. Unfortunately, as we argued in Chapter 1, except for instruction in the academic subjects for which curriculum sequences have already been established by general education, instructional objectives for persons with mental retardation tend to be selected idiosyncratically. As a consequence, programs of instruction that begin at an early age and progress consistently toward independence tend not to be available for persons with mental retardation.

Curriculum goals provide benchmarks toward which instruction can proceed in an orderly fashion over time, even when it is provided by different persons, programs, or agencies. All the schools and agencies in a local community might select the same curriculum goal for all the learners in the community, and each instructional unit might develop its own set of objectives that lead toward that goal. For example, the goal "The learners will prepare meals for a family group" can have objectives with varying degrees of complexity, ranging from "The learners will feed themselves" to "The learners will prepare evening meals" and "The learners will plan menus." Instructors can decide which specific objectives the learners should meet in each of their programs as they proceed through the community's service delivery network. Later instruction could build on earlier instruction and keep instructors at all levels working toward the same end point. Thus, teachers at the preschool level would be able to select specific aspects of meal preparation to address in their programs (such as feeding oneself, identifying and using specific foods and condiments, or pouring liquids from various containers), and the instruction that followed in later years could build on this foundation. Instruction carried out in this manner also will allow instructors at various levels to agree on the skills that learners should have when they enter upper-level programs. In other words, clear behavioral end points allow successive instructors to coordinate their efforts and to build instruction over time.

Curriculum Goals Help Maintain Instructional Consistency

It is critical to maintain consistency in the skills being taught to people with mental retardation, especially when several different staff members teach the same learners during their instructional day (as often happens in departmentalized school programs, multiservice adult agencies, and situations in which learners receive ancillary and support services). Curriculum goals can improve instructional consistency by focusing the attention of all instructional personnel on the skills the learners need to acquire at each specific point in their individualized programs of instruction.

For example, a goal for a residential program may state that "The learner will maintain the exterior of his or her living quarters." Perhaps one of the skill clusters required to meet this goal is "The learners will mow the lawn." If so, instruction can focus on the skills required to do this task, such as obtaining fuel for the mower, performing maintenance checks on the engine, judging appropriate times to mow the grass, and actually mowing the lawn. Local conventions and manufacturers' instructions will help instructors agree on such matters as where to purchase the fuel, how often to make maintenance checks, and when to mow the grass. The instructors can then construct a list of skills, analyze their associated prerequisites and lead-in skills, and arrange them in curriculum pathways. These pathways then can guide instruction and keep it consistent across instructors, even when the instruction is delivered by persons from different agencies. This list of skills will become part of the total curriculum for teaching learners to maintain the exterior of their living quarters, and all the staff can use the curriculum to further skill development. Then, even if staff turnover occurs, instruction can maintain its original direction. Moreover, a single curriculum can be shared by the various agencies in the community, and even if a learner moves from one program to another, his or her instruction can remain consistent. Clearly, such consistency makes commonly agreed-upon goals well worth the time and effort required to develop them.

Curriculum Goals Allow Accurate Judgments on the Utility and Appropriateness of Existing Curricula

At the present time it is difficult for an agency to select appropriate curricula from among the many documents that are available commercially. There are indeed a number of good curricula available commercially, and many others that have been designed by local agencies for their own internal use. All good curricula have the following two features in common:

1. they have clearly stated behavioral goals; and
2. they are very precise about what the learners must do to achieve these goals.

There are many good curricula that focus on specific skills, such as getting and keeping a job, shopping for food, or using local recreational or leisure facilities. Others address fundamental skill clusters, such as grammatical speech patterns, motor skills, and basic academic skills. Unfortunately, most of the very best curricula have very narrow foci, and instructors who wish to cover a broad range of skill clusters must hunt long and hard to identify the appropriate curricula to carry out their work.

The narrow foci of many of the good curricula can make coordinating instruction across agencies challenging. For example, two instructors might each select good curricula that focus on closely related skill clusters. But since these curricula can address different skills or areas of behavior, coordinating instruction across school or community settings becomes difficult. However, when schools and rehabilitation agencies have clearly stated curriculum goals toward which to work, instructors will be better prepared to coordinate the curricula they select and to connect instructional programs across the agencies in a community.

Unfortunately, instructors also will discover a large number of curricula in print that are not very useful in planning instruction. Typically, these curricula have poorly stated or unstated goals and contain items that are not arranged to form curriculum pathways. When the instructional staff try to use such documents, they are usually disappointed in the results. Instructional staff can select appropriate curricula more quickly if they establish curriculum goals for the learners in their programs before they begin the search. By comparing the agency's goals to those in the curricula they are examining, staff can decide when an existing curriculum will be useful and when it will not.

Terminal and Intermediate Goals

In order to develop a useful set of curriculum goals, curriculum developers must distinguish between two types of goals: *terminal* and *intermediate*. Both types serve as curriculum goals, but they are quite different in many ways.

The biggest distinction between terminal and intermediate goals is in the relationship that each has to the aim of instruction. **Terminal goals** relate directly to the aim in that they restate the aim in behavioral terms and make it instructionally operational. They are called "terminal" because each is the final point in a curriculum pathway. **Intermediate goals** consist of points along the curriculum pathways that an instructional unit selects as curriculum goals for an instructional program. Intermediate goals are less closely linked to the aim because the terminal goals come between them and the aim. Figure 3.3 depicts the relationships among the aim of instruction, terminal goals, and intermediate goals.

Characteristics of Terminal Goals

Table 3.6 lists the characteristics of terminal and intermediate goals. It shows that terminal goals have two major characteristics:

Terminal Goals Make the Aim Instructionally Operational. Terminal goals are tied directly to the aim of instruction and provide the behavioral end points for the total instructional program. When learners attain all the terminal goals, they will have accomplished the aim and will have reached the end of instruction under the aegis of the aim. It is important to

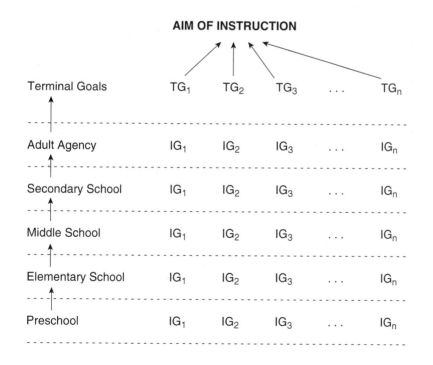

AIM OF INSTRUCTION

Terminal Goals	TG_1	TG_2	TG_3	. . .	TG_n
Adult Agency	IG_1	IG_2	IG_3	. . .	IG_n
Secondary School	IG_1	IG_2	IG_3	. . .	IG_n
Middle School	IG_1	IG_2	IG_3	. . .	IG_n
Elementary School	IG_1	IG_2	IG_3	. . .	IG_n
Preschool	IG_1	IG_2	IG_3	. . .	IG_n

FIGURE 3.3

The relationship between the aim, terminal goals (TG), and intermediate goals (IG).

TABLE 3.6 Characteristics of Terminal and Intermediate Goals

Terminal Goals

- make the aim instructionally operational; and
- have equal status with one another.

Intermediate Goals

- are subsets of terminal goals;
- pertain to specific programs;
- clarify the instructional role of the schools and agencies that have selected them;
- make required skills salient; and
- provide a rallying point for organizing services.

note that we are not saying that the learners will stop learning when they attain the terminal goals. Rather, we are saying that learners who attain all of the terminal goals will have achieved the aim of instruction and further instruction toward that aim is not warranted. If learners who have achieved the aim of instruction want to continue learning, they must move into an instructional program with a different aim, different goals, and a different curriculum. For example, when persons with mental retardation attain all the terminal goals for becoming independent, they will, in fact, have acquired all the skills and qualities that characterize this aim. At that point, they can either enter programs of instruction with other aims (such as one that could help them become qualified for higher levels of employment) or stop their formal instruction altogether.

Terminal Goals Are Equal to One Another. All of the terminal goals have equal importance relative to the aim even though learners may attain some before others. No one terminal goal can be seen as more important than any of the others because a learner must attain all of them in order to fulfill the aim. For example, two terminal goals for learners with mental retardation might be as follows: (1) "The learners will maintain bodily cleanliness," and (2) "The learners will maintain the cleanliness of living quarters." In their instructional programs, most learners are likely to learn to maintain the cleanliness of their bodies before they learn to maintain the cleanliness of their living quarters. However, despite the chronological difference in attaining these goals, both are equally important because people must attain both of them in order to become independent.

Characteristics of Intermediate Goals

As shown in Table 3.6, intermediate goals have five characteristics:

Intermediate Goals Are Subsets of Terminal Goals. Schools and rehabilitation agencies that provide instruction to persons with mental retardation will usually select at least some intermediate goals as curriculum goals that will guide their instructional programs. First, there are usually too many terminal goals for any one program to accomplish. Second, many agencies (such as those that serve young people) have to focus on teaching skills that lead to the terminal goals rather than the skills that make up the terminal goals themselves. In fact, some programs may not incorporate any terminal goals at all in their curricula if the learners are at a very basic level of skill development. For example, a preschool or elementary school program would probably not select items like "The learners will maintain cleanliness of living quarters" as a curriculum goal because the preschoolers are not yet ready to work on the necessary skills. Rather, they would select intermediate goals that young children are apt to be ready to learn, such as "The learners will clear the table after snacks" and "The learners will pick up toys."

The relationship between terminal goals and intermediate goals, and their link to the aim of instruction, allows schools and agencies to distribute curriculum goals across the various community agencies so as to provide comprehensive and continuous programs of instruction that lead to independence for all persons with mental retardation. Each agency would have its own set of curriculum goals, but all the curriculum goals would lead toward the same aim of instruction. In this manner, the distributed terminal and intermediate goals for curricula in community agencies would lay out a complete course of instruction for persons with mental retardation.

Intermediate Goals Pertain to Specific Programs. Intermediate goals should be based on the characteristics of the learners in a program because they set the stage for planning instruction that is uniquely suited to those individuals. A preschool program for children with moderate and severe retardation, for example, may select curriculum goals that focus on basic self-care, language, motor coordination, and childhood social interaction, while a multipurpose adult rehabilitation agency may choose goals that focus on competitive employment, community travel, home living, and community-based leisure activities. The goals for these two programs must be very different, partly because the learners are at very different points relative to the aim of independence, but also because the two agencies have very different purposes. The array of intermediate goals that schools and agencies select for their curricula should be based on the ages and other characteristics of the learners in the program, and the resulting curricula will help the staff plan instructional content that is appropriate for their learners. Each distinct instructional program in each school and rehabilitation agency must select a unique set of curriculum goals, but the goals of all programs in all schools and agencies must lead toward the same terminal goals and aim.

Intermediate Goals Clarify the Roles of Schools and Agencies. When an instructional unit selects a set of intermediate goals to guide its curriculum, it clarifies its role and responsibilities in its community. One of the benefits of this clarification is that the staff will be more likely to focus on doing the things that it should do, which, in turn, will help the agency keep its instructional programs focused. If curriculum goals progress across programs, the staff also will be encouraged to recognize the role that all the other schools and agencies play in the community's service delivery system and to rely on the strengths of each.

Many people assume that learners who graduate from public school programs have reached the end of their instruction. However, most persons with mental retardation require instruction beyond that which public schools can provide, and in many cases, the instruction must continue on well into adulthood. For some, it can never stop. Unfortunately, the structure of the public schools limits what can be taught in their programs. That is, public schools can provide instruction only during certain hours of the day, certain days of the week, and certain times of the year. They can teach only in certain locations and use only certain equipment and materials. These limitations prevent school personnel from providing instruction in many types of skills, and persons who require instruction in such skills must get it in other agencies. For example, public schools cannot effectively teach skills that learners would normally use on a Saturday night because the schools are not in session over the weekend. However, community residential and recreational programs often have a schedule that permits them to teach these skills. Even public school programs for 12th-grade adolescents with mild retardation probably will not be able to attend to all the goals these learners must attain. Rather, these programs must select intermediate goals that are realistic for the schools to teach, and then try to coordinate their instruction with that of the community agencies that are capable of addressing the other skill clusters. If the schools and adult agencies work together, they can develop comprehensive curricula and more effectively help learners progress steadily toward independence.

Intermediate Goals Make Required Skills Salient. Persons with mental retardation must acquire many basic skills, but the specific skills they need may not become clear until the intermediate goals have been stated in behavioral terms. Because terminal goals are usually defined broadly, it is easy to overlook the wide variety of skills that comprise or lead up to them. For example, a terminal goal such as "traveling to different locations in a community" may require learners to work on skill clusters that may vary according to the size of the community, the availability of transportation, and the interests of the learners. Thus, many basic skill clusters become apparent only after the staff lists the intermediate goals for a specific instructional program and begins to analyze the skills that define the curriculum pathways.

Intermediate Goals Provide a Rallying Point for Organizing Services. Intermediate goals allow schools and rehabilitation agencies to lay out the course of instruction for their learners regardless of how much time the instruction requires. This is an important feature of intermediate goals because persons with mental retardation often require instruction that takes place over a very long time period. If the various agencies work together to formulate their intermediate goals, they can coordinate their instructional programs and provide continuous, focused instruction that helps learners progress much further than they might progress under the current system.

At different points in their instructional programs, persons with mental retardation may require the services of several community agencies if they are to make steady progress toward independence. The curriculum goals for these programs may need to overlap, or at least complement one another, to allow the learners to receive a complete and consistent instructional program and to keep redundancy and gaps in services to a minimum. If agencies coordinate their efforts when selecting their curriculum goals, learners can progress along a consistent and continuous course of instruction leading to independence.

Concluding Statement

It is necessary to view curriculum development as a collaborative process across the entire service delivery network in a community. The curricula found in the various agencies should complement one another even though each instructional unit has its own curriculum. If the curricula in a community complement one another, each instructional unit can carry out its role in helping persons with mental retardation make progress toward independence, and all persons with mental retardation in a community can advance toward this aim. The ideal for which instructional personnel should strive, then, is for the combined curricula of all instructional units in a community to ensure that each learner progresses toward independence in an orderly and systematic manner, no matter where that person is in the service delivery network. Schools and rehabilitation agencies can meet this ideal by developing and maintaining a close working relationship with one another during the curriculum development process.

CHAPTER 4

Formulating the Aim and Curriculum Goals

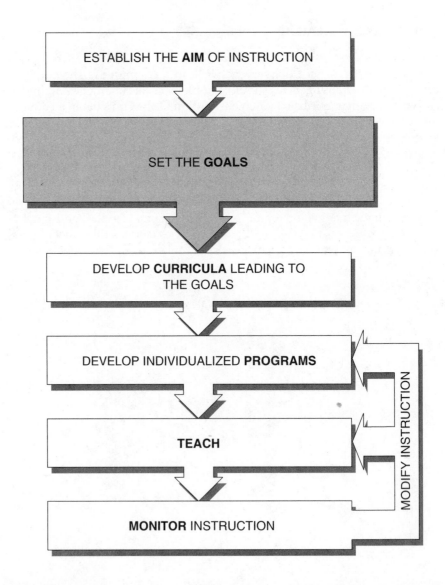

ESTABLISH THE **AIM** OF INSTRUCTION

SET THE **GOALS**

DEVELOP **CURRICULA** LEADING TO THE GOALS

DEVELOP INDIVIDUALIZED **PROGRAMS**

TEACH

MONITOR INSTRUCTION

MODIFY INSTRUCTION

When working under the Instructional Model, the first step in developing a curriculum is to establish the aim of the instructional program. Once the aim is available, the staff can formulate the curriculum goals and then develop the rest of the curriculum. In this chapter, we will show how an instructional staff can prepare a clear aim statement and list the goals that will serve as end points for its curriculum.

The aim of instruction determines the goals that can be selected. In turn, the goals determine the form the completed curriculum will take. The staff members who develop a curriculum for an instructional unit in a school or a rehabilitation facility must be very careful to prepare an aim statement that accurately reflects what they want the curriculum to accomplish. An improper aim statement might give the instructional staff the wrong mind-set, which can cause unrelenting problems during the curriculum development process. On the other hand, a good aim statement will focus the attention of the curriculum developers tightly on what they have to accomplish and allow the curriculum development process to move along at a steady pace.

We believe that all curricula, even those that focus on intermediate goals, must point toward the aim of instruction that we presented in Chapter 2: that persons with mental retardation will become independent. But this statement is too broad to guide the development process for any real curriculum, even when that curriculum is comprehensive in nature. No curriculum can possibly teach everything that learners with mental retardation need to do to become independent; rather, each curriculum must focus on its own piece of the instructional pie. For example, the curriculum goals for young persons, such as those for preschool, elementary, and middle school learners, must include many intermediate goals; instructional programs for these learners cannot use the aim of independence directly to guide the development of their curricula. Moreover, a vocational, residential, or recreational training program might focus directly on teaching learners to become independent, but only in a specific skill area, like employment, homemaking, or leisure skills. None of these programs would attempt to teach the full range of skills that are required for independence. Therefore, although each instructional program should have the ultimate aim of independence for its learners, it also must develop a more focused aim statement to guide the construction of its own unique curriculum.

Stating the Aim of Instruction

In order to state an appropriate aim of instruction, each curriculum development group must establish the limits within which it will operate. Specifically, the members of a group must understand the thrust of their agency, the purpose of the instructional unit within which they work, the strengths of the agency on which they can capitalize, and the weaknesses of the agency which serve to constrain instruction. Therefore, before we address the actual procedure for stating an aim, we must explain how these issues affect instructional programming.

Factors That Affect the Scope of a Curriculum

Establishing the operational limits requires the staff and all other concerned persons to think about the factors that influence the aim, goals, and curriculum of an instructional unit. If the staff members understand these influences prior to beginning curriculum development, they will be in a much better position to carry out the development project successfully.

An early set of decisions the administration must make is how big the curriculum should be and who should carry out the curriculum development process. For example, a school system or a large rehabilitation facility may develop a comprehensive curriculum, but decide that the easiest and most useful way to approach the task is to have each instructional unit (or some combination of units) develop a smaller curriculum that later will be integrated with the others into a single overall framework. Regardless of the way the agency decides to develop its curriculum, the decisions on how to do it should be made at an early point in the process.

There are many things for an instructional unit to think about when developing its aim. Table 4.1 presents nine factors that a unit should consider when it states an aim of instruction. If the staff considers these factors carefully, they will find that the following events will probably take place:

- they will determine the features of the school or agency that foster or constrain the overall scope of its instructional programs;
- they will analyze the strengths of the units and the current impediments to instruction;
- they will develop a realistic picture of what the curriculum should and should not include;
- they will begin to expand the scope of instruction, and possibly even begin to overcome some of the barriers that are present; and
- they will be able to prepare a clear aim statement that will guide the development of the curriculum.

Benefits like these make the difficult process of establishing the aim a worthwhile enterprise for any instructional unit.

The Mission Statement

Each school and agency should have a mission statement that defines both its role and its responsibilities in providing services to persons with mental retardation. The mission of many schools and rehabilitation agencies is assigned to them, at least in part, by a school board, a board of directors, or the local service delivery network. For example, some agencies will have responsibilities limited to areas such as vocational services, while others will have responsibilities that encompass many different service areas, such as medical, social, and/or psychological services, along with instruction in one or more curriculum content areas. Consequently, a mission statement may be very narrow or it may be very broad.

TABLE 4.1 Factors Affecting a Curriculum

- The mission of the school or rehabilitation agency
- The programmatic thrust of the instructional unit
- The clients served by the instructional unit
- The staff's talents and limitations
- The limitations of the school or agency's physical plant
- The community resources available to the school or agency
- The location of the school or agency
- The time available for instruction
- The policies and procedures of the school or agency

The mission of a school or service agency is stated in response to the following question:

What is the function of this school/agency in the community?

As the examples in Table 4.2 show, the mission statement should direct everyone's attention to the type of instruction the agency will provide to its learners and clarify the focus of its curricula in terms of the specific skill areas that will be their core. Unfortunately, the missions of many schools and agencies are often left unstated or are described in very broad and ambiguous terms. This situation can create confusion among those who develop a curriculum because without clear guidelines, the staff cannot be sure what to include or not include in the curriculum. Therefore, in situations in which the mission of a school or agency is unstated or is unclear, the staff should get together with all interested persons and define the agency's mission in terms that clarify the types of instructional services it provides. If a mission statement is already available, everyone involved should review it very carefully and consider its appropriateness before they begin to develop a curriculum. If everyone does not agree, they should take the time to work through their differences. Because the mission statement is so important, and its effects so permeating, any and all time spent developing an accurate statement is worthwhile.

Wehman, Kregel, Barcus, and Schalock (1986) have suggested that as a school or rehabilitation agency works to clarify its mission, it should also work with other agencies in the community to try to make its mission complement those of the other service providers. The missions for instructional services should be coordinated across agencies so as to form a comprehensive network of instructional services for persons with mental retardation. Ideally, even though all the schools and rehabilitation agencies in a community have different instructional thrusts, they should strive for the following:

- that all the items contained in the combined curricula of the schools and other community agencies permit any individual with mental retardation to progress toward independence in an orderly and systematic manner; and

TABLE 4.2 Examples of Mission Statements for School or Community Agencies

Our mission is
- (A preschool program)
  to prepare preschool children to participate effectively in public school kindergarten programs;
- (A public school program)
  to prepare our students to enter adult life as workers, skilled consumers, and members of the community who participate in the affairs of the community and (for the academically talented) to enter college;
- (A vocational training program)
  to prepare young adults to hold jobs in community employment settings;
- (A leisure skills program)
  to prepare adults to travel to and participate in a wide variety of age-appropriate community-based leisure activities.

- that any overlap in the provision of instructional services in the community is closely coordinated and monitored (Knapczyk, 1988).

Schools and community agencies that have clearly-stated missions will be in a position to develop curricula that accomplish these outcomes.

The Programmatic Thrust of the Agency

The areas on which the agency centers its programs will also influence the aim it selects to guide development of its curriculum. One instructional unit may focus on a limited set of goals, whereas another may focus on a much broader set because of the scope of the programs it provides.

In addition, a curriculum that teaches skills that lead to independence must focus on the behavioral demands of the settings into which the learners will go when they leave the school, the agency, or the instructional unit (Falvey, 1986; Knapczyk, 1988; Wilcox and Bellamy, 1987). For example, the aim of a curriculum for elementary-age children with mental retardation should be broad enough to reflect not only the behavioral demands of their current grades, but also of future grades. Similarly, the aim of a curriculum for adolescents and adults with mental retardation should be broad enough to account for the behavioral demands of the community settings in which they will eventually live, work, and play. Questions such as the following will be helpful in clarifying the program thrust:

- Does the instructional unit teach a wide range of community living skills, as might be true of a community residential program, or does it concentrate on a narrow range of skills, as might be true of a program for physical exercise?
- Does the agency teach skills across a broad range of age groupings, as would be true of a K–12 school program, or does it focus on a narrow band of ages, as would be true of a leisure skills program for young adults in a group home?

- In what specific areas should the unit concentrate its instruction? For example, should it focus on functional academic skills, homemaking skills, vocational skills, or some other set of skills?
- Should the instructional program be comprehensive or restricted?
- What skills must the learners acquire in order to function adequately in their present situations? What skills must they acquire to make the transition to their next placement?

Learner Characteristics

Each group of learners served by an agency or by a program in an agency is unique and may require instruction in different skill clusters. Therefore, it is necessary to appraise the characteristics of the group for whom the curriculum will be developed before trying to formulate the aim or the curriculum goals. Questions such as the following are helpful:

- What are the ages and functional levels of the learners? For example, are they teenagers with mild retardation, adults with severe retardation, or toddlers with a wide range of intellectual levels?
- What special problems or additional disabilities do the learners present? For example, do the learners have normal physical abilities or do they present orthopedic problems?
- At what level will the unit teach its learners to participate in the community? For example, a secondary school program for learners with mild mental retardation might teach its learners to participate fully in the community, while a program for students with severe mental retardation may limit its instruction to partial participation of the learners in the same community settings.

The Talents and Limitations of the Staff

Instructional units also vary in the number, quality, and expertise of the staff members that are involved in developing and delivering the instructional programs. An agency with many staff limitations would generally require a more tightly organized curriculum, while an agency with a large, well-trained, highly competent staff may address a much broader range of skills. Accordingly, questions such as the following may need to be answered:

- What professional backgrounds and skills are represented by the instructional staff members? For example, does the staff consist of a fully trained cadre of professionals? Is it composed primarily of minimum wage entry-level paraprofessionals?
- What types of support staff can be called on to assist the instructional staff?
- Schools and agencies rarely have enough staff available to provide all the instruction their learners need. How many staff hours are available in a typical work period? Is there enough time to deliver

individual instruction for all learners, or must learners be grouped? Are learners grouped for all or part of the instruction?

- Are there special requirements for staff, such as drivers' licenses for transporting learners or liability insurance?

The Limitations of the Physical Plant

The availability of facilities for instructional purposes affects the types of curriculum goals that can be included in a curriculum, and therefore must be reflected in the aim. For example, it is possible to deliver some instruction within the boundaries of the physical plant of a school or rehabilitation agency, such as academic skills for elementary-age learners with mild mental retardation, and basic motor, self-help, and social skills for learners with moderate and severe mental retardation. But the physical plant of many other schools and agencies may not allow certain skills to be taught, and the staff must take these limitations into account when they develop a curriculum. For example, if a staff wants to teach skills in the area of homemaking, they quickly will discover that the learners must have access to living quarters and to the supplies and equipment typically found in them. If such access is not available, the staff will not be able to develop effective instructional programs in these areas. The following are some important questions to consider:

- What agency facilities are available for instructional purposes?
- How often or for how long a period do learners have access to these facilities?
- Must specially trained staff oversee the activities in these facilities (e.g., in the swimming pool or in the shop)?
- Is additional staff needed to supervise the facilities?

Community Resources

Many instructional units that focus on teaching community living skills can usually reduce both the need for agency space and for purchasing supplies and equipment by providing instruction directly in the community. Community settings, such as stores, banks, and restaurants, can provide all the equipment and space necessary to prepare learners to function in these settings. Residential and vocational programs are usually well aware of the advantages of delivering instruction directly in community settings.

Every secondary school and adult rehabilitation agency should consider the fact that establishing cooperative arrangements with members of the community can greatly enhance the number of opportunities for teaching valuable skills (Beebe and Karan, 1986). Many persons in the community are able to help out in instructional programs for persons with mental retardation in the context of their day-to-day work, and are perfectly willing to do so. For example, community bus drivers could be alerted to the fact that learners with mental retardation may get confused about where they are in the community when they are on the bus, and the drivers may be willing to assist in teaching them where to get off the bus. Such actions may be well within their normal bus-driving duties; thus, an agency may find that it does not need as many staff members to carry out its travel training programs as it originally had thought.

Normally, an agency that can take advantage of local resources and expertise will be able to adopt a larger number of curriculum goals than one in which the staff works under more isolated conditions. Some questions the staff may ask are the following:

- Is the local community supportive of the agency's efforts, or is there opposition? If there is opposition, how strong and how organized is it?
- Does the agency have access to all the equipment the learners will require, or does it have constraints imposed by nonexistent, inappropriate, or out-of-date equipment? If there are equipment constraints, how severe are they?
- Does the agency have sufficient funds to carry out a wide range of programs, or is funding restricted (relative to how much is available or how the funds can be used)?
- Is it possible to rely on persons in the community to provide part of the necessary instruction?

The Location of the Instructional Unit

The location of a school or rehabilitation agency in a community can facilitate or limit the number of skills the instructional staff can teach. For example, a vocational training agency in downtown Chicago can teach a wide range of downtown travel routes, but a school or rehabilitation agency that is located in an area in which there are street gangs may be very limited in the number of walking routes it can teach its learners to use. Community settings can place constraints on the skills the staff can teach; therefore, it is important to think about the instructional program's location in the community. Some questions the staff might ask are the following:

- Is the community safe? Is it hospitable? Are there areas in the community that cannot be used for instructional purposes?
- Is the agency located in an area that has easy walking or vehicular access to the community, or is transportation a problem?

Available Program Time

Few schools or rehabilitation agencies that serve persons with mental retardation are in contact with their learners for 24 hours a day, 7 days a week. Therefore, schools and agencies that teach learners to perform skills in the community usually would not teach skills that the learners normally perform outside the hours during which the program is in operation. Moreover, the manner in which time blocks are scheduled for instruction also can limit or expand the types of skills that can be included in a curriculum. For example, if instructional time slots are scheduled in small segments to allow for things such as 50-minute instructional periods, the provision of ancillary services, or staff breaks that are timed on a rotating basis, the schedule can significantly limit the ability of staff to teach the complicated routines inherent in some curriculum goals. Such a schedule can limit instruction in areas that require large blocks of time to teach the learners to acquire and integrate all the related skills, such as vocational, homemaking, and travel skills. For example, to teach the skills that are required to prepare food, serve it, and clean up after meals, instructors will need sufficient time to show learners how to review the menu, locate ingredients and cookware, plan food preparation sequences, prepare the foods, eat, and clean up afterwards. To carry out instruction in areas as complicated as this one, the program schedule would have to allow sufficient time both to teach learners everything they must do and to show them how to integrate these skills into smooth behavioral routines.

Therefore, questions such as the following are appropriate to ask:

- What times are available for instructional purposes?
- Can the available times be scheduled as a single instructional block, or must they be divided into smaller segments?
- Can the available times be scheduled for a single instructional area, or must they be divided across curriculum areas (e.g., math/reading or vocational/leisure)?

Policies and Procedures of the School or Rehabilitation Agency

A final consideration in setting the aim of instruction is the policies and procedures that have been established by a school or rehabilitation agency. There may be strict guidelines on any number of issues that can affect instruction. For example, a school or agency may have restrictive policies on

- who can supervise learners;
- what role volunteers can play in instructional programs;
- the liability for various school/agency/community locations;
- which sexes can work alone with which learners; and
- the locations in which instruction can be conducted.

Such policies are important to think about when establishing an aim for instruction because they affect the scope of instructional programs both positively and negatively (Knapczyk, 1988). For example, the staff of an adult vocational training program may want students to learn to respond to situations like equipment breakdowns, work stoppages, harassment by fellow workers, and on-the-job emergencies. However, if the agency is unable or unwilling to permit implementation of the instructional activities that will teach the learners to handle situations like these, skills in these areas cannot be included in the agency's curriculum. Therefore, it is important to ask questions such as the following:

- Do any agency policies place limitations on
  –the type of skills that can be taught?
  –the manner in which instruction may be carried out?
  –the personnel who can teach?

–the locations in which instruction can take place?
–the times at which instruction can take place?
- If so, can these policies be changed?

Potential for Restructuring

A comprehensive review of the agency, its purpose, and its instructional strengths and weaknesses will naturally help to establish the boundaries of the curriculum and sharpen the focus of the staff who carry out the agency's instructional programs. In addition, such an examination can provide a catalyst for restructuring, upgrading, or expanding the instructional programs because it allows the staff to consider ways to overcome any barriers to instruction they may have identified (we will address possible responses to such barriers later in the chapter). This outcome alone makes the review worthwhile. In addition, the results of the review will be used at several other points during the instructional process, and the data should be preserved in preparation for those uses.

The Aim Statement

Appendix B contains a blank work sheet that will help curriculum developers establish an aim for an instructional unit. The front page of the work sheet also can serve as a cover sheet for the curriculum of an instructional program because it helps the staff describe the framework within which the curriculum was developed.

Table 4.3 presents an example of this work sheet that has been completed for the fourth- to sixth-grade unit of Thomas Jefferson Elementary School. The reader should refer to this example as we discuss the use of the work sheet.

The first page of the work sheet has a space for entering the name of the school or agency and its mission. Next are spaces for listing the name of the instructional unit and its program thrust within the overall instructional program of the school or agency. At the end of the first section is space for stating the aim of the curriculum. In stating the aim, the staff should describe very clearly what their instructional unit will actually teach the learners to become. The following format is useful for developing this statement:

The learners will become _____.

Table 4.4 provides several examples of aim statements that might be used by various schools and agencies. Note that these statements indicate the role that the instructional unit will play in teaching people with mental retardation to become independent. Given similar statements of purpose, the aim of any unit can be described in a manner that parents, administrators, instructional staff, and others involved in the instructional programs can understand easily.

The second and third pages of the work sheet provide spaces for making notes about each of the factors that can influence the scope of the instructional programs. The staff members can use these pages during their

TABLE 4.3 Work Sheet for Establishing an Instructional Aim

Name of School/Agency: Thomas Jefferson Elementary School

School/Agency Mission: To prepare students to become contributing members of their families and active participants in the community.

Instructional Unit: Intermediate Level (Grades 4–6)

Program Thrusts: Academic, social, and organizational skills that will enable students to benefit from and be successful in school activities.

Aim of the Curriculum: The students will become fully participating members of the school program, including both academic and nonacademic school settings.

Considerations/Assumptions:

Learner Characteristics: Students with mild mental retardation at the intermediate level generally have good language and motor skills (students with physical or sensory disabilities are usually served by other programs in the school district).

Talents of the Staff: Two teachers and an instructional assistant are assigned to the program. Ms. Lewis, one of the teachers, is also certified in elementary education and is very experienced in teaching the general education curriculum. All the staff members have a strong rapport with the general education teachers throughout the school, and most of the fourth- through sixth-grade teachers support or at least cooperate with inclusion efforts. However, we will need to do some in-service training in specific techniques and curricular adaptations for teaching our students.

Limitations of the Physical Plant: None for the academic areas, but we will not be able to work on many cooking, cleaning, and personal hygiene skills. Maybe we can work with parents on these.

Community Resources: About half the students have strong home support that can assist with teaching and carryover of academic and study skills. Leaders for Boy/Girl Scout troops and Boys/Girls Club programs, coaches for community sports groups, and people from other community recreational programs have close ties with our school program and usually work well with special education children.

Location of Instructional Unit: In the school building, the special education programs are in the general education intermediate classrooms. Transportation to community recreational programs is problematic for most students. Maybe we could get the school district or a community service organization to purchase a vehicle for after-school activities if we can find a driver and pay for the fuel and insurance—a fund-raising possibility. If so, we could work on more social and recreational skills.

Program Times: M–F, 9:00 A.M.–3:15 P.M., September 1–June 10.

Limiting Policies: We need to clarify the policy for having general education teachers and paraprofessional staff supervise special education students. This policy may affect the scope of inclusion activities, limiting our work to only two or three general education classrooms during any one instructional period. In addition, we can make field trips, but the children are not allowed to make daily excursions out of the school building unattended.

TABLE 4.4 Examples of the Form That Statements of the Aim of Specific
Curricula Might Take

The learners will become
(for school programs)
- functioning students in the regular third grade at _____ elementary school;
- active participants in the extracurricular activities at _____ middle school;
- citizens of _____ (community) who will be paid employees of local businesses or agencies and can handle their personal finances, travel about the community, use the local recreation and leisure sites, and fulfill their civic duties.

(for rehabilitation center programs)
- full participants in the leisure sites in _____ (community);
- apartment dwellers who meet the standards of the neighborhood in terms of neatness, cleanliness, and social interactions;
- skilled users of the public transportation system in _____ (community).

review of the resources of the school or agency to describe any variables or considerations that they feel might affect the parameters or scope of the curriculum in a significant manner. Table 4.3 shows that the staff members at Thomas Jefferson Elementary School used these spaces to indicate their reasons for including or excluding certain goal areas or skill clusters in their curriculum and for proposing strategies for overcoming or circumventing barriers to instruction.

Selecting Curriculum Goals

After stating the aim of instruction, the next step is to state the goals that make the aim operational and guide the development of the curriculum. The curriculum goals may consist of any number of combinations of terminal and intermediate goals. In Chapter 3 we stated that terminal goals are instructional end points that, taken together, make the aim of instruction operational. We also stated that intermediate goals are curriculum goals selected by an instructional unit that lead toward terminal goals.

The instructional staff who develop curricula for persons with mental retardation must understand and agree upon a set of terminal goals for persons with mental retardation, even if the curriculum for a given unit contains only intermediate goals. The reason is that the terminal goals state the end points toward which *all* curriculum goals for persons with mental retardation will progress and establish benchmarks for any intermediate goals a school or agency may choose to guide its own curriculum. Therefore, we will begin the discussion on how to formulate curriculum goals by first considering terminal goals: what they are and where to find them.

Curriculum goals should focus on the skills that people with mental retardation need to learn in order to leave us.

Photo courtesy of James L. Shaffer.

Terminal Goals

Goals are established in answer to the following question:

> What must learners be able to do to show that they have attained the aim of instruction?

The skill clusters that appear in answer to this question will constitute the end points of instruction. For example, if the aim of the unit is to prepare learners to be competent readers, the curriculum goals would consist of the skill clusters typical of successful readers; similarly, if the aim is to prepare learners to be landscapers, the curriculum goals would consist of the skill clusters typical of successful landscapers, and so forth. Thus, a curriculum goal for competent readers might be "The learners will read the local newspaper daily," and for landscapers, "The learners will plant trees and shrubs."

The terminal goals for the aim of independence consist of the things people must do to live, work, and recreate in their communities. Thus, a complete statement of terminal goals for persons with mental retardation would be a list of all the skill clusters that "successful" people perform in the course of their daily lives.

It would be a very difficult and time-consuming task to list all the behavioral end points for independence. Fortunately, the job has already been accomplished, and we are able to provide a complete list of terminal goals (Appendix A). This list of goals can be used to guide the development of all curricula for persons with mental retardation.

The List of Terminal Goals for Independence

The **List of Terminal Goals** found in Appendix A is actually a list of the skill clusters that people must exhibit to be seen as independent in any community. Instructional personnel can use it in one of two ways:

1. directly, to select terminal goals that will become curriculum goals for their schools or rehabilitation agencies; or
2. indirectly, as the referent for selecting the intermediate goals that will become curriculum goals for their schools or rehabilitation agencies.

The Structure of the List of Terminal Goals

The original version of the List of Terminal Goals was published by the American Association on Mental Retardation (Dever, 1988) as *Community Living Skills: A Taxonomy.* The List of Terminal Goals found in Appendix A is a revised version of this original document. The major features of the list are the following:

Domains. Table 4.5 presents the 60 goals in the list in Appendix A and shows that they are organized into five **domains.** Figure 4.1 depicts the relationships among the various domains. That is, the domain that focuses on the personal needs of the learner, "Personal Maintenance and Development," is represented by the circle in the center of the figure. Surrounding the person are the three domains that center on community life: "Homemaking and Community Life," "Vocational," and "Leisure." Finally, the "Travel" domain connects the learner with the community.

The contents of each domain are shown in Table 4.6. This table shows that each domain is subdivided into four categories. Three of the domains contain the skills that are performed in public places in the community (Vocational, Homemaking and Community Life, and Leisure). Each of these domains has a section related to discovering the relevant aspects of the community (finding a place to live, finding a job, and finding leisure activities). The nonpublic domains (Travel and Personal Maintenance) do not have these sections. Rather, the first sections of these two domains focus on skills that people tend to develop at early ages.

TABLE 4.5 Major Goals in the List of Terminal Goals

Domain P: Personal Maintenance and Development

P/I: Goals Related to Routine Body Maintenance

P/I A: The Learner Will Maintain Personal Cleanliness and Grooming
P/I B: The Learner Will Dress Appropriately
P/I C: The Learner Will Follow Illness Prevention Procedures

P/II: Goals Related to Illness Treatment

P/II A: The Learner Will Use First Aid and Illness Treatment Procedures
P/II B: The Learner Will Obtain Medical Advice and/or Treatment When Necessary

P/III: Goals Related to Establishing and Maintaining Personal Relationships

P/III A: The Learner Will Interact with Family
P/III B: The Learner Will Make Friends
P/III C: The Learner Will Interact with Friends
P/III D: The Learner Will Maintain Relationships with Family and Friends

P/IV: Goals Related to Coping with Personal Glitches

P/IV A: The Learner Will Cope with Changes in Daily Schedule
P/IV B: The Learner Will Cope with Equipment Breakdowns or Material Depletions

Domain H: Homemaking and Community Life

H/I: Goals Related to Obtaining Living Quarters

H/I A: The Learner Will Find Living Quarters
H/I B: The Learner Will Set Up Living Quarters

H/II: Goals Related to Community Life Routines

H/II A: The Learner Will Keep Living Quarters Neat and Clean
H/II B: The Learner Will Clean/Repair/Replace Fabric Items
H/II C: The Learner Will Maintain the Interior of Living Quarters
H/II D: The Learner Will Maintain the Exterior of Living Quarters
H/II E: The Learner Will Respond to Seasonal Changes
H/II F: The Learner Will Follow Home Safety Procedures
H/II G: The Learner Will Follow Home Accident/Emergency Procedures
H/II H: The Learner Will Maintain Food Stock
H/II I: The Learner Will Prepare Meals
H/II J: The Learner Will Budget Money
H/II K: The Learner Will Pay Bills

H/III: Goals Related to Coexisting with Others in a Neighborhood and Community

H/III A: The Learner Will Interact with Others in the Community
H/III B: The Learner Will Observe the Requirements of the Law
H/III C: The Learner Will Respond to the Inappropriate Conduct of Others in the
  Community
H/III D: The Learner Will Carry Out Civic Duties

TABLE 4.5 (*continued*)

H/IV: Goals Related to Handling Community-Related Glitches

H/IV A: The Learner Will Cope with Community Schedule Disruptions
H/IV B: The Learner Will Cope with Equipment Breakdowns or Material Depletions
H/IV C: The Learner Will Cope with Sudden Changes in the Weather

Domain V: Vocational

V/I: Goals Related to Obtaining Employment

V/I A: The Learner Will Seek Employment
V/I B: The Learner Will Accept Employment
V/I C: The Learner Will Use Unemployment Services

V/II: Goals Related to Performing Work Routines

V/II A: The Learner Will Perform the Job Routine
V/II B: The Learner Will Follow Work-Related Daily Schedule
V/II C: The Learner Will Follow Employer Rules and Regulations
V/II D: The Learner Will Maintain the Workstation
V/II E: The Learner Will Follow Safety Procedures on the Job
V/II F: The Learner Will Follow Standard Accident and Emergency Procedures on the Work
  Site

V/III: Goals Related to Coexisting with Others on the Job

V/III A: The Learner Will Interact with Others on the Job
V/III B: The Learner Will Respond to the Inappropriate Conduct of Others on the Job

V/IV: Goals Related to Handling Work-Related Glitches

V/IV A: The Learner Will Cope with Changes in the Work Routine

Domain L: Leisure

L/I: Goals Related to Developing Leisure Activities

L/I A: The Learner Will Find New Leisure Activities

L/II: Goals Related to Performing Leisure Activities

L/II A: The Learner Will Perform Leisure Activities
L/II B: The Learner Will Maintain Personal Leisure Equipment
L/II C: The Learner Will Follow Leisure Activity Safety Procedures
L/II D: The Learner Will Follow Accident and Emergency Procedures for Leisure Activities

L/III: Goals Related to Coexisting with Others During Leisure Activities

L/III A: The Learner Will Interact with Others During Leisure Time
L/III B: The Learner Will Respond to the Inappropriate Conduct of Others During Leisure
  Activity

L/IV: Goals Related to Handling Leisure-Related Glitches

L/IV A: The Learner Will Respond to Changes in Leisure Routine
L/IV B: The Learner Will Respond to Equipment Breakdowns and Material Depletions

TABLE 4.5 *(continued)*

Domain T: Travel

T/I: Goals Related to Routine Travel in the Community

T/I A: The Learner Will Develop Mental Maps of Frequented Buildings
T/I B: The Learner Will Develop Mental Maps of the Community

T/II: Goals Related to the Use of Conveyances

T/II A: The Learner Will Follow Usage Procedures for Conveyances
T/II B: The Learner Will Make Decisions Prior to Travel
T/II C: The Learner Will Follow Travel Safety Procedures
T/II D: The Learner Will Follow Accident/Emergency Procedures While Traveling

T/III: Goals Related to Coexisting with Others During Travel

T/III A: The Learner Will Interact with Others During Travel
T/III B: The Learner Will Respond to the Inappropriate Conduct of Others During Travel

T/IV: Goals Related to Handling Travel-Related Glitches

T/IV A: The Learner Will Cope with Glitches While Traveling

FIGURE 4.1

Organization of the goals.

From: *Community Living Skills: A Taxonomy.* Washington, DC: AAMR Monograph Series, Monograph #10.

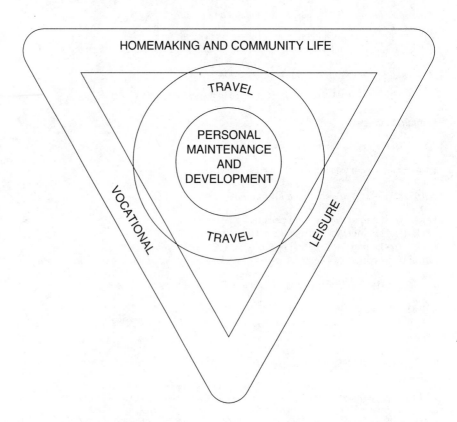

TABLE 4.6 Contents of Domains in the List of Terminal Goals

Personal Maintenance and Development	Homemaking and Community Life	Vocational	Leisure	Travel
Contains the skill clusters for caring for oneself and interacting with friends and relatives. The curriculum goals in this domain range from skills such as "feed oneself" (preschool level) to "maintain health and physical conditioning" (adolescence and adulthood); and from "interact with others" (preschool) to "establish and maintain personal relationships" (adolescence and adulthood).	Contains the skill clusters for living in a home and a neighborhood and using community facilities to carry out domestic responsibilities. The curriculum goals found in this domain range from "store one's possessions" (preschool) to "maintain one's physical environment" (adolescence and adulthood); and from "share play materials" (preschool) to "coexist with others in the community" (adolescence and adulthood).	Contains the skill clusters for obtaining and keeping a job. The curriculum goals found in this domain range from "identify work" (preschool) to "perform the jobs assigned" (adolescence and adulthood); and from "identify vocational roles" (preschool) to "interact with supervisors, fellow workers, and subordinates" (adolescence and adulthood).	Contains the skill clusters for performing activities during free times when one is required neither to work nor to do chores. The curriculum goals found in this domain vary from "identify free time" (preschool) to "budget free time productively" (adolescence and adulthood); and from "follow game rules" (preschool) to "engage in competition" and "use the community's leisure facilities" (adolescence and adulthood).	Contains the skill clusters for moving through one's environment. The curriculum goals found in this domain vary from "exhibit balance, locomotion, and manipulation" (preschool) to "travel independently" (adolescence and adulthood); and from "locate objects" (preschool) to "develop mental maps of the community" (adolescence and adulthood).

All five domains contain sections that pertain to social skills, but the social skills required in any one domain are quite different from the social skills required in any of the other four. For example, the skills that one needs to get along with one's job supervisor and fellow employees are quite different from those that one needs to get along with one's family and friends. The social skills required in each domain truly discriminate each domain from the others.

Skill Clusters. Each goal in the List of Terminal Goals was analyzed for its component **skill clusters.** They are listed under each goal found in Appendix A along with examples of skill performance situations. These skill clusters provide the structure from which an instructional unit in a school or rehabilitation agency can derive its own unique set of goals to guide curriculum development.

The skill clusters were developed by performing a skill cluster analysis (see Chapter 5 for a description of this technique) on each goal. The result was a list of the major skill clusters for each goal in the List of Terminal Goals. For example, under Goal H/II G ("The learner will follow home accident/emergency procedures"), the skill clusters are as follows:

    a. Determine when/if external assistance is required.
    b. Inform accident/emergency personnel.
    c. Follow standard home emergency procedures.

A learner who can do these things will indeed be able to respond to home emergencies or accidents. But note that all of these actions are complex, and each requires the individual to exhibit a number of skills. For example, determining whether or not assistance is required following an accident or other emergency requires a person to (1) identify the presence and severity of an injury, (2) assess the existence and seriousness of an accident, and (3) assess one's own ability to respond to the situation. This example illustrates how each skill cluster in Appendix A usually subsumes many other skills, which is why we have called them "skill clusters."

Derivation of the List of Terminal Goals

The List of Terminal Goals builds on the work of many curriculum developers in the field, such as Brolin (1993, 1995); Chalfant and Silikovitz (1972); Contrucci (1976); Ford et al. (1984); Gaylord-Ross et al. (1984); Geiger (1974); Henderson and MacDonald (1973); Kokaska and Brolin (1985); and Patton et al. (1989). Many, if not most, of the terminal goals included in the list have appeared in other publications. However, the List of Terminal Goals found in Appendix A has three features that distinguish it from most other statements. That is, the List of Terminal Goals

1. is parsimonious;
2. is complete; and
3. includes "glitches" in each domain.

Parsimony.   The terminal goals in the list are stated parsimoniously in that it is easy to understand them without having to sort through a large set of items. It would have been possible, for example, to list all the skills required to keep living quarters neat and clean and to call each item on the list a "goal." However, if the goals were stated in this much detail, the sheer physical size of the List of Terminal Goals would make it very difficult (if not impossible) to use. Therefore, each goal statement encompasses a number of skill areas that are grouped according to a common concept or theme. Thus, washing floors and cleaning furniture, drapes, walls, rugs, and linens are all aspects of keeping one's living quarters clean. But so are skills like washing dishes, dusting tables and lamps, and changing bedsheets. All of these and many other items are included under the single goal of keeping one's living quarters neat and clean. Thus, although only 60 goals appear in the List of Terminal Goals, they generate several thousand skill clusters. In addition, the examples that accompany the skill clusters generate an even larger list of skills, and any instructional staff can use this list to identify a huge number of specific skills when they begin to consider all the community locations in which they will teach.

Completeness.   The List of Terminal Goals is also comprehensive in that it encompasses a wide array of circumstances within a community; therefore, schools and agencies may find some terminal goals that do not apply to their circumstances. For example, even though "maintain exterior of living quarters" appears as a goal, not all people who live in the community must maintain the exterior of a building, or even take care of the grounds. For example, some people live in apartments or condominiums that have building maintenance staff who perform all exterior maintenance. However, because other persons with mental retardation can and do live in their own houses, this goal was included in the List of Terminal Goals.

In one sense, the List of Terminal Goals may seem incomplete because it makes no mention of the more basic skills that are often included in curricula for persons with mental retardation, such as motor skills, communication skills, or academic skills. These skill clusters do not appear because they are not terminal goals or even subcategories of terminal goals for the concept of independence (as we have defined the term). Rather, they are intermediate goals that lie someplace along the pathways that lead to the terminal goals in the list. Although they belong in many curricula for specific groups of learners, they are not terminal goals and therefore are not listed in Appendix A.

Glitches. At one time or another, everybody has felt the effects of unexpected transient problems that arise simply as a result of living. For example, sometimes the first thing that happens when we get up in the morning is that we break a shoelace, or we go to fix breakfast and find we forgot to buy milk and cannot have our morning cereal. The term *glitches* refers to such transient problems, and the List of Terminal Goals includes the areas in which people must develop the skills to handle these problems. Glitches are stated in each domain because they can and do occur anywhere and at any time. They tend to fall into one or more of three categories: scheduling problems (e.g., missing the bus); materials depletion (e.g., finding out that there is no milk after putting the cereal in the bowl); and equipment breakdowns (e.g., the electricity goes off during the night, and the alarm clock does not ring in the morning).

Persons with mental retardation, like everyone else, must learn to cope with life's glitches. However, in many schools and agencies the staff tends to handle most of the problems that arise, and from the point of view of the learners in the program, their day-to-day routines tend to go very smoothly. Unfortunately, from an instructional standpoint, such staff actions do a disservice to persons with mental retardation. If persons with mental retardation do not learn to cope with life's glitches, they may not be able to handle the vagaries of daily life successfully. Most staff members who provide services to persons with mental retardation are very much aware of how even little problems can sometimes throw their learners into a complete flap. For example, a simple change in work schedule can bring ordinary functioning to a complete halt for many individuals because they have never learned to handle life's unexpected events. Skill clusters relative to handling glitches were included in the List of Terminal Goals to make provision for teaching learners how to handle them.

Intermediate Goals

Many curricula contain a combination of terminal and intermediate goals. The staff can select at least some of their goals directly from the List of Terminal Goals. Even a preschool program might select a few terminal goals from the list, such as the Personal Maintenance and Development goals that focus on eating and personal cleanliness.

However, many school programs, especially those at the elementary and middle school level and those for younger persons with severe mental retardation, will not be able to select many goals directly from the List of Terminal Goals because they must teach the skills that prepare learners to work on terminal goals. These programs *can* derive their intermediate goals from the List of Terminal Goals by analyzing the skills required to attain the terminal goals (the techniques for doing so are discussed in Chapter 5), but other resources can be used to develop curricula for such programs as well.

The two most comprehensive sources for curriculum goals for public school programs are as follows:

1. *Life Centered Career Education Curriculum* (LCCE: Brolin, 1993). Available from the Council for Exceptional Children, 1920 Association Drive, Reston, VA, 22091.
2. *Outcome Indicators:* Available from Disability Research Systems, Inc., 2500 Kerry Street, Suite 208, Lansing, MI, 48912.

Both publications were developed primarily for use in public school programs, but could be applied at the preschool and adult levels as well in some circumstances. We will review these two resources at length because both are very useful in developing curriculum goals that are congruent with the aim of independence as defined in Chapter 2.

Life Centered Career Education Curriculum (LCCE)

The LCCE (Brolin, 1993, 1995) defines *career* as "the totality of a person's productive life experiences." These experiences are in the personal, family life, vocational, and recreational domains. Brolin further states that preparation for one's career is, or should be, a major undertaking, and the range of skills taught under the LCCE reflects this view.

Organization of the LCCE.   The LCCE is organized into three domains called "curriculum areas." These areas, in turn, are divided into 22 "competencies," or curriculum goals for public school programs. The competencies are further broken down into 97 subcompetencies. This organization is shown in Figure 4.2. A description of the three LCCE curriculum areas (domains) is presented in Table 4.7.

The LCCE Curriculum.   The **LCCE** is a curriculum (Brolin, 1993) that outlines the sequences of instruction for competencies and subcompetencies that are to be delivered under the concept of infusion. *Infusion* means that the LCCE competencies should be taught as part of a conventional academic program, especially at the elementary level. For example, teachers could include many of the LCCE objectives that pertain to daily living in their social studies lessons. Similarly, they could teach many of the personal-social skills as part of the normal school routine, such as in the structure of small or large group academic lessons under the concept of functional academics (Hamill and Dunlevy, 1993a; Missouri LINC, 1989–90). Some of the LCCE competencies, especially the ones established for the secondary level, would have to be taught outside the normal classroom framework (such as the competencies that pertain to performing a job).

Each subcompetency in the curriculum has a pathway of curriculum objectives that lead to the competencies. Furthermore, each objective in the pathway is accompanied by suggestions for teaching activities and strategies for attaining the objective. Thus, the LCCE is in concert with the Instructional Model, and the techniques for using the LCCE are similar to those discussed in this text.

The LCCE is probably most useful in planning instruction for students with mild mental retardation. A major premise of the LCCE is that academic preparation should form the bulk of a learner's instruction in the early school years because it lays a foundation for later skill development. However, as time goes by, functional instruction should play a greater and greater role in the learners' program, and formal academic instruction should play a correspondingly smaller role. For example, academic preparation may consume 90% or more of the learners' program in the first few years of schooling, but by the time the learners reach the last years of high school, functional instruction may take up 75% or more of their time, and academic instruction 25% or less. In other words, Brolin believes that the further along learners are in school years, the greater the amount of functional instruction they should receive. We share this perception relative to learners with mild mental retardation.

Brolin has been recognized for his innovative work in developing the LCCE (CEC News, 1991). He began developing the LCCE in the early 1970s, and continues to refine the curriculum as data emerge on its effectiveness. It is consonant with the parameters established by the Instructional Model and provides an excellent example of how a well-organized curriculum can be constructed by beginning with a statement of goals and developing pathways of objectives leading toward those goals.

Outcome Indicators

The State of Michigan has contracted with the Center for Quality Special Education to develop **outcome indicators,** or statements of instructional outcomes, for children and youth with disabilities at various grade levels in the public schools. These outcomes can be used to derive curriculum goals for public school programs. The project, which has been in progress since 1988, covers a very large population in terms of age, disability, and functioning level. The result of this work is presented in a series of manuals, each of which lists instructional outcome indicators for children with various disabilities at different grade levels. Manuals listing outcome indicators have been or are being developed for public school children who are classified in the following disability areas: autism, educable mental impairment, emotional impairment, hearing impairment, learning disabilities, physical and other health impairments, preprimary impairment, severe mental impairment,

Curriculum Area	Competency	Subcompetency: The student will be able to:		
DAILY LIVING SKILLS	1. Managing Personal Finances	1. Count money & make correct change	2. Make responsible expenditures	3. Keep basic financial records
	2. Selecting & Managing a Household	7. Maintain home exterior/interior	8. Use basic appliances and tools	9. Select adequate housing
	3. Caring for Personal Needs	12. Demonstrate knowledge of physical fitness, nutrition & weight	13. Exhibit proper grooming & hygiene	14. Dress appropriately
	4. Raising Children & Meeting Marriage Responsibilities	17. Demonstrate physical care for raising children	18. Know psychological aspects of raising children	19. Demonstrate marriage responsibility
	5. Buying, Preparing & Consuming Food	20. Purchase food	21. Clean food preparation areas	22. Store food
	6. Buying & Caring for Clothing	26. Wash/clean clothing	27. Purchase clothing	28. Iron, mend & store clothing
	7. Exhibiting Responsible Citizenship	29. Demonstrate knowledge of civil rights & responsibilities	30. Know nature of local, state & federal governments	31. Demonstrate knowledge of the law & ability to follow the law
	8. Utilizing Recreational Facilities & Engaging in Leisure	33. Demonstrate knowledge of available community resources	34. Choose & plan activities	35. Demonstrate knowledge of the value of recreation
	9. Getting Around the Community	38. Demonstrate knowledge of traffic rules & safety	39. Demonstrate knowledge & use of various means of transportation	40. Find way around the community
PERSONAL-SOCIAL SKILLS	10. Achieving Self Awareness	42. Identify physical & psychological needs	43. Identify interests & abilities	44. Identify emotions
	11. Acquiring Self Confidence	46. Express feelings of self-worth	47. Describe others perception of self	48. Accept & give praise
	12. Achieving Socially Responsible Behavior	51. Develop respect for the rights & properties of others	52. Recognize authority & follow instructions	53. Demonstrate appropriate behavior in public places
	13. Maintaining Good Interpersonal Skills	56. Demonstrate listening & responding skills	57. Establish & maintain close relationships	58. Make & maintain friendships
	14. Achieving Independence	59. Strive toward self-actualization	60. Demonstrate self-organization	61. Demonstrate awareness of how one's behavior affects others
	15. Making Adequate Decisions	62. Locate & utilize sources of assistance	63. Anticipate consequences	64. Develop & evaluate alternatives
	16. Communicating with Others	67. Recognize & respond to emergency situations	68. Communicate with understanding	69. Know subtleties of communication

4. Calculate & pay taxes	5. Use credit responsibly	6. Use banking services	
10. Set up household	11. Maintain home grounds		
15. Demonstrate knowledge of common illness, prevention & treatment	16. Practice personal safety		
23. Prepare meals	24. Demonstrate appropriate eating habits	25. Plan/eat balanced meals	
32. Demonstrate knowledge of citizen rights & responsibilities			
36. Engage in group & individual activities	37. Plan vacation time		
41. Drive a car			
45. Demonstrate knowledge of physical self			
49. Accept & give criticism	50. Develop confidence in oneself		
54. Know important character traits	55. Recognize personal roles		
65. Recognize nature of a problem	66. Develop goal seeking behavior		

FIGURE 4.2

Life Centered Career Education Competencies.

From *Life Centered Career Education* by Donn Brolin, pp. 10–11. © 1987 by The Council for Exceptional Children. Reprinted with permission.

Curriculum Area	Competency	Subcompetency: The student will be able to:		
OCCUPATIONAL GUIDANCE AND PREPARATION	17. Knowing & Exploring Occupational Possibilities	70. Identify remunerative aspects of work	71. Locate sources of occupational & training information	72. Identify personal values met through work
	18. Selecting & Planning Occupational Choices	76. Make realistic occupational choices	77. Identify requirements of appropriate & available jobs	78. Identify occupational aptitudes
	19. Exhibiting Appropriate Work Habits & Behavior	81. Follow directions & observe regulations	82. Recognize importance of attendance & punctuality	83. Recognize importance of supervision
	20. Seeking, Securing & Maintaining Employment	88. Search for a job	89. Apply for a job	90. Interview for a job
	21. Exhibiting Sufficient Physical-Manual Skills	94. Demonstrate stamina & endurance	95. Demonstrate satisfactory balance & coordination	96. Demonstrate manual dexterity
	22. Obtaining Specific Occupational Skill			

TABLE 4.7 Curriculum Areas in the LCCE

Curriculum Area	Contents
Daily living skills	The skills in this area are those required for managing a home and family. They focus on managing money; caring for personal needs such as grooming and hygiene; handling family responsibilities; purchasing food and other goods; using leisure for recreation; developing mobility; and exhibiting citizenship.
Personal-social skills	The skills in this domain are those required to make a satisfactory adjustment to the community. They focus on developing self-awareness; gaining self-confidence; demonstrating socially responsible behavior; acquiring interpersonal skills; exhibiting problem-solving skills; developing communication skills; and attaining independence.
Occupational guidance and preparation	The skills in this area are those required to make a satisfactory adjustment to work. They focus on exploring occupations; planning occupations; developing work habits; seeking, securing, and maintaining employment; acquiring physical dexterity and manual skills; and developing specific occupational skills.

FIGURE 4.2

(*continued*)

73. Identify societal values met through work	74. Classify jobs into occupational categories	75. Investigate local occupational & training opportunities	
79. Identify major occupational interests	80. Identify major occupational needs		
84. Demonstrate knowledge of occupational safety	85. Work with others	86. Meet demands for quality work	87. Work at a satisfactory rate
91. Know how to maintain post-school occupational adjustment	92. Demonstrate knowledge of competitive standards	93. Know how to adjust to changes in employment	
97. Demonstrate sensory discrimination			
There are no specific subcompetencies as they depend on skill being taught.			

severe multiple impairments, speech and language impairments, and trainable mental impairment (the terminology in this list is that used by the Michigan Department of Education).

An Example of Outcome Indicators: Educable Mental Impairment.

For space reasons we will discuss only the outcome indicators for educable mental impairment (EMI) (the Michigan Department of Education's term for mild mental retardation). Since the same process was used to generate the outcome indicators for all groups, the major difference between this set of indicators and the indicators for learners with moderate and severe or profound mental retardation is in the specific content of the outcome statements.

Categories.   Table 4.8 presents the overview of expected outcomes for EMI (Disability Research Systems, Inc., 1991). They are organized into six categories: academics, social competence, community integration, personal growth and health and fitness, vocational integration, and domestic living environment. Each of the outcomes is broken down into five different grade levels, that is, outcomes appropriate for children who are exiting kindergarten, the third grade, the fifth grade, the eighth grade, and finally, those who are leaving high school.

Performance expectations.   Each set of outcomes is preceded by a description of the **performance expectations** for the outcome-related behaviors. For example, Outcome 3.1, "Ability to travel efficiently within the

TABLE 4.8 Overview of Expected Outcomes: Educable Mental Impairment

Category 1: Academics
 1.1 Ability to understand and use the spoken language to communicate effectively
 1.2 Ability to interact with print material to comprehend and convey main ideas, draw conclusions, and make judgments
 1.3 Ability to use math processes

Category 2: Social Competence
 2.1 Ability to interact appropriately within the course of daily social, vocational, and community living
 2.2 Ability to develop and maintain friendships and a support network

Category 3: Community Integration
 3.1 Ability to travel efficiently within the community and beyond
 3.2 Ability to access the community to meet personal and daily living needs
 3.3 Ability to follow basic safety precautions and procedures to protect self and others
 3.4 Ability to act as a responsible citizen

Category 4: Personal Growth and Health and Fitness
 4.1 Ability to advocate for self
 4.2 Competency in personal decision making
 4.3 Ability to manage personal health and fitness
 4.4 Ability to maintain appropriate hygiene, grooming and appearance
 4.5 Ability to participate in leisure and recreation activities

Category 5: Vocational Integration
 5.1 Knowledge of realistic vocational options and a comprehensive plan for career development
 5.2 Ability to organize self, complete tasks, and maintain job performance standards

Category 6: Domestic Living Environment
 6.1 Knowledge of personal rights and responsibilities
 6.2 Ability to maintain a personal living environment
 6.3 Understanding of the personal responsibilities inherent in family, communal, or other living arrangements

Adapted and printed with permission from *Addressing Unique Educational Needs of Individuals with Disabilities—An Outcome Based Approach: Educable Mental Impairment.* Disability Research Systems, Inc., 2500 Kerry Street, Suite 208; Lansing, MI 48912.

community and beyond," is accompanied by the performance expectations shown in Table 4.9. These and the other statements of performance expectations are presented to guide the instructional staff in understanding what to expect from learners if they can produce all the outcomes in the section.

Outcome sequences.   Tables 4.10 and 4.11 illustrate the manner in which the outcomes are stated according to different grade levels. Table 4.10 presents the outcomes listed under Outcome 3.1, "Ability to travel efficiently within the community and beyond," for children exiting Grade 3, while Table 4.11 presents the equivalent list of outcomes for children exiting Grade 5. A comparison of these lists will show clearly the sequential nature of the outcome statements.

Use of the Outcome Indicators.   The collection of outcomes found in the *Outcome Indicators* does not constitute a curriculum as we have defined it.

TABLE 4.9 Performance Expectations for the Outcome "Ability to Travel Efficiently Within the Community and Beyond"

Clarification: The ability to travel effectively within the community and beyond enables persons to achieve many different purposes and accomplish a wide variety of tasks. This mobility enables them to actively participate in community activities, conduct daily transactions, and access community resources. In addition, it provides a foundation for travel experiences beyond the familiar confines of community "boundaries." While experiences gained in the course of daily living are often sufficient to enable persons to develop necessary travel skills, persons with mild mental impairment often require direct instruction and guided practice to acquire skills and apply them in real-life travel situations. At a minimum, their mobility within the community and beyond is dependent on ability to access different forms of transportation, familiarity with commonly used community and other travel signs, familiarity with other helpful reference points (e.g., streets, guideposts), basic map-reading skills, ability to generalize practical usage skills (e.g., using money, asking for assistance, using phone books and pay phones), appropriate interpersonal skills, and ability to plan for successful travel experiences. In addition, such individuals need opportunities to travel within their communities and beyond and strategies for dealing with the experiences and unexpected events that can occur while traveling. The ability to travel effectively within their community and beyond allows for more complete integration into community living and exposure to living options.

Performance Expectations

The expected result of meeting these needs is individuals who travel effectively within the community and beyond by

1. planning for travel requirements (e.g., obtaining information about the destination, figuring amount of time required, deciding on a mode of transportation;
2. accessing an appropriate mode of transportation;
3. anticipating and taking precautions to prevent unwanted situations (e.g., flat tires, being approached by strangers, getting rained on);
4. engaging others appropriately;
5. using strategies to accommodate unexpected events that occur while traveling; and
6. following basic rules and regulations associated with various modes of travel.

Adapted and printed with permission from *Addressing Unique Educational Needs of Individuals with Disabilities—An Outcome Based Approach: Educable Mental Impairment.* Disability Research Systems, Inc., 2500 Kerry Street, Suite 208; Lansing, MI 48912.

Rather, it lists only expected outcomes that can be used to develop curriculum goals for each of the grade levels specified. To use the outcome indicators, it is necessary to realize that they are not stated in terms of behaviors; therefore, they must be transformed into behavioral statements in order to derive curriculum goals. This transformation requires some thought on the part of curriculum developers, because one outcome may be addressed by several different curriculum goals, and one curriculum goal may address several different outcomes. To illustrate this statement, let us assume that a middle school has chosen the goal "The learners will use the telephone directory to make local telephone calls." If the learners in this program learn to use the white, yellow, and business pages to locate telephone numbers, they will

TABLE 4.10 Expected Travel Outcomes for Children Exiting Grade 3

- Knows items needed for travel (e.g., way to travel, money for payment, attire for specific weather conditions)
- Knows and has skills to recite name, house number, street, city, phone number, or has compensatory strategy for identifying self
- Knows location of his/her home from somewhere on same block
- Knows the main cross-streets most appropriate for his/her address
- Has a coping strategy to use if he/she gets lost (e.g., not hiding, but persisting until appropriate assistance is given, knowing the type of person to approach for help)
- Knows the procedure he/she follows traveling to/from school
- Knows the advantages and disadvantages of different modes of travel within his/her community and which modes are more appropriate for travel beyond the community
- Knows that he/she has to prepare him/herself for traveling (e.g., prepares schoolbag, follows routine of dressing)
- Knows the parameters within which he/she is allowed to travel
- Has the skills to move about independently within the school (e.g., library, gym, appropriate entering and exiting doors)

Adapted and printed with permission from *Addressing Unique Educational Needs of Individuals with Disabilities—An Outcome Based Approach: Educable Mental Impairment.* Disability Research Systems, Inc., 2500 Kerry Street, Suite 208; Lansing, MI 48912.

TABLE 4.11 Expected Travel Outcomes for Children Exiting Grade 5

- Knows the advantages and disadvantages associated with different modes of transportation
- Knows appropriate attire and necessary items for specific modes of travel
- Knows location of his/her house when placed two blocks away
- Has skills to recognize a safe house
- Has a strategy for dealing with emergencies such as getting lost (i.e., knows where to find a public phone, knows how to make an emergency call with or without money)
- Knows name, house number, street, city, phone number, or has compensatory strategy for identifying him/herself
- Knows emergency symbols common to many communities (e.g., hospital, police, fire, helping hand, neighborhood watch)
- Knows the parameters within which he/she is allowed to travel alone
- Has the skills to use public transportation with supervision

Reprinted with permission from *Addressing Unique Educational Needs of Individuals with Disabilities—An Outcome Based Approach: Educable Mental Impairment.* Disability Research Systems, Inc., 2500 Kerry Street, Suite 208; Lansing, MI 48912.

TABLE 4.12 Partial List of EMI "Exiting Eighth Grade" Outcome Indicators Related to the Curriculum Goal "The Learners Will Use the Telephone Book to Locate Local Telephone Numbers"

1.1 Communicate Effectively through Oral Language
- Know how to ask questions and answer questions with appropriate information
- Know how to break down complex directions
- Have an age-appropriate functional vocabulary

1.2 Integrate the Use of Print Material into Daily Living
- Have the skills to read at the 3.5 grade level
- Know how to alphabetize words
- Know the role of guide words in a dictionary, encyclopedia, and phone book
- Know the purpose and function of different reference books

2.1 Interact Appropriately Within the Course of Daily Social, Vocational, and Community Living
- Know how to use a telephone appropriately for different reasons
- Know typical groups found in school and community settings

2.2 Develop and Maintain Friendships and a Support Network
- Have a group of boys and girls to associate with on a regular basis
- Have the skills to arrange to meet friends at two or more locations

3.1 Travel Effectively in the Community and Beyond
- Have the skills to accomplish travel preparations

3.2 Access Community Resources and Services as Needed to Meet Personal and Daily Living Needs
- Know how to use the telephone to call for assistance and information
- Are willing to ask for repetition and clarification, when necessary, when seeking assistance or information
- Have the skills to use various conveniences in a public place (e.g., rest room, elevator, escalator, public telephone)
- Know agencies, services, and resources available to assist with meeting needs for independent living and how to access each
- Know to call an appropriate individual or agency for help with personal situations
- Have the skills to make personal appointments

Adapted and printed with permission from *Addressing Unique Educational Needs of Individuals with Disabilities—An Outcome Based Approach: Educable Mental Impairment.* Disability Research Systems, Inc., 2500 Kerry Street, Suite 208; Lansing, MI 48912.

have (at least partially) attained the outcomes listed in Table 4.12. On the other hand, if this school wished to address the single outcome "Have the skills to assist with meal preparation," the staff would find that the outcome could be addressed by comprehensive curricula encompassing all the terminal goals listed in Table 4.13.

The importance of the outcome indicators is that they give school personnel an organized framework from which to derive curricula for an entire school system and a structure for developing sequential, coordinated, school-based curricula for all children and youth with mental retardation. We believe that the best way for school personnel to choose curriculum goals is to use a set of goals such as those in the LCCE or the List of Terminal Goals

TABLE 4.13 Terminal Goals That Address the "Exiting Eighth Grade" Outcome "Have the Skills to Assist with Meal Planning and Preparation"

The learners will
- maintain nutrition;
- prepare their own meals;
- clean up after meals;
- shop for food;
- store food;
- keep living quarters neat and clean;
- perform acceptable interactions with family members;
- cope with changes in daily schedule;
- cope with equipment breakdowns or materials depletion;
- follow home safety procedures;
- budget money; and
- pay bills.

and relate them to the outcome indicators. If any of the outcome indicators are not addressed by goals in one of these lists, new goals would have to be derived using the technique we will present later in the chapter. This goal selection process can be very effective in establishing a comprehensive set of goals to guide the development of curricula.

Outcomes and Grade Groups. Curriculum developers do not have to consider the outcomes for all of the grade levels simultaneously when they use the outcome indicator manuals. Rather, the staff for each group of grades specified in the *Outcome Indicators* can review the outcomes and develop a curriculum for each group separately. For example, personnel for Grades 1, 2, and 3 could develop a curriculum from the list of outcomes for exiting Grade 3, and the teachers from Grades 4, 5, and 6 could develop a curriculum for exiting Grade 6, and so on. Once the curriculum for each grade level grouping is complete, the teachers from the adjacent grade groups could adjust their lists of curriculum goals for entering subsequent levels accordingly. The object of these meetings would be to develop coordinated curricula that would span the public school years. In this manner, the curriculum for Grades 1, 2, and 3 will lead directly to the curriculum for Grades 4, 5, and 6, and the curriculum for Grades 4, 5, and 6 will lead directly to the curriculum for Grades 7, 8, and 9, and so on. At the end of the process, the school system will have a complete and comprehensive curriculum that links all the individual instructional programs together with a common set of curriculum goals.

The List of Terminal Goals, the LCCE, and the Outcome Indicators as Sources of Curriculum Goals

The List of Terminal Goals, the LCCE, and the *Outcome Indicators* were designed for general use in special education and rehabilitation services, and their major role is to suggest the kinds of goals that instructional units might select for their curricula. They provide instructional personnel with excellent frameworks for developing curricula that are suited to the requirements of the community agencies in which they work.

A Procedure for Formulating Curriculum Goals

Formulating curriculum goals requires an instructional unit to specify the curriculum end points toward which the learners will work. Collectively, these curriculum goals should give the aim a clear behavioral representation and provide a realistic picture of what the instructional programs will teach.

The personnel in most schools and agencies will find that they can choose skill clusters that are directly applicable in their programs from one or more of the three resources described previously. However, some instructional units will find that nothing in print completely fills the needs of the learners they serve and that they must derive at least some of their curriculum goals themselves. For example, many programs that serve adults will be able simply to decide which items in the List of Terminal Goals best describe their program's focus and to interpret these items in light of their particular circumstances. However, the staff of preschool and elementary programs and of programs for younger learners with severe mental retardation may find that few or none of the goals in the List of Terminal Goals can serve as end points for their curricula because their learners are at such basic levels. In such circumstances, staff either will have to rely on the LCCE or on one of the outcome indicator manuals in combination with the List of Terminal Goals to derive their own unique set of curriculum goals.

Instructional personnel can follow the four steps listed in Table 4.14 to formulate a detailed list of the curriculum goals that will guide instruction for their school or agency. A work sheet to help organize the effort appears in Table 4.15, and it shows some of the goals that the Big Horizons Agency developed for its curriculum in the area of Maintenance of Living Quarters. A blank copy of the work sheet is included in Appendix B.

TABLE 4.14 Steps to Formulating Curriculum Goals

To develop a curriculum:
- Identify the important goals the instructional unit will address in its instructional program.
- Define the goals in terms of the skill clusters the learners must acquire.
- Organize the curriculum goals and skill clusters.
- Assign skill clusters to the units that will teach them.

TABLE 4.15 Work Sheet for Formulating Curriculum Goals

Agency:	Big Horizons Residential Agency
Instructional Unit:	Main Street House
Curriculum Area:	Maintenance of Living Quarters
GOALS:	
Goal 1:	The learners will keep living quarters neat and clean.
Skill Clusters:	Follow assigned cleaning schedule.
	Use all household cleaning techniques.
	Store cleaning supplies in designated location.
Goal 2:	The learners will keep household fabrics clean.
Skill Clusters:	Wash, dry, and store clothes.
	Follow assigned cleaning schedule for linens and towels.
	Store linens and towels in assigned locations.
Goal 3:	The learners will perform interior maintenance on the residence.
Skill Clusters:	Replace burned-out lightbulbs.
	Replace cleaning fluids, kitchen and toilet supplies as needed.
	Collect trash for discard.
	Collect recyclable materials for recycling.
	Call repair personnel for needed repairs.
Goal 4:	
Skill Clusters:	

Step 1: List the Important Goals That the Instructional Unit Will Address in Its Programs

After staff members of an instructional unit have reviewed the features of the school or agency and have stated the aim of the curriculum, they should review the lists of curriculum goals and/or outcomes and establish the goals that will guide the instruction for their unit. The manner in which an instructional staff completes this step will depend on the age and/or ability level of its learners.

Preschools and Elementary Schools

If a school selects the LCCE to guide its programs, the curriculum is already complete and is ready for use in instruction. The staff will not have to select goals or develop a curriculum, although it may decide to modify the LCCE by adding or deleting some goals. Additions can come directly from the List of Terminal Goals or they can be derived from the *Outcome Indicators.*

The outcomes in the *Outcome Indicators* are not stated in behavioral terms; therefore, the staff must transform them into goal statements. To do so, they must consider each outcome in turn and decide what the learners must do to achieve the outcome. For example, one EMI travel outcome in the community integration area is

"Has the skills to move about independently within the school."

This outcome might be transformed into a goal using the standard goal statement pattern as follows:

The learners will <u>travel between the following locations in the school: entry door, principal's office, assigned classroom, boys'/girls' rest room, playground, library, resource room, cafeteria, and auditorium.</u>

When some aspect of the physical environment is used as part of the goal, the staff must understand the environment and its requirements. In this example, the school has several locations to which the children normally travel, and each is listed in the goal. For purely academic goals, it may not be necessary to consider the environment, but it is imperative to state the goal in a manner that clarifies expected learner behavior.

Secondary Schools and Adult Rehabilitation Agencies

A secondary school or adult program may elect to use the *Outcome Indicators* to create goals for older students. For example, one EMI outcome indicator for exiting 12th grade in the community integration area states the following:

"Know how newspapers can be used to find out what is happening in their community and gain information for personal involvement activities."

This outcome might tranform to a goal statement in the following way:

The learners will <u>use the local morning newspaper to get information on the following: events in the community of interest to them; housing; purchases (food, clothing, etc.); and leisure activities.</u>

When learners have attained this goal, they will be able to read the local newspaper and obtain the information that is specified in the goal statement.

When the instructional staff in a secondary school or rehabilitation agency uses the List of Terminal Goals, it must decide which terminal goals provide appropriate end points for its programs and which ones do not. Given the structure of the List of Terminal Goals, this step is mostly one of elimination and requires the unit to delete the skill clusters that the agency should *not* address.

Some agencies will list a broad range of goals, while others will list narrower ranges. Table 4.16 lists some goals that a vocational training agency and a residential provider might address in their programs.

TABLE 4.16 Examples of Goals That Might Be Selected by a Vocational Training Agency and a Residential Provider

Vocational Training Agency:

- The learners will perform a job.
- The learners will follow the work schedule.
- The learners will maintain their workstation.
- The learners will observe all job-related safety regulations and procedures.

Residential Provider:

- The learners will keep their living quarters neat and clean.
- The learners will keep their fabrics neat and clean.
- The learners will perform interior maintenance procedures.

Step 2: Define the Goals in Terms of the Skill Clusters the Learners Must Acquire

After the initial goals have been listed, the process of goal definition must go one step further, and the staff must list the skill clusters that they will include in the curriculum. These skill clusters become the actual curriculum goals.

The skill clusters form the heart of the agency's curriculum because they describe the specific sets of behaviors that learners must exhibit in order to attain the curriculum goals. To determine the skill clusters, the curriculum developers should ask the following question:

> Given the characteristics of the instructional unit, what must learners do to meet this goal under the existing conditions?

As an example, consider the newspaper-reading goal in the previous section. In the authors' community, learners would attain this goal if they could perform the skills listed in Table 4.17. Note how each of the skill clusters in this table encompasses a number of specific skills when the clusters are considered in relation to the local newspaper and local community. That is, the classified section in the local newspaper has a format that is peculiar to the local newspaper, and to find the section, a learner must do specific things. Similar statements can be made for the other skill clusters in Table 4.17. (Table 4.15 shows how skill clusters would be entered on the work sheet under each goal area.)

Curriculum Goals Delimit Instruction

A unit that selects "The learners will ride the bus to various community locations" as one of its travel goals has stated a focal point toward which the instructors will teach. Now, the staff should state what this goal means in terms of the specific skill clusters the learners must exhibit in the community. If the staff decides to teach the learners to take the bus to the local shopping mall, they focus on a different set of skill clusters than if they decide to

TABLE 4.17 Skill Clusters for the Goal "Learners Will Read Local Newspapers to Obtain Information About Events in the Community of Interest to Them; Housing; Purchases (Food, Clothing, Etc.); and Leisure Activities"

- Obtain the local newspaper.
- Find and read specific newspaper sections:
  - lists of entertainment activities of various types;
  - lists of meetings of various groups in the community;
  - sections that focus on current topics in which citizens get involved for one reason or another;
  - classified ads; and
  - other advertisements for food, clothing, household goods, and so on found in various sections of the paper.
- Identify how various events relate to their own interests.
- Identify when and where events relevant to their interests occur.
- Develop techniques for getting to the events.

teach learners to take the bus to the local farmers' market. Thus, when described in terms of its manifestations in the community, a skill cluster defines the specific skills and behaviors the learners must attain and the types of instruction that will be required to teach these skills.

Note that by *not* listing some skills, the list also specifies what the unit will not teach. That is, if this same agency decides not to teach certain skill clusters, such as "to use bus schedules to determine departure times" or "to use bus transfers when changing buses," the omissions further clarify the limits of the agency's instructional thrust.

Skill Clusters in the List of Terminal Goals

If the instructional unit uses the List of Terminal Goals, the analysis of skill clusters already has been carried out, at least in part. For example, an instructional unit may select the curriculum goal "The learner will dress appropriately." This unit now must decide what skill clusters it can actually address in its instructional program. The List of Terminal Goals contains the statements found in Table 4.18 under the goal "Wear appropriate clothing" (PI.B.3). The problem is that the goal is very comprehensive, and the list contains more skill clusters than some programs actually could address. For example, a junior high school program may not be able to teach learners how to dress for a Saturday night date or for church on Sunday morning. The instructional staff might conclude that teaching weekend dressing skills is more appropriate to teach at home or in a residential program and that their program should focus on only the skills that pertain to selecting weekday clothing, such as clothing for school, work, exercise, and running errands. In doing so, the staff sharply clarifies the focus of the instructional program.

Therefore, to list the skill clusters for the curriculum, the instructional staff should consider each of the skill clusters under the chosen goals in the

a. Identify activity.
b. Identify location.
c. Identify weather conditions.
d. Identify level of formality.
e. Select clothing appropriate to activity, location, weather conditions, and level of formality.

List of Terminal Goals and ask how each skill cluster will be realized in the local community. In this manner, the staff of a unit should define the specific skill clusters it will address for each of the curriculum goals it selects.

A Strategy for Selecting Skill Clusters

Many factors will influence the selection of skill clusters by an instructional program. Typically, these factors will relate either to the characteristics of the learners who are served by the unit or to the characteristics of the unit itself. Earlier in the chapter we discussed how factors inherent in a school or agency can influence the selection of an aim, such as its location, schedule, resources, and staff expertise. Curriculum developers should now consider how these factors may also affect the selection of specific skill clusters for a curriculum.

Some of these limitations will become barriers to instruction. When they do, the staff may find that they cannot teach the learners to perform certain skill clusters. They may also find that they may be able to cope with the barriers in certain ways.

One strategy for handling barriers to effective instruction is the following: As the instructional staff begins to consider the types of items to include in the curriculum, it can also evaluate what is required to teach them. Then, they can place the items into one of four categories based on their decision:

Category One: skill clusters for which the school or agency can provide instruction within the existing organization and structure of the program;

Category Two: skill clusters that cannot be added to the curriculum until there is a change in policies, procedures, staffing patterns, or schedules;

Category Three: skill clusters that cannot be added to the curriculum until additional resources are allocated or facilities become available; and

Category Four: skill clusters that cannot be added to the curriculum until the mission of the school or agency changes.

As potential skill clusters are placed in the second and third categories, staff and administrative personnel can sketch out a plan for generating the resources or revising the policies, procedures, or organization of the program that will enable the inclusion of these items in the curriculum at a later point in time. The staff also will be able to refer the items in the fourth category to another agency whose mission encompasses those areas of instruction or to personnel responsible for the overall service delivery network if no agency in the community currently addresses these areas. By using a strategy like this one, those engaged in curriculum development can provide input into decisions that affect instructional programming so that those decisions are made deliberately and systematically, based on sound educational practices.

Step 3: Organize the Curriculum Goals and Skill Clusters

A well-organized curriculum gives instructional personnel quick and easy access to its contents during instructional planning activities. Good organization is especially important when the curriculum is comprehensive and contains a wide array of curriculum goals and skill clusters. When a curriculum contains many items, the goals and skill clusters should have some sort of cataloging system.

The organization of curriculum items should begin by categorizing the curriculum goals and their associated skill clusters according to one or more dimensions that can provide a framework for the total curriculum. For example, public schools may categorize their curriculum goals according to the age levels of the students, such as primary level, intermediate level, and middle school level. Schools may wish to categorize the goals further according to subject matter (e.g., reading, mathematics, art, and physical education) or according to skill clusters (e.g., academic skills, social skills, and study habits). Community agencies, on the other hand, may wish to categorize their curriculum goals using the indexing system in the List of Terminal Goals or according to the community settings to which the goals apply (e.g., home, work, and recreational). In most cases the skill clusters for the goals should be listed as subheadings under the goals.

Perhaps the easiest way to organize a set of curriculum goals and skill clusters would be to use an already existing organization, such as those found in the List of Terminal Goals, the LCCE, or the *Outcome Indicators.* These organizational schemes allow schools and agencies to reference their goals to an external source that is known (or can be made available) to others.

Step 4: Assign the Skill Clusters to the Instructional Units That Will Teach Them

Schools and agencies that have several instructional units also may want to assign curriculum goals and skill clusters to these units according to the areas in which each unit concentrates its efforts. For example, an agency with two major instructional programs (e.g., residential and vocational) may divide the curriculum goals into two broad areas. One unit might concentrate on all the goals in the vocational domain, and the other unit might concentrate on the goals in the personal maintenance, homemaking, and leisure domains. The staff could assign the goals in the travel domain to both programs so the programs complement one another. Under ideal conditions, the process of assigning goals and skill clusters to instructional units would be expanded further to include all the schools and agencies in a community.

Securing ownership of the curriculum is a key factor in offering well-coordinated and high-quality services to persons with mental retardation. The best way to develop ownership is to encourage everyone who delivers the instruction, and who supports and oversees the activities, to agree on the final list of curriculum goals and skill clusters. Group meetings to clarify and revise the goals and to gain consensus on the skill clusters are important activities for agencies and communities because when everyone providing instruction agrees on its content, instruction will be focused and continue on course toward the aim.

Concluding Statement

Curriculum goals link the aim of instruction to the actual skills that will lead the learners toward fulfilling the aim. These goals serve as behavioral end points for the curriculum pathways and help lay out the sequence of skills and objectives on which the school's or agency's instructional programs will focus. They give direction to the total instructional program and provide benchmarks for keeping teaching on course.

For persons with mental retardation, the curriculum goals must correspond to the skill clusters that people who live in the community need in order to become independent. Public schools and community agencies can use commercial materials, such as the List of Terminal Goals, the LCCE, and the *Outcome Indicators* to gain an overview of the curriculum goals that may apply to the aim of independence. They can formulate the appropriate curriculum goals for their programs by considering the mission or purpose of the agency and the characteristics of the learners it serves.

The next step in developing a curriculum is to work out the curriculum pathways that lead to the goals. We will address this topic in Chapter 5.

Developing a Curriculum

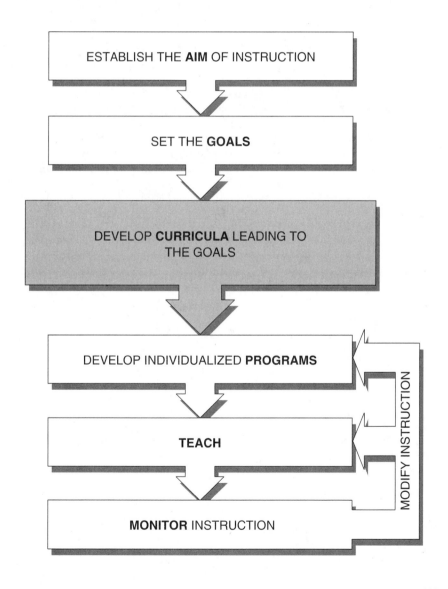

ESTABLISH THE **AIM** OF INSTRUCTION

SET THE **GOALS**

DEVELOP **CURRICULA** LEADING TO THE GOALS

DEVELOP INDIVIDUALIZED **PROGRAMS**

TEACH

MODIFY INSTRUCTION

MONITOR INSTRUCTION

BOX 5.1
Two Situations for Curriculum Development

SITUATION 1

The learners in the first situation are adults with moderate and severe retardation who live in a group home in Community A. They are nonreaders who have only a few minor physical problems; for example, some have low physical endurance and/or strength limitations that make some actions involving standing, lifting, and carrying heavy objects difficult. However, none have life-threatening conditions, all can see and hear relatively well, and all have relatively full range of motion.

The overall group home program consists of five sequenced residential settings and a semi-independent living program (SILP). The instructional program is designed to help these learners make the transition from group homes to independent living. The homes are graded in terms of proximity to independent living, and on intake, clients are assigned to a home on the basis of their level of community functioning. As clients acquire the skills taught in one home, they go to the next level of independent living by moving into a different home. Eventually, most clients move into the SILP program, and some even progress to complete independence.

The mission of the residential program is to prepare the learners to live in private living quarters (with or without roommates or spouses). The curriculum will focus on the skills that are relevant to residential and community life found in the List of Terminal Goals (Appendix A). Since the learners are essentially nonreaders, they must learn to perform these skills without relying on academic skills.

The staff is now developing a curriculum they hope will help them (a) to make better placements, (b) to decide when the time has come to move a learner from one home to another, and (c) to select appropriate skills to teach each of the learners in each home. Thus, the curriculum that will result from this effort will be comprehensive in nature. One of the skill clusters with which they are concerned involves food, because the learners cannot go to a SILP placement if they cannot prepare their own food.

SITUATION 2:

The learners in the second example are enrolled in a secondary public school program in Community B. The young people in this group are ages 14–19 and have mild mental retardation. None have physical disabilities that would restrict their movements in any significant way.

During their elementary years the school system's inclusion program began to integrate these students into the regular school population and attempted to develop their social and academic skills to the fullest possible extent. Most of the students in the secondary program can now read at the fifth- to sixth-grade level, and their math skills are commensurate. The staff of the secondary program will now concentrate on teaching them the skills they will need to live in the community without extraordinary assistance. Vocational training is a big part of this program, but the staff knows they must teach other skills necessary for community functioning, as well, and are beginning to develop the curricula to do so.

The teachers in this school program are convinced that they can have a major effect on the ability of the students to function appropriately in the community and are determined to make the greatest possible progress toward this end during the four years the students are in high school. They reason that the students with mild retardation will have few or no services available to them when they leave school and enter adult life and that they must develop the greatest possible number of community functioning skills before they "age out" of the program.

Because the instructional programs for both the elementary and secondary grades are at the beginning stages of development and should naturally be linked together, the teachers are working toward the development of a comprehensive curriculum that uses the *Outcome Indicators* to guide goal selection. One of the skill clusters that they have chosen to address is handling finances, which includes, among other things, budgeting one's income and paying bills.

In Chapter 4, we showed how the staff of an instructional unit can establish a set of curriculum goals. Now, in this chapter, we will explain how the staff can use this list of goals to develop a curriculum. To show how the process works, we have set up two situations (see Box 5.1) that we will use to illustrate the various principles of curriculum development discussed throughout the chapter.

We selected one goal from the sets of goals established by the staff in our two examples. Obviously, there are other goals in each program, but our purpose here is to show how to develop a curriculum, and a single goal from each program will fulfill our needs. These goals are as follows:

Situation 1: The learners will prepare all their own food.
Situation 2: The learners will budget money and pay bills.

Curriculum Format

Table 5.1 shows a standard format for laying out a curriculum and gives examples of each of the component parts. The aim for this curriculum and all other examples in this chapter is independence (see Chapter 4).

Schools and agencies often develop curricula that have many goals. These goals will probably be organized into instructional areas, each of which requires a separate section in the curriculum with its own heading. For example, a school curriculum may have one area for applied academics, one for social skills, one for travel skills, and one for leisure skills. Similarly, a residential curriculum may have one area for homemaking skills, one for personal maintenance skills, one for travel skills, and one for leisure skills. Furthermore, each curriculum area may have subareas. For example, the applied academics area of a curriculum might be subdivided into mathematics,

TABLE 5.1 Illustration of the Curriculum Format

Curriculum Area: Personal Maintenance and Development
Goal 1:   The learner will wear appropriate clothing.
Conditions:

    Location: At home
    Time: Evenings, mornings
    Tools & Materials: Clothing, television, calendar, umbrella, writing pad, pencil, temperature chart

Behavior Pattern: To achieve this goal, the learners will:

Each evening, immediately preceding the local news program on TV, the learners will look at the calendar, locate "today," and point to "tomorrow." They will read aloud the activities that will take place the next day. They will turn on the TV, tune to the news, watch the weather report, and write down the forecast for "tomorrow." They will then look at the temperature chart to determine what clothing they should wear. On the following day, the learner will follow these rules:

1. Bring umbrella if there is a chance of rain.
2. Always carry a light jacket in the spring and fall.
3. Do not wear sandals if the temperature will be below 65 degrees.

The learners will state the location of an activity (church, home, work, etc.) and whether the activity is routine (work, exercise, shopping, etc.) or occasional (weddings, parties, etc.). For routine activities, the learners will choose regular clothing that is appropriate for precipitation and temperature. If occasional, the learner will call a friend to ask if the activity is formal, semiformal, or informal, and what to wear. The learners then will choose the appropriate clothing for temperature, precipitation, and level of formality.

Curriculum Objectives

The learners will

Elementary School:

1.1 Dress self
1.2 Select channels on TV
1.3 State the days of the week
1.4 Discriminate "today" and "tomorrow"
1.5 Locate "today's" day of week on calendar
1.6 Locate "tomorrow" on the calendar
1.7 State months of the year
1.8 State city of residence
1.9 Discriminate "dry/wet" weather
1.10 Discriminate "clear/cloudy" weather
1.11 Tell time to the minute
1.12 Tune to local TV station
1.13 Locate an intermediate number in a range of numbers
1.14 Read at third-grade level
1.15 Write at third-grade level
1.16 State current activity
1.17 Follow daily routine
1.18 Define "occasional"
1.19 Discriminate "routine/occasional"
1.20 Identify location of next activity
1.21 Locate specific dates on a calendar
1.22 Identify weather symbols: rain, cloudy, partly cloudy, sunny, snow, cold, hot
1.23 Locate row-column intersection on chart
1.24 Locate words sequenced in alphabetical order

1.25 Make local telephone calls
1.26 Use white pages of telephone book

Junior High School:
1.27 Get station and time of TV program from TV guide in local newspaper
1.28 Identify weather segment of news program
1.29 State weather forecast: precipitation and temperature
1.30 Select appropriate clothing for precipitation
1.31 Select appropriate clothing for temperature
1.32 Identify person to ask about appropriate clothing for level of formality when unsure

Clothing Selection Chart

Temperature	Dry Weather	Wet Weather
<25 degrees	Long pants, long-sleeved shirt or turtleneck, winter coat, gloves, hat, scarf, ear protection	Long pants, long-sleeved shirt or turtleneck, winter coat, gloves, hat, scarf, ear protection, boots
25–45 degrees	Long pants, long-sleeved shirt, winter coat, gloves	Long pants, long-sleeved shirt, winter coat, scarf, boots
45–60 degrees	Long pants, long-sleeved shirt, light jacket	Long pants, long-sleeved shirt, heavy jacket
60–70 degrees	Long pants, short-sleeved shirt	Long pants, long-sleeved shirt, light jacket, umbrella
70–80 degrees	long/short pants, short-sleeved shirt	Long/short pants, short-sleeved shirt, umbrella
80+ degrees	Short pants, short-sleeved shirt	Short pants, short-sleeved shirt, umbrella

Curriculum material developed in response to a course assignment for the course K351, "Vocational Assessment and Instruction in Special Education," at Indiana University, first semester 1994–1995. Used by permission of Barbara J. Hubbard.

reading, social studies, and science; and the personal maintenance area of a residential curriculum might be subdivided into personal cleanliness, health care, clothing, and social skills. Each of these areas and subareas should have separate sections in the curriculum. For example, the portion of the curriculum presented in Table 5.1 would be found in the "Personal Maintenance and Development" section of the curriculum.

The goal appears next and is followed by the behavior pattern that states precisely what the learners must do to attain the goal (note that the goal should be stated in the standard format provided in Chapter 4).

Finally, the objectives leading to each goal are listed in a pathway that shows the sequence in which the instructional staff will assess and teach them. Each goal and each objective should be numbered when they are listed in the curriculum. The earliest-taught objectives will have the lowest numbers, and the last-taught objectives will have the highest numbers.

Curriculum Variables

Two variables affect the complexity of the curriculum that an instructional staff develops:

1. the scope of the curriculum; and
2. the degree of specificity found in the curriculum goals.

We will begin the chapter by explaining these variables.

Curriculum Scope

In Chapter 4, we mentioned that an instructional staff can develop either a restricted or a comprehensive curriculum. These two types of curricula require further description.

Restricted Curricula

A **restricted curriculum** is self-contained and typically is developed for a single instructional program that is not formally linked to other instructional programs. A restricted curriculum contains few or no curriculum objectives, and instruction focuses directly on the goals selected by the instructional unit.

Many agencies have instructional programs that are relatively limited in instructional scope. Restricted curricula are most appropriate for instructional units that have the characteristics listed in Table 5.2. A residential program, for example, may serve only adults with moderate or severe mental retardation. The staff of such a program may decide that the learners must work directly on acquiring the skills they need to participate as members of the community even though they lack certain basic skills, such as reading and writing skills. The curriculum for this agency probably would center on teaching skills such as those found in the personal maintenance, homemaking, travel, and leisure domains. The goals can be derived directly from the List of Terminal Goals in Appendix A. We call the resulting curriculum

---

TABLE 5.2 Characteristics of Instructional Units That Would Use Restricted Curricula

- The instructional program teaches skills to a specific group of learners with similar characteristics.
- The curriculum consists mostly of the skills required for functioning in specific community settings.
- The instructional program has a single theme (such as one that would be found in a vocational training program).
- The curriculum focuses on terminal goals.
- The curriculum is constrained by some circumstance.

Goals and Curricula

"restricted" because the instructional scope is very limited, and the teaching that takes place is not closely connected to the instruction of other programs in the community, such as those found in the public schools or adult vocational agencies.

Note that the developers of a restricted curriculum assume two things: (1) that the learners enter the agency's programs with few or no prerequisites and (2) that the learners will be able to achieve the curriculum objectives even if they must use special techniques to perform them.

Comprehensive Curricula

A **comprehensive curriculum** covers a wide range of skills and skill clusters; thus, learners often must spend a number of years in the instructional programs that have them. These curricula are organized by levels of instruction that are linked in closely related instructional chains, and each level of instruction prepares learners to go on to the next level. Comprehensive curricula are found in instructional programs in which learners "move up" through various levels. Such curricula are most appropriate for schools and agencies that have the characteristics found in Table 5.3.

A very good example of a comprehensive curriculum is found in general education, in which learners acquire basic skills in the elementary years and higher-level skills in the secondary and postsecondary years. Such curricula are "comprehensive" because the elementary program prepares students to go on to the secondary program, and within each level, students prepare to go on to the next level. Parenthetically, a school system that uses either the LCCE or the *Outcome Indicators* to select its goals will generate a comprehensive curriculum because these systems are organized progressively.

In schools and agencies that develop a comprehensive curriculum, learners progress from level to level because the curriculum connects each of the levels instructionally. For example, an agency may provide residential training in which the learners can "move up" from one level to another, as from highly structured group homes to less structured group homes to semi-independent apartment programs, and finally, to independent living. Although comprehensive curricula are quite common in both general and vocational education, they have not been the norm in special education and rehabilitation services.

TABLE 5.3 Characteristics of Instructional Units That Use Comprehensive Curricula

- The learners in the instructional program have a wide age range.
- The instructional program teaches a wide range of skill levels.
- The learners in the instructional program move to different settings as they acquire skills.

Degree of Specificity in a Curriculum

Not all curricula require the same degree of detail in describing the skills and behaviors the learners need to achieve the curriculum goals. Some groups of learners need a lot of detail in their instruction while others require much less, and the respective curricula will have to reflect these differences in learner capabilities. As a general rule, the more severe the mental retardation, the greater the amount of detail that will be needed to describe the instructional content. Conversely, the less severe the retardation, the less the detail, and the more the learners can be expected to figure out for themselves. However, learners with mental retardation nearly always require more detail than learners without mental retardation; thus, clarity of instructional content is the watchword throughout the curriculum development process for the entire group.

Steps in Developing a Curriculum

Let us now turn to the task of specifying the content of instruction and the sequences in which that content should be taught. The process of developing both a restricted and a comprehensive curriculum is approximately the same except that a comprehensive curriculum requires more steps. To develop a comprehensive curriculum, the staff would accomplish all of the steps in the list found in Table 5.4, whereas to develop restricted curriculum, usually they would complete just the first and fourth steps in this list, and occasionally, the second step.

Step 1: Establish Behavior Patterns

In Chapter 2 we discussed how everyone generally goes through daily life by following specific routines that get us up and out of the house, to our places of work, through our workday, back home, through our meals, finished with our chores, and into bed. The routines we follow consist of patterns of behavior that we perform without having to think about them very much. These patterns allow us to concentrate on solving the problems we encounter while we are performing the patterns. In formal terms, a **behavior pattern** is

> A ROUTINIZED SEQUENCE OF SKILLS THAT PEOPLE PERFORM IN ORDER TO COMPLETE A PURPOSEFUL ACTIVITY.

Behavior patterns minimize the amount of attention people need to give to routine activities in their daily lives. To illustrate just how important behavior patterns are, consider the fact that most of us rarely think about specific behaviors while we are performing them. Instead, most of us focus almost exclusively on selecting the "NEXT" activity. For example, when we drive a car, we rarely consider each of the individual actions involved in starting the car or in applying the brakes and stopping the car (except when

TABLE 5.4 Sequence of Actions Required to Develop a Curriculum

Curriculum developers must
1. establish behavior patterns for each curriculum goal;
2. analyze the skills required for each behavior pattern;
3. analyze the prerequisite and lead-in skills for each behavior pattern;
4. arrange all the skills in a list to form a logical instructional sequence; and
5. assign segments of the sequence to the various levels of the instructional program.

first learning to drive). It is clear that making a left turn against traffic requires many discrete actions, but few people stop to consider how they will make a left turn. Rather, most of us think in terms of where we are going and what route we will follow to get there, and we produce the individual behaviors for performing the action in a smooth pattern. The exceptions occur when we encounter a new, unexpected, or especially complicated situation in which we need to produce deliberate, thoughtful actions in order to complete the activity. But, in general, most of the routine things we do involve the use of behavior patterns, and it is these patterns that allow us to go though our daily routines in a smooth and efficient manner.

Because behavior patterns are important in carrying out our daily routines, the curricula for persons with mental retardation should focus on teaching them. Therefore, the instructional staff in a school or rehabilitation agency should examine each curriculum goal and describe one or more behavior patterns that will allow learners to accomplish that goal. The behavior pattern has the following format:

To show that a learner has attained this goal, the learner will _____

_____.

The statement made in response to this stimulus will produce a sequence of steps that the learners must accomplish in order to do things such as prepare meals, perform a job, or travel downtown. The behavior patterns will become the focus of the learner's instruction, and when the learner can perform a behavior pattern successfully, he or she will have attained the curriculum goal.

To describe a behavior pattern, the instructional staff must accomplish the three steps that appear in Table 5.5. These steps also appear on the blank

TABLE 5.5 Steps in Stating a Behavior Pattern

1. State the conditions under which the learners will perform the skills.
2. List the major skill clusters the learners must accomplish.
3. Select a behavior pattern that allows the learners in the program to accomplish each major skill cluster.

TABLE 5.6 Work Sheet for Developing a Behavior Pattern

Step One: State the goal:
                  The learners will inventory food stock.

Step Two: List the conditions:
                  Location(s): At home
                  Time(s): Friday evenings prior to food shopping trip
                  Person(s) Present: Mother and Father
                  Tools and Materials: "To Buy" list, pencil

Step Three: List the major skill clusters:
  1. Locate items for potential purchase on the "To Buy" list
  2. Assess need to purchase each item on list
  3. Mark list for purchase if below level indicated on list

Step Four: State the behavior pattern:
To show that the learners have attained this objective, they will assess the food stock
and make a grocery list as follows: On Friday evening after dinner and before completing
any chores, the learners will obtain their "To Buy" list and check the pantry, refrigerator,
and each storage cabinet, locate each item listed, and assess the current quantity of the
item available. If the item has a greater quantity than indicated in the "Reference" column
on the list, they will go on to the next item. If the item has an equal or lesser amount than
indicated in the "Reference" column, the learners will write the name of the item on a sheet
of paper along with the size or amount required, as stated in the "Amount" column. They
will then check the Big Food store ads to find coupons corresponding to as many items on
the list as possible.

"To Buy" List

Item	Amount	Reference
Apples	8	Less than 2
Bread	1 loaf	Less than 6 slices
Butter	1/4 lb.	Less than 2 finger widths
Cheddar Cheese	1/2 lb.	Less than 1 finger width
Coffee	1 lb. can	Less than 1 finger joint deep
Corn Flakes	1 box	Less than 2 finger joints deep
Detergent	1 bottle	Less than 2 finger widths
Eggs	1/2 dozen	2 or less
Grape Jelly	1 jar	Less than 1 finger width
Ham	1/2 lb. (sliced)	Less than 2 slices
Milk	1 qt.	Less than 3 finger widths
Oatmeal	1 box	Less than 1 finger joint deep
Orange Juice	1/2 gal. can	Less than 1/4 can
Pears	4	Less than 1
Potatoes	6	Less than 2
Soup (Chicken)	2 cans	1 can
Soup (Tomato)	2 cans	1 can
Tea	1 small box	Less than 4 bags
Toothpaste	1 medium tube	Less than one finger width
Vegetables:	1 small bag ea.	Less than 1/2 bag
Broccoli, Carrots,		
Corn, Green Beans,		
Peas & Onions, Succotash		

work sheet provided in Appendix B. An example of a completed behavior pattern for the goal "The learners will inventory food stock" appears in Table 5.6.

State the Conditions

The first step in specifying a behavior pattern is to define the conditions under which the learners will perform the skills in the curriculum. These conditions will have a direct effect on which skills the learners must acquire to attain the curriculum goals and how they will perform them. For example, anyone who would cash a check at the local bank would do it differently under each of the following conditions:

- inside the bank at 10:00 A.M. in the middle of the month;
- inside the bank at five o'clock on the day the local factory pays its workers; and
- at the drive-up window on Friday afternoon.

The staff must specify the conditions under which the learners will perform before they can describe a behavior pattern. To complete this step, the staff should consider each goal and ask the following question:

Where, when, with whom, with what, and/or how often should the learners perform the skills required for this curriculum goal?

The answers to this question will vary a great deal. For example:

- a preschool or an elementary school may decide that a curriculum goal should be met in a general education classroom during the ordinary course of the school day;
- a secondary school may decide that its learners must achieve a goal by going to a number of different settings in the community during the middle of the day; and
- a residential program may decide that its learners must meet a goal in two places: (1) in and around the residence during normal home-living hours and (2) in the community during the evenings and on weekends.

The skills that the learners would use in each of these settings and the manner in which they will achieve each goal will vary widely because the conditions place different demands on the learners' performance (Knapczyk and Rodes, 1996).

Conditions have two major variables: settings and circumstances.

Settings. The settings in which the instruction will take place could be the physical plant of the school or other service agency, or they could be other locations. For example, residents of a group home would probably learn homemaking and home maintenance skills within the confines of the group home itself, while learners in a secondary school vocational program would probably learn to perform jobs by going into various work settings in the community. Whatever the thrust of the instruction, the settings in which the staff chooses to teach will largely determine not only the specific skills that learners must acquire, but also the manner in which they will perform them.

There are many examples that illustrate how changes in location can affect the content of instruction. For example, consider the following goal: "The learner will perform five recreational activities." This goal encompasses a wide array of settings in which the learners might learn goal-related behaviors, and instructional personnel must make decisions about which specific settings will be the focus of the curriculum. Obviously, it makes a difference if the staff teaches leisure skills in a movie theater or in a gymnasium. Similarly, suppose the staff of an elementary program establishes the following goal: "The learners will play recess games with the other children." The instructors will find that many of the recess games that children play are performed differently in different schools, and may even be performed differently in different locations within a single school. For example, a game of "catch" with a football will probably be played differently out on a football field than in a gymnasium because the distances are greater on the football field, and learners who play there may throw the ball farther and do more running than they would in the gymnasium. Therefore, instructors must define the settings in which they will teach the different types of game-playing skills.

Ideally, staff would limit the range of possible settings for each goal to those that best represent the conditions under which the learners will actually perform the goal-related behavior after instruction is complete. The lower the functional levels of the learners, the more critical it is for the conditions to represent those under which the learners will have to perform when instruction is complete.

Falvey (1986), Ford et al. (1984), Wilcox and Bellamy (1987), and others have identified several factors to consider when selecting settings in which to teach skills. These factors are listed in Table 5.7.

Some skills can be performed in so many different locations that it may be necessary to select a representative sample of settings. The following examples illustrate this idea:

- "Travel around the community."
- "Eat evening meal at a restaurant."
- "Play games with peers."

In other instances, a single setting contains all the conditions necessary for learning the goal-related behaviors. For example, many learners will live in one general location for their entire lives, and for them, only one setting for an activity may be available within a reasonable travel distance. The following examples illustrate this idea:

- "Shop for food."
- "Attend religious services."
- "Purchase medicines at the pharmacy."

Surveys that assess the preferences of learners and their families and friends (Falvey, 1986; Ford et al., 1984) or those that inventory community

TABLE 5.7 Factors to Consider When Selecting Settings for Instructional Purposes

The setting should
- be age-appropriate to the learners in the program;
- be preferred by the learners (i.e., be aligned with their interests, aptitudes, and physical characteristics);
- be consistent with the lifestyles of the learners and their families, friends, and acquaintances;
- be proximate to the primary settings in which learners live and work;
- provide variety for the learners; and
- provide opportunities for further skill development across functional areas of behavior (e.g., give the learners access to other learning environments).

settings (Easterday and Sitlington, 1985; Moon, Goodall, Barcus, and Brooke, 1985) can be very useful when devising samples of locations in which to teach skills. For example, the State Departments of Labor and Chambers of Commerce often conduct surveys of various job types and use the resulting information to make projections about the future job markets, such as which categories of jobs will expand in the future, and which will shrink. Such projections can help the staff in a vocational training program focus their instruction on jobs that are in the expanding or stable job categories and avoid teaching jobs that are in the shrinking categories.

When selecting settings, it is necessary to consider both the settings the learners currently frequent and the settings they are likely to encounter after they leave the instructional agency (Brown, Branston, Hamre-Nietupski, Johnson, et al., 1979; Snell, 1987). For example, some goals for upper-elementary school grades may focus on skills that are required by the middle or junior high school to which the students will go. These skills would be taught near the end of the elementary school program to help learners make successful transitions from one program to the next. The instructional staff in the elementary programs (or any program from which learners regularly advance to another program) should take into account the conditions of the subsequent settings as much as possible.

Circumstances. The circumstances under which the learners perform the skills they learn also have an effect on the way in which they will perform them. For example, the skills that are required to drive a car downtown are different at noon on a weekday than they are at 1:00 A.M. when the area is empty (or nearly so); and a game of basketball is played differently when only two players play "horse" under a single basket than when a full complement of five players per team plays on a full court under competitive game conditions. Thus, the circumstances of performance should be considered as part of the conditions under which the learners will carry out the behavior patterns.

As a rule, people with mental retardation should acquire skills in the circumstances in which people normally perform them because they must learn to respond to the situational cues and outcomes that are typical for those circumstances. If instructors teach the skills in other circumstances, that instruction should be considered only preparatory to the instruction that actually will help the learners become functioning members of the community.

The most important circumstances to consider usually involve the variables of time, persons present, and tools, equipment, and materials.

Time. The description of the behavior pattern should reflect the time at which learners will use the skills. Some skills should be taught within very limited time frames. For example, a program that teaches learners to attend the religious service of their choice should carry out instruction on Sunday morning and/or on whatever other days and times people normally attend the service. It would be most inappropriate to teach learners to participate in religious services on Monday mornings because most people normally do not attend services at this time.

Persons present. Other people who are present while the learners are performing in a setting may affect the behavior pattern markedly. For example, a crowded restaurant may require its customers either to make reservations or to stand in line to wait for a table, and other people in an empty theater may tolerate more boisterous behaviors than would those in a full theater. At the elementary school level, the inclusion movement is predicated on the hypothesis that a general education classroom is a better site for students with disabilities to learn social and academic skills because of the demands set by the teachers and other students in these settings and the behavioral models they provide (McLaughlin, 1993). The general rule, then, is that it is best to teach skills with the persons and under the conditions that normally would be present in a location. The behavior pattern should reflect these conditions.

Tools, equipment, and materials. The tools, equipment, and materials used during the performance of a behavior pattern can also make a tremendous difference in the skills the learners would have to use. For example, if instructors want to teach learners how to grow a garden, it is clear that they will use different skills to prepare soil with a hand shovel than they will when they prepare it with power-tilling equipment. Similarly, fastening nuts and bolts is done differently with a pair of pliers than it is with a set of socket wrenches.

Tools, materials, and equipment are not limited to hand tools or things that the learner must manipulate. For example, travel skills can be taught in taxis or on public transportation systems that include buses, trolleys, or trains, all of which are types of equipment that some learners must learn to use. The behavior pattern should reflect the variations introduced by different types of equipment because they can make a vast difference in what skills are taught and how the learners perform them. Therefore, a list of all tools, equipment, and materials should be part of the process of stating a behavior pattern.

Adjustments.   It may be necessary to make adjustments in settings and circumstances to facilitate the performance of skills. For example, agency considerations may require the staff to teach aspects of vocational, leisure, and travel skills at times when the skills might not ordinarily be performed, such as when workloads of other people are light or when safety hazards are at a minimum. Under such conditions, it is likely that the circumstances will not completely match those under which learners will perform the skills when instruction is complete, and the differences must be noted. For example, an understaffed agency may decide to have the learners work toward goals in one specific bank, church, restaurant, or leisure site near the grounds of the agency. This staff must remember that other banks, churches, restaurants, and leisure sites will present other demands on behavior, and if learners eventually will use other facilities, it may be necessary to teach them to respond to those demands before concluding instruction.

List the Major Skill Clusters

The next step in describing a behavior pattern is to analyze the major skill clusters (White, 1980). For our purposes, the definition of major skill clusters is as follows:

> **MAJOR SKILL CLUSTERS** ARE THE IMPORTANT STEPS THAT ANYONE MUST ACCOMPLISH TO EXHIBIT A BEHAVIOR PATTERN IN A SETTING.

From an instructional standpoint, there are many ways in which a learner can perform the skills required to meet an objective. For example, there are many ways a learner could mow a lawn, shop for food, or walk to the mall. When the instructional staff has considered the possible ways in which to accomplish a curriculum goal, they must select the one particular behavior pattern from among these possibilities that they will teach their learners to perform.

Analyzing Major Skill Clusters.   Ecological psychologists have long noted that, in any community setting, people regularly do what everyone else in the setting does (Barker, 1968). Examples abound to illustrate this point, three of which appear in Table 5.8. The manner in which people do these things varies from location to location, but the things they must accomplish in most locations are quite predictable. For example, in order to shop in a supermarket the learner would have to complete the steps found in Table 5.8. A person who does these things successfully will make purchases in a supermarket.

The list of major skill clusters states only the things that a learner must accomplish. In Table 5.8, note that the lists make no mention of *how* the skill clusters will be accomplished, and in fact, people can accomplish each skill cluster in somewhat different ways and still complete the activities in an acceptable manner. The list of major skill clusters describes only *what* learners must do to produce a behavior pattern. It never describes how an individual learner might do it. Curriculum developers specify the manner in which a

TABLE 5.8 Examples of How People Behave Similarly in Any Setting

At a swimming pool, people
- go into the dressing room;
- change into a swimsuit;
- shower;
- go out to the pool;
- lay on the deck;
- go into the water;
- swim;
- play water games with other people;
- dry off;
- gather belongings;
- change back into street clothes; and
- leave.

In a bank, people
- fill out forms;
- stand in line;
- approach a teller's window;
- exchange greetings with the teller;
- exchange money and/or papers with the teller; and
- leave.

In a supermarket, people
- get a cart or basket (optional);
- go up and down aisles taking foods and other items from the shelves and tables;
- bring the selections to the checkout counter;
- pay for the selections; and
- leave with the purchases.

group of learners might accomplish such behaviors later, when describing the behavior pattern.

Each major skill cluster states an outcome, which means that it is possible to analyze skill clusters of the major skill clusters. In fact, the analysis of skill clusters is very much like peeling the layers off an onion: Each time one layer of skill clusters is exposed, another comes into view. For example, consider the second major skill cluster in the supermarket example in Table 5.8 ("go up and down aisles taking foods and other items from the shelves and tables"). This one skill cluster requires a person to use a number of more basic skills:

- identify various foods;
- locate aisles containing various foods;
- locate various foods on shelves and tables;
- stack cans, packages, and bottles of varying shapes and sizes appropriately in basket; and
- maneuver food cart in crowded aisles.

In a similar manner, major skill clusters for curriculum goals usually contain a number of skills that learners must acquire to attain the goal.

Curriculum developers must go out into the community to identify the skills their learners need.

Photo courtesy of Jean-Claude Lejeune.

Finally, in Table 5.8, note that each list of major skill clusters is rather short: It is not unusual for a list of major skill clusters to contain only two or three entries. More items appear for complicated behavior patterns, such as a job with many different duties.

The staff of a school or other agency can analyze the major skill clusters for each of their curriculum goals by observing how people in community settings act and interact. If staff members are familiar with a location, they can accomplish this step simply by recalling what they themselves usually do in this location. However, in unfamiliar locations they have to engage in direct observation to identify an appropriate list. Observation is especially necessary when analyzing unique behavior patterns, such as those required to perform a specific job.

Once the list of major skill clusters is complete, it should be preserved in some way, such as on a computer disk, in a notebook, or in a file of some kind, because the instructors may have to use the list again when developing instruction for an individual. An individual learner may need to learn a pattern that is different from the one that most learners acquire, perhaps even a special behavior pattern that the instructional staff develops specifically for that person. If the staff saves all the lists of skill clusters developed during the curriculum construction period, they will be available when such situations arise.

Example of Major Skill Clusters.   Box 5.2 presents the major skill clusters for Situations 1 and 2 (presented earlier in the chapter). The behavior patterns that we will develop later must account for these skill clusters. We will use the concept of skill clusters again when we address the development of individual programs and the use of certain teaching procedures. It is a useful instructional tool that has many applications.

BOX 5.2
Major Skill Clusters for Each Curriculum Goal

1. *Group Home:* **Preparing all meals**
   To learn to prepare all their own food, the residents must perform the following *major skill clusters:*
   a. Name the day of the week.
   b. Name the meal to be prepared.
   c. Name the foods to be prepared.
   d. Locate the foods to be prepared.
   e. Prepare foods in an appropriate manner and with appropriate timing.

2. *Secondary School:* **Budgeting Money and Paying Bills**
   To budget money and pay bills, the students must perform the following *major skill clusters:*
   a. Determine expenses.
   b. Allocate funds.
   c. Identify bills.
   d. Pay bills.
   e. File receipts.

State the Behavior Pattern

Once analyzed, the list of major skill clusters provides instructors with a set of parameters for describing a behavior pattern that will allow the learners to accomplish each major skill cluster. The problem is to specify a pattern that allows the learners to perform the activity efficiently and in a manner that does not attract negative attention. To arrive at an appropriate behavior pattern, the staff should consider each major skill cluster separately and ask the following question:

"How could this group of learners perform this skill cluster?

When instructors respond to this question, useful ways to perform each major skill cluster will emerge. That is, not only will the learners be able to learn to produce the major skill clusters, but also, their performance probably will be acceptable to the other people in the setting.

Special Behavior Patterns. Most often, it is appropriate to select the behavior pattern that most people ordinarily use in the community. However, sometimes learners must develop special patterns because they do not have the ability to perform an activity the way people usually perform it. For example, most people identify the bus they want to get on by reading the sign on the front of the bus as it arrives at the bus stop. However, learners who cannot read may have to use special techniques to identify the appropriate bus when they are standing at the bus stop. If they do, they can learn to ride the bus independently, but if they do not, they will be unable to perform the activity correctly and will always need assistance to ride the bus. A learner who cannot read may have to learn to ask the driver, "Does this bus go to ____(X location)____?" Such a question would not be too much out of the ordinary and would get the job done.

When a group consists of learners who have similar characteristics, it usually is possible to define a common behavior pattern for all of them, even when the learners have disabilities that prevent them from behaving in the typical way. For example, a major skill cluster for performing an assembly job in a factory might be to "re-order spare parts." Ordinarily, workers in this factory might perform a periodic inventory and then make out the order form. If the learners are nonreaders, it may not be possible for them to inventory the spare parts the way other workers ordinarily do it. However, they might be able to accomplish the activity by using a picture list of spare parts and a tally mark-off system. If the system is set up so that spare parts are ordered when the tallies reach a certain level, the learners will be able to accomplish the skill cluster and the work required. Alternatively, parts may be kept in boxes, and when the next-to-the-last box is empty, a standard number of parts can be ordered. Other techniques could be developed as well. The advantage of having a list of major skill clusters is that it focuses the attention of staff on what has to get done to meet a curriculum goal and allows them to be as creative as necessary in figuring out *how* a specific group of learners will actually accomplish each goal.

Physical or intellectual limitations often require instructors to find creative ways for learners to perform a major skill cluster. Sometimes the accommodations are easy to make and are well within typical behavior patterns. For example, a learner who lacks the strength to operate a push lawn mower may be able to guide a self-propelled mower. Since many people use self-propelled mowers, the learner will not be doing something "different" when mowing the lawn with one. But sometimes the special patterns must really be "special," and instructors must figure out a behavior pattern that makes it seem as though the learner can do what others do, but which actually is a kind of "trick." To use an example from White (1980), a learner who can count only to 10 can learn to make any purchase up to $11.00 by looking at the price tag, counting out a number of dollar bills equal to the numbers to the left of the decimal, and adding one more dollar for all the numbers to the right of the decimal. The clerk who takes the money will make change (which is nearly always correct). At some point, the learner will have a pocket full of coins, but if he or she goes to a bank, puts the coins on the counter, and says, "Dollars, please," the teller will count the coins and give him or her the right number of dollar bills. Instructors can work out many special behavior patterns similar to this one that allow learners with limited academic, physical, cognitive, and sensory abilities to perform such skills as preparing their own meals, shopping, budgeting, traveling, and performing jobs.

The behavior pattern for preparing meals that we will develop for our first situation must be special because these learners cannot read. Obviously, teaching them to use standard cookbooks and menus will not work. Development of a behavior pattern begins with a menu that the learners will learn to prepare, such as the Seven Day Menu that appears in Table 5.9. That is, the agency has decided that "making meals" means preparing all the foods that appear in this menu on the days and at the meals specified in the menu. Now, the only remaining problem is to find a way for the learners to prepare the foods even though they cannot read or write.

Unfortunately, in real group homes, this response is too simplistic. Many readers who are familiar with residential work will realize that certain government regulations for residential facilities require that no meal can be repeated within a 21-day period. The Seven Day Menu does not meet this regulation, but fortunately, setting up a pattern to prepare foods for periods longer than seven days does not have to be more complicated than this menu suggests. For example, we know one agency that has a seven-day rotation of foods with three weekly variations. On Tuesday (or whatever day) of the first weekly rotation, the meal may be a chicken breast baked in sauce made with a can of onion soup; on Tuesday of the second weekly rotation, the chicken breast may be baked in a sauce made with a can of mushroom soup; and on Tuesday of the third rotation, the sauce may be made with a can of cheese soup. Thus, the meal preparation process is the same each Tuesday, that is, a chicken breast baked with a can of soup, but the requirement that meals not repeat is also satisfied. The net effect is that learners with moderate and severe mental retardation are able to learn to cook all their meals and have a balanced diet, yet still must contend with only a one-week menu. This example illustrates how special behavior patterns are limited only by the imagination of the staff.

Limitations of Special Behavior Patterns. Special behavior patterns do pose a problem: They are not as flexible as the patterns used by people who have the usual array of skills and abilities. Consequently, their performance often is limited to the context in which they are learned. A person who can only use the "dollar more" behavior pattern described previously, for example, will not be able to compare prices to get the "best buy." In fact, some learners may even be limited to using this skill only in the store in which it was taught. Hence, a special behavior pattern is more restrictive than one that people ordinarily would use. Nevertheless, some people must learn to use them because, in doing so, they attain a measure of independence they might not attain otherwise.

Range of Special Behavior Patterns. Special behavior patterns can be developed for nearly any skill. They are often required when learners have academic, physical, language, or sensory disabilities that limit their interactions, range of motion, strength, or other attributes. Learners with visual disabilities often require different patterns of locomotion than sighted learners, learners with orthopedic disabilities often require special patterns for skills that require the use of the body's motor system, and learners who cannot read or write require special patterns to perform many community-living

TABLE 5.9 Seven Day Repeating Menu

Meal	Sunday	Monday	Tuesday	Wednesday	Thursday	Friday	Saturday
Breakfast	Juice Poached Eggs Whole Wheat Toast Butter/Jelly Milk/Coffee/Tea	Juice Cold Cereal Milk Whole Wheat Toast Butter/Jelly Milk/Coffee/Tea	Juice Hot Oatmeal Milk Whole Wheat Toast Butter/Jelly Milk/Coffee/Tea	Juice Soft Boiled Eggs Toast Butter/Jelly Milk/Coffee/Tea	Juice Cold Cereal Milk Toast Butter/Jelly Milk/Coffee/Tea	Juice Cold Cereal Milk Toast Butter/Jelly Milk/Coffee/Tea	Juice Hot Oatmeal Milk Toast Butter/Jelly Milk/Coffee/Tea
Lunch	Soup Grilled Cheese Sandwich Fruit Milk/Coffee/Tea	Ham Sandwich Fruit Milk/Coffee/Tea	Ham Sandwich Fruit Milk/Coffee/Tea	Roast Beef Sandwich Fruit Milk/Coffee/Tea	Roast Beef Sandwich Fruit Milk/Coffee/Tea	Turkey Sandwich Fruit Milk/Coffee/Tea	Turkey Sandwich Fruit Milk/Coffee/Tea
Dinner	Baked Ham Baked Potato w/ Butter Cauliflower Bread/Butter Cookies Milk/Coffee/Tea	Meat Loaf Rice Green Beans Bread/Butter Milk/Coffee/Tea	Roast Beef Mashed Potato w/ Gravy Carrots Bread/Butter Pie Milk/Coffee/Tea	Pork Chop Mashed Potato w/ Butter Peas and Onions Cake Milk/Coffee/Tea	Roast Turkey Breast Stuffing w/ Gravy Broccoli Cookies Milk/Coffee/Tea	Baked Fish Baked Potato w/ Butter Corn Cookies Milk/Coffee/Tea	Hamburger Potato Chips Succotash Cookies Milk/Coffee/Tea

Note: This menu is for demonstration purposes only. Any balanced and nutritious menu could be used in its place.

skills. In fact, most disabilities result in behavioral limitations that could require the use of special behavior patterns under at least some circumstances. Special education, rehabilitation services, and occupational therapy have long focused on developing special behavior patterns, and with the advent of adaptive devices using new technology, some techniques have become very sophisticated.

Special behavior patterns can be developed for persons at all levels of mental retardation. We have addressed the issue of complicated special patterns, such as those required for interacting in the community, but behavior patterns in areas such as personal care are often much less complicated. For example, learners who have trouble putting their shoes on the correct feet may require a dressing pattern that involves putting the shoes on the floor and lining them up "just so." Similarly, learners in wheelchairs may require a behavior pattern for entering a vehicle that is different from the one used by people who are not in wheelchairs (and which is likely to be different for different vehicles). Doubtless, staff will have to figure out many ways for learners to accomplish a skill cluster even when the learners have unique limitations.

Special behavior patterns can help many learners with mental retardation perform successfully in settings when they do not have the ability to learn the typical behavior patterns. Therefore, special behavior patterns have an important place in the instruction of persons with mental retardation. They should be used only when necessary, however, due to their limiting nature.

Written Behavior Patterns

When a curriculum development group describes a behavior pattern, it should be written as part of the curriculum. Most behavior patterns should be stated in some detail, but some do not require very much detail at all, especially those developed for learners who are very young or very severely disabled. For example, Gold (1980a) pointed out that objectives such as "drink liquids from a cup" or "use over-the-head method to put on overcoat" generally need little additional detail to be useful.

Boxes 5.3 and 5.4 present the behavior patterns for the learners in our two hypothetical situations. Note how they differ in terms of how much detail appears: The pattern that the group home residents with no academic skills will use to prepare meals is presented in much more detail than is the pattern that youngsters with mild retardation will use to budget money.

Step 2: Analyze the Skills Required for Each Behavior Pattern

The second step in constructing a curriculum is to make a list of the separate skills required to produce each behavior pattern. This list is the foundation for formulating the sequence of objectives leading to each goal in the curriculum. In general, most restricted curricula require the analysis of skills for every behavior pattern, and *all* comprehensive curricula require it.

BOX 5.3
Performance Pattern for Preparing All Meals

To show that the learners have attained this goal, they will do the following:
Learners will mark the days on a kitchen calendar with an *X* prior to going to bed each night. The next day, the learner responsible for the meal to be

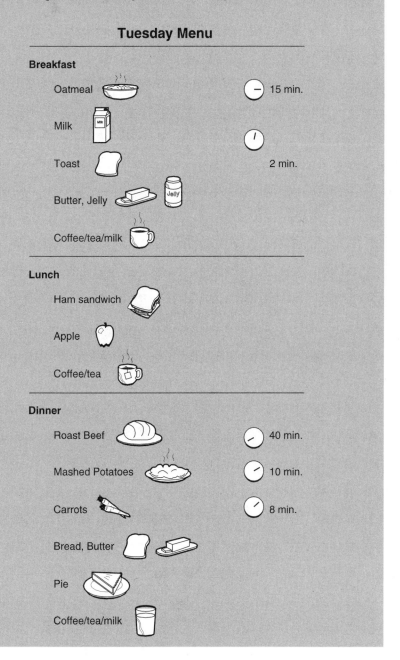

Tuesday Menu

Breakfast

Oatmeal		⊖	15 min.
Milk		⊘	
Toast			2 min.
Butter, Jelly			
Coffee/tea/milk			

Lunch

Ham sandwich	
Apple	
Coffee/tea	

Dinner

Roast Beef		⊘	40 min.
Mashed Potatoes		⊘	10 min.
Carrots		⊘	8 min.
Bread, Butter			
Pie			
Coffee/tea/milk			

prepared will identify the correct time for meal preparation and identify "today" by counting the Xs on the calendar (i.e., saying, "Sunday, Monday, Tuesday," etc.) until arriving at the first day without an 'X'. The learner will then identify the correct page in a notebook by counting an equal number of colored side tabs to get to "today" (again by saying, "Sunday, Monday, Tuesday," etc.). When the notebook page is opened, "today's" food will be on the page in picture form, as in Figure 5.1.

Foods will be prepared in the order shown in the cookbook; that is, foods at the top of the picture list get cooked first, the next in the sequence get cooked next, and so forth. For cooked meals, each pictured food has a circle next to it with the line in the circle indicating the length of time (to 60 minutes) each food should cook. This line represents the position of the handle on a 60-minute dial timer and indicates where to set the dial before placing the next food in or on the heat source. The longest-cooking food is listed first, the next longest second, and so forth, until all the foods are accounted for. When the learner places a food on the heat source, he or she sets the timer as indicated by the cookbook. When the timer sounds, the learner places the next food on the heat and sets the timer as indicated. When all the foods have been placed on the heat and the timer sounds for the last time, all the food has been cooked and is ready to eat.

The learners will prepare all their meals in the group home using the home's kitchen equipment. They will prepare 21 meals (seven each of breakfast, lunch, and supper) each week. They will prepare breakfasts in the morning and suppers in the evening. They will prepare weekday lunches in the mornings after breakfast and weekend lunches at noon before lunch.

Learners will prepare each meal using only the foods specified in the menu. When making cold sandwiches, the learners will place two pieces of meat and two lettuce leaves on a piece of bread, spread the condiment of their choice on the other slice of bread, and close the sandwich. Sandwiches for weekday lunches will be wrapped in plastic and bagged along with fruits and drinks. Breads and pastries will be purchased prepared, mashed potatoes will be made from instant potatoes, turkey stuffing will be made from prepared stuffing, and all vegetables will be frozen. Gravy will be made from meat drippings. Rice will be cooked in a rice cooker. Coffee and tea will be decaffeinated and milk will be skim. Cold cereals will be selected from bran flakes, oat squares, or corn flakes. Coffee will be prepared in an electric percolator and tea will be made with bagged tea and water boiled in a teapot, both using standard procedures. Eggs will be boiled or poached in an open pot following standard procedure, and oatmeal will be cooked in a covered pot, also following standard procedure. All hot meals will be hot and ready to eat, and all meals will look appetizing.

BOX 5.4
Performance Pattern for Budgeting Money and Paying Bills*

To show that the learners have attained this goal, they will do the following:

Learners will identify and list all liabilities requiring payment over the course of the year. They will subdivide this list into <monthly expenses> and <other schedule expenses>.

The learners will subdivide the two lists of liabilities into lists of <fixed> (rent, etc.) and <variable> expenses. They will establish "Budget Billing" for all utilities for which this option is available in order to regularize as many of their bills as possible. They will establish a monthly average expense for each recurring <variable> expense for which Budget Billing is not possible. They will calculate a <monthly total> of all recurring fixed and averaged variable expenses and record the total for each coming month on the calendar in the space for the first day of the month containing the due date. They will then note the due date for every expense on a yearly calendar.

The learners will calculate net income for one month after identifying all possible sources of income and adding them together. They will subtract the monthly average total of recurring expenses from their total income and identify the remainder as funds available for <occasional> expenses. The learners will place an individually determined portion of their <occasional> funds into a savings account for use as an <emergency> fund. The remainder will be placed in their checking accounts along with the amount set aside for paying monthly liabilities.

The learners will prioritize their preferred leisure expenses and other occasional expenses and list these expenses by priority. They will estimate an average monthly cost for each leisure activity using this formula:

$$\text{cost of the activity} + \text{travel}$$
$$+ \text{ peripheral expenses (equipment, food, tips, etc.)}.$$

They will then calculate a cumulative yearly cost for each activity by its priority and identify which activities on the list of occasional expenses and leisure activities they can afford for each month. They will then mark the total monthly cost for these expenses on the calendar along with the total of <fixed> and <occasional> monthly expenses for each month and calculate a grand total. They will now have a complete list of expenses and a grand total for each month on the calendar.

---

*Our thanks to Deanna Heckman and Linda Zabel for this example.

The learners will establish a weekly bill-payment schedule for each month. On the average, one-fourth of the total of their bills for the month will be paid each week, but bill due dates may "bunch" and require periodic surplus checkbook balances and carryover of money to successive weeks. The learner will mark a line through each expense on the calendar as it is paid.

When paying bills, the learners will identify each bill, payment book, or other expense indicator and match it to its corresponding entry on the calendar. They will compare the <amount due> to the budgeted allocation for each expense. They will identify which expenses have an excess and which have a deficit. If there is more than a dollar difference, they will add all the bills for the week together and compare the total to the budgeted total to see if the budgeted amount is sufficient to cover the deficits. If it is insufficient, they will consider one or more of the following strategies:

1. eliminate one or more optional expenses not yet incurred;
2. withdraw money from emergency fund;
3. petition assisting agency (e.g., welfare, county relief office) for assistance;
4. increase household income (e.g., get second job, change jobs for higher wages, have other member of household get job, or use a combination of these strategies);
5. obtain loan from financial institution; or
6. borrow from friend or relative.

If income exceeds expenses, they will consider using one or more of the following strategies:

1. add to savings;
2. prepay a bill;
3. increase monthly payments of installment bill; or
4. invest in mutual fund.

The learners will rebudget using the previously specified budgeting procedures (1) if the amount for one or more fixed expenses changes (e.g., the rent is raised or lowered); or (2) if a deficit appears in two consecutive months.

The learners will note the date and check number on the receipt portion of each bill they pay and place it in a file box containing file folders for each fixed expense and a set of alphabet folders for filing the receipts from other expenses. In the last week of December of each year, they will establish a new file box for the coming year and place the previous year's file in storage. They will maintain each file box for seven years, at which point they can discard files older than seven years.

Table 1.1 Yearly Fixed and Occasional Expenses by Month

	JAN.	FEB.	MAR.	APR.	MAY	JUNE	JULY	AUG.	SEPT.	OCT.	NOV.	DEC.
ALLOCATION LIST												
FIXED EXPENSES												
AUTO/TRANSPORTATION												
Insurance												
License												
Payments/Fees												
Fuel												
CLOTHING												
FOOD/HOUSEHOLD SUPPLIES												
HEALTH												
Insurance: Health/Life												
Medical/Dental Fees												
Prescriptions/Aids												
SERVICES												
Barber/Stylist												
Other												
HOUSING												
Rent/Mortgage												
Insurance/Taxes												
Utilities:												
Cable TV												
Electricity												
Heat												
Sewage/Water												
Telephone												
OCCASIONAL EXPENSES												
EMERGENCY FUND												
Miscellaneous												
Repairs												
GIFTS/CONTRIBUTIONS												
INTEREST/CREDIT CARD												
LEISURE ACTIVITIES												
Equipment												
Fees/Subscriptions												
Newspaper/Magazine												
Peripheral Expense												
SAVINGS												
TOTAL												
WAGES												
SOCIAL SECURITY												
ALIMONY												
GIFTS												
WELFARE BENEFITS												
INTEREST/DIVIDENDS												
OTHER												
TOTAL												

TABLE 5.10 Skills Required to Produce the Behavior Pattern "Inventory Food Stock"

Identify "Friday."
Identify "after dinner."
Follow schedule of chores.
Locate pantry, refrigerator, and storage cabinets.
Locate items on list: apples, bread, butter, cheese, cornflakes, coffee, detergent, eggs, grape jelly, ham, milk, oatmeal, orange juice, pears, potatoes, soup (chicken and tomato), tea, toothpaste, and vegetables (broccoli, carrots, corn, green beans, peas & onions, and succotash).
Count to six.
Identify 1/2 and 1/4 container contents.
Judge finger width.
Judge finger joint depth.
Locate row/column intersection.
Copy words and numbers from a list to a sheet of paper.
Judge "equal to or less than."
Read at third-grade level.
Relate coupons to "to buy" item.
Identify Big Food store advertisements.

The technique for analyzing skills is rather straightforward: Sentence by sentence, the staff reviews what the learners must do to exhibit the behavior pattern and makes a list of all the individual skills. Table 5.10 presents a skill analysis of the behavior pattern for making a food inventory prior to going to buy groceries found in Table 5.6.

Stating Skills

Like everything else that we have discussed, skills have to be stated in behavioral terms, and the following is a useful format for doing so:

The learners will _____

At this point there is no need to worry about specifying the order in which to teach the skills. The instructional staff can analyze them in any order and can add any skills they overlooked as they make revisions of the work.

Boxes 5.5 and 5.6 present the lists of skills needed to perform the behavior patterns in each of our two situations. Note that there is nothing magical or complicated about these lists: They are not listed in any particular order and do not have any significance beyond listing the things the learners will have to do to produce the behavior patterns specified in the previous set of boxes. The significance will come later when the skills and their prerequisite and lead-in skills are arranged, in the order in which they will be taught, to form a pathway of objectives.

BOX 5.5
Skills Inherent in Preparing Foods for the Seven Day Menu

Retrieve stored foods.
Retrieve pots, pans, and utensils from storage.
Pour juice.
Boil water in pot.
Poach eggs.
Make toast.
Butter bread or spread jelly or peanut butter.
Pour cold cereal into bowl.
Pour milk on cereal.
Make coffee in electric percolator.
Make tea.
Boil water in teapot.
Pour hot water from teapot.
Pour milk.
Make oatmeal.
Soft boil eggs.
Make cold sandwiches: ham, roast beef, and turkey.
Make hot sandwich: grilled cheese.
Bag sandwiches, fruit, and drinks.
Bake ham.
Bake potato.
Place butter in baked potato.
Cook frozen vegetables.

Place cookies on plate.
Make meat loaf.
Shred bread slices.
Chop vegetables.
Take meat dish from oven.
Slice meat loaf.
Roast meat loaf.
Cook rice.
Scoop rice from cooker.
Scoop ice cream.
Roast beef.
Make mashed potatoes.
Stir frozen juice concentrate.
Stir hot liquid.
Stir viscous substances (e.g., potatoes and cookie dough).
Make gravy.
Slice pie.
Grill pork chops.
Slice cake.
Roast turkey breast.
Prepare stuffing.
Bake fish.
Grill hamburgers.
Form hamburgers.
Serve potato chips.

BOX 5.6
Skills Inherent in Budgeting Money and Paying Bills

List fixed expenses: rent/mortgage; food; utilities (telephone, gas, electric, water/sewage, heat, and cable TV); transportation (work or other); taxes; clothing; supplies (home and work); payments (car, household, and personal equipment); and personal care (routine medical and dental care, personal grooming, and health care).

List occasional expenses: leisure activities (equipment, fees, transportation, and other); repairs (home, auto, and personal equipment); expendables (cleaning equipment and materials, personal care materials, and treats); emergencies; contributions; and savings.

Discriminate required and optional expenses.

Set priorities for expenses.

Identify billing techniques: payment schedule (Budget Billing, fixed, and occasional); due dates; minimum payments; late charges; payment books; and finance charges.

Identify information on a bill: due date(s); amount due; minimum payment; finance charge; telephone number for billing information; address for remittance; reason for bill; and late payment charges.

Calculate averages, cumulative totals, surplus funds, and deficits.

Relate amount of bill to budgeted amount (surplus and deficits).

Money skills: read and write money symbols; make purchases; make change; identify paycheck; identify deductions (FICA, state tax, federal tax, local tax, medical insurance, and other); identify gross pay; identify net pay; and identify other sources of income (welfare, pension, refunds, and other).

Calculate total monthly income.

Banking skills: cash checks; relate passbook data to actual cash amount; write checks; keep running record of checks; identify parts of bank statement (specific account, current balance, initial balance, checks cleared, deposits, and closing date); reconcile checkbook running record with bank statement; and establish Budget Billing.

Establish emergency fund.

Discriminate financial emergency from routine expense.

Use telephone: use white pages (personal names, addresses, and telephone numbers) and yellow pages (business categories, business names, addresses, and telephone numbers).

Calendar skills: identify points in time (dates, end of month, beginning of month, weekend, days of week, months of year, week of month, and year-end); identify span of time (day, week, month, year, or seven years); identify order of time (dates, months, seasons, and years); relate due date to actual date; file bills by date; identify payday; and identify monthly payment dates for each bill.

Identify investments (money market, mutual funds, certificates of deposit, stocks, and bonds).

Mail letters: mail bills (self-addressed, hand-addressed, and window envelopes); identify appropriate postage; purchase stamps; and identify mail drops.

Make appointments.

Fill out forms: W-4, employment, welfare requests, unemployment, Budget Billing, and loan requests.

Make file.

Identify appropriate file storage.

When and When Not to Analyze Skills

A skill analysis is not always necessary. That is, under the following conditions, the statements of behavior patterns themselves may be sufficiently detailed to teach the learners:

- when the aim of instruction is narrowly defined, and the curriculum goals focus on a limited number of skills;

- when learners have mild retardation and well-developed skill repertoires, and instruction is provided only in community sites; or
- when learners with any degree of mental retardation must use special behavior patterns that have no prerequisite and lead-in skills.

Some instructional programs use restricted curricula that are community-based in nature and do not provide instruction anywhere but directly in the community. Supported-employment programs often demonstrate these characteristics. In these programs, jobs are found for individual learners, and a job coach accompanies them to the job and performs it with them while they learn to do it for themselves. When learners learn skills in natural settings and circumstances, all instructional information is contained in the setting, and the learners may be able to acquire the behavior pattern as a single unit or as a series of major subunits. Moreover, if the learners have well-developed skill repertoires, or if they learn special behavior patterns that have no prerequisite and lead-in skills, it may not be necessary to teach each individual skill as a separate entity. In such cases, a skill analysis would be superfluous.

On the other hand, learners in a comprehensive curriculum progress from one level to another. In such a program, it is often possible to group the learners by the skills they must learn and teach the skills to groups of learners. Then, upper-level instructors can anticipate that the learners will have acquired these skills before they come to the upper-level programs. To accomplish this result, however, it is necessary to describe clearly the skills that the learners need to move from level to level.

If a skill cluster is particularly complicated, it also will require a skill analysis, even in the case of restricted curricula. For example, one of the major skill clusters for Situation 1 is to "prepare foods using appropriate timing." This skill cluster requires learners to have many skills that range from opening a bag of chips to scheduling the cooking of various foods while preparing evening meals. Instruction will go much more smoothly in such a complicated curriculum area if the staff identifies all the necessary skills before trying to teach any of them.

Step 3: Analyze Prerequisite and Lead-in Skills

In all comprehensive curricula and most restricted curricula, behavior patterns are made up of both skills and prerequisite and lead-in skills. The learners must acquire all of them to produce the pattern, and all three types of skills should be stated as objectives in most curricula. Comprehensive curricula, because they must advance learners from level to level, tend to contain many prerequisite and lead-in skills because developers must determine what to teach at early levels that will make instruction at the upper levels possible. Restricted curricula, because they often focus directly on teaching behavior patterns, usually do not need to be as concerned with prerequisite and lead-in skills, especially if they contain many special behavior patterns.

Prerequisite and Lead-in Skills Defined

The following is a definition of prerequisite and lead-in skills:

> **Prerequisite** and **lead-in skills** are basic skills that are closely associated with skills in the behavior pattern that learners should or must have before beginning to acquire the behavior pattern.

A prerequisite skill is one that *must* be present before another skill can appear. For example, it is impossible for a learner to learn to walk if that learner cannot stand. Thus, standing is prerequisite to walking.

Lead-in skills are skills that, while not prerequisite, make instruction of a behavior pattern easier if they are present. For example, it is not necessary to know how to read a thermometer before learning to dress for weather conditions, but if learners have this skill, it will be easier to teach them how to figure out what kind of clothes to wear. Therefore, from the instructor's point of view, it could be helpful to teach thermometer reading as a lead-in skill for dressing to go outside.

Thus, prerequisite and lead-in skills are the skills that the instructional unit should or must teach before trying to teach the skills in the behavior pattern (Howell, Fox, and Morehead, 1993). A curriculum that lists prerequisite and lead-in skills in an instructional sequence will help instructors determine if a learner is ready to begin working on a behavior pattern and allow them to plan instruction accordingly. An analysis of the prerequisite and lead-in skills for a behavior pattern will supply the information the staff needs to construct the curriculum pathways that guide learners toward the goal in an orderly and systematic manner. Thus, a curriculum that includes the prerequisite and lead-in skills for the behavior patterns will lay out a unified course of instruction that proceeds directly toward the goals.

Analyzing Prerequisites and Lead-in Skills

The techniques for analyzing prerequisite and lead-in skills are as follows:

Prerequisite Skills. The technique used to analyze prerequisites is to consider each of the skills analyzed in the previous step and ask,

> "What must a learner be able to do before beginning to work on this skill?"

Many prerequisites will involve basic skills, such as physical, social, communication, and academic skills. For example, learners would have to have certain addition and subtraction skills before they could learn to budget money and pay bills.

Prerequisites may not be presumed: They must be analyzed separately for each skill because many skills that are assumed to be prerequisite to another skill are not. The examples of "prerequisites" in Table 5.11 are commonly taught in school and rehabilitation center programs, though each has been shown to be false many times. Learners who are color-blind often learn to read; many learners with jobs in competitive employment never put nuts onto bolts (or even use the movements associated with this skill); and some

TABLE 5.11 Examples of False Prerequisites

Learners must
- be able to identify colors before learning to read;
- be able to screw nuts onto bolts prior to learning job skills in a competitive job setting; and
- be able to control inappropriate behaviors prior to going out into the community.

forms of nonaversive behavior management are predicated on the fact that the community itself provides sufficient management of inappropriate behaviors (Baker and Salon, 1986; Berkman and Meyer, 1988).

When learners must use special behavior patterns, the list of prerequisites will usually be very small or nonexistent. The specific reason for teaching special behavior patterns in the first place is because learners lack certain prerequisite skills. For example, most learners learn to count and to read and write numbers beyond 100 before they begin to learn to shop for food and clothing. But learners who cannot do these things may still perform limited shopping skills by using the "dollar more" method discussed previously. For people who use this special behavior pattern, the counting, reading, and writing skills would not be prerequisites.

Lead-in Skills.   We can illustrate what lead-in skills are by referring to the food preparation curriculum in Situation 1. In this curriculum, pouring liquids from various containers would be lead-in skills, because it would be very difficult to teach learners to perform many useful cooking skills if they have not learned to pour liquids. Similarly, learners will benefit more from instruction in cooking if they know how to use certain condiments, set a table, and butter a slice of bread. Such skills would logically be taught prior to teaching more advanced cooking skills and therefore would be listed as lead-in skills. Similarly, in Situation 2, it would be logical to teach learners to use a city bus before trying to teach them to travel to the bank unassisted. Bus skills and mental map skills could be taught simultaneously, but most instructors would probably want the learners to acquire the bus skills first because it would make it easier to teach the mental map skills required for traveling to specific locations at a later time.

There is no firm rule about what should or should not be considered a lead-in skill. For example, it is not necessary for learners to be able to read dials before they start to learn to drive a car, nor is it necessary for learners to be able to use a knife and fork to eat before learning to make a tossed salad. But many instructors would feel more comfortable if such skills were in place prior to beginning instruction in the second set of skills in each example. Therefore, they could be listed as lead-in skills. On the other hand, they might also be taught as part of the behavior pattern, in which case they would not be listed at all.

The value of a lead-in skill analysis is that such a list indicates which skills would be best to teach in the early stages of instruction, along with the more obvious prerequisite skills. When the skills for performing a behavior pattern are arranged in an instructional sequence along with the prerequisite and lead-in skills, the staff will have a sequenced list of skills that leads directly to the curriculum goal. Such a list has several instructional uses, chief among which is that it provides a complete sequence of curriculum objectives to guide instruction and an assessment tool for deciding what to teach "next" to an individual learner.

Listing Prerequisite and Lead-in Skills

Schools and agencies should use the characteristics of the learners in the program to gauge which prerequisite and lead-in skills to include as objectives in a curriculum. As a general rule, comprehensive curricula are developed for learners with a wide age range and contain many prerequisite and lead-in skills. For learners who are lower functioning, or for learners who are less experienced in the goal areas, curricula should include many more prerequisite and lead-in skills than curricula for learners who are older, higher functioning, or more experienced in the areas. Also, the range of prerequisite and lead-in skills contained in the curriculum should be broad enough to accommodate all the learners in the program regardless of their age and functioning levels.

The prerequisite and lead-in skills for each of our two situations are presented in Boxes 5.7 and 5.8.

Cautions

All the prerequisite and lead-in skills that are listed in a curriculum should be well within the limitations imposed by the physical, cognitive, and academic abilities of the learners for whom the curriculum was developed. After the staff begins to perform a skill analysis, they may find some basic skills that, for one reason or another, the learners are not likely to acquire. In such a case, they should change the behavior pattern so that these prerequisite skill(s) do not have to be in the curriculum. However, when behavior patterns are changed, the new behavior patterns will have their own skill requirements, and the list of skills produced in Step 2 will need to be reanalyzed.

Step 4: Sequence Objectives to Form a Curriculum Pathway

The fourth step in the curriculum development process is to arrange all the skills and prerequisite and lead-in skills for each curriculum goal into a curriculum pathway. When this step is complete, the instructional unit will have a curriculum that can be used to decide what to teach "next" to any individual learner.

Pathways of objectives can vary from program to program because the staff must make judgments about which skill or behavior pattern they must teach first, and which to teach next, and so on, until they account for all the skills that have been identified in the previous steps. Objectives consisting of prerequisite and lead-in skills should be taught earlier than the skills for producing the behavior pattern.

PREREQUISITES:

1. Feed self.
   Foods: finger foods; vegetables; soup; meat
   Using: fork; spoon; knife
2. Discriminate hot/cold.
3. Match foods to pictures, line drawings to dials, and meal to time of day (breakfast, lunch, or dinner).

LEAD-IN SKILLS:

1. State food preferences.
2. Use condiments: salt, pepper, ketchup, mustard, relish, and tartar sauce.
3. Name foods on the table at each meal.
4. Discriminate cooked/raw.
5. Pour from sauce pan, frying pan, teapot, coffeepot, milk carton, and measuring cup.
6. Pass foods and condiments on request at table.
7. Make cold sandwich: meat, peanut butter, or cheese.
8. State days of week by rote.

BOX 5.8
Preskills for Budgeting Money and Paying Bills

Make purchases.
Make change.
Ride public transportation.
Make payments.
Read at sixth-grade level.
Drive automobile.
Maintain personal cleanliness.
Maintain cleanliness of domicile.
Identify need for repairs (home, auto, and personal equipment).
Establish savings account.
Establish checking account.
Make donations.
Establish routines (school or personal).
Discriminate "wants" and "needs."
Obtain employment.
Add five-figure numbers.

Add five-figure numbers with decimals.
Calculate "one-fourth."
Identify "emergency."
Fill out forms.
Alphabetize words.
Make lists.
Locate information at row-column intersection in a table of values.
Tell time to the nearest minute.
Make telephone calls.
Address letters.
Pay bills.
Prioritize personal activities.
List activity likes and dislikes.
Make labels.
Obtain social security number.

For restricted curricula, it also may be necessary to sequence the behavior patterns. Not all patterns can be taught simultaneously, and choices must be made about which patterns to teach before others. Such choices are necessary if for no other reason than to maximize the efficiency of staff efforts. In our experience, instructors have little difficulty deciding which skills are easy to teach and which are difficult and can produce a very good pathway of objectives in relatively short order.

Preparing Pathways of Objectives

The question to ask when sequencing curriculum objectives into curriculum pathways is as follows:

> Should this objective be taught before or after this other objective?

When experienced instructors respond to this question for each objective in the curriculum, they eventually will develop a systematic and well-organized list of objectives that forms a curriculum pathway. The staff can then use this list to guide the development of individual instructional programs.

Assembling the Document

The resulting curriculum should be assembled in a loose-leaf notebook because it will be a dynamic, changeable document. Two features, inherent in a curriculum constructed in the manner we have suggested, will make it dynamic: the community referents and the sequence.

Community Referents. In any community-based curriculum, the contents must be revised periodically because conditions change; for example, buildings get constructed or torn down, transportation routes change, new supplies and equipment are purchased, and key persons move away or retire. Behavior patterns that once were accurate will become obsolete and unworkable, and objectives that once were appropriate will no longer apply. Consequently, the curriculum must also change.

Sequence Variation. When two different groups of instructors construct a pathway of objectives, one group may decide to teach one objective before teaching another, while the other group may decide the opposite. The fact that two groups of instructors do not develop identical sequences of objectives for a pathway is not important. What is important is for a staff to agree on the final pathway of objectives because they must use it to make judgments about what to teach and when to teach it to a specific group of learners. In fact, the staff should expect to make adjustments as they grow in experience and develop new ideas.

Step 5: Assign Pathway Segments to Instructional Units

After the pathway analysis is complete, one last task remains: assigning segments of the pathways of objectives to the various instructional units in the school or agency. Like the previous step, this step requires the consensus of the instructional staff, but in our experience, most people who teach tend to make very good decisions about who should teach which objectives.

Boxes 5.9, 5.10, and 5.11 present examples from our two situations. Note in Box 5.11 how the staff organized their list of curriculum objectives according to the instructional units in the school system. Each of these documents

---

BOX 5.9
Pathway of Objectives for "Preparing All Meals from the Seven Day Menu"

1. Feed self.
2. Discriminate hot/cold.
3. Place on plate: potato chips and cookies.
4. Spoon out ice cream, vegetables, mashed potatoes, and rice.
5. Stir juice concentrate.
6. Pour from milk carton, coffeepot/teapot, and juice bottle.
7. Prepare cold cereal.
8. Retrieve bread, cold meats/cheese/butter, condiments/jellies, ice cream, eggs/milk, cereals/oatmeal, and cookies/pies.
9. Spread butter and jelly.
10. Make cold sandwiches: meat.
11. Pass foods and condiments on request.
12. Locate pots, pans, and utensils.
13. Use condiments: salt, pepper, ketchup, mustard, relish, and tartar sauce.
14. Wrap and bag sandwiches and cookies.
15. Slice pie and cake.
16. Name foods on table: breakfast, lunch, and dinner.
17. Match line drawings to dials.
18. Prepare coffee.
19. Heat toast, and heat water for tea.
20. Stir hot liquid.
21. Butter baked potato.
22. Set table: breakfast, lunch, and dinner.
23. State food preferences.
24. Retrieve meats, frozen vegetables, and rice.
25. Make grilled cheese sandwich.
26. Pour from sauce pan and frying pan.
27. Chop vegetables.
28. Boil frozen vegetables, potatoes, soft-boiled eggs, and poached eggs.
29. Prepare oatmeal and rice.
30. Bake potato and fish.
31. Slice meat loaf, ham, roast beef, and turkey.
32. Fry pork chop and hamburger.
33. Prepare mashed potatoes and turkey stuffing.
34. Prepare hamburger and meat loaf.
35. Roast ham, roast beef, turkey, and meat loaf.
36. Prepare gravy.

BOX 5.10
Pathway of Objectives for Budgeting Money and Paying Bills

1. Maintain personal cleanliness.
2. Tell time to nearest minute.
3. Establish school routines.
4. Read at fourth-grade level.
5. Obtain social security number.
6. Add/subtract five-figure numbers.
7. Add/subtract numbers with decimals.
8. Identify money symbols.
9. Purchase stamps.
10. Identify points in time.
11. Calculate "one-fourth."
12. Locate information at row-column intersection in a table of values.
13. Calculate averages.
14. Make lists.
15. Identify span of day, week, and month.
16. Establish personal routines.
17. List activity likes and dislikes.
18. Make telephone calls.
19. Address letters.
20. Identify mail drops.
21. Identify appropriate postage.
22. Ride public transportation.
23. Make change.
24. Establish savings account.
25. Relate passbook data to real cash amount.
26. Discriminate "wants" and "needs."
27. Identify need for repairs of personal equipment.
28. Identify "emergency."
29. Identify span of a year.
30. Fill out school forms.
31. Make donations.
32. Maintain cleanliness of domicile.
33. Identify need for home repairs.
34. Alphabetize words.
35. Make file folders.
36. Drive automobile.
37. Use white pages.
38. Fill out employment forms.
39. Fill out W-4 form.
40. Identify order of events.
41. Obtain employment.
42. Identify paycheck.
43. Cash check.
44. Identify payday.
45. Identify net pay.
46. Identify deductions.
47. Establish checking account.
48. Write checks.
49. Make payments.
50. Identify bank statement.
51. Calculate cumulative totals.
52. Keep running record of checkbook.
53. Identify gross pay.
54. Relate "due date" to "today's date."
55. Identify need for auto repairs.
56. Use yellow pages.
57. Prioritize personal activities.
58. Identify information on a bill.
59. Pay bills.
60. Mail bills.
61. Identify billing techniques.
62. Discriminate emergency and routine expense.
63. Make appointments.
64. List fixed expenses.
65. List occasional expenses.
66. Discriminate "required" and "optional" expenses.
67. Establish emergency fund.
68. Reconcile checkbook running record with bank statement balance.
69. Identify surplus funds.
70. Identify deficits.
71. Relate amount of bill to budgeted amount.
72. Identify monthly payment date of bill.
73. Establish Budget Billing.

74. Identify total monthly income.
75. Identify other sources of income.
76. Fill out unemployment forms.
77. Fill out welfare forms.
78. Fill out loan forms.
79. Identify appropriate bill storage.
80. Identify investments.

ELEMENTARY SCHOOL

1. Maintain personal cleanliness.
2. Tell time to nearest minute.
3. Establish school routines.
4. Read at fourth-grade level.
5. Obtain social security number.
6. Add/subtract five-figure numbers.
7. Add/subtract numbers with decimals.
8. Identify money symbols.
9. Purchase stamps.
10. Identify points in time.

JUNIOR HIGH SCHOOL

11. Calculate "one-fourth."
12. Locate information at row-column intersection in a table of values.
13. Calculate averages.
14. Make lists.
15. Identify span of day, week, and month.
16. Establish personal routines.
17. List activity likes and dislikes.
18. Make telephone calls.
19. Address letters.
20. Identify mail drops.
21. Identify appropriate postage.
22. Ride public transportation.
23. Make change.

HIGH SCHOOL

24. Establish savings account.
25. Relate passbook data to real cash amount.
26. Discriminate "wants" and "needs."
27. Identify need for repairs of personal equipment.
28. Identify "emergency."
29. Identify span of a year.
30. Fill out school forms.
31. Make donations.
32. Maintain cleanliness of domicile.
33. Identify need for home repairs.
34. Alphabetize words.
35. Make file folders.
36. Drive automobile.
37. Use white pages.
38. Fill out employment forms.
39. Fill out W-4 form.
40. Identify order of time.
41. Obtain employment.
42. Identify paycheck.
43. Cash check.
44. Identify payday.
45. Identify net pay.
46. Identify deductions.
47. Establish checking account.
48. Write checks.
49. Make payments.
50. Identify bank statement.
51. Calculate cumulative totals.
52. Keep running record of checkbook.
53. Identify gross pay.
54. Relate "due date" to "today's date."
55. Identify need for auto repairs.

56. Use yellow pages.
57. Prioritize personal activities.
58. Identify information on a bill.
59. Pay bills.
60. Mail bills.
61. Identify billing techniques.
62. Discriminate financial emergency and routine expense.
63. Make appointments.
64. List fixed expenses.
65. List occasional expenses.
66. Discriminate "required" and "optional" expenses.
67. Establish emergency fund.
68. Reconcile checkbook running record with bank statement balance.
69. Identify surplus funds.
70. Identify deficits.
71. Relate amount of bill to budgeted amount.
72. Identify monthly payment date of bill.
73. Establish Budget Billing.
74. Identify total monthly income.
75. Identify other sources of income.
76. Fill out unemployment forms.
77. Fill out welfare forms.
78. Fill out loan forms.
79. Identify appropriate bill storage.
80. Identify investments.

Curriculum material developed as one of the requirements of a course assignment for K541, "Assessment and Remediation of Special Needs Adolescents and Adults" at Indiana University, Second Semester 1993–1994. Used by permission of Deanna Heckman and Linda Zabel.

can now be used to find out what skills the learners in the program have and what skills they should be working on next. At this point, the staff has agreed upon (a) a sequence of skills that their learners should acquire and (b) when the learners should acquire them.

Concluding Statement

In this chapter we have shown how to take the curriculum goals that were developed through the techniques shown in Chapter 4 and use them to carry out the curriculum development process. We have presented two different kinds of curricula, restricted and comprehensive, that schools and adult agencies can develop, and we have shown how to construct each type.

If a school or agency uses the process explained in this chapter, the staff will find that the development of IPs, the preparation of teaching lessons, and the scheduling of activities can be carried out logically and in a focused manner. They will have a framework for grouping learners for instructional purposes and for deciding which aspects of the curriculum can be carried out within the physical boundaries of the school or agency. They will also discover that some instruction must be carried out in community settings because they are the only places in which some skills can be taught well. The instructional programs that result from such curricula will take on a direction and a purpose that is difficult to achieve under any other system.

PART III

Assessment and Planning of Individual Instructional Programs

A school or an agency develops a curriculum to create a tool that the staff can use to plan individualized instructional programs for their learners. The subject of the next two chapters will be how to use this tool to perform an instructional assessment and how to select skills to include in an instructional plan for an individual learner.

The term **assessment** has been used in many ways. Following Cone and Hawkins (1977), Gresham and Elliot (1984), and Knapczyk and Rodes (1996), we will use it to refer to the investigative process that helps instructors answer the following questions:

- Do individual learners have the skills to meet the objectives found in the list of skills in the curriculum?

and, if they do,

- Do they actually use these skills in the settings and circumstances in which they should use them?

In Chapter 6, we will explain how to plan an assessment that allows the instructor to answer these questions. The results of the assessment will help decide which skills to teach to learners "next" and provide a framework for evaluating their instructional programs.

We also will show how to develop **individualized instructional plans,** or the various documents that instructors use to plan and monitor a learner's instruction. These documents will provide the framework within which to describe instructional activities for each learner. In Chapter 7 we will discuss how to carry out the assessment, summarize the results, and set the priorities for learners' instruction.

The next two chapters concentrate primarily on what a school or rehabilitation agency must do to plan and conduct an assessment. We will not focus on how to use commercially developed assessment instruments because most of the skills that learners need to become independent are specific to community settings, and commercially prepared instruments cannot take into account the demands posed by these settings. Cartwright and Cartwright (1984), Howell and Morehead (1987), McFall (1982), and Salvia and Hughes (1990), among others, have stated that most of the requirements for being successful in home, school, and community settings are established by two factors:

1. the people who are in the settings; and
2. the circumstances presented in the settings.

Commercial and standardized instruments cannot define the behavioral demands posed by these settings because each setting is unique and has its own performance requirements. Therefore, instructional personnel must develop many (if not most) of their own assessment tools and procedures to find out what skills their learners need to acquire. If they have a good curriculum available, the techniques presented in Chapters 6 and 7 will provide the information that is required to do so.

CHAPTER 6

Planning an Assessment of Curriculum Objectives

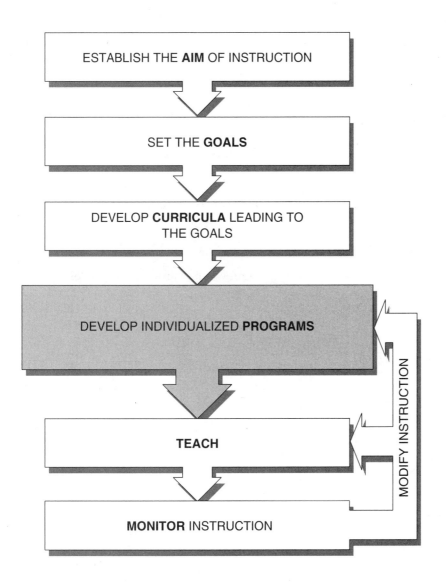

A well-designed curriculum gives instructors a clear picture of the full range of both the skills that learners must acquire to reach the goals of the curriculum and the sequences in which to teach those skills. Given such a curriculum, instructors can conduct an assessment that tells them where in the curriculum to begin teaching a specific learner.

An assessment compares a learner's current behavioral repertoire to the sequence of skills that lead to the curriculum goals. The results of an assessment provide a broad overview of the skills that the learner has now and the skills that he or she has yet to acquire in each curriculum pathway. An assessment not only shows where in those curriculum pathways to begin teaching, it also provides a framework for setting priorities among the many curriculum objectives that the learner has not yet attained. Thus, a well-conducted assessment reduces or eliminates the possibilities that instructors will

- select curriculum objectives that the learners have already met; and
- choose objectives that are presently beyond the learners' ability levels.

For these reasons, assessment is an extremely important activity within the Instructional Model.

Benefits of Performing an Assessment

Conducting an assessment helps the instructional staff carry out two important tasks in planning individualized programs of instruction.

Placing Learners in the Curriculum Pathways

An assessment is particularly useful when instructors need to place learners in the curriculum pathways for the very first time, such as when they first enter an instructional program in a school or agency or when they begin to work in a new instructional area. At such times, instructors must find out where in the curriculum pathways each learner currently functions relative to the goals of the curriculum. Because an assessment shows which curriculum items the learners have attained and which they have not, the curriculum objectives that are sequenced "next" in the pathways should become the immediate focus of the learners' instruction. These objectives contain the skills the learner must acquire next.

It is not necessary for instructors to conduct an assessment every time they must decide what to teach to a learner. If the curriculum has been designed appropriately, and if the instructors do a good job of placing the learners in the curriculum the first time, instruction will proceed from one objective to the next in the curriculum pathway without requiring reassessment because the attainment of one curriculum objective signals the learner's readiness for instruction on the next one.

Setting Priorities Among Curriculum Objectives

After instructors determine where in the curriculum to begin teaching, they often will find that they have identified so many curriculum objectives toward which the learners could work that it is impossible to focus on all of them right away. In these cases, it is necessary to specify a reasonable and attainable number of curriculum objectives to include in their instructional plans. The instructors can reduce the options by setting priorities among the various instructional possibilities for each learner. At this point, the instructor's task is to choose the few items that will have the greatest impact on the learners' overall performance and that will allow each of them to make optimum progress toward the curriculum goals. Setting priorities is especially important when the learners have to acquire many skills during instruction.

Principles for Performing an Assessment

Table 6.1 contains three fundamental principles for conducting assessments. Adherence to these principles will help ensure that the assessment process yields the most accurate and useful information. We do not think that standardized assessment instruments (such as those used to assess aptitude and achievement levels) are very useful in finding out what to teach to learners. While it is true that standardized tests play an important role in making decisions about identification and classification and about the eligibility of learners for certain programs, these tests usually provide little useful information about the skills and curriculum objectives to include in individualized programs of instruction (Choate, Enright, Miller, Poteet, and Rakes, 1995; Howell et al., 1993; Salvia and Ysseldyke, 1995).

With this idea in mind, let us consider the principles under which assessments should be conducted.

Assessments Should Focus on the Demands Expressed by the Curriculum Objectives

Instructional personnel will usually be able to select from a wide variety of procedures and activities with which to assess the skill levels of their learners. Among other things, they can use questionnaires, work samples, chapter tests, simulations, and direct observations of behavior in the settings in which learners must perform skills. Furthermore, instructors can conduct assessments under many different conditions and at many different times. The examples in Table 6.2 illustrate the range of possible variations for where and when assessments can be conducted.

Any instructor might be able to choose from a wide variety of procedures to assess learner behavior. For example, a vocational instructor might be able to choose from among written tests to assess computational skills, hands-on activities to assess performance skills, simulated activities to

TABLE 6.1 Principles for Conducting Assessments

Assessments should
- focus on the demands expressed in the curriculum objectives;
- be conducted under natural conditions; and
- be individualized.

TABLE 6.2 Illustrations of When and Where to Conduct Assessments

Assessments can be conducted
- during regularly scheduled activities in a classroom, residential setting, work setting, or leisure setting;
- during one-on-one testing situations that are designed to investigate the limits of the learners' abilities;
- during random interactive moments throughout the regular course of the day; and
- during activities that are scheduled to assess a particular set of skills.

assess language and interpersonal skills, and/or observations of on-the-job behavior to assess specific job skills. From among the possibilities, the best and most accurate assessments always will be those in which the procedures and conditions allow a direct examination of the skills the learner needs to meet the specific demands of the curriculum objectives. The instructor should base all decisions about which assessment procedures and activities to use on the skill demands of the curriculum objectives being assessed. Thus, if the instructor is interested in finding out how a learner responds to actual job variables, direct observation of on-the-job activities would be the best source of information about the learner's skill level.

An elementary-level special education teacher who is preparing his or her learners to go to a middle school program might assess some of the same areas as the instructor in the vocational program, such as computational skills and language skills. But this teacher would probably use different assessment procedures to assess these skills than would the vocational teacher; for example, he or she might use paper-and-pencil tests, work sheets, or simulations to obtain the necessary information. These examples indicate that even though different instructors may focus on assessing the same skills, they may need to obtain very different kinds of information about their learners' skill levels.

It is important to plan an assessment carefully and to develop a clear, unbiased estimate of the learners' current skill levels relative to the curriculum objectives toward which they will work. To do so, it is necessary to ensure valid comparisons of their behavior to the requirements presented by the curriculum objectives.

Assessment investigates the skills that learners need to have in order to meet curriculum goals.
Photo courtesy of Cleo Photography.

Assessments Should Be Conducted Under Natural Conditions

The best and most reliable means of assessing performance are normally those that occur under the natural conditions in which learners will use their skills when instruction is complete. As we indicated in Chapter 5, the natural conditions define the actual skills the learners must perform to meet the curriculum objectives; thus, the instructor's job is to find out how the learners actually respond when faced with the demands imposed by the environment (Knapczyk and Rodes, 1996). The assessment results will give a clear indication of where the learners are relative to achieving the curriculum objectives. Therefore, they will ensure the most accurate placement in the curriculum.

In some curriculum areas, observation of behavior under the natural performance conditions provides the only possible way to obtain reliable measures of learner performance. To illustrate, consider the fact that many "travel" curriculum objectives must be tied directly to characteristics of the community, such as the local geography, the available means of transportation, commonly observed safety rules, and the regulations and local conventions for travel. Such dimensions set the parameters for each curriculum objective and largely define how the learners must meet these objectives. Instructors who assess learners under natural conditions create the best opportunities for observing whether the learners can actually exhibit the required skills. Conducting an assessment of travel skills under artificial or atypical circumstances (such as having learners draw diagrams or answer questions on work sheets) usually will not give an accurate estimate of how well they can use their skills in community settings.

Assessing curriculum objectives under natural performance conditions allows instructors to attend closely to two things:

1. the ways in which most people typically behave in the setting; and
2. the circumstances under which they exhibit this behavior (Knapczyk and Rodes, 1996).

From an instructional standpoint, it is advantageous to attend closely to these variables because the information gained about them will indicate what learners must do to meet the demands and requirements of a setting. In addition, this information may suggest approaches to teaching the required skills.

Assessments Should Be Individualized

Instructors should conduct assessments that fit the characteristics of each individual learner in a program. This approach gives the most complete and accurate account of the ability levels of the learners and assists in the planning of instructional lessons and activities that suit their specific needs. Table 6.3 presents three ways to individualize assessments.

Assess Only Objectives That Need to Be Assessed

In most cases, instructors should design assessments to investigate a different set of curriculum objectives for each learner in the program. When the selection of curriculum items is individualized, the instructors can conduct the assessment in an efficient and straightforward manner and more easily place the learners in the curriculum based on the abilities, skills, and experiences that each brings into the instructional program.

Also, instructors should tailor their assessments to the needs of individual learners in order to take advantage of whatever information they already may have about the learners' abilities to meet the objectives in the curriculum. For example, instructors who have worked with learners for a while may find that it is unnecessary to conduct an assessment on some curriculum items because they already know enough about the learners' skill level on these items to make an instructional decision. When instructors know their learners well, they can use their knowledge to choose only a few curriculum objectives to assess and quickly decide which items each learner is ready to learn "next."

Finally, the results obtained from individualized assessments will allow the instructors to prepare different instructional plans for each learner even though several of them may be working on the same curriculum objectives and participating in the same instructional activities. For example, several learners may work at the same job site, but each may have to learn completely different skills: One may be learning job skills, another may be developing interpersonal skills, and another may be trying to increase his or her level of productivity. If so, the instructional staff will have to seek different information about each learner.

TABLE 6.3 Ways to Individualize Assessments

Assessments can be individualized by
- assessing only the curriculum items that an individual learner needs to have examined;
- using assessment procedures that are tailored to both the learner's characteristics and the skills being assessed; and/or
- examining behavior in the settings and situations in which the learner actually uses (or will use) the skills.

Tailor Assessment Procedures to Learner Characteristics

Each learner may react more or less favorably to some procedures than to others. Even though several learners may be evaluated on the same curriculum objectives, it often is necessary to modify the assessment to obtain a reliable estimate of the ability of each learner. For example, an instructor may obtain the most accurate information about some learners by assessing their skills under very controlled circumstances but gain the best information about other learners by assessing under very flexible conditions. Similarly, some learners may demonstrate their skills while being observed in applied settings and circumstances, while others may respond poorly to these conditions and require assessment in the context of interviews, role playing, skits, or written activities. Thus, instructors will find that they can assess skill levels with the greatest efficiency when they tailor an assessment to each individual learner.

Assess Behavior in the Settings and Situations in Which Skills Are Used

Instructors also must individualize assessments to make them correspond to the circumstances in which learners actually will use their skills after they have acquired them. When planning assessments, instructors should take into account how each setting may make very different demands on the way in which learners will demonstrate their skills. For example, two students with mild mental retardation who are in different general education classrooms might need to apply their skills in very different ways because the teaching formats, grouping arrangements, instructional activities, and materials are likely to vary markedly across two programs. The teacher who conducts assessments of these students must modify the approach to reflect these differences so that the results give a clear indication of how the students respond to the demands of the settings in which they must use their skills.

Planning an Assessment

Conducting an assessment can be a very complicated process because instructors often have many questions and concerns about each of their learners' skill levels. Moreover, activities and interactions can take place so quickly that instructors may lose valuable information about their learners if they depend on haphazardly structured procedures to observe behavior. Therefore, it is best to develop a well-planned approach that allows the instructor to obtain information deliberately.

We will present a comprehensive step-by-step procedure that organizes assessment activities. Our approach to assessment will enable instructors to do two things:

1. investigate the specific curriculum objectives that pose the most problems for learners; and
2. examine the objectives about which the instructor needs more information in order to plan instructional lessons.

The approach we espouse will help instructors organize their procedures before they begin an assessment and understand exactly what skills they need to observe when they do begin. This organization will allow them to record their observations, interpret the results, and move on to the task of planning instruction. If our procedure is followed, it also will increase the precision and accuracy of the assessment results.

Table 6.4 outlines the steps required to prepare an assessment, and Table 6.5 presents a sample of a completed assessment work sheet. Note that Table 6.5 uses a portion of the applied mathematics curriculum for learners with mild mental retardation (budgeting and paying bills) from Chapter 5 to show examples of the types of information instructors would enter on the work sheet. A blank copy of the work sheet appears in Appendix B.

Step 1: Select Which Learners to Assess

The process of planning an assessment should begin by deciding which learners to assess and reviewing the available background information on these learners. Ideally, instructors should conduct an assessment of each learner before preparing an individualized program of instruction (IP) in order to ensure that the objectives listed in the IP represent the most important skills for each learner. It is especially necessary to assess learners closely when they are new to an instructional unit or when a learner is just starting to work on a new curriculum area. However, it is often advantageous to hold off the assessments until an instructor has had an opportunity to develop

---

TABLE 6.4 Steps to Take in Preparing to Assess Curriculum Objectives

- Select which learners to assess.
- Select curriculum objectives to assess.
- Choose settings and conditions under which to carry out assessment.
- Specify standards for curriculum objectives.
- Select assessment procedures.
- Prepare to record results.
- Schedule assessment activities.

TABLE 6.5 Example of an Assessment Work Sheet

ASSESSMENT WORK SHEET

NAME OF LEARNER: ___Phil Weatherspoon___ **AGE:** ___15___
DATES OF ASSESSMENT: ___October 4–October 25___
GRADE/PROGRAM AREA: ___Grade 9/Functional Academics___
NAME OF INSTRUCTOR/ASSESSOR: ___Mrs. Franklin___
LOCATION OF ASSESSMENT: ___School and First American Bank and Trust___

ASSESSMENT SETTING/SITUATION: ___Classroom during math period___

CURRICULUM OBJECTIVES	STANDARDS	PROCEDURES	RESULTS
Tell time to nearest minute.	90% correct in 15 minutes	Work sheet of clock face examples	
Add/subtract five-figure numbers.	15 of 20 problems correct in 15 minutes	Math workbook page	
Add/subtract numbers with decimals.	15 of 20 problems correct in 15 minutes	Math workbook page	
Calculate one-fourth.	95% correct	Test using oral word problems	
Make lists.	90% of items on lists Items legible	Observation while helping with inventory	
Alphabetize words.	80% in correct order in 10 minutes	Work sheet of 30 words	

COMMENTS:

ASSESSMENT SETTING/SITUATION: ___School office___

CURRICULUM OBJECTIVES	STANDARDS	PROCEDURES	RESULTS
Make telephone calls.	All steps correct in telephone checklist before connection drops	Observation/Mrs. Peters	
Address envelope.	5 of 5 correct: has complete address, items legible and in correct positions	Observation/Mrs. Peters	
Identify appropriate postage.	Postage correct on 5 of 5 envelopes	Observation/Mrs. Peters	
Establish personal routine.	All steps complete office work routine checklist Completes routine in 40 minutes	Observation/Mrs. Peters	
Make file folders.	5 of 5 correct: label matches folder contents	Observation/Mrs. Peters	
Use white pages of telephone book.	9 of 10 correct: number matches name and address in 10 minutes	Observation/Mrs. Peters	

COMMENTS:

TABLE 6.5 (*continued*)

ASSESSMENT SETTING/SITUATION: ___School bookstore___

CURRICULUM OBJECTIVES	STANDARDS	PROCEDURES	RESULTS
Make change.	10 of 10 correct on purchases	Observation	
Identify money symbols.	10 of 10 correct on purchases	Observation	
Cash check.	All steps correct on check-cashing checklist	Observation	

COMMENTS:

ASSESSMENT SETTING/SITUATION: ___First American Bank and Trust___

CURRICULUM OBJECTIVES	STANDARDS	PROCEDURES	RESULTS
Establish a savings account.	All steps correct on account checklist	Interview bank official	
Identify bank statement.	Identifies statement 5 of 5 times	Observation	
Calculate totals.	3 of 3 correct in checking statement	Observation	
Locate information at row-column intersection in a table.	5 of 5 correct on bank statements	Oral quiz	

COMMENTS:

---

rapport with the learner and has gained sufficient experience to make the assessments focused and productive.

Instructors should make a special effort to conduct assessments on the learners who present the most complicated and perplexing instructional problems. Assessments of these learners usually will uncover new information about their abilities and performance levels and help place them more accurately in the curriculum. It will also help the instructor prepare instructional activities and procedures for these learners.

Not all learners require an assessment. An instructor may choose to conduct only a cursory assessment, or no assessment at all, before preparing IPs for some learners. For example, it usually is possible to bypass an assessment and start instruction at the beginning of a curriculum pathway when the instructor knows that a learner has few or no skills in that pathway. Similarly, it may be necessary to do only a preliminary check of the learners' skill levels when the instructor feels they are well placed in the curriculum as judged by their previous behavior during instruction. In this case, any new objectives the instructors would add to the learners' IPs would be whatever objectives happen to be next in the curriculum pathway.

When an instructor decides to conduct an assessment of a specific learner's skill level, he or she should start the preparation by entering certain background information about the learner on the assessment work sheet. Since much detailed information about the learner's personal history will already be on record, the entries on the work sheet can be limited to information that is pertinent to the assessment activities. Common entries would include the following:

- the learner's name, age, and grade or program level;
- the date(s) of the assessment;
- the curriculum areas on which the assessment will focus;
- the person(s) conducting the assessment; and
- the location of the assessment activities.

This type of information is important because it can mitigate the inevitable effects of time, other work, and fading memory that quickly can make a document meaningless if it does not contain the proper information. This basic information allows the instructional staff to refer to the work sheet weeks or months after the assessment takes place and accurately recall details about a learner's behavior.

The top section of Table 6.5 gives an example of a partially completed assessment work sheet containing background information about a learner named Phil Weatherspoon. This information will allow instructors to separate this learner's assessment from any others they may conduct. Furthermore, the information will help them remember many important details about the assessment activities if they must refer to the work sheet sometime in the future.

Step 2: Select the Curriculum Objectives to Assess

The next step in planning an assessment is to choose the specific curriculum objectives that will be the focus of the assessment. In practice, the instructional staff would probably select objectives by going through the curriculum and deciding which items are important enough to examine in some detail. These decisions should be based mostly on what the instructors already know about each learner's skill level relative to the curriculum objectives. That is, rather than assess all the objectives in the curriculum, an instructor would individualize the assessment by selecting objectives only if he or she is uncertain about the learner's ability to meet them. The instructor should ask two questions, the first of which is the following:

> Does the learner have the skills to meet the demands posed by these objectives?

If the instructor is unsure of the answer to this question in regard to a particular objective, he or she should include that objective in the learner's assessment plan. Thus, the instructor should pick out objectives about which the learner's ability level is unclear. This process allows instructors to use their time efficiently and focus assessment on the areas of behavior about which they know the least. For example, if the staff teaches food preparation skills and an instructor already knows that a learner can pour liquids from various containers proficiently, the instructor would not need to assess this skill.

The second question to answer is the following:

Can the learner use his or her existing skills under the particular circumstances in which the objectives apply?

An instructor should assess curriculum objectives when a learner can use his or her skills under one set of conditions but may not be able to use them under all the other conditions that have been stated for the objective.

For example, a curriculum objective for a residential program may state that learners will display appropriate table manners in the group home, when dining in restaurants, and when eating in friends' homes. This objective should be selected for assessment anytime there is a question about a learner's ability to use his or her skills in any of these settings. Similarly, an applied mathematics curriculum in a school program for students with mild mental retardation may require the students to perform basic math operations, both when they go to the bank to make a deposit or withdrawal and when they are in a restaurant and must figure a tip. If the teacher is uncertain whether or not the student can perform proficiently in either of these circumstances, the teacher should assess performance in the locations in which it applies.

At this point in the assessment-planning process, the objectives to be assessed can be checked off on a copy of the curriculum document or they can be listed on a separate page. It is usually best not to enter the curriculum objectives directly on the assessment work sheet until after making the decisions on the settings and situations in which the assessment will take place (the next step in the process).

Step 3: Select the Conditions Under Which to Carry Out the Assessment

The next step in planning an assessment is to choose the settings and circumstances under which the assessment will take place. Since assessments should be carried out under circumstances that are as close as possible to the natural conditions, it is best to choose the settings and circumstances that are already described in the curriculum goals and objectives. Doing so will ensure that the conditions of the assessment coincide with the normal circumstances under which the learner's behavior will be expected to occur (Knapczyk and Rodes, 1996). During the assessment, instructors will be able to observe not only if the learner knows what to do, but also if he or she knows where, when, with whom, with what, and how to do it.

For example, a learner who stocks shelves at a hardware store may be required to stop what he or she is doing to assist customers. During assessment of this objective, the conditions should correspond to the circumstances under which the employee would usually be expected to display these skills, such as in the store during the times when it is open for business. If the instructor tried to assess this objective under different performance conditions, such as with a paper-and-pencil test or after closing hours, he or she would not obtain valid information about the learner's actual skill level. Similarly, if a curriculum objective states that learners should go to and from recreational activities by themselves, the assessment should take place under the conditions in which they have to make their own travel arrangements, not when others do it for them.

There are three times at which assessments could be conducted:

1. during normally scheduled activities;
2. during impromptu and unstructured activities; and
3. during preplanned activities.

Using Normally Scheduled Activities

Many of the activities that are already part of normal home, school, or community routines provide the best opportunities for assessing curriculum objectives and should be used whenever possible (Borich, 1988; Salvia and Hughes, 1990). In preschool and school settings, examples would be found during regularly scheduled lessons, projects, quizzes, discussion groups, text assignments, and recess games. In adult programs, examples occur during the times in which learners normally engage in personal care, homemaking, travel, work, and leisure tasks.

These natural activities not only create the best circumstances under which to assess the learners' skills relative to the curriculum objectives, they also allow instructors to observe many related skills as well. For example, normally scheduled activities may help instructors investigate such broad-based skills as seeking information, contributing appropriately to discussions, initiating activities, staying on task, cooperating with others, and other social and organizational skills that are fundamental to meeting a wide variety of curriculum objectives (Eisler and Fredericksen, 1980; Greenwood and Carta, 1987). Similarly, regularly scheduled activities will allow instructors to assess such critical skills as the learners' ability to follow the sequences and routines inherent in a behavioral pattern or their ability to transfer previously learned skills to a wide range of community settings. Because of these benefits, normally scheduled activities should be used for assessment whenever possible.

Using Impromptu and Unstructured Activities

Impromptu activities can provide excellent occasions for conducting assessments because they provide opportunities to observe skills under normally occurring, but relatively unstructured conditions. For example, in order to assess many objectives that involve social behaviors, instructors may want to observe activities that the learners themselves select or to watch the chance encounters they have with other people. Unstructured activities can offer many of the best occasions for observing whether learners can exhibit skills in such areas as initiating social interactions, selecting and following through on leisure activities, cooperating with other people in performing tasks, handling disagreements, and responding to glitches in daily routines and activities.

Using Special Assessment Activities

Sometimes, instructors may have to design special assessment activities in order to offer learners opportunities to use their skills when few or no such opportunities are available in the assessment setting (Bellack, 1979). These activities may involve any one or a combination of the things found in Table 6.6.

Special assessment activities can help instructors obtain a wealth of useful information in a short period of time. For example, an instructor may wish to assess the conversational skills of learners who usually keep to themselves during the times in which people normally engage in conversations. The instructor may have to plan activities that encourage or even require these learners to interact with other people. One possibility would be to ask other people to approach the learners and engage them in conversations. Another would be to set up a situation in which the learners have to talk with other people to obtain information about a game they enjoy playing (Asher and Hymel, 1981).

Instructors can also focus observations on a narrower range of skills during special assessment activities or can increase the number of opportunities they have to observe how learners handle a particular situation. For example, it is possible to create glitches in a normal daily routine; that is, soap can be made to run out, electrical fuses can be made to blow, and learners can be caused to be late for a bus or to get lost. Such activities can provide very good opportunities to find out how a learner reacts under what could be very real conditions some day. Special assessment activities may not always be ideal, but they can provide some very useful information about certain skills.

Entering Descriptions of Settings and Conditions on the Work Sheet

Instructors should describe their choices of assessment settings and situations as headings on separate pages of the work sheet. Then, on each page of the work sheet, they should list the curriculum objectives that they will assess in each of the settings and situations. The observation of objectives should be sequenced according to the learners' normal daily routine or according to the way in which activities are normally scheduled in the settings.

For example, a schoolteacher might place all the curriculum objectives he or she plans to assess in the applied math classroom on the "Applied Math" work sheet and those he or she plans to assess during recess on the "Recess" work sheet. Furthermore, the teacher should sequence each list of objectives so it coincides with the routine the students usually follow in the settings. Thus, in the mathematics class, the teacher would list the objectives for class start-up activities first, then those for homework review, then those for individual work time, and so on, through class dismissal time. For recess, the teacher should list the objectives for lining up to go outside before the

TABLE 6.6 Types of Assessment Modifications When Natural Opportunities Are Not Available

- Vary the content and presentation format of normal instructional lessons and activities.
- Alter the schedule in which activities are normally sequenced.
- Modify the physical structure or layout of a setting.
- Change other characteristics of the school, home, or community environment.

objectives for playing recess games. Table 6.5 provides a good example of how to list objectives by location and sequence.

With this type of organization, instructors will use only the sections of the assessment work sheet that correspond to the specific settings and situations they are observing at the moment. Moreover, they can proceed down the list of objectives on the work sheet as the learners go from one activity or situation to another. Instructors can then be selective about the objectives they assess, especially on occasions in which there are changes in routine or constraints in time.

Step 4: Specify the Standards for the Curriculum Objectives

Instructors must specify the **standards** they will use to evaluate learner behavior during the assessment of each curriculum objective. There are two reasons for doing so:

1. it is very difficult to evaluate the proficiency of behavior without clear standards; and
2. standards provide an unbiased referent for assessing learner behavior.

The contrast between Table 6.7 and 6.8 illustrates why it is necessary to specify standards. Note that each of the questions posed in the examples in Table 6.7 cannot be answered, but those in Table 6.8 can. The reason is that Table 6.8 provides standards against which to evaluate performance, but Table 6.7 does not. For example, in Table 6.8, the standard for Mrs. Ellison's class indicates that Michael's performance (an average of 12 items correct on quizzes) does meet the objective for answering questions. In contrast, the standard for selecting items on a grocery list indicates that Harriet's performance (10 items in the shopping cart) does not meet the objective for grocery shopping.

Functions of Standards

Standards serve two major functions in the assessment process:

- they designate the criterion levels instructors can use to judge if and when learners meet curriculum objectives; and
- they indicate the types of measures instructors should record during the assessment activities.

TABLE 6.7 Examples Showing Need for Standards

SETTING: Mrs. Ellison's Second-Grade Reading Class

CURRICULUM OBJECTIVE	PERFORMANCE OBSERVED
Answer questions on daily quizzes.	Michael averages 12 items correct each day.

Question: Would Michael's performance meet the objective for Mrs. Ellison's class?

SETTING: Hillside Grocery Store

CURRICULUM OBJECTIVE	PERFORMANCE OBSERVED
Select items on the grocery list.	Harriet selects 10 grocery items and puts them in her shopping cart in 14 minutes.

Question: Would Harriet's performance meet the objective for selecting grocery items?

SETTING: Mrs. Wilson's 10th-Grade Shop Class

CURRICULUM OBJECTIVE	PERFORMANCE OBSERVED
Complete class projects for the semester.	Larry completes 4 projects during the semester.

Question: Would Larry's performance meet the objective for Mrs. Wilson's class?

SETTING: Farnsworth Appliance Store

CURRICULUM OBJECTIVE	PERFORMANCE OBSERVED
Complete the day's work assignment.	On Tuesday Jack finishes about 75% of his day's work assignment and leaves all his tools, supplies, and unfinished work on his workbench.

Question: Would Jack's performance meet the objective for working at Farnsworth Appliance Store?

Criterion Levels. One of the functions of standards is to establish the minimum level of behavior that is required to meet an objective. Performance that equals or exceeds the standard meets the objective, and performance that falls below the standard does not. Standards fulfill this function by stating what the learner must do to exhibit "successful" performance. For example, a mathematics teacher may say that a learner will be successful if he or she gets 70% of the answers to test questions correct, and an instructor who is teaching travel skills may say that the learner must perform the skills required to cross a street without error.

Standards enable instructors to assess curriculum objectives in a straightforward and unbiased manner because they describe the precise level or amount of behavior that the learners must display. That is, they indicate how much or how well learners must perform to be judged proficient (Burden and Byrd, 1994; Knapczyk and Rodes, 1996).

Types of Measures. Standards also indicate how to measure the learners' behavior during the assessment activities by specifying the exact behavior to track when evaluating the learner's performance (Knapczyk and Rodes, 1996).

TABLE 6.8 Examples of Standards to Clarify Whether Learners Meet Curriculum Objective

SETTING: Mrs. Ellison's Second-Grade Reading Class

CURRICULUM OBJECTIVE	STANDARD
Answer questions on daily quizzes.	Answer 10 questions correctly to earn a C grade.

Conclusion: Michael's performance would meet the objective.

SETTING: Hillside Grocery Store

CURRICULUM OBJECTIVE	STANDARD
Select items on the grocery list.	Put all the items specified on the list in the shopping cart (there are 15 items on Harriet's list). Complete shopping in 15 minutes.

Conclusion: Harriet's performance would not meet the objective.

SETTING: Mrs. Wilson's 10th-Grade Shop Class

CURRICULUM OBJECTIVE	STANDARD
Complete class projects for the semester.	Complete at least 5 projects to earn a passing grade.

Conclusion: Larry's performance would not meet the objective.

SETTING: Farnsworth Appliance Store

CURRICULUM OBJECTIVE	STANDARD
Complete the day's work assignment.	Finish at least 65% of the day's work assignment. On Mondays-Thursdays leave tools, supplies, and unfinished work on workbench.

Conclusion: Jack's performance would meet the objective.

For example, if students must earn a grade of at least 70% to pass a math test, the instructor would have to

- administer a test to obtain the students' answers;
- determine which of their answers are correct; and
- compute percentage scores of each student's correct responses.

The instructor would then compare the resulting measures of behavior to the criterion level to determine which students meet the objective and which do not.

On the other hand, if a learner must cross a street without error, the instructor must

- take the learner to places at which he or she must cross streets;
- have the learner cross the street; and
- record any errors.

Again, the instructor would compare the data to the criterion level and, if the learner exhibits any errors, provide instruction.

It is possible that some curriculum objectives may have an evaluation measurement procedure already in place. For example, an objective like "arrives at work on time" is easy to assess if the employer already has a standardized procedure for logging employees into the work site (such as with a time clock). Similarly, schoolteachers usually record attendance and grades in grade books, and residential personnel keep various types of records to fulfill medicaid or state requirements. When these measurement procedures provide information that allows an instructor to evaluate learner proficiency, instructors can use them for assessment purposes.

Identifying Standards

Every objective in a curriculum will have standards; however, not all of them will have explicitly stated criterion levels and/or procedures for measuring them. In this regard, it is important to consider that the behavior of each individual is constantly being evaluated by other people in all community settings. For example, the customers and employees in a supermarket are likely to notice when a person does not seem to be engaging in "supermarket behavior." When an instructor prepares to assess a learner's grocery-shopping skills, the instructor must understand the kinds of things that people watch for and the standards they use to judge the adequacy and appropriateness of behavior.

Since standards are usually set by the people who participate in the activities of a setting, instructors may find that the standards for some curriculum objectives change from setting to setting or from time to time. For example, standards for an academic skill, such as when homework assignments must be completed, may change from assignment to assignment, from teacher to teacher, from grade level to grade level, or from subject matter to subject matter. Similarly, employers may set standards that vary significantly for skills that employees perform at different times of work, such as during peak sales hours and during slack hours. In cases in which the same curriculum objective applies to different settings and/or circumstances, it may be necessary to state the standards differently according to the settings and circumstances in which they will apply.

Instructors often have to observe activities and interactions closely to determine what standards they should state for an assessment, especially for objectives that involve community settings. These observations should focus on what the people who are in the setting look for when they judge whether or not behavior is "correct." For example, employers and fellow workers on a job site may expect other employees to do things like return greetings, volunteer assistance to fellow workers when their own work is caught up, and comply with directions and suggestions that have a positive effect on productivity. Even though these actions are not stated formally, and in fact, people may not be able to state clear standards for performance, they usually have some kind of system for evaluating performance. These standards should become the basis for assessing curriculum objectives. Similar informal standards operate in all school and community settings. Instructors can usually ascertain the best ways of assessing learner's behavior by conferring with the people who oversee or frequent the settings and/or by closely observing the activities and interactions involved in meeting the curriculum objective.

Types of Standards

Standards for curriculum objectives usually consist of quantity or quality statements.

Quantity Standards. The standards for many curriculum objectives can be quantified in some manner because they allow learner performance to be measured or counted. Quantity standards usually fall into one or more of four categories: occurrence, frequency, duration, rate, or other measure (Cartwright and Cartwright, 1984; Kerr and Nelson, 1989; Knapczyk and Rodes, 1996; Kruger, 1990). Examples of each of these categories appear in Table 6.9.

Occurrence. Occurrence is perhaps the most basic way to state standards. It responds to the following question:

Does performance occur when it is supposed to occur?

Occurrence standards describe how learners should act when they are presented with specific opportunities to perform a behavior or task. For example, an objective in the area of travel may be "The learner will ride a bus to (destination)." An occurrence standard for meeting this objective might be "gets to the bus stop in time to catch the bus." That is, either the learners perform the required behavior (they are "on time"), or they do not. This type of standard can be used with most curriculum objectives.

In many areas of behavior, learners will have several opportunities to show whether or not they can meet the standard. Instructors may have to observe both the number of behaviors learners perform *and* the number of opportunities they have to perform them. If the learners act "correctly" when presented with the opportunities to do so, then occurrence will be noted; if the learners do not, then nonoccurrence will be noted. In the bus example, learners may have a number of opportunities to demonstrate whether they can arrive at the bus stop on time, such as before and after work every weekday or when going to stores or recreation sites.

Occurrence standards are usually stated as percentages, or as ratios of behaviors relative to opportunities, such as "gets to bus stop on time 9 of 10 opportunities" or "90% of the time." In assessing this curriculum objective for an individual learner, the instructors would tally the number of occurrences of "successful bus catching" *and* the number of occasions the learner has to be at the bus stop on time. They would then compare the results to the 90% criterion level and determine whether the learner meets the standard. The first set of examples in Table 6.9 show occurrence standards.

When establishing a standard, it is important to keep in mind that it may not always be possible to observe the learners' opportunities to perform

TABLE 6.9 Examples of Standards for Curriculum Objectives

QUANTITATIVE STANDARDS: Occurrence

Curriculum Objective	Standard
Turn in homework assignment on time.	Turn in 80% of homework assignments on time.
Make appointments for medical and dental checkups.	Make all appointments on a yearly schedule.
Pour liquids from a pitcher.	Pour liquids without spilling 95% of the time.
Find one's way when lost.	Find way when lost 10 of 10 times.

QUANTITATIVE STANDARDS: Frequency

Curriculum Objective	Standard
Answer questions correctly during class discussions.	Answer at least 3 questions correctly during the class period.
Stir ingredients before placing in cake pan.	Stir between 25 and 35 times.
Complete chores on weekly list.	Complete at least 5 chores each week.
Ask questions about job assignment.	Ask no more than 2 questions each day.

QUANTITATIVE STANDARDS: Duration

Curriculum Objective	Standard
Complete daily art project.	Complete project within 30 minutes.
Start work on time.	Start work within 5 minutes of arriving at job site.
Talk with friends about personal experiences.	Talk with friends at least 5 minutes but no more than 15 minutes.
Stay on task during independent time.	Stay on task for at least 10 work minutes.

QUANTITATIVE STANDARDS: Rate

Curriculum Objective	Standard
Run laps around the track.	Run 3 laps within 20 minutes.
Complete a math work sheet on addition.	Complete 100 problems in 10 minutes.
Package items for delivery.	Package 10 items per hour.
Make sack lunches for residents.	Make 6 lunches in 30 minutes.

QUANTITATIVE STANDARDS: Other Measures

Work on loading dock.	Move 50-pound crates with handcart.
Swim in the pool at the YMCA.	Swim 50 meters without stopping.
Dig a ditch.	Dig a hole 3 ft $\times$ 8 ft $\times$ 2 ft.

TABLE 6.9 (*continued*)

QUALITATIVE STANDARDS:

Curriculum Objective	Standard
Set table settings for dinner.	Set settings with plates, silverware, glasses, napkins, etc. Place flatware in correct location—refer to place-setting chart.
Leave home with clothing that suits the day's weather.	Based on weather forecast: 80 degrees and above—short sleeves 70–80 degrees—long or short sleeves 50–70 degrees—light coat or sweater 30–50 degrees—heavy coat or light coat and sweater
Mow and rake lawn.	Lawn area looks neatly maintained from sidewalk area (e.g., lawn evenly cut, no more than a few leaves on lawn).
Make bed.	Sheets and bedspread are about equidistant from floor on all four sides of bed.
Clean work area.	Area looks clean from the supervisor's table.

a behavior. For example, it may be impossible for instructors to keep a tally of the number of opportunities that learners have to ask a stranger for directions, to volunteer comments in group discussions, or to start an appropriate conversation on a date. In such instances, the standard would have to involve some measure other than occurrence.

Frequency.   **Frequency standards** pertain to the number of times learners must perform a specific skill during a predetermined time period. These standards address the following questions:

> How many times must the learners do something?
> or
> How often must they do it?

Instructors would state frequency standards in one of two ways:

1. as the total times learners must perform a behavior; or
2. as a range of behavior if the upper and lower limits of performance are important.

For example, an objective in the personal maintenance area may state that "The learners will wash their hands before all meals." A frequency standard for this objective might be "washes hands before every meal." Similarly, an objective in the vocational area may be that "The learners will check the work area and pick up litter." A frequency standard might be "checks for litter at least two times an hour but no more than five times an hour." To meet this objective, a learner would have to make checks with a frequency that stays within these limits.

During assessment the instructor would observe the learner's behavior for the time interval specified and would count the number of times he or she performed the behavior correctly. The instructor would then compare the totals with the standard measure and judge whether the totals meet the objective. For example, if the learner in the previous example checks for litter four times an hour, he or she meets the objective, whereas a learner who checks either once each hour or six times an hour does not. Other examples of frequency standards are given in Table 6.9.

Duration.   **Duration standards** indicate the amount of time it should take learners to perform a behavior or task and responds to the following question:

How long should performance last during any performance opportunity?

Instructors should describe duration standards in terms of minutes, hours, or any other useful unit of time. For example, an objective in the personal maintenance area may state that "The learners will get dressed to leave the house for the day." A duration standard for this objective might be "gets dressed within 15 minutes of arising." Learners would have to stay within this time limit to meet the objective. Similarly, in the leisure area, an objective may state that "The learners will work on their personally chosen recreational activity each weekday evening." The standard for this objective might include "works on activity for at least 20 minutes each evening." Learners would have to stay with their chosen activity for at least this long each evening to meet the objective.

When checking to see if learners meet duration standards, instructors would record the time at which the learners begin to perform a specified behavior *and* the time at which they end it. Instructors would then compute the total amount of time the learners engage in the specified behavior, compare the total to the standard, and evaluate whether the total meets the criterion for the objective. In the example of working on a recreational activity, if a learner worked on an activity for 5 minutes on one occasion and 15 minutes on another in a single evening, he or she would meet the objective. Similarly, a learner who takes any longer than 15 minutes to get dressed would not meet the objective stated in the dressing example. Table 6.9 gives more examples of duration standards.

Rate.   **Rate standards** focus on issues of time in which the major concern is not just whether or not the learners perform a behavior or task, but the speed at which they perform it. Rate standards respond to the following questions:

How quickly do learners perform a skill or skill cluster?
and
How much performance must occur during a preset time interval?

Instructors can describe rate standards either as an average time per performance or as the amount accomplished per unit of time. For example, a vocational objective for working in a veterinary clinic may state that "Learners will clean animal cages." A rate standard would focus on the average number of cages they should clean in a given time period, such as "cleans four cages per hour." An academic objective may state that "Learners will write out the week's spelling words," and the standard might be "writes ten words per minute."

When measuring rate, instructors keep track of both the number of behaviors the learners complete *and* the time interval in which they complete them. Instructors then convert the measure to a ratio, such as the number of behaviors that occur in the time interval, and compare the results to the standards. In the spelling example, if a learner wrote 20 words in 4 minutes, the ratio would be five words per minute and the learner's behavior would not meet the "ten words per minute" standard for the objective.

Other types of quantitative standards. Many other types of quantitative standards can be used to state the standards for curriculum objectives, and instructors must examine each curriculum objective closely to determine which type accurately reflects the demands performance of the objectives. Some examples of other quantitative measures are the following:

- *Distance.* A physical fitness objective may pertain to how long learners should jog. The standard could be stated in terms of distance, such as "jogs 100 yards without stopping."
- *Strength.* A vocational objective may involve how strong the learners should be. The standard might be described in terms of the learner's strength, such as "lifts boxes weighing at least 40 pounds to table height."
- *Volume.* A communication skills objective may pertain to how loud learners should speak when talking in front of a group of people. The standard might be described in terms of the learner's voice level, such as "speaks loud enough to be heard by everyone in the room."

Note that each of these statements involves a measurement of some type, and successful performance can be checked with some kind of rule or scale. If the learner meets the standard, he or she exhibits "successful" performance.

Quality Standards. Despite the importance of quantity standards, many times it is impossible to quantify learner behavior, and instructors must use some sort of qualitative standard to judge whether or not the learner meets an objective. For example, what quantity standard can be applied to how well a learner sweeps a floor, dresses, or fries an egg? The mere fact that someone pushes a broom for a given period of time by no means guarantees that the floor will be clean when the sweeping is finished. Nor does the fact that a person puts on the correct clothing guarantee that he or she will be neatly dressed. Judging how well a learner performs such skills requires the instructor to describe the quality of performance, or what the finished product should look like, before evaluating whether or not a learner meets the objectives. For example, in the case of sweeping the floor, it is possible to state that the floor is clean when "no dirt or debris can be seen when standing in the doorway of the room." Such a statement has no real measure built into it but does provide a clear idea about what the instructor must look for when assessing a learner's performance of this skill cluster. The last block in Table 6.9 presents other examples of quality statements.

Stating Standards on the Assessment Work Sheet

On the assessment work sheet, instructors should determine standards that have as much in common as possible to how others in the setting(s) usually evaluate behavior under normal performance conditions. For example, if the general education teachers in an inclusion program usually are concerned about how often students ask for help or about how many ideas they contribute to group discussions, then the standards for curriculum objectives in these areas should be expressed in terms of frequency (the number of questions students should ask or the number of ideas they should give). Similarly, if employers ordinarily monitor how much time employees take to perform a job, such as how long they take to start a job after it has been assigned or how long they take to complete the job once they start it, then the standard should be described in terms of duration (number of minutes it should take to do the job). And if performance is evaluated in terms of the number of responses or tasks that occur within a specified time period, then the standard should contain a rate measure.

Occurrence standards are often used in combination with qualitative standards or one or more of the other types of quantitative standards. For example, when employers assign tasks, they usually note whether the workers complete the assigned tasks (occurrence) and how well they do them (frequency, duration, rate, or quality of performance). In other words, instructional personnel must observe the settings closely to determine the type of standards that apply to each curriculum objective before describing them on an assessment work sheet.

Examples of Complete Standards Statements

Most of the examples we have given consist of bits and pieces of complete standards statements. In practice, standards statements should be stated for the performance of the entire objective and often will contain different types of standards. Examples to illustrate this point appear in Table 6.10.

Step 5: Select Assessment Procedures

The next step in planning an assessment is to describe the procedures that the instructors will use to assess each of the curriculum objectives. In carrying out this step, it is necessary to select procedures that allow the instructors to give their full attention to what the learners are doing so they can record their observations without being distracted by other obligations. These observation techniques should enable instructors to obtain the most accurate and reliable measures of the learners' behavior, yet minimize the effects the

TABLE 6.10 Examples of Complete Standards Statements

Skill Cluster	Standards
Making coffee	The learner will prepare two cups of coffee with his or her breakfast meal (two cups of water, two spoonfuls of coffee grounds); the coffee will be neither weak nor strong; it will be steaming hot and poured into a cup, ready for consumption.
Washing clothes	The learner will wash his or her clothes once a week; the clothes will be clean and dry; no clothes will be damaged due to improper sorting, temperature, or cycle used.
Bandaging a cut	The learner will bandage a cut each time blood flows from a wound; the cut area will be completely clear of dirt and grime; the bandage will cover only the cut area.
Washing windows	The learner will wash windows at a rate of 4 per hour; the windows will be clear and free of streaks when viewed from a distance of 4 feet; there will be no water or cleanser on either the window or the surrounding area.
Purchasing food	The learner will purchase the exact amount of each item on the shopping list; he or she will hand the clerk an appropriate amount of money and place the change in his or her wallet; he or she will return home with the groceries and store them in the appropriate locations.
Assembling widgets	The learner will assemble 10 widgets per hour with less than 3% assembly errors.

assessment procedures might otherwise have on the way in which the learners typically perform (Bellack, 1979; Cartwright and Cartwright, 1984).

Direct observation is usually the best way to assess most curriculum objectives because it allows instructors to watch the learners' performance firsthand. But there are also many other procedures that instructors can use, including paper-and-pencil tests, work samples, questionnaires, interviews, and simulated task performance.

Knapczyk and Rodes (1996) state that the assessment procedures instructors select should allow them to:

- determine whether the learners clearly demonstrate the ability to meet the curriculum objectives; and
- measure the learners' behavior easily and accurately based on the standards defined for the curriculum objectives.

Considerations in Selecting Assessment Procedures

Table 6.11 presents important considerations for planning assessment procedures.

Choose Unobtrusive Procedures. Instructors should use assessment procedures that do not greatly affect the manner in which the learners typically act under natural performance conditions (Knapczyk and Rodes, 1996). In general, the activities within which instructors carry out assessment should

TABLE 6.11 Considerations in Selecting Assessment Procedures

- Choose unobtrusive procedures.
- Consider using videotapes to collect data.
- Consider using other observers to collect data.

appear to be part of the normal routine; the learners should not notice anything unusual about the assessment techniques that their instructors use. If the procedures are unobtrusive, it is possible to minimize the changes in behavior that can result when learners know they are being observed (Merrell, 1994; Salvia and Ysseldyke, 1995). The most unobtrusive procedures and activities are those that instructors already use in their teaching and supervision and that are a normal part of the learners' performance environment.

For example, an instructor who assesses social interactions in a leisure setting should observe and record behavior in such a manner that the learners do not realize that they are being assessed. To do so, the instructor may have to act preoccupied with some other task, such as reading a newspaper or appearing to look at something else, even though he or she is attentively observing the learners' performance. The more unobtrusive the instructor's behavior, the more likely the learners will act naturally during the assessment, even to the point where they might "get away" with behavior that they would not exhibit if they were aware of the observation. When conducting assessments during more structured situations, such as during closely supervised activities, instructors should also act as they normally do under those circumstances.

Consider Using Videotapes to Document Assessment Activities.
When direct observation is not feasible, videotaping can provide a very effective alternative (Dowrick, 1986; Knapczyk, 1989, 1992). In fact, using video during assessment procedures offers the four advantages listed in Table 6.12.

Videotaping can be helpful, especially when instructors are busy teaching an instructional lesson or when they are trying to keep track of several variables at once. For example, an instructor who is observing leisure activities might want to assess variables such as the following:

- which activities learners select;
- whether the learners' attention fades quickly from an activity or whether they stick with it;
- how much time the learners spend completing an activity;
- how many interactions the learners have with others; and
- how often the learners do what is expected or not expected.

The instructor could assess these and many other variables readily and precisely by videotaping the learners' performance. Under these conditions, the observations are likely to be more precise and reliable than direct observation.

TABLE 6.12 Advantages of Videotaped Data Collection in Assessment

- Videotaping can capture much information that would otherwise be overlooked or difficult to obtain.
- Videotaping can eliminate the need to hover over learners to closely watch their performance.
- Videotaping can make it possible to assess the behavior of several learners simultaneously.
- Videotaping can allow instructors to watch learner performance several times in order to pick up nuances they may not notice during on-site observations (Knapczyk and Rodes, 1996).

Videotaping is also useful when two or more persons (such as instructors and parents) want to assess the learners' skills jointly. They can each watch the videotape segment, record their observations, compare their findings, and discuss the results (Knapczyk, 1992).

Before using videotaping for assessment, instructors should allow the learners to become accustomed to being videotaped. The instructors should put the camera in place for a period of time before actually beginning to collect the assessment data. This preparation will ensure that the learners will act more naturally than they would if they noticed the camera for the first time.

Consider Using Other Observers to Assist During Assessment. On many occasions, teaching and supervisory duties must take precedence over conducting assessments. When they do, they interfere with the instructors' ability to devote full attention to the assessment activities. For this reason, it is sometimes helpful to have other people, such as instructional assistants, supervisors, parents, and volunteers, carry out the observations. However, such people must first be adequately prepared to conduct the observations to ensure that the information they collect is accurate and reliable. They must be given the information found in Table 6.13 prior to beginning assessment.

Prior to an assessment, outside observers will also need to become familiar with the setting, if it is one in which they have not been before, and will need to identify the specific learners they are to observe. Also, they must clearly understand the types of responses they must observe and the recording procedures they must use. It is usually helpful to prepare a separate observation form for outside observers that gives them a detailed explanation of the observation procedures. Such a form could contain the information found in Table 6.14. Although the instructor must make extra preparations to have other observers assist during an assessment, these people can help overcome many of the scheduling and logistical difficulties that busy instructors may encounter in assessing learners.

TABLE 6.13 Information Needed by Other Observers Prior to Attempting to Collect Assessment Data

Additional observers must know
- the purpose of the assessment procedures;
- the skills they are to observe;
- the difference between appropriate and inappropriate performance of the skills; and
- the procedures for measuring performance and making the recordings.

TABLE 6.14 Information Required for Observation by Outside Observers

- Name of the learner being assessed
- Name of the person doing the observation
- Days and times during which the assessment will take place
- Description of the assessment situation
- Instructions for the observer
- Description of curriculum items or behavior to be assessed
- Explanation of the recording and observation procedures
- Space to record observations and tally results

Describing Procedures on the Assessment Work Sheet

Instructors should describe the assessment procedures in enough detail to allow them to plan ahead and modify schedules, set up activities, coordinate timetables with other personnel, develop recording forms, and complete all the other preparation that is needed before conducting the assessment. These descriptions should be placed on the work sheet next to the curriculum objectives they will assess. Table 6.5 shows how descriptions of the assessment procedures can be entered on a work sheet.

Step 6: Prepare to Record the Assessment Results

The next step in planning an assessment is to prepare recording forms for summarizing the assessment results. Table 6.5 shows that spaces for entering results can be added directly to the assessment work sheet. Such additions maintain a single document on which to tabulate all the information pertaining to the array of curriculum objectives that will be assessed.

Instructors can use the space on the work sheet to transcribe test scores, tally averages, and list observation totals. They should keep the original response materials, performance samples, and other assessment products in a separate folder or file. For example, job coaches may develop note cards or check-off sheets on which to record the learners' behavior during the workday. They can keep the forms and note cards in a separate folder and add their summaries of the observations to the work sheet at the end of the day. Similarly, teachers can enter the learners' scores from work samples, quizzes, and projects and store the actual materials in a cumulative folder to which they can refer if the need arises. It is also good practice to add extra space to the work sheet for comments about learner performance and for jotting down ideas about possible teaching strategies that come to mind during the assessment (Cartwright and Cartwright, 1984). Table 6.5 shows how spaces for recording assessment results and comments can be added to the assessment work sheet.

There are also other types of information that instructors may wish to obtain during an assessment, such as updated information on the learners' medical status or changes in their home situations. However, the primary purpose for planning the assessment is to lay the groundwork for choosing curriculum objectives for the learners' individual instructional plans. Therefore, it is essential to keep the work sheet as orderly and concise as possible.

Step 7: Schedule Assessment Activities

The last step in preparing for assessment is to schedule and coordinate the assessment activities well ahead of time. The assessment work sheet is a valuable tool for planning specific assessment activities, but it should be used in conjunction with an overall assessment schedule. Such a schedule should help everyone involved in the assessment carry out the tasks shown in Table 6.15.

An assessment schedule provides an advanced organizer that ensures that the time available for conducting the assessment is used as effectively as possible. It not only allows instructors to maintain a clear focus on what is supposed to happen during the assessment, it also guards against gaps in information that could require the staff to repeat activities or that could result in their overlooking crucial information. In the long run, taking the extra time to prepare a schedule will make it much easier to keep track of exactly what should be assessed in the various circumstances under which the observations will be made. It is especially important to devise an assessment schedule under the conditions outlined in Table 6.16.

Preparing an Assessment Schedule

Developing a schedule need not be a particularly lengthy or involved process. Still, the instructional staff should do enough planning to ensure that they have a clear idea of the procedures and purposes of the activities and that they have provided enough time to do a comprehensive assessment of learner behavior. An assessment schedule should include the five sets of information found in Table 6.17. Note that the third and fourth items in this list can be taken directly from the assessment work sheet.

Table 6.18 continues the example we began in Table 6.5. It presents a format that instructors can use to prepare a schedule, and it shows a sample schedule that Mrs. Franklin prepared for Phil Weatherspoon. Notice that Mrs. Franklin has spread the assessment activities over a 3-week period to allow for several repetitions of the behaviors in question and to pace observations so as to guard against fatigue and other adverse factors. The first week's assessment activities take place in the classroom setting, the second

TABLE 6.15 Outline of Assessment Tasks

To perform an assessment, it is necessary to
- select which curriculum objectives to assess on a particular day;
- specify who will observe and record behavior;
- specify which samples of work and learner products to collect;
- specify which materials and equipment to prepare; and
- state any other logistical factors that will make the assessment proceed smoothly and efficiently.

TABLE 6.16 When to Establish an Assessment Schedule

Establish an assessment schedule
- when there are many curriculum objectives to assess;
- when there are many learners to assess; and
- when there are several different settings in which observations will take place.

TABLE 6.17 Information to Include in an Assessment Schedule

- Name of the learner to be assessed
- Dates, days, and times during which the assessment will take place
- Activities that will occur during assessment times
- Procedures for measuring the standards
- Lists of the personnel and supplies needed to conduct the assessment

week's activities in out-of-classroom settings, and the third week's activities complete the observations begun in the previous weeks or follow up on areas in which the results were inconclusive. Similar schedules for assessments in a residential setting might involve scheduling some observations at the residence and other observations in community locations.

Guidelines for Preparing an Assessment Schedule

The guidelines contained in Table 6.19 will help instructors prepare an assessment schedule.

Provide Several Opportunities for the Performance of the Skill(s) Being Observed. It is important to give learners sufficient opportunity to show whether they have the skills to perform the curriculum objectives that are being assessed, and to allow for normal variations both in learner behavior and performance conditions during the assessment. The more occasions on which instructors assess an area of behavior, the greater the likelihood that the results will truly represent the learners' actual skill levels (Borich, 1988). The rule of thumb is to give learners at least five opportunities to show

TABLE 6.18 Example of an Assessment Schedule

ASSESSMENT SCHEDULE

NAME OF LEARNER: Phil Weatherspoon   **AGE:**   15
DATES OF ASSESSMENT: October 4–October 25

SETTING: Classroom

Days/Times	Activities	Procedures	Personnel/Materials Needed
Week 1, MWF	Independent work time	Work sheets	Math workbook
Week 1, TTh	Test/Quiz	Test	Oral test questions

SETTING: School office

Days/Times	Activities	Procedures	Personnel/Materials Needed
Week 2, MWF	Work/Study period	Observation	Mrs. Peters Observation checklist

SETTING: School bookstore

Days/Times	Activities	Procedures	Personnel/Materials Needed
Week 2, MWF	Lunch period Class break	Observation	Bookstore supplies

SETTING: First American Bank and Trust

Days/Times	Activities	Procedures	Personnel/Materials Needed
Week 2, TTh	Work/study period	Observation Interview Oral quiz	Checklist Quiz questions

SETTING: School bookstore and office

Days/Times	Activities	Procedures	Personnel/Materials Needed
Week 3, MWF	Lunch period	Observation	Mrs. Peters Observation checklist
	Work/study period		Bookstore supplies

SETTING: First American Bank and Trust

Days/Times	Activities	Procedures	Personnel/Materials Needed
Week 3, TTh	Work/study period	Observation Interview Oral quiz	Checklist Quiz questions

TABLE 6.19 Guidelines for Preparing an Assessment Schedule

- Provide several opportunities for the performance of the skill(s) being observed.
- Take advantage of normally scheduled activities.
- Schedule assessment activities to take place during several short time periods rather than one long one.

whether they have the skills to meet a curriculum item (Howell and Morehead, 1987). For example, a group-home supervisor who is assessing a learner's vacuuming skills should conduct observations on several occasions to ensure that the results are unbiased. If the supervisor were to obtain only one or two observations, it would be possible to obtain results that would generate erroneous conclusions about the learner's skill level (e.g., the learner was having a particularly good day or a particularly bad day).

The schedule should also provide enough opportunities to find out

- whether the learners can display the full array of skills required to meet the curriculum objectives; and
- how learners respond in a variety of circumstances.

In the vacuuming example given above, the amount of clutter in the room or the amount of dirt and debris might change from day to day; therefore, the supervisor would need to assess the learner under varying conditions in order to obtain an accurate estimate of his or her range of skills. Instructors may have to schedule more than five assessment opportunities for a particular curriculum objective if the initial assessment results are inconclusive. The important factor in deciding how long or how often to assess a skill area is whether or not the results give a reliable estimate of learner performance. Instructors should repeat assessment activities until they are sure they have achieved this outcome.

Take Advantage of Normally Scheduled Activities. Assessment activities should be scheduled to coincide with the normal routine of the setting. Such a schedule will minimize any disruptions to the normal sequence of activities in which the learners usually engage. As we mentioned before, normally scheduled activities present the best and the most natural opportunities for skill performance and allow instructors to observe the manner in which learners usually employ their skills. During the course of a normal routine, the learners' behavior will be most characteristic of their typical performance, and the assessment results will give the best estimate of their skill levels.

Using normally scheduled activities to conduct assessments will also reduce the amount of extra planning and preparation that goes into the assessment. That is, scheduling assessment activities should be a relatively straightforward activity in which there is little need to develop extra activities or to make special provisions for conducting assessments. For example, assessment activities that take place in a vocational setting should be coordinated with the employees' regular daily schedule, and both the employees and supervisor(s) should act the way they normally do while the assessment is being conducted. Similarly, assessment in a residential setting should coincide with the daily routine so the residents interact with each other and conduct their lives in their usual ways. In unstructured or informal settings, such as those found in many recreational settings, the assessment activities, equipment and materials, grouping arrangements, and interaction patterns should also be those that are typical of the learners' normal leisure routine. Under such conditions the amount of special planning of the procedures and activities can be held to a minimum.

Schedule Assessment Activities to Take Place During Several Short Time Periods Rather Than in a Single Long Time Period. Assessment activities should be scheduled for shorter but more frequent time periods (as opposed to a few long ones) to allow instructors to concentrate on the specific items they are assessing and to be more attentive to factors that affect the learners' behavior. For example, short observation periods allow observers to avoid the mental fatigue and distractions that often accompany an extended assessment period. Furthermore, short observations make it easier to scrutinize events, activities, or interactions that may contribute to skill limitations or problem behaviors. The exception to this guideline is when instructors wish to check skills that are exhibited across time spans, such as a learner's knowledge of a routine or schedule or the physical endurance level of a learner. For example, an instructor may have to schedule a fairly lengthy activity to determine whether a learner can plan and prepare an evening meal or whether the learner has the stamina to remain on his or her feet for a full day's work.

Assessment activities of shorter duration will usually be easier to schedule in the settings in which the assessment is to take place. It can be very difficult to find a long time block within which to schedule extended assessment activities, but it generally is easy to find a number of short time blocks for this purpose.

Concluding Statement

The primary purpose in conducting an assessment is to obtain insight into the skill levels that learners bring with them into an instructional setting. An assessment gives instructors a straightforward means of determining whether learners have the skills to meet the objectives in a curriculum and helps instructors plan appropriate and effective teaching activities.

An assessment should be comprehensive, well organized, unbiased, and tied directly to the objectives in a school's or agency's curriculum. Instructional personnel should carefully select the circumstances for the assessment and, whenever possible, use activities and tasks that are already a part of the learners' normal routine. The assessment should be carried out under natural performance conditions, be individualized for each learner, and provide multiple opportunities for the learners to demonstrate whether they have the skills being examined. In addition, the assessment should be scheduled in a manner that permits instructors to give their full attention to learner behavior and that allows learners to demonstrate their skills clearly and fully.

Preparing an assessment work sheet is a helpful way of organizing the assessment because it assists in the cataloging of curriculum objectives that will be the focus of the assessment, in selecting assessment procedures, in scheduling the activities, and in keeping track of the results. After preparing a work sheet, instructional personnel will be well prepared to conduct an assessment of their learners. In the next chapter we will explain how to carry out an assessment, summarize the results, set priorities for instruction, and develop an instructional program plan.

CHAPTER 7

Conducting an Assessment and Developing an Individualized Program of Instruction

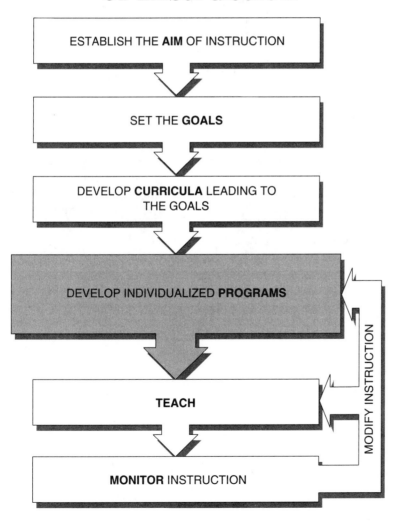

If instructors prepare as we suggested in Chapter 6, they will be able to conduct an assessment and interpret the results in a relatively straightforward manner. The main concern at this point is to ensure that the assessment yields the clearest, most accurate results possible. If instructors keep the activities and procedures tightly focused on the specific curriculum objectives they have selected for assessment, they will find what they need to know about the learners' skill levels. Then they can plan appropriate instruction, which is the reason for conducting an assessment in the first place.

In this chapter we will explain how to carry out an actual assessment of curriculum objectives and how to summarize the results. We will also discuss how to use these results to set priorities for instruction and to develop individualized instructional program plans (IPs).

Conducting an Assessment of Curriculum Objectives

Table 7.1 contains a set of guidelines for conducting an assessment. We will begin the chapter by discussing these guidelines.

Stay Focused on the Curriculum Objectives Being Assessed

It may seem self-evident that instructors should focus on the particular curriculum objectives they are investigating, but we present this guideline because it is easy to become distracted by other activities while conducting an assessment. For example, instructors may discover that their duties toward other learners interfere with their ability to observe the behavior of a particular learner. Under these circumstances, they should adjust their schedules to give full attention to the learner's performance. If they cannot adjust their schedules, they should either reschedule the assessment activities or use a different assessment approach, such as videotaping the activities or asking another person to conduct the observations for them.

It is also easy to lose one's focus when the learners are involved in complex activities, and the instructor may begin to focus on behavior that was not in the original assessment plan. The instructor should avoid observing tangential areas too closely because it may cause him or her to miss some crucial information about the learner's performance. For example, while assessing a learner's ability to use public transportation, the instructor may have an opportunity to examine many different types of skills, such as

- handling money and dealing with travel expenses;
- planning travel routes;
- estimating required travel times;
- identifying landmarks along the route;
- interacting with fellow passengers;
- negotiating tight spaces;
- displaying various personal habits; and
- using social etiquette conventions.

TABLE 7.1 Guidelines for Conducting an Assessment

To conduct an assessment, the instructor must
- stay focused on the curriculum objectives being assessed;
- minimize reactive effects of the assessment activities;
- conduct assessment activities within the limits of the instructor's ability; and
- be flexible in carrying out the assessment plan.

Even though an instructor may be able to assess many of these areas in some depth, not all of them will be pertinent to a particular learner's instructional program, and those that are not may not be worth investigating under these complicated and demanding conditions.

To avoid straying from the original intent of the assessment, instructors should periodically review the curriculum objectives on the work sheet and follow the plans carefully. In this way, they can refrain from being distracted by extraneous or tangential factors and from observing behaviors for which information is already available. On the other hand, during the course of an assessment, if instructors find some skill areas that seem to require closer examination, they should add these areas to the assessment work sheet, determine the standards that apply, and systematically plan procedures that will help them obtain accurate and valid results.

Minimize Reactive Effects of the Assessment Activities

Instructors must take special precautions when they carry out assessment activities in settings where they do not normally go, such as when a job coach conducts observations in a classroom or in the learner's residence. The reason is that during an assessment, other people in the setting can react to the assessment activities by altering their normal behavior. Because these behavioral changes might affect the accuracy of the assessment results, instructors should take steps to minimize any such changes.

Special precautions are also required when people who are not normally present in a setting assist in conducting the assessment. It is usually necessary to give outside observers specific directions on how to act to prevent their presence from changing either the learners' behavior or the behavior of the other people in the setting.

Knapczyk and Rodes (1996) list seven safeguards that will help instructors and others who assist in an assessment minimize any disruptions they might cause when conducting observations. These safeguards appear in Table 7.2. If those who conduct the observations follow these safeguards, they will ensure that the learners, instructors, and supervisors act as they normally would during the assessment activities.

TABLE 7.2 Safeguards for Conducting Assessment Observations

- Arrive on site some time before beginning assessment activities to minimize the attention visitors usually attract.
- Remain away from the areas in which the learners' interactions are taking place.
- Stay out of the traffic flow of the activities.
- Keep out of the line of vision of those being observed and avoid establishing eye contact with people.
- Avoid talking to people in the setting and making gestures or sudden moves.
- Allow people to become acclimated to you (the observer) before making observations.
- Try to look engaged in some task to reduce learner curiosity about what you (the observer) are doing.

Conduct Assessment Activities Within the Limits of the Instructor's Ability

When assessing some learners, instructors may have to gather information on a broad spectrum of skills, all of which might appear within a short time period. For example, an instructor may wish to assess several different interpersonal and recreational skills while the learner is playing a game. This instructor may wish to find out whether the learner

- gets into the flow of the activities;
- follows the rules for playing the game;
- plays the game skillfully;
- interacts with teammates during the game;
- responds to criticism and disagreements with opponents; and
- cheers and supports teammates.

In such a case, the number of skills the instructor plans to assess, the circumstances under which the assessment will take place, and the time limitations for conducting the assessment may make it very difficult to observe all of these skills accurately. But, when assessing several skills in a single activity or time interval, it is possible to maintain the integrity of the assessment by taking the precautions listed in Table 7.3.

Divide Assessment Items Across Observations

One approach instructors can use to assess several curriculum items at once is to change the focus of the assessment each time they conduct an observation. For example, an instructor could attend closely to a few specific behaviors during one set of observations and look at a few other behaviors during another set of observations. By varying the focus of the observations across repetitions of the assessment activity, instructors systematically can conduct a complete assessment in all pertinent curriculum areas. For example, an instructor who assesses learners in a competitive game situation would be able to observe only a few specific skills during each of several games. On some occasions, the instructor could assess only how the learners enter the game

TABLE 7.3 Precautions to Take While Observing Several Behaviors in a Single Time Interval

To maintain integrity of assessment, instructors can
- divide the assessment items across observations;
- coordinate observations with other observers; or
- videotape activities.

and how they follow the rules of the game. On other occasions, the instructor could watch for how skillfully the learners play, how well they interact with and support teammates, and how they handle criticism and disagreements. By structuring observations in this way, the instructor would be able to devote full attention to each of the individual curriculum areas being assessed.

Coordinate Observations with Other Observers

A second approach is to divide the observations among one or more observers. For example, during a single time segment, one person could record how the learners exhibit one set of skills while another observer records how the learners exhibit another set. In the example of the competitive game, an assistant might observe how learners enter the game and how they follow the rules while the instructor observes the learners' interactions with teammates and responses to opponents. The instructor and the assistant could then put their findings together to gain a complete picture of the learners' behavior during the game. As we stressed in Chapter 6, instructors should prepare those who help with an assessment ahead of time to make sure that they have a clear idea of what to look for and how to record it.

Use Video to Record Performance

As a final consideration, we again must underscore the usefulness of videotaping assessment activities: Videotaping alleviates many scheduling conflicts and reduces the need to recruit other observers. Instructors will find that videotaping can be especially helpful when other duties make it difficult for them to pay close attention to learner performance. It allows them to make a much more complete and detailed observation, since the tape can be viewed as often as necessary. Videotaping has the added benefit of providing a permanent record of the assessment activities. Once a videotape has been made, it can be stored and retrieved at any time. These "historical accounts" of the assessment can be used later for planning and evaluation purposes.

If instructors decide to videotape assessment activities, they must take into account that videotaping can affect learner behavior. These effects, however, quickly dissipate as the learners become acclimated to the videotape equipment. Furthermore, instructors may find it helpful to cover the recording indicator light on the camera so the learners do not realize when the machine has been turned on.

Be Flexible in Carrying Out the Assessment Plan

We stated that instructors should give learners about five performance opportunities to show whether they can meet each curriculum objective. However, instructors should keep in mind that the primary goal of an assessment is to determine clearly and accurately whether learners are able to meet the standards established for the curriculum objectives that are being assessed. The important factor in deciding how long or how often to continue assessing a skill is whether or not the assessment results give a reliable estimate of learner performance. Instructors should repeat assessment activities until they are sure they have achieved this outcome.

There are two factors to consider when deciding how many times to assess an objective. Instructors should

1. provide sufficient performance opportunities for the learner to demonstrate skill levels adequately; and
2. challenge the limits of the learner's ability.

Provide Sufficient Performance Opportunities

Any number of factors can affect learner performance, and it often is necessary to adjust the number of opportunities in order to determine whether the learners meet curriculum objectives. More replications of the assessment activities are usually needed when the learners

- are not experienced in a skill area;
- are not prepared adequately for an activity; or
- do not have the right disposition to perform at the times the assessment takes place (Salvia and Ysseldyke, 1995).

For example, before evaluating whether a learner can carry on a conversation with strangers in a community setting, the learner must have some experience in talking to people he or she does not know very well. If the learner lacks this experience or is intimidated by the new circumstance, it may be necessary to extend the assessment (or suspend it temporarily) until the learner has gained more background in this area. Otherwise it will be unclear whether problems that appear in the learner's performance stem from a lack of experience or from specific conversational skill deficits. Similarly, if a learner is ill, unusually tired, or overly preoccupied with something else at the time of the assessment, the results are likely to be unreliable. Under these circumstances, the assessment should be rescheduled for a time when the learner is more cooperative or attentive.

As a general rule, when any of the three conditions listed above are present, instructors should provide several additional performance opportunities either prior to or as part of the assessment to make sure that they obtain an accurate, unbiased accounting of the learners' skill levels.

Challenge the Limits of the Learners' Ability

The second consideration pertains to adjusting assessment activities to determine the limits of the learners' performance on the curriculum objectives. The original assessment schedule should give the learners a wide range of performance opportunities that correspond to the various conditions they will encounter in the course of their daily circumstances. But when the learners are successful in their initial attempts, it may be advantageous to broaden the scope or complexity of the performance conditions in order to examine the range of settings and circumstances in which the learners can perform their skills. On the other hand, if the learners' attempts are unsuccessful, it may be beneficial to simplify the performance conditions to see at what point their abilities begin.

For example, travel skills should be assessed across the range of locations that learners typically frequent. Instructors may wish to challenge successful learners even further to determine whether or not their skills extend beyond the initial estimates. This approach can help instructors decide whether the learners are ready to move up to the next instructional level. Conversely, with unsuccessful learners, instructors may adjust activities to have learners perform under more controlled and structured circumstances that would clarify where to begin instruction. Thus, in order to obtain a representative sample of their behavior, it is important to ensure that learners have sufficient opportunities to show what they can do.

In summary, then, instructors should carry out their assessment carefully and obtain a complete and accurate record of the learners' behavior. By being well organized from the start, instructors will find it much easier to keep track of the different curriculum items and activities that are in the assessment plan. However, instructors should be prepared to adjust their plans to account for factors they may not have anticipated.

Recording the Results of an Assessment

The assessment work sheet we presented in Chapter 6 contains a "Results" column in which to record the results of the learners' assessment (See Table 6.5). Instructors should record their results in this column in the form of tally marks, averages, percentages, totals, or other recordings that accurately describe the learners' performance. The manner in which instructors record the assessment results should allow them to easily compare the performance they observe to the standards for the curriculum objectives. The record-keeping procedures should help them tell at a glance whether the learners have the necessary skills for each of the curriculum objectives assessed. Table 7.4 shows examples of how assessment results can be recorded in the "Results" column of a work sheet. It uses the same portion of the assessment plan that was presented in Table 6.5.

Table 7.5 contains three guidelines that instructors should follow when they record the results of an assessment.

TABLE 7.4 Example of an Assessment Work Sheet with Results

ASSESSMENT WORK SHEET

Name of Learner: Phil Weatherspoon   **Age:**   15

Dates of Assessment: October 4–October 25

Grade/Program Area: Grade 9/Functional Academics

Name of Instructor/Assessor: Mrs. Franklin

Location of Assessment: School and First American Bank and Trust

Assessment Setting/Situation: Classroom during math period

CURRICULUM OBJECTIVES	STANDARDS	PROCEDURES	RESULTS
Tell time to nearest minute	90% correct in 15 minutes	Work sheet of clock face examples	90%- 13min 100%- 15min 80%- 12min 90%- 14min 95%- 13min
Add/subtract five-figure numbers	15 of 20 problems correct in 15 minutes	Math workbook page	16/20- 16min 14/20- 14min 15/20- 13min 16/20- 15min 15/20- 14min
Add/subtract numbers with decimals	15 of 20 problems correct in 15 minutes	Math workbook page	10/20- 14min 12/20- 13min 9/20- 15min 8/20- 14min ***
Calculate one-fourth	95% correct	Test using oral work problems	80% 75% 75% 80% ***
Make lists	90% of items on lists Items legible	Observation while helping with inventory	95%- leg 90%- leg 100%- leg 95%- leg
Alphabetize words	80% in correct order in 10 minutes	Work sheet of 30 words	90%- 10min 85%- 10min 80%- 9min 90%- 9min 80%- 10min

Comments: Phil consistently has difficulty putting numbers into neat rows or columns—sometimes he adds the wrong numbers.

TABLE 7.4 (CONT.) Example of an Assessment Work Sheet

Assessment Setting/Situation: School office

Curriculum Objectives	Standards	Procedures	Results
Make telephone calls	All steps correct in telephone checklist before connection drops	Observation/Mrs. Peters	3 missed 4 missed 2 missed 5 missed ***
Address envelope	5 of 5 correct: has complete address, items legible and in correct positions	Observation/Mrs. Peters	5/5 5/5 5/5 5/5 5/5
Identify appropriate postage	Postage correct on 5 of 5 envelopes	Observation/Mrs. Peters	no, no, no, yes, no ***
Establish personal routine	All steps complete office work routine checklist Completes routine in 40 minutes	Observation/Mrs. Peters	yes- 38min yes- 40min yes- 41min yes- 35min yes- 40min
Make file folders	5 of 5 correct: label matches folder contents	Observation/Mrs. Peters	5/5 5/5 5/5 5/5 5/5
Use white pages of telephone book	9 of 10 correct: number matches name and address in 10 minutes	Observation/Mrs. Peters	4/10 6/10 8/10 7/10 7/10 ***

Comments: Phil continued to act apprehensive about answering and talking on the phone. We should give him more experience in this area and assess again later. He works comfortably with the office staff and asks for help when he needs it. He does tend to interrupt the work of the staff, so we need to work on his timing in asking for assistance.

Assessment Setting/Situation: School bookstore

Curriculum Objectives	Standards	Procedures	Results
Make change	10 of 10 correct on purchases	Observation	3/10 8/10 10/10 7/10 7/10 7/10 ***
Identify money symbols	10 of 10 correct on purchases	Observation	5/10 10/10 10/10 10/10 10/10

TABLE 7.4 (CONT.) Example of an Assessment Work Sheet

Curriculum Objectives	Standards	Procedures	Results
Cash check	All steps correct on check-cashing checklist	Observation	No, No, Yes, No, No ***

Comments: Monday was unusually hectic this week because the bookstore staff had to inventory and stock a new shipment of supplies. Phil seemed very distracted by the amount of activity going on.

Assessment Setting/Situation: First American Bank and Trust

Curriculum Objectives	Standards	Procedures	Results
Establish a savings account	All steps correct on account checklist	Interview bank official	No, No, No, No, No ***
Identify bank statement	Identifies statement 5 of 5 times	Observation	Yes, Yes, Yes, Yes, Yes
Calculate totals	3 of 3 correct in checking statement	Observation	Yes, Yes, Yes
Locate information at row-column intersection in a table	5 of 5 correct on bank statement	Oral quiz	3/5 4/5 2/5 3/5 4/5 ***

Comments: Ms. Davis, a bank clerk, said she would talk to her supervisor about working with Phil on banking procedures. She will work out a schedule of the times she would be available. Phil seemed to interact well with Ms. Davis, so this might be a good arrangement.

TABLE 7.5 Guidelines for Recording the Results of an Assessment

When recording assessment results, instructors should
- use procedures that match the standards for the curriculum objectives;
- keep a daily account of the results; and
- record other information that may assist the planning of the learners' instruction.

Use Procedures That Match the Standards
for Curriculum Objectives

Instructors will find it easy to interpret the results of their assessment if they use recording procedures that correspond to the standards outlined on the assessment work sheet. For example, when occurrence standards have been established, instructors can record whether or not learners can use a particular set of skills with either a simple "Yes" or "No" or a "+" or "−" tally procedure. For example, an instructor who assesses theater-going skills might be observing whether learners can "buy a ticket and refreshments." The standard for this part of the objective may be "obtain a ticket and get desired refreshments." When the instructor assesses this skill, the instructor could simply enter a "Yes" or "+" in the "Results" column of the work sheet each time the learners are successful in meeting the objective and a "No" or "−" each time they are unsuccessful.

When assessing other quantitative standards such as frequency, duration, and rate, instructors should enter tallies or scores in the "Results" column and the total for each day's observation. For example, a residential supervisor might be assessing the completion of evening chores, and the standard may be "complete 75% of assigned tasks." When recording the learner's behavior, the supervisor should count the number of chores the learner is supposed to complete and the number of chores he or she actually completes and convert the totals to a percent score. The supervisor should enter *both* the raw number counts and the percent score on the assessment work sheet next to the curriculum item. Note that in Table 7.4, Mrs. Franklin's results match the standards that apply for each objective. Instructors will be able to interpret the results quickly if the recording procedures are consistent with the standards.

Keep a Day-by-Day Record of Results

Instructors should also catalogue each day's entries according to the day or date on which the results were obtained. For example, when counting the number of times a learner completes an assigned task, the instructor should keep each day's tallies separate, even when intending to average the results over the whole week. Keeping a daily account of observations will allow the instructor to take any anomalous scores into account when summarizing the results. For example, if an instructor is tracking the results of a program of physical conditioning, and a learner jogs a total of 25 laps around the track during a week, it would be important to note whether all 25 laps were completed on a single day or whether they were spread across the entire week. This information can indicate when the learner had a particularly good or bad day or can provide information about the learner's performance under differing conditions, such as heat, cold, rain, or dry weather.

This guideline also applies to objectives that require performance that spans several days, such as is often true of complex tasks or lengthy routines involved in doing school projects, home maintenance and repairs, and budgeting. Periodic records of the learners' progress can indicate the steps that pose the most difficulty for the learners or the places in the performance pattern in which behavior becomes very slow or inconsistent.

Instructors should also note on the work sheet any variations from natural conditions that occur during an assessment activity. For example, an instructor might note the days on which a learner has a bad cold or when a substitute instructor oversees activities. Any extraordinary event that seems to affect a learner's behavior should be described so the day's results are more interpretable. As a general rule, measures derived from unusual circumstances should not be used in the summary of assessment results if a learner's performance is atypical under those circumstances. Inclusion of these measures in the results can cause the average score to misrepresent typical learner behavior and lead to erroneous conclusions about the learner's performance.

Record Other Information That May Assist the Planning of the Learners' Instruction

The time that instructors devote to assessment provides an excellent opportunity to think about both the requirements for meeting curriculum objectives and the performance conditions that may facilitate the learners' instruction. For example, during an assessment, instructors may discover requirements or prerequisite skills that they had not identified during the curriculum development process, but which could prove very important in planning the learners' instruction. These types of serendipitous information should be noted in the "Comments" section of the work sheet.

Assessment also provides an ideal time to begin thinking about instructional activities. For example, while conducting an assessment, a learner's reactions to events may show that he or she particularly likes or dislikes certain activities. Not only would this information be extremely valuable in interpreting the assessment results, it is also very useful when making decisions about instructional procedures and lesson plans. This type of information can give insight into the source of the learner's problem behaviors and may even suggest possible solutions for changing them. Such information, therefore, should also be entered in the "Comments" section of the work sheet.

In summary, instructors should record the assessment results in a way that matches the standards for the curriculum objectives and should keep a daily account of the results. Any major factors or variables that influence learner performance should be noted because they can assist in interpreting the results and planning instruction.

Comparing Assessment Results to Standards

The next step in the assessment process is to compare the assessment results to the standards for the curriculum objectives. If the instructors have entered the results on an assessment work sheet according to the guidelines described in the previous section, they should be able to compare them directly to the measures entered in the "Standards" column of the work sheet. That is, assessment results that equal or exceed the standards indicate that the learners meet the objective, while results that do not meet the standards do not. In this straightforward manner, instructors can easily determine whether the performance they observed during assessment meets the requirements for meeting the objectives.

As they compare the results to the standards, instructors should use the assessment work sheet to highlight the curriculum objectives on which the learners' performance falls below the standards, or they can tabulate these items on a separate page. They should also compile a list of any other objectives they had previously determined that the learners could not meet, even though they may not have assessed these objectives. By completing these tasks, instructors will create from their assessment a detailed, complete, and (most importantly) accurate list of the curriculum objectives that the learners do not meet. This list will ensure a tight focus on the important skills to teach when planning instruction.

In Table 7.4, asterisks (***) were used to highlight assessment results that did not meet the standards. They indicate that Phil Weatherspoon met the standard for telling time, adding and subtracting five-figure numbers, and making lists, but that he did not meet the standards for adding and subtracting decimals, calculating one-fourth, and making telephone calls.

Setting Priorities for Instruction

The process of comparing the assessment results with the standards for the curriculum objectives will help instructors decide which curriculum items posed the most difficulties for the learners. Now it is time to show how to use these items to set priorities for instruction.

After completing a comprehensive assessment of the learners' performance, the instructor still may find that there are too many areas on which to work given the time available for instruction. Instructors must avoid trying to concentrate on too many areas simultaneously because they will not be able to implement, monitor, and evaluate all the lessons and activities. By trying to work on too much at once, it is possible to end up accomplishing very little in terms of improving the learners' overall skill levels because no single objective will receive as much attention as it needs.

To give instruction a clear, tight focus, instructors should set priorities among curriculum objectives and target specific skill areas for immediate instruction. The objectives they list as the highest priorities should be the areas they plan to address within the next few days, weeks, or months, and these objectives should be included in the learners' instructional program plans (IPs). If the learners attain these objectives, the instructors can then attend to the objectives that are ranked lower on the priority list.

TABLE 7.6 Guidelines for Setting Priorities Among Curriculum Objectives

- Objectives that are more functional and/or more frequently used by learners should take priority over those that are less functional or less frequently used.
- Objectives that are more likely to carry over to other settings and situations should take priority over those that are less likely to carry over.
- Objectives that improve the learners' ability to learn from other people should be given priority over those that do not.
- Objectives that learners value and that improve their self-esteem and self-image should be given priority over those that do not.
- Objectives that lead up to or that are prerequisite to more advanced skills should be given priority over those that do not lead to more advanced skills.
- Objectives that are valued and judged to be especially important by other people in a setting should be given priority over those that are judged to be less important.

Knapczyk, D., and Rodes, P. (1996). *Teaching social competence: A practical approach for improving social skills in students at-risk.* Pacific Grove, CA: Brooks/Cole.

Guidelines for Setting Priorities Among Curriculum Objectives

Table 7.6 contains guidelines for assigning priority rankings to the curriculum objectives learners do not meet. These guidelines are *not* presented in a particular order because the unique circumstances of each individual learner will cause some guidelines to assume greater importance than others at different times and under different circumstances.

Objectives That Are More Functional and/or More Frequently Used Should Take Priority over Those That Are Less Functional or Less Frequently Used

The skill clusters that are represented by curriculum objectives can vary widely in how often learners actually need to use them and how important they are in achieving success and independence in school and community settings (Solity and Bull, 1987; Wasik, 1990; Wolery, Bailey, and Sugai, 1988). The skills that learners will use more often or that relate more closely to furthering their independence should be listed before skills that are less important. For example, elementary and middle school teachers may wish to give priority to objectives involving the use of basic skills, such as those found in Table 7.7.

Instructors in secondary school and adult programs might wish to give priority to objectives involving other kinds of skills, such as those found in Table 7.8.

The skills listed in Tables 7.7 and 7.8, and other skills that learners must use frequently in community settings, can contribute significantly to many areas of achievement. They should be ranked higher than those that would have less impact on the learners' participation in instructional activities and should be given priority in the learners' individualized programs of instruction.

TABLE 7.7 Examples of Skills That Could Be Priorities for Elementary and Middle Schools

Elementary and middle school instructors should give priority to
- skills that promote attention to and participation in a wide range of instructional activities, such as staying on task, seeking assistance, and following directions;
- motor skills that improve the learners' ability to engage in physical activities, such as increasing endurance, agility, coordination, and strength;
- communication skills that are useful in carrying out interactions in the community, such as conducting conversations, following lists of instructions, and specifying problems that require resolution; and
- functional academic skills that are used in community settings, such as reading signs and labels, figuring costs, locating information, and finding specific values in tables of values.

TABLE 7.8 Examples of Skills That Could Be Priorities for Secondary Schools and Adult Programs

Instructors in secondary school and adult programs should give priority to
- skills that are required during travel to and from frequented locations in the community, such as using public transportation, knowing what to do when lost, and interacting with fellow travelers;
- skills that pertain to obtaining and holding a job, such as showing up to work every day on time, doing things without being told, and interacting with supervisors and fellow employees;
- skills that are used in maintaining health and personal appearance, such as identifying illnesses and injuries that require medical attention, keeping clothing clean and neat, and making regular visits to beauty or barber shop; and
- skills that are required in interactions with other people in the community, such as imitating expected behavior, identifying the roles others play, and listening for the topics of conversation that are appropriate for the circumstances.

Objectives That Are More Likely to Carry Over to Other Settings and Situations Should Take Priority over Those That Are Less Likely to Carry Over

Another consideration in setting priorities is the number and range of settings and circumstances in which learners will actually use the skill clusters represented by the curriculum objectives. Especially in school programs, instructors should teach skill clusters that learners can use in several settings before working on those they can use in only a single setting. The frequent opportunities the learners have to use these skills will allow them to practice and refine their actions quickly and to experience an immediate improvement in their ability to function in a number of situations. Such skills will take advantage of any carryover effects that may result from instruction (Kerr and Nelson, 1989; Wolery, Bailey, and Sugai, 1988).

Some skill clusters are naturally easier for learners to carry over to several settings because there are many opportunities to perform them or because the conditions of performance are fairly consistent. Other skill clusters may carry over quickly if the learners are provided with a little additional instruction in the other settings. In both cases, the skills learners can use in a number of different settings soon will become a part of their performance pattern and produce discernible improvements in overall school and community functioning. For example, many social skills, such as exchanging greetings and conversing with other people, can transfer naturally to several settings because the people in those settings may use similar language patterns and discuss similar topics. Skill clusters such as using rest room facilities, checking one's personal appearance, using acceptable table manners, and showing common courtesy to others can carry over to many settings, as well. Therefore, curriculum objectives for skill clusters that learners will use in more than one setting should be given special consideration in IPs.

Objectives That Improve a Learner's Ability to Learn from Other People Should Be Given Priority over Those That Do Not

Learners must broaden the scope of their behavior and increase its complexity as they grow, mature, and participate in an ever-widening variety of school and community settings. In order to achieve this outcome, they must learn to develop skills incidentally by watching and imitating the behavior of the people around them. Working on curriculum objectives that involve interacting with other people will usually encourage learners to imitate and practice new behaviors, and such opportunities will often lead to more mature and more advanced performance patterns. Furthermore, as learners experience success in learning from and interacting with other people, they are likely to begin to show generalized and continuing improvements in their behavior (Renshaw and Asher, 1982).

In setting priorities among curriculum objectives for younger learners, instructors may wish to give a higher rank to items that will teach learners to do such things as cooperate on assigned tasks and participate in group activities. Objectives for these types of skills will help the learners become more integrated into group activities and encourage them to observe and learn from other people's behavior (Johnson and Johnson, 1990; Slavin, Karweit, and Madden, 1989). For example, a middle school teacher should give priority to objectives that require learners to work with nondisabled classmates on school activities and projects as opposed to objectives that primarily involve solitary activities. Similarly, an instructor who teaches vocational skills may wish to give higher priority to objectives that promote collaborative teamwork among employees.

Objectives That Learners Value and That Improve Their Self-Esteem and Self-Image Should Be Given Priority over Those That Do Not

We believe that self-esteem comes, in large measure, from doing things that are wanted or needed by somebody else (Gold, 1980a). For example, an employer hires an employee because the employer needs to accomplish something. The

Instructional plans provide the framework for teaching individual learners.
Photo courtesy of James L. Shaffer.

fact that the employer is willing to give the employee money to perform work indicates that the employee has value; therefore, paid employment is an activity that by its nature builds self-esteem. Similarly, people feel good when they volunteer their time and effort to help other people because volunteers do something that someone else needs to have done. Thus, volunteer activities that learners believe to be important and activities that are developed within the construct of service assist learners in building self-esteem (Cairn and Kielsmeir, 1995; Hamilton, 1980). In fact, any curriculum objectives that will help learners do things that are wanted or needed by somebody else should take priority over those that will not.

In addition, curriculum objectives that allow learners to pursue personal interests and achieve personal goals will naturally create more intrinsic motivation than those that hold less interest for the learners (Miller and Harrington, 1990; Peterson and Miller, 1990; Wolery, Bailey, and Sugai, 1988). Such objectives can also foster self-confidence and encourage camaraderie and trust between learners and other people who can help them acquire and master skills. Such benefits are especially important for learners who have poor self-images or who show a lack of initiative (Lehr and Harris, 1988). Therefore objectives that are likely to have these positive effects on learners should be listed before those that do not.

An instructor may wish to give priority to improving the particular skill clusters in which learners have a special interest because they will usually pay close attention to the instruction directed toward acquiring these skills. Furthermore, while teaching such skill clusters, the instructors may be able to take advantage of the learners' inherent motivation and concentration by having them develop other related skills as well, such as following the rules required to participate in the activity or being more attentive to the tedious and mundane aspects of performance. The spin-off effects of establishing a learning pattern that attends to these areas of performance can prove to be invaluable when the learners are reluctant to participate in the instructional activities.

Objectives That Lead Up to or Are Prerequisite to More Advanced Skills Should Be Given Priority over Those That Do Not Lead to More Advanced Skills

When prioritizing curriculum objectives, instructors should also consider whether the skills under consideration will help learners progress satisfactorily toward integration in school and community settings. There are some objectives that may be especially important for younger learners because these objectives will help them make successful transitions to higher-level programs. For example, classroom teachers may wish to give higher priority to curriculum objectives that involve cooperating with classmates because cooperation may increase the benefits the learners can gain from inclusion programs. Similarly, instructors in community-based settings should consider giving precedence to such areas as forming mental maps of travel routes because these skills provide the foundation for traveling to a wide variety of community settings.

Objectives That Are Valued and Judged to Be Especially Important by Other People in a Setting Should Be Given Priority over Those That Are Judged to Be Less Important

As we mentioned in previous chapters, other people in a setting usually define the parameters for successful performance in the setting. Therefore, when establishing priorities for instruction, instructors should consider the way in which other people in the setting perceive the relative importance of curriculum objectives. Doing so will add greater "social validity" to the process of planning IPs (Cartledge and Milburn, 1986; Gresham and Elliott, 1984; Wolf, 1978).

For example, the employees in certain work settings may place more value on group participation, teamwork, and "fitting in" than on proficiency in performing specific tasks and activities. On the other hand, the employees in other work settings may give more importance to complying with directions and completing assigned tasks than to group cooperation and interaction. The relative value people place on skills can be an especially important aspect in planning instruction for learners who are being prepared for general education and community placements.

Using the Guidelines

As we mentioned at the beginning of this section, the guidelines are not listed in any particular order, and their relative importance probably will change from learner to learner. Instructors should review them frequently as they plan each learner's IP and should weigh the considerations in light of the assessment results and the learner's circumstances. To do so, it is necessary to take into account variables such as

- the learner's age, skill level, interests, abilities, and talents;
- the characteristics of the learner's peer groups; and
- the various attributes of the instructional environment that can influence the learner's behavior.

The overall intent behind the application of the guidelines is to help instructors decide which curriculum objectives will have the greatest impact on improving a learner's performance and thus have the greatest effect on the learner's progress toward independence. As a general rule, instructors should try to anticipate the effect that the attainment of any particular curriculum objective will have on a learner's level of performance. They should consider whether there are some skill areas that can improve the learner's overall independence more than others or that can provide a framework for developing other important or more advanced skills.

It is often the case that some curriculum objectives will be more important than others for a specific learner in a specific set of circumstances. The priorities that instructors assign to these curriculum items will create the central focus for a learner's IP. These priorities will enable instructors to direct their full attention to a few specific areas of behavior and to avoid trying to teach all of the objectives that may attract their attention.

The Individualized Instructional Plan

Schools and adult service agencies use many different terms for documents that contain individualized instructional plans. Regardless of what it is called, an IP must consist of a plan for the instruction that persons with mental retardation will receive. It should always be based on the results of a sound assessment of learner behavior and on the priorities that instructors give to curriculum objectives.

The Reason for Individualized Instructional Plans

An IP contributes to the overall success and effectiveness of instruction by helping instructors become well-organized and systematic in their implementation of instructional procedures. An IP is a guide that serves the following functions:

- it gives each learner's instruction a sharp focus;
- it allows instructors to evaluate the learner's reactions to instructional activities;
- it enables instructors to monitor the learner's acquisition of skills and curriculum objectives; and
- it helps instructors judge whether the learner sustains his or her performance of recently acquired skills.

In most cases, instructors must adjust their teaching procedures as they carry out instruction. All modifications should be based on the responses made by the learners and their progress in developing and using the skills. Instructors can use the IP to determine whether the procedures produce the desired effects and to decide when to modify or end instruction that focuses on specific curriculum objectives (Smith, 1989).

An IP is especially useful when instructors must coordinate their teaching with the actions of other instructional and supervisory personnel. The IP will help everyone involved in the instruction do two things:

1. understand clearly what their responsibilities are in carrying out the instruction; and
2. maintain a steady focus on the overall outcome of the instruction.

IPs help keep the teaching procedures consistent with the overall focus of the instruction. In doing so, they help bring about quicker and more orderly changes in learner behavior. An IP facilitates communication about instructional procedures among everyone who is concerned with the learners' instruction and enhances consistency in carrying out activities across all the settings in which instruction takes place.

Best of all, an IP does not take much work to develop. After instructors have conducted the assessment and selected the priority areas from the curriculum, they will have completed much of the preparation and established a focus for instruction. After completing the assessment, drawing up the IP becomes a matter of documenting the priority curriculum items, setting a schedule for carrying out lessons, coordinating personnel and resources, and outlining the procedures for monitoring the learners' behavior.

The IP Should Be Consistent with Assessment Results

IPs should be directed toward assisting learners in overcoming the skill deficits that have been noted during assessment (Greenwood and Carta, 1987; Salvia and Hughes, 1990). Although this principle should be self-evident, we state it deliberately because it is easy for instructors to get so involved in planning instructional lessons and activities that they lose the clear focus that results from the assessment. For example, they may start with a definite idea of the skills they need to teach to a learner but lose their focus because of the other difficulties a learner presents, such as behavior problems. Or they may become engrossed in trying out new instructional techniques or materials for teaching skill clusters that are only slightly related to the overall intent of the instruction. In either case, such sidetracking inevitably diffuses the instructors' teaching efforts. When instructors try to address a broad range of skills or try to deal with problems that are only indirectly defined in the assessment results, instruction tends to lose its focus quickly. Therefore, to do the most good for their learners, instructors should base their planning on the decisions they have already made and on the information they gathered during the assessment process. After the teaching activities begin to produce their desired effect on the learners' behavior, the instructors will be able to conduct some follow-up assessments and to shift the focus of the instruction to other areas if it proves necessary to do so.

Preparing an Individualized Instructional Plan

The following procedures and format provide a generalized approach for preparing IPs in both schools and adult agencies. The approach, perhaps with some minor modifications, will be applicable to any type of IP development process.

The format we will present for an IP work sheet is similar to the assessment work sheet we described in Chapter 6, and serves a similar purpose. As before, the work sheet provides a place to list information and plans that will keep the instruction on track. The main difference is that the IP work sheet is a planning document that relates to organizing, scheduling, and coordinating *instructional* activities rather than assessment activities. Table 7.9 shows a portion of an IP for Phil Weatherspoon. Table 7.10 lists the steps involved in preparing the work sheet.

Step 1: List Basic Information About the Learner and the Program Planning Process

Instructors should begin preparing the IP by listing their name, the date, the name of the learner, and any other background information that is pertinent to the planning process. For example, they should note the other people who are assisting in developing the IP, such as administrative and instructional support personnel and the learner's family member(s) or guardian(s). Space for this type of information should be provided on the cover sheet of the IP document. Table 7.9 shows an example of information that could be entered in this portion of the work sheet.

Step 2: List the Curriculum Objectives That Are the Focus of the Plan

The next step is to list the curriculum objectives that were chosen as the top priority areas for the learner's instruction. These curriculum objectives then will become the *program objectives* for the learner's IP. Listing these objectives at the beginning of the IP document will center everyone's ideas around specific, concrete objectives for the learner (Harris and Schutz, 1986).

We suggest the use of a multiple-page work sheet with each of the program objectives serving as a separate heading at the top of a page. This approach will help those who develop the IP focus on each objective as a distinct program outcome. It also will keep discussions about how to plan instruction toward each objective fairly separate from the discussions on the other objectives. Table 7.9 shows the way in which program objectives can be entered on the IP work sheet.

Some instructional planning documents have terms like *short-term objectives* or *short-term goals*. These items usually refer to the specific skill

TABLE 7.9 Sample Format for an Instructional Program Plan

Learner's Name: Phil Weatherspoon   **Date:** November 7
Instructor's Name: Mrs. Franklin
Grade/Program Area: Grade 9/ Functional Academics
Participants in plan: Mrs. Weatherspoon
                    Mrs. Curry
                    Mr. Filmont
                    Ms. Waterford

Program Objective: Add/subtract numbers with decimals
Instructional Settings and Situations: Classroom, during small group and independent work times
Personnel: None
Resources: Computer and software, work sheets, Kyle—Phil's tutor

Time Line:	*Week of*	*Tasks*
	November 14	Provide one-on-one instruction
		Provide peer tutoring
	November 21	Present computer practice drills
	December 5	Continue with tutoring and computer drills
	December 12	Give timed test, evaluate responses, and plan further work, if needed

Program Objective: Calculate one-fourth
Instructional Settings and Situations: Classroom, during small group and independent work time
Personnel: None
Resources: Math workbook, work sheets, manipulatives from math kit

Time Line:	*Week of*	*Tasks*
	November 14	Prepare practice work sheets
		Provide one-on-one instruction—work with manipulatives
	November 21	Provide one-on-one instruction—use work sheet examples of objects
	December 5	Provide one-on-one instruction—use workbook examples using numbers
	December 12	Use practice drills within small groups
		Practice for quiz
	December 19	Give test, evaluate responses, and plan further work, if needed

TABLE 7.9 (CONT.) Sample Format for an Instructional Program Plan

Program Objective: Make telephone calls

Instructional Settings and Situations: School office, also classroom area for simulations

Personnel: Mrs. Kelly, school secretary

Resources: Telephones, coins, telephone-use checklist, two-way internal telephone system (order from Resource Center)

Time Line:	Week of	Tasks
	November 21	Prepare work sheet for Phil that outlines steps for making calls
		Have Mrs. Kelly list the different types of calls that Phil could make dealing with school business
	December 5	Go over outline with Phil, covering steps he does not know
	December 12	Practice steps using internal phone system—simulate different phone-use situations
	December 19	Practice making calls—teacher supervised
		Evaluate performance and plan further work if needed
	December 19	Practice making calls—Mrs. Kelly supervised
		Evaluate performance and plan further work if needed

Program Objective: Identify postage

Instructional Settings and Situations: School office

Personnel: Mrs. Kelly, school secretary

Resources: School's supply of stamps, envelopes of various sizes and weights—already addressed

Time Line:	Week of	Tasks
	November 21	Prepare a chart showing the scale readings for weight and postage
		Cover how to decide whether a letter or package must be weighed before placing postage on it
	December 5	Go over scale chart with Phil
		Check Phil's ability to read and understand weight/postage scale (provide instruction if needed)
		Highlight weight-to-postage relationship
	December 12	Work on calculating postage and assembling stamps that fit the readings on postage scale
	December 19	Continue with instruction
	January 9	Evaluate Phil's performance, and plan further work, if needed

TABLE 7.10 Steps in Preparing an Individual Instructional Plan

1. List basic information about the learner and the instructional setting.
2. List the curriculum objectives that are the focus of the plan.
3. Describe the settings and situations in which the instruction will take place.
4. List the personnel who will carry out the instruction and assist with activities.
5. List the resources to be used during instruction.
6. Develop a time line for the instructional lessons and activities.

clusters that appear in the curriculum objectives. As a general rule, the curriculum objectives that have the highest priority rankings should become the short-term objectives for a learner. If a school or agency requires the IP to state long-term goals, they should consist of the goals that serve as end points for the curriculum pathways from which the program objectives were selected.

Some documents also have a space next to each objective or goal for listing *criteria*. This term corresponds to the performance measures we have been calling "standards." It is usually a good idea to list the standards next to the program objectives to call attention to the level of behavior the learner must achieve before instruction in that area is complete. However, we did not include a place in Table 7.9 for entering standards; instead, we will discuss how to prepare a separate work sheet that can be added to the IP to assist in monitoring instruction because monitoring activities include the process of comparing the learner's performance to standards.

Step 3: Describe the Settings and Circumstances in Which the Instruction Will Take Place

A description of the settings and situations in which the instruction of each program objective will take place should also be entered on the IP work sheet. These descriptions should include both the principal settings in which the instruction will be carried out and any other settings in which the learner's performance will be monitored to check for transfer or generalization of performance.

For example, instructors will often begin their instruction in a fairly structured or controlled set of circumstances, such as a classroom, in order to judge the effectiveness of the procedures and to adjust them to the learners' characteristics. These types of circumstances may also help learners develop some basic skills or experiences in the instructional area. As the procedures become more refined and the learners begin to progress beyond the level of basic instruction, instructors may move the instruction to more natural settings, such as to general education settings or to community residential, leisure, or vocational settings. All the settings and circumstances that will be used during the course of instruction should be listed in the IP to allow lessons to be prepared and coordinated.

Assessment and Planning of Individual Instructional Programs

Step 4: List the Personnel Who Will Carry Out the Instruction and Assist with Activities

A list of the personnel who are involved in the instruction will remind instructors to include them in major decisions relative to developing, implementing, and monitoring the instructional lessons and activities (Harris and Schutz, 1986; Salvia and Hughes, 1990). For example, the IP should contain a list of those individuals who will help judge the effectiveness of the IP and decide whether the plan needs modification. It should also list the administrative staff members if their approval is required to make changes in routines, class assignments, grouping arrangements, schedules, or other factors related to the conduct of instruction. Finally, listing the people who will be involved in various aspects of instruction, such as those in the community who will oversee the learners' performance, will remind the instructors to contact these people well in advance of the time that they become involved in the learners' programs.

Step 5: List the Resources to Be Used During Instruction

The instructional lessons and activities may entail the use of equipment, supplies, commercial materials, tutors or learner helpers, videotapes, and other instructional aids. Instructors should list any and all needed tools, materials, and supplies in the IP to ensure that they are available at the time the instruction begins (Harris and Schutz, 1986).

Step 6: Develop a Time Line for the Instructional Lessons and Activities

A time line should be included in the IP that lists the major steps for implementing the plan, the sequence in which each step will be carried out, and the dates and times of implementation. A time line that includes these and similar elements will allow instructors to review the entire schedule of activities, select the necessary instructional settings, and assign responsibilities accordingly. If instructors have a schedule, they will not lose sight of their overall plan of instruction or overlook a crucial component of the individual learner's instruction (Harris and Schutz, 1986). A time line is especially useful when the instruction in program objectives will begin at different times.

Note that instructors do not have to explain the instructional activities or procedures they will use because they will work out these details later as part of the development of instructional lessons. However, the descriptions should be clear enough to organize, direct, and oversee the activities over time and should contain sufficient detail to ensure their understanding by those directly involved in the planning process (Harris and Schutz, 1986).

An IP, then, is a document that instructors can use to organize and coordinate various aspects of learners' instructional programs before instruction in curriculum objectives begins. Completing an IP work sheet will help center everyone's planning on the particular objectives that are priority areas for the learners.

Concluding Statement

The insights about learner behavior that instructors can derive from an assessment depend on the care with which the assessment is organized and carried out. This chapter has suggested that there are three important areas to consider:

1. Conduct the Assessment Carefully

Instructors should coordinate an assessment with normally scheduled routines and activities to take advantage of the naturally occurring circumstances for observing the learners' behavior. An assessment should take place over several days and should include enough different performance opportunities to make the results as accurate and representative as possible.

Instructors should also be careful to keep the goals of the assessment firmly in mind and focus on the particular curriculum objectives with which they are concerned. Similarly, when other people assist in the assessment, they must understand the important details of the assessment in advance and have clear directions for recording the information they need to obtain. Everyone involved in the assessment should recognize the limits of their ability in carrying out the assessment procedures and try to be unobtrusive while making the observations.

2. Keep a Tally of the Results

The results from the assessment should be recorded in a way that matches the standards for each curriculum objective. It is usually a good idea to keep a daily tally of results so that anomalous or erratic performance will be easy to spot. It is also helpful to record any variables or conditions that may have an effect on the learners' performance or that may suggest useful instructional approaches.

After the assessment, the results should be compared to the standards to clearly show which curriculum objectives the learners do and do not meet. When learners show problems in several areas, it is best to prioritize the objectives they did not meet according to the guidelines presented in this chapter and to focus on the top priority items when developing instructional lessons and activities.

3. Prepare an Instructional Program Plan

Instructors should also develop a sound individualized instructional program plan before beginning the learners' instruction. Preparing the IP will clarify the instructional outcomes for learners and assist in structuring the instructional activities in an organized and consistent manner. The information on the IP provides a framework for collaborating with other instructional personnel in carrying out the instructional procedures.

PART IV

Overview of the Teaching Process

Instruction can be seen as an information transmission process in which instructors have information that learners need, and their job is to see to it that the learners somehow get the information. The process of providing learners with information is called *teaching* in the public schools and *training* in rehabilitation and residential services, but it is the same process in both cases. We will discuss this process in this section of the book.

The instructional act can be represented by a continuous "loop" in which some person, thing, or event presents the learner with information that pertains to meeting a program objective in an IP (see Figure IV.1). When the learner responds to this information, someone, something, or some event in the environment must inform the learner as to the appropriateness of the response, and if necessary, indicate what the learner must do to improve his or her behavior; when the learner demonstrates an understanding of the information by showing proficiency in using the required skills, instructional activities are "faded," and the learner is expected to continue using the skills without outside assistance. Thus, when instruction has been carried to completion, the learner will be able to perform the skills without the presence of an instructor, in the natural environment, and under natural conditions.

This section of the book contains four chapters that focus on the topic of providing instruction. The first two, Chapters 8 and 9, focus on the steps that are illustrated in Table IV.1. Chapter 8 explains how to find out exactly what information the learner needs, or the content of instruction. Once the instructors understand the instructional content, they can decide on the methodology they will use to present the information to the learner and to inform the learner about the accuracy of his or her responses. Once the learner responds appropriately and consistently, the instructor can fade from the scene and leave the learner to perform the relevant skills on his or her own. Chapter 9 is concerned with these three steps.

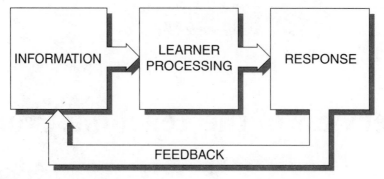

FIGURE IV.1
The instructional loop.

TABLE IV.1 Basic Processes Used in the Instructional Act

To teach, someone or something in the learner's environment must
- provide the learner with information;
- confirm learner responses that are appropriate;
- correct learner responses that are inappropriate;
- adjust instruction that is not progressing satisfactorily; and then
- fade from the instruction.

Despite the most meticulous preparation, the instructor must monitor the process to ensure that the learner makes steady progress toward the objective. If the learner is doing well, little or nothing needs to change, but if the learner is not acquiring skills at the rate at which he or she should, something may be wrong. The instructors must discover what is interfering with the learning process and make corrections to the procedures. In Chapter 10 we will present techniques for monitoring the instructional progress of the learner, and in Chapter 11 we will discuss how to plan follow-up courses of action to ensure that instruction produces steady progress in the learner's performance.

CHAPTER 8

Preparing to Teach:
Program Objective Analysis

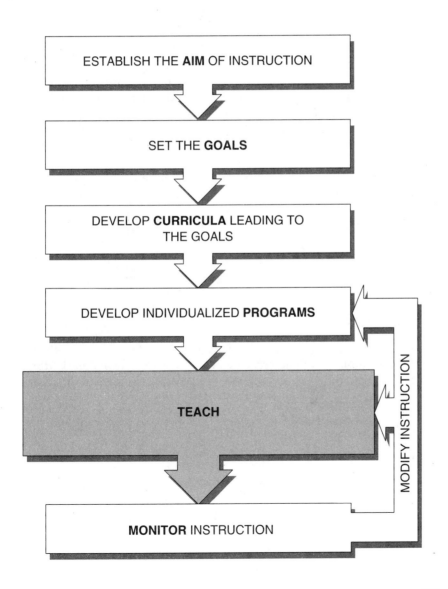

ESTABLISH THE **AIM** OF INSTRUCTION

SET THE **GOALS**

DEVELOP **CURRICULA** LEADING TO THE GOALS

DEVELOP INDIVIDUALIZED **PROGRAMS**

TEACH

MODIFY INSTRUCTION

MONITOR INSTRUCTION

The instructor's last step before actually beginning to teach is to decide what the learner must do to attain each program objective that has been listed in the IP. This step requires the instructor to select an objective from the IP and ask the following question:

> What must this learner do to show that he or she has attained this program objective?

Instructors often must answer this question differently for different learners, even when they are trying to help them reach the same objective. A useful process for developing an answer to the question was introduced to special education and rehabilitation services by Marc Gold (1980a, 1980b), who called the process "task analysis." The analytical procedure that we will present in this chapter is based on Gold's work but reflects the modifications that we ourselves have made to his procedures over the years (e.g., Knapczyk, 1975; Knapczyk and Rodes, 1996). In order to keep our terminology consistent throughout this text, we will call the process **program objective analysis** rather than task analysis. This term more directly reflects what instructors must do to identify the type of information that will help the learner achieve the objectives in his or her IP.

The procedure for analyzing program objectives is outlined in the work sheet for analyzing program objectives found in Appendix B. The program objective analysis work sheet has two parts: a cover sheet for entering basic information and a form for performing an analysis of skills. A completed example of this work sheet appears in Table 8.1, and we will refer to it during the discussion that follows.

To perform a program objective analysis, the instructor would accomplish the steps found in Table 8.2. The analysis of skills and cues, as indicated by the third and fourth steps in this table, may be omitted in many instances. However, the other steps should be completed in all cases.

The Cover Sheet

The cover sheet for a program objective analysis contains information that is useful in both planning and carrying out instructional activities. During instruction, the cover sheet is available for periodic reminder of the objective and the scope of instruction. When instruction is complete, the cover sheet can be placed in the learner's file folder as evidence of what the learner has learned to do and when he or she has achieved the objective.

Learner(s)

The first entry contains basic information about the learner or learners for whom the analysis was performed. This information includes the learner's name (if the analysis was performed for an individual learner) and a description of the learner's characteristics that affect performance of the skill clusters for the objective.

TABLE 8.1 Analysis for the Objective: The Learner Will Scramble Eggs

COVER SHEET

Big Sky Residences, Inc.

Unit: Fourth Street Home   **Date:** _____June 9_____

Learners: Residents with no physical disabilities that restrict range of motion and no sensory disabilities

Objective: The learners will scramble two eggs and clean up the cooking area

Learner Characteristics: Severely retarded 18- to 25-year-olds with no uncorrectable visual deficits or other physical disabilities that restrict range of motion.

Major Skill Clusters:

_____ 1. Assemble tools and materials (3 min.)
_____ 2. Mix eggs and other materials (2 min.)
_____ 3. Cook (3 min.)
_____ 4. Serve (1 min.)
_____ 5. Clean up area (6 min.)

Outcomes: The learners will be able to prepare their own breakfasts of scrambled eggs

Standards: The eggs will be completely cooked, but not overdone or burnt; no liquid will run from the eggs when they are placed on the dinner plate, and no shell fragments will be found in the eggs. The eggs will be placed on the center of the plate, and the plate will be placed on the table at the correct place setting. No spills will be evident. All dishes and utensils will be clean and in dish drainer, and the learner's hands will be dry.

Mastery Criteria: Eight consecutive attempts with no errors and no assistance.

Settings and Circumstances: In the group home, using the home's equipment, on Sunday morning before going to church.

Tools and Materials: Electric stove; frying pan; mixing bowl; dinner plate; spatula; tablespoon measure; small whisk; church-key-style can opener; 1 can of condensed milk; two eggs; bacon fat; sink with running water; sponge with handle for soap; dish drainer.

Instructors: Jack Moran, Ellen Sanchez, Marty Speer

Date Completed: _____

Completion Certified by: _____

_____

LIST OF SKILLS

A. *Assemble Tools and Materials*
  1. Obtain frying pan from cupboard and place on cold burner on stove.
  2. Obtain two eggs and bacon grease from refrigerator and place on counter next to stove.
  3. Obtain condensed milk from refrigerator (if previously opened) or from cupboard (if none in refrigerator) and place on counter next to stove.
  4. Obtain plate and bowl from cupboard and place next to eggs.
  5. Obtain whisk, spatula, and tablespoon from drawer and place next to bowl.
B. *Mixing Eggs*
  6. Pick up egg with two fingers under egg and thumb on top, and position over center of the bowl.
  7. Strike center of egg with edge of spatula so that egg develops a visible crack.
  8. Put down spatula and grasp egg with other hand, mirroring original grasp.
  9. Press egg and move thumbs apart, cracking open egg. Egg yolk and white will drop into bowl.
  10. Repeat for second egg.
  11. If condensed milk is unopened, place church key across can with point resting just inside edge of can.
  12. Steady handle and strike head of church key with heel of hand, driving point into the can. Hole will be shaped like an arrowhead.
  13. Repeat on opposite side of can to make second hole.
  14. Pour milk into tablespoon and dump into bowl.
  15. Repeat.
  16. Put spoon on counter.
  17. With whisk, stir egg mixture vigorously.
  18. Put whisk on counter.
C. *Cooking Eggs*
  19. Place pan on burner.
  20. Turn burner control on "Med High."
  21. Place approx 1 tbs. bacon grease into pan.
  22. When grease melts completely, pour egg mixture into pan and place bowl on counter next to plate.
  23. With spatula held upside down, place tip of spatula into pan and push eggs back from several directions. Eggs will roll up and off spatula and cook on all sides.
  24. When eggs are fluffy and all liquid has been cooked out of mixture, pour eggs onto plate, scraping pan to remove all residue.
  25. Turn burner control to "Off" and place pan on cold back burner.
D. *Serving Eggs*
  26. Place plate on table at place setting.
  27. Check to make sure all utensils, condiments, napkins, and dinnerware are on table at place setting. Add anything that is missing.
E. *Cleanup*
  28. Put covers on bacon grease can and evaporated milk can.
  29. Put bacon grease and evaporated milk in refrigerator.
  30. Bring pan, bowl, plate, tools, and silverware to sink.
  31. Run warm water on each item to wet it.
  32. Wet soap sponge.
  33. Rub sponge around inside and outside of pan until clean.
  34. Rinse pan and place in dish drainer.
  35. Repeat with bowl and plate.

TABLE 8.1 (CONT.) Analysis for the Objective: The Learner Will Scramble Eggs

36. Rub sponge on spatula, both top and bottom of blade and handle.
37. Rinse and place in silverware holder in dish drainer.
38. Repeat with whisk, knife, and fork.
39. Check for other dirty utensils or dishes and wash if necessary.
40. Rinse sink.
41. Dry hands.

TABLE 8.2 Steps for Performing a Program Objective Analysis

- State the program objective.
- List the major skill clusters.
- Analyze the skills the learner(s) will acquire.
- Describe the cues in the behavioral pattern.
- Specify the outcomes of performance.
- List the tools and materials.
- Establish the performance criteria.
- List the instructor(s).
- Provide a sign-off space.

We stated in Chapter 5 that some learners may have to learn to use a different pattern of behavior from other learners in order to perform a major skill cluster. For example, a learner who is blind must learn to cross a busy street differently from a learner who is sighted, and a learner who is in a wheelchair must board a bus differently from a learner who has full range of motion. Any learner characteristics that affect the way in which the learner(s) will achieve the program objective should be noted, including variables such as functioning level, performance abilities, or the presence of sensory, physical, or emotional disabilities. When an analysis is performed for a group of learners with similar characteristics, their common characteristics would be noted on the cover sheet.

There are two primary reasons for noting learner characteristics on the cover page:

1. A note on characteristics will establish expectations for the kinds of behaviors that will be found in the analysis on the following page(s). For example, if the statement on the cover sheet notes that the analysis was conducted for learner(s) with severe visual disabilities, those who use the analysis will expect that the analysis is likely to contain behavior patterns that are characteristic of people with visual disabilities.
2. This information will be helpful in deciding whether the analysis can be used again with other learners who need to learn the same program objective.

Table 8.1 shows that the analysis for scrambling eggs was performed for young adults who live in a group home and who have severe mental retardation and no outstanding physical or visual disabilities. This analysis now is available for any similar learner or group of learners and may require only minor modifications to be useful when teaching them.

Program Objective

The second step is to state the program objective on the cover sheet, and the instructor would simply copy the objective directly from the learner's IP. However, if a complete IP is not available, the instructor must clarify the objective so that it provides an accurate statement of the following:

- the skills the learner will develop; and
- the settings and circumstances under which the learner will use the skills.

These topics were covered in detail in Chapter 6.

Table 8.1 shows that the program objective for this analysis is, "The learner will scramble eggs."

Major Skill Clusters

The next entry on the cover sheet should contain a list of the major skill clusters for the program objective (see Chapter 5). Placing this list on the cover page provides a clear, concise, and easy-to-find statement of what the learner must do to achieve the objective.

Note the short line that precedes each major skill cluster in Table 8.1. These lines form a checklist that allows the instructor to check off the major skill clusters as the learner becomes proficient in performing each of them, and provide a record of what the learner has learned. As a learner becomes proficient in each of the skill clusters, the instructor can make a check in the appropriate space and shift attention to teaching only the skill clusters that the learner does not yet perform. In addition, note that a statement of how much time it should take a learner to perform each major skill cluster accompanies the entry. These time estimates will become useful during the monitoring of the instructional process and will be discussed in detail in Chapter 10.

The analysis in Table 8.1 has five major skill clusters. Other analyses could have more or fewer major skill clusters, depending on the objective being taught.

Outcomes

The cover page should contain a statement of the outcomes the learner will produce when he or she performs the skill clusters proficiently. Outcomes give purpose, direction, and meaning to performance and establish clear reasons for *why* a learner should perform the skill clusters after instruction is over and the instructor is no longer present. For example, a learner who uses an umbrella when it is raining can stay dry. Therefore, staying dry is an outcome of using the umbrella and gives the learner a reason to check the weather and carry an umbrella when rain is in the forecast.

Experience with outcomes will help learners take control of their lives by giving them the incentive to maintain the level of performance that is required to live in the community (Knapczyk and Rodes, 1996). For example, a person who likes to eat eggs is likely to scramble eggs now and then after he or she learns how to do it.

Many learners with mental retardation will attend to instruction because their instructors provide some sort of incentive for them to do so. But if they do not understand the outcomes, they may have little or no motivation to perform the skill clusters after instruction is complete. In the long run, learners' incentive for meeting program objectives depends largely on their experience with outcomes, and the most effective way to get learners to understand outcomes is to provide them with firsthand experiences. For example, learners may learn how to groom themselves, but in order for them to continue to perform this skill when no instructor is present, they must also learn why they should do so. That is, they may have to learn that grooming makes them presentable to other people or that not grooming may cause others to react negatively to them. Note that, since people respond differently to various outcomes, sometimes it is necessary to emphasize the outcomes that will be the most meaningful to a particular learner.

Table 8.3 gives examples of outcomes that may result from the performance of skill clusters for various program objectives. Unlike the objective, these outcomes are not stated behaviorally because they describe what will happen to the learners rather than what the learners will do. That is, they refer to what will happen at some time in the future after the learners perform the skill clusters proficiently. It is important to specify the outcomes on the cover sheet of an analysis so that instructional personnel will focus attention on them during the instructional activities.

Performance Standards

The statement of performance standards also appears on the cover page of the analysis. This statement describes what successful performance should look like to an observer and tells others what to expect the learner to do after instruction is over. The performance standards can be taken directly from the IP, but if for some reason the IP does not contain a statement of standards, the instructor will have to develop one. The procedure for doing so is described in Chapter 6.

Mastery Criteria

The next entry on the cover sheet is the statement of the criteria by which the instructors will judge the learner's mastery of the objective. This statement tells the instructor when to stop teaching and begin to require the learner

TABLE 8.3 Examples of Outcomes

Objective	Outcome
The learner will dress	Being presentable to others; being comfortable for the activities of the day
The learner will use public transportation	Having mobility in the community
The learner will read at the fourth-grade level	Locating information without assistance; having no embarrassment at being illiterate
The learner will use five leisure facilities external to home and job	Enjoying leisure time; potential to make friends; opportunity to develop new skills
The learner will participate in classroom activities	Being part of the group; earning teacher praise; getting better grades
The learner will explain his or her rights if arrested	Getting legal representation if needed; getting treated with greater respect

to control his or her own performance of the skills required to meet the objective.

A statement of mastery criteria does three things:

1. it tells how many times the instructor should observe "correct" performance of a skill before assuming that the learner has acquired it;
2. it tells how many and what kinds of errors the instructor will accept *after* the learner has reached the performance criterion for the program objective; and
3. it specifies when all forms of instruction toward the objective can stop.

An example of mastery criteria appears in Table 8.1. It states that when the instructional staff observes the learner scramble eggs eight consecutive times without error or assistance, they can assume that he or she has mastered all the skill clusters inherent in this objective. At that point, the learner will require no further instruction toward this objective.

An instructor should be very reluctant to stop instruction the first time a learner performs successfully. At this point, most learners with mental retardation probably are just beginning to meet a program objective, and learner behavior still can be erratic for a period of time. For example, learners often perform a skill cluster correctly a few times and then forget to watch for some important cues or to coordinate their actions properly. Sometimes learners become lackadaisical, and if they have not yet developed a solid behavioral pattern, their performance may deteriorate. The first time a learner performs a skill cluster successfully, he or she usually has not had enough practice using it, and probably does not control it yet. Therefore, it is typical for an instructor to require several successful performances before being willing to

stop teaching. The instructor can use these trials to help the learner further refine skills and to correct any errors that throw performance off target.

Establishing Mastery Criteria

In establishing the mastery criteria, the instructor should consider the four variables found in Table 8.4.

Complexity of Skills.   Learners will have more difficulty mastering complicated program objectives than simple ones, and the more severe the retardation, the greater the difficulty they will have. As a general rule, the more complex the behavior, the more successive repetitions the instructor should require before ending instruction. Thus, an instructor who is teaching a fairly basic skill cluster, like putting on a coat or making a sandwich for lunch, may be able to stop teaching after just a few correct repetitions of the skill, but an instructor who is teaching a more complicated skill cluster, like traveling around a big city using several different public conveyances, may want to see errorless performance for a longer time before stopping instruction.

Level of Functioning.   When teaching learners who have difficulty acquiring and retaining information, instructors should be very reluctant to stop teaching after just a few successful repetitions. The more difficulty the learners have, the greater the need for them to demonstrate continued competence before ending instruction. Of course, there are always times when such learners acquire skill clusters rapidly and dependably, but in general,

TABLE 8.4 Considerations for Establishing Mastery Criteria

When thinking about mastery criteria, the instructor must consider
- the complexity of the skills;
- the level of learner functioning;
- the number of opportunities the learner has to practice the skills; and
- any dangers that may be inherent in performing the skills.

the fact that some learners take longer to solidify their skill performance must be taken into account when setting mastery criteria.

Amount of Practice. The amount of practice learners get in using skills during the course of their daily routines may also be a factor in setting mastery criteria. When learners are acquiring skills that people perform regularly in the course of their daily lives, frequent practice may reduce the number of observations required to convince the instructor that they have acquired the skills. For example, when teaching a learner to make a bed, the fact that the learner can practice this skill cluster every day might allow the instructor to end instruction if the learner makes the bed correctly five days in a row without error and without prompts. Conversely, when a learner has opportunities to perform skills only occasionally, more repetitions may be necessary because the intervening time may allow the learner to forget the skills. For example, when teaching a learner to make a pizza, it may not be practical to work on the objective more than once every other week or so, and less often in certain settings. Under these circumstances, the learner will probably forget some things between instructional sessions, and the instructor may not be able to stop teaching until the learner has made ten or more pizzas without errors and without assistance.

Dangerous Skills. Some program objectives may place learners at risks of cuts, burns, falls, and trauma of many sorts. When teaching skills like these, the instructor must see to it that the learner meets the three conditions in Table 8.5 before ending supervision of the learner's performance. *If any one of these conditions are not met, the instructor should not allow the learner to perform the skill unsupervised.*

When teaching a skill that may present danger to the learner and/or others, the rule of thumb is to require enough supervised performance to ensure that the learner can perform the skill flawlessly and with complete self-assurance before removing supervision. For example, if a learner is learning to use an industrial table saw, the instructor may want to watch the learner perform a cutting operation several hundred times before walking away.

Settings and Circumstances

The settings and circumstances for a program objective must appear on the cover sheet. This list does two things:

1. it establishes the conditions under which the learners will perform the skills clusters after instruction is complete; and

TABLE 8.5 Three Conditions for Allowing Learners to Perform Potentially Dangerous Skills Unsupervised

1. The learner follows all safety rules and procedures.
2. The learner performs the behavior in the way it is supposed to be performed.
3. The learner understands the possibly dangerous outcomes of the objective.

    2. it lets other people know where and when the learners can be expected to perform the skill clusters, and by omission, where and when they might not be expected to perform them in the absence of further instruction.

The settings and circumstances under which a learner will meet the program objectives will greatly affect how the learner must perform the skill cluster. For example, there are major differences between the way in which learners would cross a busy city's downtown street at noon and the way they would cross a street late in the evening in a small town after all the stores have closed.

An instructor may choose to teach a learner to perform a program objective under different conditions from those in which he or she must perform after instruction is complete. However, instruction carried out in this manner should be considered preliminary, not final. For persons with mental retardation, it is necessary to make sure that any skills they learn out of the context they are able to transfer to the appropriate settings and circumstances before ending instruction.

Tools and Materials

Program objectives often require a learner to use a set of tools and materials. A *tool* is anything the learner uses to perform a skill, and *material* is anything consumed while performing the skill. In washing dishes, the sponges, dishcloths, and dishwasher are tools, while the water and soap are materials. An example of a list of tools and materials appears on the cover page in Table 8.1.

It is important to recognize that the choice of tools and materials can dramatically affect how the learner meets a program objective; therefore, instructors must select them carefully. For example, learners will have to learn to perform very different behaviors when washing dishes under the following conditions:

- in a sink filled with soapy water and using a sponge or a dishrag;
- with a sponge on a stick with a hollow handle that is filled with soap; and
- with a dishwasher.

For many program objectives, the circumstances will dictate which tools and materials the learner must use: They should be the ones that are most readily available when instruction is complete. For example, if learners live in a house that has a dishwasher, they should learn to use it.

Instructors often have considerable discretion over the selection of tools and materials that learners might use to meet an objective, and sometimes may need to find special tools and materials to solve a performance problem presented by a specific learner. For example, people with limitations in strength and dexterity often need special tools to perform even the most mundane skills, like buttoning a shirt or filling a glass with juice. The guiding principle for deciding whether to have the learner use common or uncommon tools or materials is that the more closely the person's performance resembles that of other people, the greater that person's potential to "fit in" to a setting. Thus, tools and materials should be selected to make the learner's behavior seem as typical as possible. For example, in the community in which the authors live, it is preferable to teach a person who does not drive a car to take a taxi to the grocery store rather than ride a bicycle. The reason is that people in our community tend to not ride bicycles to the grocery store, but frequently use a taxi service. In another community, however, it might be preferable for learners to use a bicycle to go to the grocery store because that is the way many people do it there. Therefore, as is true of all other aspects of performance, learners should be taught to use the tools and materials that are commonly used by others in the community whenever possible.

It is sometimes necessary to develop special kinds of tools, especially for learners with severe physical or sensory disabilities. For example, learners who have problems grasping objects may need to use a special tool to turn a doorknob or button a shirt. Other learners may need special jigs to hold tools and materials steady when they perform an assembly procedure in a factory. Instructors in rehabilitation services have been building special tools and jigs for many years. Indeed, rehabilitation engineering is a specialty that focuses on precisely this activity, and we encourage instructors to seek the assistance of people in this specialty area when they work with learners who have physical or sensory problems that severely limit their behavioral repertoires.

Instructors

A note should appear on the cover sheet listing all those who are involved in teaching the program objective. This information could assist another instructor who is considering whether to use the analysis to teach another learner or learners. That instructor can check with the staff who used it before to find out what their experiences were and whether any modifications should be made in the analysis.

Sign-Off

The last entry on the cover sheet is for signing off on the objective. When an instructor signs this line and dates it, he or she certifies that the learner has met the objective and can perform all the skill clusters in the list. The cover sheet can then be separated from the rest of the analysis and placed in the learner's file for future reference. This sheet can assist both in record keeping and setting expectations for learner performance. The latter is especially useful for events such as the arrival of new staff and the departure of old staff because a review of the file can bring the new staff quickly up to date.

Skill Cluster Analysis

The second part of the work sheet is designed to help instructors perform a skill cluster analysis. A **skill cluster analysis** describes, in more or less detail, the specific skills a learner must have to achieve the program objective. The result of a skill cluster analysis will be a behavior pattern that is similar to the behavior pattern developed for a curriculum goal. It is different from that behavior pattern in two ways:

1. it is for a program objective rather than a curriculum goal; and
2. it lists the individual skills separately rather than in paragraph form.

To perform a skill cluster analysis, the instructor considers the major skill clusters and works out a behavior pattern in much the same way that curriculum developers work out one for a curriculum goal (see Chapter 5). Then the instructor makes a list of the specific skills and cues required to perform each major skill cluster and lists the skills in the sequence in which the learner must perform them (Knapczyk, 1975). The result is a list of skills that are numbered.

Note that the list of egg-scrambling skills in Table 8.1 has five divisions that correspond to the list of major skill clusters on the cover page. Note, too, how the list provides an accurate description of how the learner will perform the skills that are required to scramble eggs successfully and that the skills appear in the sequence in which the learner must perform them. This description includes clear information on matters such as how the learners should use a "church key" can opener to make holes in a can of condensed milk and how the learners must hold the eggs in order to crack them and have them fall into the bowl. The analysis gives instructors a complete list of skills the learners must have in order to scramble eggs.

To perform a skill cluster analysis, the instructor finds a way for the learner to perform major skill cluster, and lists the skills in the sequence in which the learner should perform them. The list must account for the following three variables:

1. behavior pattern;
2. skills; and
3. cues.

The list of skills found in the second part of Table 8.1 provides an example of what the results of an analysis might look like. However, the reader should remember that "a skill" may be different for each individual learner (see Chapter 3) and that each learner may require a different list of skills for each major skill cluster. Consequently, each skill cluster analysis is unique.

Describing Behavior Patterns

When doing a skill cluster analysis, the whole is truly greater than the sum of its parts: Individual behaviors do not occur in a vacuum, but rather are affected by other behaviors in the pattern. In fact, the same behavior may be performed in very different ways when it is embedded in two different patterns. For example, the behavior of snapping one's fingers is different when it appears in the context of calling a dog than when it appears as part of certain dances. Variations occur in things like the number of snaps, the rhythm of the snaps, the position of the hands, and the position of the rest of the body.

Pike (1967) once pointed out that individual behaviors performed in a pattern are analogous to ocean waves. When we look at the ocean and see the crests of the waves, it is easy to discriminate one wave from another. But when we look at the troughs between waves, it is difficult to tell where one wave ends and another begins. In a similar manner, a skill cluster analysis lists the different behaviors in a behavior pattern separately, but when people perform the pattern, the behaviors tend to flow together and it is difficult to tell where one stops and another begins. For example, consider the analysis of a somersault in Table 8.6. It is very difficult to observe where the behavior "push with legs" ends and the behavior "begin roll on back of head" begins. Although the two behaviors are different from one another, the point at which one ends and the other begins is blurred. The distinctions between most behaviors performed in patterns are similarly blurred. This fact suggests that learners not only must acquire individual behaviors, but also, that they must learn to perform behaviors in patterns in which the behaviors flow together in a smooth and well-integrated manner.

Instructors can often teach learners with mental retardation to perform entire behavior patterns as a unit. But when learners have trouble understanding what they are supposed to do, an instructor should be able to separate the behaviors for instructional purposes. Once separated, the instructor can teach each skill individually to the learners if necessary, and afterwards, teach the learners how to link the behaviors together in a well-integrated, smoothly performed pattern. This two-stage approach can make very complicated skill clusters much easier for some learners to acquire.

Behavior patterns are most accessible for instructional purposes when they are described according to the five guidelines found in Table 8.7.

Behavior Patterns Should Contain Only the List of Skills the Learner Must Perform to Meet the Objective

When first performing an analysis, some instructors want to describe the things that *they* plan to do during instruction (e.g., "tell the learner to stand straight" or "place the learner's hands on the mat"). But an instructor who

TABLE 8.6 List of Skills for "Performing a Somersault" for Seven-Year-Old Children with Moderate Mental Retardation and No Restrictions in Mobility

Skills

1. Stand on edge of mat.
2. Spread legs 20″ apart.
3. Squat to balance point.
4. Place both hands on mat, 10″ in front of feet.
5. Lean forward to new balance point.
6. Lower chin as far as possible toward chest.
7. Push with legs.
8. Begin roll on back of head.
9. Move hands to center line when shoulders touch mat.
10. Straighten arms when back touches mat.
11. Straighten legs when buttocks touch mat.
12. Stop roll when heels touch mat.
13. Stand when roll is complete.
14. Return to edge of mat.

TABLE 8.7 Guidelines for Selecting a Performance Pattern During a Skill Cluster Analysis

A performance pattern should
- indicate what learners must do, not what instructors do;
- list the sequence of skills in the order in which they should occur;
- indicate the way in which the learners will perform each skill;
- show how skills are interrelated; and
- account for the conditions of performance.

does so ignores the basic principle that it is the learner's behavior we must understand, not the instructor's. It is only after we examine the skills that the learner must perform that we can begin to focus on the problem of how to get the learner's performance to improve. Note that the steps listed in the various examples throughout this chapter describe what the learner should do and make no mention of what the instructor will do.

Behavior Patterns Should List the Sequence of Skills in the Order in Which They Should Occur

The instructors should list the individual skills in the behavior pattern in the order in which the learner will perform them when instruction is complete. The list will then provide a clear description of the sequence of behaviors the learner will perform to meet the objective. For example, Table 8.6 shows the sequence of steps necessary for a learner to perform a somersault.

*Behavior Patterns Should Indicate the Manner
in Which the Learner Will Perform Each Skill*

The manner in which any individual performs a skill is not necessarily the way anyone else would do it, and most skills can be performed in more than one way. The reader who looks closely at how other people achieve program objectives will quickly see that they use many techniques to perform even the most common skill, such as tying their shoelaces, fixing a sandwich, or washing one's face. The patterns that some people use to perform the most ordinary skill clusters can be quite remarkable and creative.

The instructional implication of using different behavior patterns to accomplish program objectives is that learners can meet the requirements of the objectives in alternative ways, either by using a different set of actions or by changing the order or the timing of their behaviors. Some of these ways may be defined very narrowly by the circumstances in which the learners will use their skills, such as when a learner must always take the same bus to school. But learners may have considerable leeway in how they do things such as getting dressed for work or making their lunch, as long as they accomplish the major skill clusters of the objective.

When instructors plan instruction, they usually have a number of choices about which behavior patterns they can teach to a specific learner. In most cases, it is best to teach the most commonly used patterns to meet the objective, but instructions should consider exceptions to this rule if the results might benefit a learner. Instructors often must explore alternative ways to accomplish objectives that might be easier for learners with physical, sensory, or severe cognitive limitations.

Behavior Patterns Should Show How Skills Are Interrelated

The behavior pattern should highlight the interrelationship among the individual skills that make up the pattern. These interrelationships are often essential to meeting an objective because each behavior tends to affect the performance of the behaviors that come before and after it. Teaching learners about the interrelationships among their actions will help them make the necessary refinements in their behavior. For example, when performing a somersault (see Table 8.6), pushing with the legs actually puts the learner in the correct position to begin the forward roll. The links between balancing and pushing allow the learner to modify speed and body position. Thus, the learner could plan and adjust the speed of the roll based on how well he or she is expected to control the location and position of the landing. The instructor can teach the connections among behaviors like these as part of instructional lessons and activities.

Behavior Patterns Should Account for the Conditions of Performance

The conditions under which a learner meets a program objective include any environmental factors that would give meaning and purpose to the learner's actions. The context within which behavior patterns occur usually affects the manner in which the individual actions are performed and linked together because it defines the overall purpose or function that the actions must have. To illustrate, performing a somersault is likely to be done quite differently when "fooling around" in the gym than when performing floor exercises in a gymnastic meet. The actions involved in performing somersaults during the gymnastics meet must be more planned and precise than those that take place during play.

Skills

Not all learners will be able to achieve program objectives based on the same skill cluster analysis. Therefore, the list of skills may have to be different for different learners. For example, let us consider the analysis of the skills for the objective "the learner will put on a pair of pants" that appears in Table 8.8. This analysis was developed for young children with moderate mental retardation who have no extraordinary physical or sensory disabilities. Note that the list of skills is relatively detailed and quite clear about what these learners must do and the sequence in which they must do it.

Table 8.9 presents a different analysis of the same objective. This analysis was performed for a slightly older child with severe mental retardation. Since this learner had more difficulty processing information, what was considered a "skill" for the first set of learners would contain too much information for this learner to process, and the instructor had to develop greater detail in the skill cluster analysis. Note that it focuses on the same objective as Table 8.8, but the skills are much smaller and the analysis more detailed.

Even the analysis in Table 8.9 may not be sufficient to allow instruction to take place smoothly and efficiently for some learners. Although the skills are very small and the analysis very detailed, it is possible to create more detail if needed. Table 8.10 contains an analysis for a teenager who has been institutionalized all his life and who has very little experience in doing things for himself. The analysis found in Table 8.10 focuses on just one aspect of putting on pants: fastening the flat hook on a pair of pants. It illustrates how instructors can create as much detail in an analysis as they need to plan a learner's instruction.

The first and subsequent attempts to do an analysis of a program objective always are an educated guess (Gold, 1980a). Experienced instructors who know a learner well can be quite correct in their first analysis, but they can miss, too (e.g., they might list skills that are too large or too small for a learner to aquire). Such mistakes present no problem as long as the instructors are aware of the learner's instructional needs and make the necessary revisions when the need arises (see Chapter 11).

In many cases, the list of critical functions provides enough detail for instruction to proceed smoothly and efficiently, especially when only one instructor carries out instruction. But even learners with mild mental retardation may require skill analyses for complicated program objectives. When it is necessary to perform an analysis for a learner, the major factor in making

TABLE 8.8 List of Skills for "Putting on Pants" for Five-Year-Old Children with Moderate Mental Retardation

1. Pick up pants by waistband.
2. Orient zipper away from body.
3. Sit.
4. Put right leg into right pants leg.
5. Put left leg into left pants leg.
6. Push feet through cuffs.
7. Stand.
8. Pull pants to waist.
9. Tuck in shirt.
10. Fasten hook.
11. Zip zipper.

TABLE 8.9 List of Skills for "Putting on Pants" for an Eight-Year-Old Child with Severe Mental Retardation

A. *Orient Pants*
  1. Pick up pants with one hand.
  2. Shake to unfold and loosen.
  3. Locate waistband.
  4. Grasp pants by waistband with other hand.
  5. Release first hand grasp.
  6. Locate zipper visually.
  7. Grasp waistband 90° to the (left) of zipper with first hand (zipper should now be away from learner's body).
  8. Release second hand grasp.
  9. Grasp waistband 180° from point at which first hand is grasping.
B. *Put Legs in Pants*
  10. Sit on chair or edge of bed.
  11. Lower waistband to within 4″ of floor.
  12. Raise right foot 8″ off floor.
  13. Move waistband toward chair (bed, etc.) until right leg opening is under foot.
  14. Place right foot on right leg opening.
  15. Place foot into leg hole.
  16. Pull waistband up to knee while pushing foot into hole.
  17. Lower foot to floor and allow it to rest there.
  18. Lower waistband to ankle level of right foot.
  19. Repeat 12–16 for left foot.
  20. Raise right foot 8″ off floor (both feet now off the floor).
  21. Pull waistband over knees and up thighs as far as possible.
  22. Lower both feet to floor.
  23. Release both grasps on waistband.
  24. Grasp pant leg on right leg about 4″ below knee with both hands.
  25. Raise right leg about 4″ off floor.
  26. Point toes forward.
  27. Pull pant leg toward thigh until foot clears cuff of pant leg.
  28. Lower foot to floor.
  29. Release grasp on pant leg.

30. Repeat 24–29 for left foot.

C. *Pull Pants to Waist*

31. Grasp waistband at sides of body, one hand on each side.
32. Stand.
33. Pull waistband up over hips to waist.

D. *Tuck in Shirttail*

34. Spread feet 18″–24″ apart to support pants while tucking shirt.
35. Release left hand grasp.
36. Cross left hand over to right front and grasp waistband.
37. Release right hand grasp.
38. Grasp shirttail on right side at bottom with right hand.
39. Insert inside waistband so that shirttail hangs smoothly (adjust if necessary).
40. Release left hand grasp.
41. Cross right hand over to left front and grasp waistband.
42. With left hand, grasp shirttail on left side at bottom.
43. Insert inside waistband so that shirttail hangs smoothly (adjust if necessary).
44. Release right hand grasp.
45. With right hand, grasp waistband at right rear.
46. Cross left hand behind back and grasp shirttail at right rear bottom.
47. Insert into waistband so that shirttail hangs smoothly (adjust if necessary).
48. With left hand, grasp left rear waistband.
49. Cross right hand behind back and grasp left rear shirttail.
50. Insert into waistband so that shirttail hangs smoothly (adjust if necessary).
51. Release left hand grasp.

E. *Hook Pants*

52. Grasp front of waistband with left thumb 1″ from left edge of male hook.
53. Release right hand grasp.
54. Grasp front of waistband with right hand (ball of thumb should be directly under female hook).
55. Move right hand to the left until the female hook is beyond the male hook.
56. Align male and female hooks horizontally.
57. Move left hand toward the body until male hook touches waistband.
58. Allow right hand to slide to the right until hooks engage.
59. Release right hand grasp.

F. *Zip Zipper*

60. With right hand, locate zipper tab by touch.
61. Grasp tab with pincer grasp.
62. Lift left hand 2″ raising waistband.
63. Pull zipper tab to the top of its run.
64. Release right hand grasp.
65. Move tab to its "lock" position using index finger of right hand.
66. Release left hand grasp.

TABLE 8.10 Increased Detail for "Hooking Flat Hook Pants Fastener" for a Fourteen-Year-Old Adolescent with Profound Mental Retardation Who Has Been Institutionalized

(Note: On pants for males, the male hook is on the left and the female hook is on the right of waistband.)

1. Locate male hook.
2. Place thumb and fingers of left hand in opposition.
3. Place thumb of left hand inside waistband, 1″ to left of male hook.
4. Pincer grasp waistband securely.
5. Release right hand grasp on waistband (from previous steps).
6. Locate female hook.
7. Place right thumb inside waistband.
8. Touch right thumb to waistband directly under female hook.
9. Place fingers of right hand on outside of waistband, ½″ to right of female hook, and form secure scissors grasp against first knuckle of index finger.
10. Move right side of waistband to the left until female hook is 1″ to the left of male hook.
11. Touch female hook to inside of left waistband.
12. Align female hook with male hook.
13. Allow right side of waistband to slip to the right until hooks almost touch.
14. Recheck alignment of hooks.
15. If alignment is okay, allow right side of waistband to complete its travel to the right; if alignment is not okay, repeat steps 10–13.
16. Release right hand grasp when hooks engage.

the initial attempt is the instructor's perception of what constitutes "a skill" for that specific learner or group of learners. Learners who acquire information easily usually can handle larger skills, and learners who acquire information with difficulty may require objectives to be broken down into much smaller skills or even individual movements. The challenge for the instructor is to strike a balance between developing too much and too little detail so that instruction can proceed smoothly and efficiently. If the skills are too small, the learner may get bored; even worse, the learner may become so dependent on the instructor that he or she is not able to attain the objective. On the other hand, if the instructor makes the skills include too much, the learner may have difficulty comprehending what he or she is required to do and either flail about in confusion or lose his or her incentive to learn. The balance point between too little and too much detail will vary from learner to learner and from circumstance to circumstance.

Analyzing Cues

Cues are features in the environment that indicate how, when, where, with whom, with what, how much, how often, in what order (and so forth) to perform either a behavior pattern or the actions in the pattern. There are two types of cues that relate to program objectives: behavioral cues and situational cues. Instructors should describe both types of cues when they analyze skill clusters.

Behavioral Cues

Behavioral cues indicate when specific behaviors should occur in a pattern. They are the movements, forms, sounds, previous behaviors, and other perceptually identifiable features in the environment that give people information about when, where, with whom, with what, how often, how far, in what order, and so on to perform *each behavior* in the pattern. For example, when riding a bus, certain landmarks indicate when it is time to get off the bus; and when locking a door, an audible click or the feel of a key hitting the detent tells when to stop turning the key. When a learner comes to recognize features such as these and relate them to specific actions, they become behavioral cues. For example, in reference to Table 8.6, learners performing somersaults must learn to recognize specific cues that tell them how much to squat, when to begin the roll, and how fast to push off with their feet. They must also learn that they cannot push with their legs until after they squat and lower their chins to their chests, and that they cannot do a complete roll until they first feel their heads touch the mat and then feel their backs touch it. When they are able to perceive these and other cues and relate them to their behaviors, they will be able to do somersaults.

Describing Behavioral Cues

Table 8.11 repeats the list of steps for doing a somersault found in Table 8.6 but separates the behaviors from the behavioral cues in each statement. Note that each skill in the analysis contains at least one behavior and one cue: The only exception to this rule occurs when the cues are so self-evident that there is no need to list them, such as in Step 3 in Table 8.8, in which the behavior is to "Sit." That is, sitting behavior is so obvious that it does not require the instructor to list the cue unless the sitting must take place in a specific location or occur in a specific manner, such as "in the lotus position."

Whatever the cues to which the learner must attend, the statement of cues in the list of skills should always be stated from the instructor's perspective. To illustrate what we mean, note that Skill 2 in Table 8.11 states that the learner is to "spread legs 20 inches." It is unlikely that any learner will ever use a ruler to measure how far apart his or her feet are placed or even think about whether they are "20 inches apart." Rather, the learner will have a different set of cues, such as certain muscle tensions in his or her legs and body when in the correct stance. But the *instructor* must be able to see that the learner's feet are placed at the appropriate distance from each other; thus, the cue is stated so the instructor will know what to look for when the learner tries to perform the behavior. Learners will come to identify their own internal behavioral cues and their relation to the behaviors in the pattern when the instructor ensures the following:

- that the learners can perform the behavior correctly; and
- that the learners have sufficient practice to gain proficiency in using the pattern.

TABLE 8.11 Separation of Behaviors and Cues in the Skill Cluster Analysis for Doing a Somersault

Skill #	Behavior	Cue
1.	Stand	on *edge* of mat.
2.	Spread legs	*20" apart.*
3.	Squat	to *balance point.*
4.	Place hands	on *mat, 10" in front of* feet.
5.	Lean forward	to *new balance point.*
6.	Lower chin	as far as possible toward *chest.*
7.	Push	with *legs.*
8.	Begin roll	on *back of head.*
9.	Move hands	to *center line,* when *shoulders* touch *mat.*
10.	Straighten arms	when *back* touches *mat.*
11.	Straighten legs	when *buttocks* touch *mat.*
12.	Stop roll	when *heels* touch *mat.*
13.	Stand	when roll is *complete.*
14.	Return	to *edge* of mat.

Under these conditions, they will learn when, where, in what sequence, and so forth to perform each of the individual behaviors.

Situational Cues

The second type of cue is the situational cue. Unlike the behavioral cue, which informs the learners when or where (etc.) to perform each step in the list of skills, the **situational cue** informs learners about when to perform the skill clusters themselves. That is, these cues indicate when, where, with whom, and so forth to perform the behavior pattern itself.

Situational cues are external to the behavioral pattern and indicate the conditions under which program objectives apply. They trigger the performance of the pattern by signaling the need to use it. Examples appear in Table 8.12. One example, going to the store to buy a loaf of bread, consists of a series of behaviors performed in relation to a set of behavioral cues. However, over and above these cues, the lack of bread in the house provides a situational cue that indicates that it is time to go to the store and buy some more bread. Note that the list of settings and circumstances on the cover sheet generally provides an appropriate and sufficient statement of situational cues.

It is just as necessary to teach situational cues as it is to teach any other aspect of performance. Situational cues indicate the various circumstances under which particular behavior patterns are to be used, and learners who learn how and when to watch for them will have a framework for transferring skills to settings and situations other than those in which instruction takes place.

The authors have found many instances in which learners were taught to perform skills, but were not taught when, where, or under what circumstances to use them. As a result, their knowledge of how to perform the skills

TABLE 8.12 Potential Situational Cues

Skill	Potential Situational Cues
Get dressed	Awakening in the morning Completing a shower Leaving the beach
Mow the grass	Sunny Saturday morning Shaggy grass Return from vacation
Go on a movie date	Arrival of weekend Possession of sufficient money Friend agrees to a date
Prepare breakfast	Breakfast time Hunger
Answer telephone	Ringing telephone
Buy bread	Lack of bread in the house Friday trip to grocery store
Shave	Completion of shower Presence of facial hair Morning routine

did not contribute much to their ability to participate effectively in community settings where these skills would have been useful. Instruction that focuses on responding to situational cues will provide learners with the background they need to decide whether or not to use their skills. Thus, an important benefit of making a list of settings and circumstances for an analysis of program objectives is the aid it gives the instructor in teaching learners with mental retardation to transfer or generalize their performance to settings other than the ones in which they learned it. Such instruction will foster performance in all the settings and situations to which the objective applies.

When to Do Skill Cluster Analyses

The reader will recall from Chapter 2 that people with mental retardation need instruction to help them learn to do what others generally learn to do in the absence of formal instruction. The technique of skill cluster analysis is based on the presumption that when compared to others, people with mental retardation have difficulty doing two things: (1) sorting through all the information in their environment that tells them what to do and when to do it, and (2) interpreting information that would help them develop new skills. The more severe the mental retardation, the greater the difficulty a person has in doing these things.

We have found that it is necessary to teach directly and deliberately many (if not most) of the skills that people with mental retardation need in order to live productive and independent lives in their communities.

Therefore, instructors should do three things in order to teach people with mental retardation:

1. sort through all the information in the learners' environment;
2. figure out what bits of that information the learners need in order to acquire necessary skills; and
3. present the information to them in a form they can understand and use.

A skill cluster analysis focuses on the first two of these steps and helps to identify the specific skills and cues that a learner needs in order to perform the skill clusters in a program objective.

However, it is not always necessary to perform a skill cluster analysis. As a general rule, an analysis is necessary only when one or more of the following three conditions are present:

1. the learner(s) have difficulty discovering the information they need by themselves;
2. the learners must use a special behavior pattern; and/or
3. more than one instructor is going to provide the instruction.

If the learners can acquire the information they need when the instructors work directly from the list of major skill clusters, analysis beyond this level is unnecessary. But the presence of any one of the three conditions listed above indicates the need for a skill cluster analysis.

Difficulty Discovering Information

Anytime learners have difficulty figuring out what to do for themselves, someone will have to figure it out for them (Gold, 1980a). Under these circumstances, instructors will usually have to go beyond the list of major skill clusters and develop a list of the specific skills for performing a program objective. Thus, instructors are likely to have to develop a relatively detailed list of skills for learners with severe and profound mental retardation because these learners have great difficulty identifying the information they need. On the other hand, if and when learners with mild retardation need a skill cluster analysis, they tend to need fewer and less detailed lists of skills than people who function at lower levels.

Special Behavior Patterns

In Chapter 5 we discussed the concept of special behavior patterns. Just as is true for curriculum goals, learners sometimes must use special behavior patterns to attain program objectives. An individual learner who has a physical or sensory disability, has difficulty processing information, or lacks prerequisites may be a candidate for a special behavior pattern and a skill cluster analysis.

Everyone who is involved in teaching a learner should agree on a special behavior pattern before instruction begins because the learner who uses it usually may not be able to generalize it to many circumstances other than the one in which it is taught. Any limitations in performance that accompany the use of a special behavior pattern should be made clear before instruction begins. A description of how the learner will perform the skill cluster also will help other persons understand what the learner is supposed to do. Thus, anytime that a learner needs a special behavior pattern, an analysis of skill clusters serves to facilitate communication and perhaps forestalls any counterproductive instruction that can decrease independence.

Multiple Instructors

A skill cluster analysis can also help prevent instructional variations when more than one instructor teaches a learner to do something. For example, both a job coach and a residential staff member may teach travel skills to a learner. Given a written skill cluster analysis, both instructors will know what the learner is supposed to do and how he or she is supposed to do it, and each instructor can teach the learner to perform the travel skills the same way and in the same sequence. Under these conditions, learning can proceed smoothly and efficiently.

Must the Analysis Be Written?

Instructors who have performed analyses of skill clusters for awhile will become very skilled at figuring out the proper amount of detail. In a relatively short time, it becomes possible to do an analysis "in one's head," and the temptation is to not bother to write it down. In general, however, instructors should resist this temptation and write out every analysis they perform. A written analysis not only provides a record of the work the instructor did, it makes that work available for future use. It also provides the foundation for coordinating teaching activities with other instructors and for achieving consistency in the skills the learners must perform. That is, when analyses are written, all the instructors who work on the same program objective can make sure they are teaching the learners to meet the same performance requirements in a consistent and well-coordinated manner. In addition, other instructors who teach a learner may be able to think of a better way for that learner to meet the objective, and a written analysis will allow them to provide suggestions.

Other Examples

The examples we have provided show analyses that might be useful for persons with moderate and severe mental retardation. Tables 8.13 and 8.14 present two more examples, but these were developed for persons with mild mental retardation and illustrate the level of detail that might be appropriate for learners in this group.

TABLE 8.13 Going on a Movie Date

Objective: The learners will ask for date. If accepted, they will bring date to a movie; get snack after movie; and return date to her home

Learners: Mildly retarded 17-year-old high school students with no visual or orthopedic restrictions

Major Skill Clusters: Note: Standard times are not appropriate for this analysis.

_____	1.	Ask for date
_____	2.	Leave home at appropriate time
_____	3.	Pick up girl
_____	4.	Go to movie
_____	5.	Get snack
_____	6.	Return to girl's house
_____	7.	Return home

Standards: The learner will bring girl to movie in time to watch entire movie; he will engage in appropriate conversation during travel and snack; saying "good night" will take place outside house and will not exceed ten minutes; he will return home after leaving girl at her home.

Outcomes: Boys will be able to find and make female friends

Conditions: When the boy meets a girl he likes and would like to get to know better

Tools and Materials: Sufficient money for movie, bus, and snack

Mastery Criteria: Three consecutive dates

Instructor: _____

Completion Certified by: _____

Date: _____

List of Skills

A. *Asking for Date*
1. Contact girl by phone or in person at school.
2. Ask for date on specified evening.
3. Wait for confirmation or denial.
4. If girl answers "yes," decide which movie to see.

B. *Leaving Home*
5. In early afternoon, check movie time and decide which bus to take.
6. Inform date of pickup time by telephone.
7. On evening of date, obtain sufficient funds from money storage.
8. Take bus to date's house.
9. Knock on door and
   a. state reason for presence to person answering, or
   b. greet date if she answers door.
10. Take bus to movie.

C. *Going to Movie*
11. Purchase tickets and enter movie.
12. Leave when movie is over.

D. *Purchasing Snack*
13. Mutually select restaurant and enter it.
14. Purchase snack and consume.
15. Leave restaurant.

E. *Returning Home*
16. Take bus to girl's house.
17. Say "good night" at door.
18. Leave when girl enters house.
19. Take bus home.

TABLE 8.14 Skill Analysis for Shaving with an Electric Razor

Objective: The learners will shave facial hair with an electric razor
Learners: Moderately retarded 15-year-olds with no uncorrected visual or orthopedic deficits
Critical Functions:

_____ 1. Assemble tools and materials (1 min.)
_____ 2. Shave facial hair (3 min.)
_____ 3. Store tools and materials (1 min.)

Standards: The learner's face will be devoid of hair when viewed from conversational distance (arm's length)
Outcomes: The learner will be presentable for work and social occasions
Mastery Criteria: Five consecutive mornings with no errors and no assistance
Conditions: At home, in the morning before going to work
Tools and Materials: Electric razor; odorless preshave lotion; aftershave lotion; bathroom cabinet with mirror; electric outlet
Instructor: _____
Completion Certified by:

_____

Date: _____

List of Skills

A. *Assemble Tools and Materials*
  1. Remove razor from storage and place on countertop.
  2. Remove preshave and aftershave lotion from storage and place on countertop.
B. *Shave*
  3. Pour quarter-sized amount of preshave lotion into palm of hand.
  4. Rub hands together and rub beard with wet hands.
  5. Plug razor into outlet and turn switch on razor to "on" position.
  6. Starting at center bottom of throat, shave neck on right side.
  7. Return to center bottom of throat and shave neck on left side.
  8. Starting at center bottom of chin, shave right side of face.
  9. Return to center bottom of chin and shave left side of face.
  10. Shave under nose.
  11. Turn razor switch to "off" position and put razor down on counter.
  12. Pour quarter-size amount of aftershave lotion into palm and rub on shaved area.
  13. Rinse and wipe hands.
C. *Storing Tools and Materials*
  14. Return razor to storage area.
  15. Return preshave and aftershave lotion to storage area.

Concluding Statement

By discussing how to analyze program objectives, this chapter begins our presentation of how to provide instruction to learners. By analyzing program objectives instructors determine precisely what learners must do to meet the objectives in their IPs. An analysis of program objectives includes the following information:

- the learners for whom the analysis was performed;
- the program objective;

- the critical functions;
- the outcomes;
- the standards and mastery criteria;
- the tools and materials; and
- the skill cluster analysis:
  - pattern,
  - behaviors, and
  - cues.

Preparing a work sheet that lays out the step-by-step process will assist instructors when planning their instruction and help them coordinate teaching activities.

CHAPTER 9

Providing Information

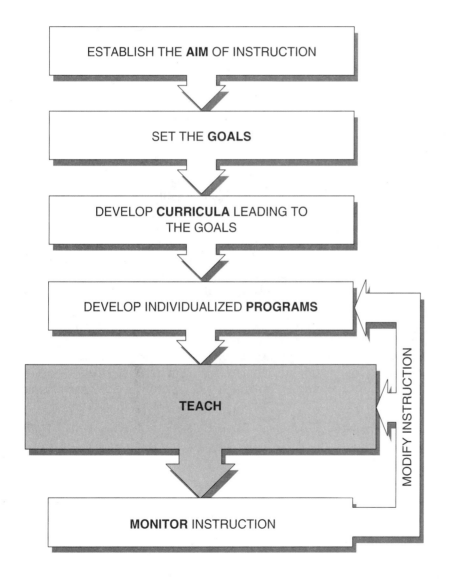

ESTABLISH THE **AIM** OF INSTRUCTION

SET THE **GOALS**

DEVELOP **CURRICULA** LEADING TO THE GOALS

DEVELOP INDIVIDUALIZED **PROGRAMS**

TEACH

MODIFY INSTRUCTION

MONITOR INSTRUCTION

TABLE 9.1 Techniques for Providing Information

To provide information to a learner an instructor can
- tell the learner what to do (verbal instructions);
- point to whatever the learner should attend to (gestures);
- show the learner what to do (demonstration);
- guide the learner's body through the motions (physical guidance); and/or
- have the learner find out what to do for himself or herself (learner search).

The next step in planning instruction is to find a way to deliver the content to the learner. Education libraries and instructional materials centers are full of books and manuals that focus on instructional methods, and when we look at the shelves, it may seem as if there are a million different ways to teach. As it turns out, there are actually only five ways to provide learners with the information they need to improve their skill levels (see Table 9.1). All teaching methods, techniques, and strategies described in the literature present variants of or combinations of one or more of these five procedures. In explaining them, we will present some guidelines and principles for choosing which procedure to use under a particular set of circumstances. Although we will discuss each technique separately, each of them can and should be used in combination with one another. In fact, it is quite natural to combine them while teaching.

The reader will note that this chapter, unlike most of the others, does not begin with a work sheet to fill out. In the final analysis, it is impossible to provide a rigid set of rules to guide the manner in which to give learners the information they need to meet program objectives. If one thinks of the analysis of curriculum and program objectives as the science of instruction, then providing information must be the art of teaching. The important thing about information techniques is not to state which ones *should* be used, but to know which ones *could* be used. The reason is that actual instruction depends, just as it always has, on an instructor who is sensitive to the learner's limitations, strengths, and needs and who understands the potential range of instructional possibilities. Thus, just as a painter needs to know what paints, brushes, and so forth are available, and just as a composer needs to know what the various musical instruments can do, an instructor needs to understand the possible techniques for providing information. Then, when it comes time to teach a particular skill to a particular learner, the instructor will be able to consider all the alternatives and employ the most appropriate ones.

Information Provision Techniques

Verbal Instructions

One way to provide information is to *tell* the learner what behaviors to exhibit, what cues to attend to, or what outcomes to expect as a result of performing the skill. Certainly, verbal instructions are often (but not always) the most economical technique in terms of the amount of information that can be provided at any moment and the size of the group to which verbal instructions can be addressed. That is, a verbal instruction can transmit one or many bits of information, and it can be directed toward a single person or to a large crowd of people. It is no wonder that verbal instructions seem to be the most basic, broadly applicable, and commonly used information provision technique.

Verbal instructions can be spoken or written.

The Spoken Word

For most learners in the United States, the primary language is English, but for others it may be sign language, Spanish, one of the Native American tribal languages, or any one of a number of other languages spoken in various communities across the country. Instructors will usually give verbal instructions in the language the learner understands most easily, at least until the learner has enough facility with spoken English to use it in his or her daily life. Whatever the language used, delivering instruction through the spoken word often allows the instructor to expend less energy than is true of other information transmission techniques and to deliver instruction across greater distances.

The instructor can transmit many different kinds and amounts of information through use of the spoken word. For example, any of the following statements could be made during instruction:

> "Here is the one you should use next."
> "The big one needs a push."
> "First the red one, then the blue one goes here."
> "Everyone who works faster gets a bonus."

Notice that each of the above examples is couched in a declarative form. But statements are not the only way to give information. Imperatives and questions can provide just as much information:

> "Hold the handle and wait until the flap closes."
> "Put that one on first."
> "Why don't we carry it over to the oven now?"
> "Think, now: Have you put them in the correct order?"

Note, too, that each of these verbal instructions contains information on both the individual behaviors or the behavioral pattern and the behavioral cues. Both types of information can be included in any verbal instruction, or they can be presented separately when it is advantageous to do so. Some variations in using verbal instruction are shown in Table 9.2.

Although some people may think it necessary to speak in "complete sentences," the only really important thing to do during instruction is to provide the information in a form the learner can understand. Note that many learners (especially those with severe mental retardation, but also many with mild mental retardation) find it difficult to process information when an instructor uses too many words in an instruction. For these learners it is

TABLE 9.2 The Use of Verbal Instructions for Different Types of Information

Information	Examples
Behaviors only	"Grab hold" "Stand up and walk"
Behavior pattern only	"Do all the steps in long division" "Be sure you turn the lights off when you leave"
Cues only	"Now the big one" "The bump is on top"
Outcomes only	"It's going to fall" "This is the best part: Now we can eat it"
Situational cues only	"Now it is time to take it out" "Listen for the click, then begin"
Combined situational cues and behavior patterns	"Don't stand until after you put it down" "When morning comes, take it out of the oven"
Combined behaviors and outcomes	"Prop it up or it will fall"

often necessary to reduce the instruction to its "bare-bones" content to allow them to process the information. For example, an instructor might tell a learner:

> "The green light tells you that the machine is on."

Because the grammar of such an instruction is complicated (it contains a subordinated clause), many learners with severe retardation would have trouble understanding it. We can reduce its complexity, however, by focusing on the essential information that must be transmitted:

> "Green light. Machine on."
> "Green light. Machine."
> "Light . . . on."

Only the two most essential bits of information are included in the latter statement. It is probable that this statement will have to be accompanied by a gesture or two (see the next section) and that the learner will have to be in the presence of both the light and the running machine in order to comprehend the information. But a learner who must have information truncated to such a degree would probably need these cues anyway.

Written Instructions

In a fundamental sense, writing is little more than speech made permanent (Hockett, 1958), and the difference between the spoken word and written instructions is mostly one of form, not structure. However, the ability to put instructions down on paper (or some other medium) enables instructors to remove the time, space, and location constraints inherent in the spoken word. That is, a spoken instruction usually requires both instructor and

TABLE 9.3 Guidelines for Using Verbal Instructions
• Use verbal instructions whenever possible.
• Limit instructions to essential information.
• Employ the best means of communicating with each learner.

learner to be in direct contact, even if the contact occurs through a mechanical intermediary, such as a telephone. If the instruction is written, however, the instructor and learner can be in different places, and time is not a critical factor. If for no other reason than this one, it is important that learners acquire reading skills if at all possible. Those who do not will always require the presence of others for information.

Since writing is simply an alternate form of verbal instructions, all comments made in the previous section apply to the written word as well, and we will not repeat them here.

Guidelines for Using Verbal Instructions

A set of three guidelines for using verbal instructions appears in Table 9.3.

Use Verbal Instructions Whenever Possible.   Verbal instructions are usually the most flexible and economical way to provide the information learners need to achieve program objectives. Consequently, when planning a lesson, instructors should think about using verbal instructions before considering other ways to transmit information. In addition, before using any of the other teaching techniques, instructors should try to couple them with verbal instructions in order to facilitate the eventual substitution of the verbal instructions.

It is important to realize that verbal instructions are effective only when the learners have the ability to comprehend and act on verbally presented information. Therefore, it is important for learners to develop the ability to follow these instructions. Learners who have problems understanding a language should participate in programs that are designed to increase their language facility, and after they have gained good use of a spoken language, they should have an opportunity to learn the corresponding written system if at all possible (Dever, 1978).

Limit Verbal Instructions to Essential Information.   One problem often found in instructional settings, especially those in which low-functioning learners are located, is that many instructors talk too much. Everyone who teaches learners with mental retardation should realize that it can be counterproductive to use verbal instructions that are too complex, too repetitious, or that are given too rapidly because any of these approaches can cause confusion for a learner. Instructors should always make a conscious attempt to gear instructions to both the cognitive capabilities and the immediate instructional needs of the learners.

Many learners with perceptual and processing problems have difficulty following verbal instructions. For these learners, instructors must speak quietly, slowly, and with a minimum of complexity in order to communicate effectively. Instructors must always attend to how well they are communicating with their learners and be aware that, for many learners with mental retardation, too much talking actually may obstruct communication, especially in the early stages of instruction.

A comparable problem can arise when using written instructions. For example, learners can be given materials in which there are too many words or words that are too small, too closely spaced, or beyond the learners' reading ability. Instructors must realize that when learners do not act on a verbal instruction (whether spoken or written), it simply may be that they are confused by the instruction. Therefore, when learners do not respond to verbal instructions, the instructor should consider one or more of the following options:

- modify the form or content of the verbal instructions; or
- choose another information provision technique.

The choices would include switching to physical guidance, demonstration, or learner search, or combining one or more of these techniques with a verbal or written instruction that has been reduced in complexity.

Employ the Best Means of Communicating with the Learner. It is often possible, and many times desirable, to have other people, or even objects or machines, provide instructions to learners if these other options are able to communicate quickly and effectively what the learners need. For example, another instructor, a peer, a parent or relative, or anyone else in the learner's environment may be able to provide the information in the most effective manner under a given set of circumstances. Such other persons may have the clearest understanding of the learner's instructional needs, or they may have the closest rapport with the learner. They also may have a special talent for communicating certain kinds of information clearly and efficiently.

It is also possible to use an audiotape or a videotape of a set of instructions to provide information to some learners. Tapes can give learners access to instructions when they need them even when the instructor is not available. Tapes may also help the learners listen more attentively to instructions by reducing distractions and interruptions. Similarly, computers are being used more and more often to provide information, and under the right conditions, can provide information to learners with mental retardation as effectively as they can for any learner. Therefore, as with all instructional techniques, instructors should consider the available options for providing verbal instructions and choose the approach that will help learners quickly achieve the objectives in their IPs.

Gestures

Gestures involve the use of *body movements* or *directed actions* to communicate information about behaviors, cues, and outcomes to learners. Examples of gestures include instances in which an instructor points to something, touches an object, motions in a particular direction, or nods his or her head. In the following examples, notice how easily instructors can use gestures instead of speech to indicate bits of information:

"Attend to this feature" (by touching part of an object);
"Move in that direction" (by looking toward a specific location);
"Pick up that object" (by motioning to the object); and
"Hold it on this end" (by pointing to the end of the object).

Thus, simply by indicating with some gesture, the instructor can transmit the same information that would appear in a verbal or written instruction, and do so effectively. In many instances, gestures can transmit information just as well as verbal instructions and with a lot less environmental noise. For many persons with mental retardation, the latter feature can be a big plus.

The major considerations when choosing gestures to transmit information are that the learners must

- be able to comprehend what is being communicated by the gesture; and
- be able to carry out the actions that the gestures suggest.

Gestures work especially well while teaching learners to identify and respond to situational and behavioral cues and when teaching them to sequence and link behaviors to form patterns. Therefore, this technique can be used most effectively and most often in the later stages of instruction, after learners have acquired basic skills.

Guidelines for Using Gestures

The guidelines in Table 9.4 should help instructors decide when to use gestures to provide information.

Gestures Can Substitute for Verbal Instructions. Instructors will often find it beneficial to use gestures when working with learners who have difficulty comprehending the spoken or written language. Many learners with mental retardation, especially those who also have auditory-perceptual problems, may find even relatively simple verbal instructions very confusing. Very often, instructors will discover that a gesture that is combined with a one- or two-word verbal instruction will communicate efficiently and effectively. Afterwards, they can stop using the gesture, switch to using only the verbal instruction as a prompt, and start to fade their presence from the interaction.

Gestures are also useful when other people are present and the instructor does not want to call attention to the fact that the learner is receiving instruction. This situation arises quite often when instruction takes place in the community. In such a setting, the instructor can use a gesture rather than trying to say something to a learner, and instruction often can proceed without calling attention to the fact that it is going on.

Gestures Can Supplement Verbal Instructions. Instructors, when in the act of teaching, will often find that a verbal instruction is insufficient to transmit all of the information the learner requires. For example, it is one

Gestures can be used to
- substitute for verbal instructions;
- supplement verbal instructions; and
- focus attention on the cues found in the environment.

thing for an instructor to say to a learner, "place the widget on the end of the flugbudget," and another for the learner to understand what the instructor is talking about. While it may be important for the learner to develop the vocabulary that refers to the performance of a skill, an instruction may sound like gibberish to a learner if there is no supplemental information. In the example provided, communication would increase greatly if the instructor pointed to both the "widget" and the "flugbudget" while giving the verbal instruction. Under these conditions, the learner would be learning both what to do and the appropriate vocabulary associated with the performance of the skill.

Gestures Can Focus Attention on the Cues Already Present in the Environment.   It tends to be a lot easier to use gestures to transmit information than it might first appear. Not only will the activity itself usually contain a lot of important cues, but the behavior pattern always contains much crucial information. When the instructor points out a cue to a learner or gestures that the learner should do what everyone else is doing, there is already a great deal of information available in the setting, and the bits of information that the learner needs can be provided rapidly and smoothly.

When an instructor uses gestures, the learner must glean part of the information he or she needs from the physical environment and couple it with the information contained in the gesture. This focus on the activity provides an important advantage because gestures can direct the learner's attention toward the behavioral cues that are already a natural part of the performance environment (and that will continue to be there after instruction is complete). Thus, gestures rely on the environment to supply learners with important information, and their use can help learners quickly move toward independent performance of activities. As long as the learners can figure out what is being communicated, the use of a gesture to transmit instructional information is possible, often appropriate, and frequently very useful.

Demonstration

The third technique for providing information to learners is to *show* them what to do, how to do it, or when to do it. To use **demonstration,** somebody or something illustrates either what the learner is supposed to do or what the finished product of the learner's behavior will be like. That is, somebody

TABLE 9.5 Range of Uses of Demonstration

Use	Examples
To teach specific behaviors	How to hold a tennis racquet How to fold a bedsheet after washing and drying it How to put money into the fare box on a subway
To highlight behavioral cues	How much chocolate sauce to spoon onto a sundae How far to push the jack under the car when changing a flat tire Where to hold the rope to make secure knots when replacing clotheslines
To show sequencing and linking of behaviors	The order in which to set dishes on a table What to do after causing a spill What steps to follow to handle a disagreement
To point out situational cues	When to ask the boss for a day off When to begin cleaning up the play area When to carry the trash to the curbside
To communicate outcomes	Show what happens when classmates "get along" Indicate the benefits of a job "well done" Point out the advantages of maintaining a well-organized work space

or something provides a model for the learner to imitate. Demonstration always occurs in two phases:

1. a model of some sort, either animate or inanimate, illustrates in some way what the learner is supposed to do; and
2. the learner tries to imitate exactly what the model has done (Bandura, 1986).

Demonstration can be very efficient because the learner can actually see what to do to meet the objective, and there are many situations in which it is extremely useful. Table 9.5 gives some examples of the range of information transmission possibilities inherent in demonstration. Under circumstances similar to the ones in this list, demonstration is often the best way to provide information to a learner. Furthermore, demonstration can be used to teach not only simple skills, but also very complicated ones. For example, it can be used very efficiently to teach important social skills, such as appropriate manners, conversational skills, and other social behaviors that one should exhibit in school settings, playgrounds, restaurants, job settings, churches, and other community settings.

Some skills *require* the use of demonstration because they can be taught in no other way. The only way to give learners information about many language skills, for example, is to demonstrate them, and it is probably impossible to teach many basic music skills without using demonstration. On the other hand, there are things that *could* be taught through demonstration, but probably should not. The largest class of these behaviors are those with social constraints of one kind or another, such as those involving the sex act.

Models

The somebody or something that provides a demonstration is called a *model*. There are two kinds of models: animate and inanimate.

Animate Models. Anything that moves can serve as an animate model. Beginning instructors may think that only teachers and staff can model behaviors, but the actual range of potential models is much greater. Peers, for example, can provide very good models for desired behaviors, just as they often provide excellent models of undesirable behaviors (much to the chagrin of instructors and parents). In addition, many other persons or things can provide animate models for behavior, including a school principal, the man who lives next door, a fellow worker, older learners, puppets, and even animals. Whoever or whatever can perform the skill being taught can function as an animate model for the learner to imitate if an instructor should choose to employ it.

Animate models are not limited to things that are alive. They also include the people and the animations that appear on film, on videotape, and in computer programs. Actions can be captured on film or videotape, and learners can view them later when they need a model. Learners who can follow the videotaped action may be able to imitate the model's behavior even if the instructor is not present. Videotapes, audiotapes, and other media have many advantages because they allow instructors to demonstrate behaviors that would otherwise be difficult to point out or reconstruct under natural conditions. They also enable instructors to "freeze" actions in time and to repeat them as often as is needed to allow learners to see the appropriate behaviors and the circumstances under which they should be performed (Dowrick, 1986; Knapczyk, 1988).

Inanimate Models. Information also can be provided using inanimate models. There are three types of inanimate models: mock-ups, plans, and schematic diagrams. Definitions of these models appear in Table 9.6.

Plans, schematics, and mock-ups can be as simple or as complex as necessary. For example, the wiring diagram for a stereo audio system is a very complicated schematic, whereas a picture cookbook is an example of a much simpler one (e.g., a drawing of a little blue spoon can represent a "tablespoonful," while a little red spoon can indicate a "teaspoonful"). Such models are called schematics because they use symbols instead of pictures.

The use of plans in instruction is well known and goes back many years. Like schematics, they can be simple or complex. For example, a house plan is complicated, but the plan for a weekly schedule is simple. A calendar is a sort of plan, as are certain types of maps, such as those used to indicate bus routes. The range of things that can be included in this category is enormous, and the major limiting factor to the use of plans is the instructor's imagination.

TABLE 9.6 Types of Inanimate Models

Mock-ups:	Three-dimensional models of an object
Plans:	Two-dimensional models that use pictures (either photographs or drawings) to represent objects or processes
Schematics:	Two-dimensional models that use symbolic representations of objects or processes

TABLE 9.7 Guidelines for Using Demonstration to Present Information

Instructors can use models to
- demonstrate discrete skills and actions;
- focus the learners' attention on information in their environment;
- develop imitative responses;
- show standards for performance; and
- promote spontaneous imitation in learners.

Mock-ups can also be simple or complex. A mock-up of the human body would be very complex, but a letter holder made from two paper plates would present an uncomplicated model for an elementary school student to follow as a Christmas crafts project. Again, the number of potential mock-ups is enormous, and they range from a minibusiness in a school (Hamill and Dunlevy, 1993b) to a driver-training simulator.

Inanimate models are especially valuable because once a learner learns how to use them, the instructor need not be present to provide the information contained in the model. Rather, the instructor can stay in the background and respond only to questions and problems that may appear.

Guidelines for Using Demonstration

The demonstration technique has many uses. Table 9.7 presents some guidelines for using demonstration as an instructional technique.

Models Can Demonstrate Discrete Skills and Actions. One use of demonstration is to teach learners how to perform part of an activity. This use can be important in the initial stages of teaching a complex objective to persons with mental retardation, when it may prove necessary to break down the skill clusters into discrete skills to allow learners to comprehend and perform the required actions more easily. That is, when teaching a learner how to play a sports activity, to make a meal, or to operate a complicated piece of machinery, the instructor may need to isolate some of the required skills for specific instruction. Demonstration often can be used successfully to inform the learner about these actions and allow the learner to imitate the elements of performance being illustrated. After the learner has had an opportunity to practice the individual components or actions, the instructor can teach the learner how to combine them into a more complicated behavioral pattern, perhaps again by using demonstration.

Models Can Focus the Learners' Attention on Information in Their Environment. The learner assumes part of the burden for discovering relevant information when demonstration is used as an information provision technique. Instructors can take advantage of this feature of demonstration by carefully choosing the types of animate and inanimate models they use and by showing learners how to attend more closely and critically to their surroundings. In doing so, instructors will help learners become less dependent on staff for information and more dependent on themselves as learners. For example, a peer or person in the community can often demonstrate the skills that are required to meet an objective, the cues that inform the learner about necessary behaviors, and the circumstances under which to display behavior patterns. The learner who becomes skilled at looking for these things may be able to acquire important skills even when the instructor is not present.

Similarly, a well-planned drawing or schematic can direct a learner's attention to key elements of an activity and hold his or her attention for extended lengths of time. That is, the model can significantly reduce or even eliminate a learner's dependence on the instructor's directions or the need for ongoing direct feedback, reinforcement, or redirection. Therefore, the use of models should be a part of every learner's instruction from a very early point in the instructional process.

Models Can Develop Imitative Responses. Most learners begin to imitate models spontaneously as a normal part of their growth and development, but many persons with severe retardation or severe autism do not. Since knowing *how* to imitate is a prerequisite to learning from models, it is necessary to teach such learners to display an imitative response. The act of imitating can usually be taught through a combination of demonstration, verbal instructions, and physical guidance. The first step is to demonstrate a behavior for the learner to imitate and to pair the action with a specific instruction, such as "Do this." Then the instructor physically guides the learner through the action.

Since the earliest actions often have little or no relevance to the learner's perception of outcomes, and the learner may not understand why he or she should perform the actions, it may be necessary to provide external rewards when the learner cooperates and participates in the instruction. In cases such as this, the use of external rewards may be warranted at the early stages of instruction because the objective at this point is to teach the learner to perform the action only in the presence of the demonstration and the verbal instruction. Rewards probably will not be required if the activity has inherent motivators, however. For instance, if the activity is couched in a gamelike format (such as "pat-a-cake"), external motivators may be superfluous.

Instruction in how to imitate a model usually begins by focusing on a skill that the learner already knows how to perform. It should be one that is simple, straightforward, and very obvious to the learner. It is often useful to employ large muscle movements, such as those involved in lifting an arm over the head, in clapping hands, or in standing up. After the learner begins to imitate whatever action is selected, the same procedure is used to teach a second response, then a third, and so forth. As the imitative response develops, the complexity of the activities can increase. Moreover, the instructor should fade both the physical guidance and any external rewards as quickly as possible and move on to instruction that is more closely tied to the objectives in the program plan. Eventually (the length of time required varies with the learner) the learner will generalize the imitative response, and instructors can then use it to carry out instruction in the normal manner.

Models Can Present Standards for Performance. Either animate or inanimate models can serve as performance exemplars to highlight the standards for program objectives. That is, models can be used to show learners how to judge the accuracy and effectiveness of their own performance, or at least, to indicate how others will make the judgment. For example, in learning to kick a football, the learners' objective would be to do it in a manner similar to that of the model and to achieve similar results, such as kicking the ball at least 25 yards. The standard demonstrated by the model in each case can show the learners how their performance will be measured (e.g., the distance that the ball travels) and the criterion they must reach (e.g., a kick of 25 yards). Thus, a model can help the learners direct their attention to achieving the standards that apply in the natural environment under normal conditions rather than to other factors that may have little or no relevance to how behavior is evaluated.

Models Can Promote Spontaneous Imitation in Learners. No instructor has the time or the resources to teach every skill and provide all the information learners must have to become independent. Therefore, it is crucial that all learners, regardless of their functioning level, acquire some information by themselves. Learners who are unable or unwilling to learn through their own initiative stand very little chance of becoming independent. Demonstration and learning from models can be key factors in the process of learning to seek information because the more learners engage in spontaneous imitation, the more incidental learning they will acquire. Therefore, if learners do not spontaneously acquire skills by watching and imitating what others do in their everyday behavior, it is necessary to teach them to do so.

The first and most important way to facilitate spontaneous imitation is to give learners access to models who (a) have prestige for the learners and (b) exhibit higher-level skills than those exhibited by the learners. In fact, the constant availability of nondisabled models in community settings may be enough to increase the frequency of spontaneous imitation, a fact that alone is sufficient justification for providing community-based instruction for all learners with mental retardation.

Another way to increase spontaneous imitation is to establish an atmosphere in which learners are encouraged or even expected to use one

TABLE 9.8 Strategies for Promoting Spontaneous Imitation in Learners

- Have learners go to one another or to other people in the "real world" for assistance.
- Send the learners to each other for judgment on skill performance.
- Set up activities that require learners to share materials, supplies, and talents.
- Use cross-age teaching and peer tutoring activities.
- Have people from the community with specific talents assist with instruction.
- Use cooperative learning assignments and projects in which everyone in the group has something important to contribute and learn.

another as models, such as when using peer tutoring and cooperative learning strategies (Knapczyk, 1989; Knapczyk and Rodes, 1996). Our experience indicates that most instructional activity currently originates from staff members. If instructors encourage learners to focus on other people for at least part of their information, they can create a more economical learning environment and are likely to increase greatly the number of things learned.

Some strategies instructors might use to promote more spontaneous imitation appear in Table 9.8.

Cautions in the Use of Models. Demonstration is most effective when it focuses on behavior that learners are willing to observe and imitate. For this reason, instructors must choose models carefully because people and things serve as models with varying degrees of effectiveness. For example, some learners will eagerly imitate the actions of an instructor, while others will imitate peers but not adults. Still other learners will learn best from samples of a finished product. Therefore, instructors should set up demonstration situations ahead of time and base them not only on the information the learner needs, but also on how the learner is to attend to and try to imitate the actions of the model. For example, there will be many times when a peer will be the most effective model to illustrate an activity. But when using a peer as a model, it is necessary for the peer to have good status with the learner, or the learner may refuse to imitate the actions the peer displays. In other words, factors such as a human model's sex, age, race, relative competence, and relative standing in a group can influence the degree to which learners will imitate the model's actions (Bandura, 1986; Sharan, 1980). Under certain circumstances, instructors may have to manipulate the status of peers or other models (or the learner's perception of the status) using behavior management procedures, such as praise for continuous accurate performance (Goldstein, 1988).

Physical Guidance

The fourth technique for providing information is **physical guidance.** To use it, the instructor *physically guides* the learner's body through all or part of the behavioral pattern either by touching the learner's body or by using a mechanical intermediary to do so. The degree to which physical guidance can provide information varies along a continuum ranging from a "nudge" to "total physical control."

Athletic instructors (such as gymnastics coaches and others) have used physical guidance for many years to teach difficult skills to budding athletes because it allows them to present information in the following ways:

- accurately, especially when the learner must learn to rely on internal physical feedback for judging correct performance;
- in a deliberate manner; and
- at a slow pace.

Similarly, teachers of persons with mental retardation have found physical guidance very useful in helping learners quickly make adjustments in their movements (Gold, 1980a). It is a useful information transmission technique when learners find it difficult to figure out what they are supposed to do, and instructors often can use it to transmit information rapidly and efficiently.

Guidelines for Using Physical Guidance

Instructors can use physical guidance in many ways when working with persons with mental retardation (see Table 9.9).

Use Physical Guidance to Teach Behaviors. Physical guidance is often a useful technique for teaching gross motor skills, athletic skills, and other skills in which physical movements must have a lot of refinement. For example, physical guidance can quickly teach the appropriate stance to take when holding a baseball bat, or it can emphasize and isolate the movements required to swing a golf club. Physical guidance is not limited to teaching athletic behaviors, however; it can be used to teach learners an enormous number of skills that range from tying shoelaces to cutting boards with a power saw.

Physical guidance does not always require one person to touch another, although many instructors think of it only in terms of "hand-over-hand" instruction. Certain kinds of mechanical equipment can provide physical guidance. One example is a driver-training automobile that has dual controls that allow the instructor to sit at the controls in the passenger seat while the learner sits at the controls in the driver's seat. Using this machine, the learner can actually feel the correct movements while the instructor makes them. Such machinery is especially helpful in teaching the movements that tend to cause difficulty, such as the coordination required to operate the clutch and accelerator in a car with a standard transmission. Other mechanical devices are available or can be invented by instructors to teach skills in a similar manner.

Use Physical Guidance to Teach Cues. Physical guidance can teach more than just behaviors. For example, there are a number of situations in which instructors will use physical guidance to focus a learner's attention on cues. In such cases, the use of physical guidance can cause learning to take place more quickly than either verbal instruction or demonstration (Gold,

Instruction is the process of providing the learners with information about the skills they are acquiring.

Photo courtesy of James L. Shaffer.

TABLE 9.9 Guidelines for Using Physical Guidance

Instructors can use physical guidance to
- teach behaviors,
- teach cues,
- provide strategic physical support,
- prevent injury, and
- initiate activity performance or encourage activity completion.

1980a). One of these instances is when the behavioral cues have a physical prominence of some sort to which learners must attend. Physical guidance can be used to point out these cues very effectively, such as a peculiar bump on one of the parts of the assembly unit that lets the learner know the correct way in which to orient the part for assembly. An instructor could make the cue salient to a learner by placing the part in the learner's hand in its proper physical orientation or by rubbing the learner's finger on the bump.

Physical guidance can also be used to highlight other crucial cues the learner must recognize to perform an activity, such as whether something is at the correct temperature or has the correct texture or whether something is traveling at the right speed or in the proper direction. In situations like these, instructors can often provide information about the important cues more quickly using physical guidance than any other way.

Use Physical Guidance to Provide Strategic Physical Support.   Physical guidance is an effective technique to use when learners lack the strength, stamina, steadiness, or muscle control to perform a skill or a behavior pattern. If the instructor provides support correctly and strategically, the learner will be able to perform the activity, and the lack of physical ability will not interfere with achievement. For example, it may be necessary to provide a learner who is physically weak with support when teaching him or her to serve others at mealtime, such as when pouring coffee for guests. In such a case, as the coffee carafe empties and becomes lighter, the instructor may be able to withdraw the physical support and allow the learner to perform at least part the activity unaided. Similarly, it may be necessary to assist a learner with spasticity to dress by helping to orient various articles of clothing or by assisting through some of the more strenuous dressing activities. Whenever possible, the assistance should be given in a way that both communicates information about the program objective and increases the learner's strength, dexterity, and other physical attributes needed to improve performance.

By using physical guidance in these ways, instruction can proceed until the learner develops the physical abilities necessary to attain the program objectives. When the instructional staff works toward both physical and instructional goals in a coordinated fashion, the learners often make quick and steady progress toward performing program objectives completely unaided.

Use Physical Guidance to Prevent Injury.   When teaching learners to perform an activity in which there is a potential for injury, it may be very wise to use physical guidance not only to provide the learners with the information they need, but also to reduce the potential for injury. In performing a somersault, for example, there is a point immediately prior to beginning the roll at which the learners must lower their chins to begin the roll on the back (rather than the top) of their heads. Many young learners with mental retardation do not perform this step without instruction and actually tend to hold their heads upright when they start the roll. Under these conditions, a learner's head can twist backward at the midpoint of the roll just when his or her entire weight is on his or her head. This situation is very dangerous because it can result in a broken neck. Instructors could use physical guidance to make the learner lower the chin just prior to beginning the somersault. This procedure would be especially important in the early stages of instruction when the risks of injury are highest.

Instructors should always be on the lookout for potential injury to learners while they are learning to perform the skills. Even though other information techniques can provide the necessary information effectively, instructors should be prepared to employ physical guidance any time a learner might be subject to injury. For example, instructors should consider using physical guidance while teaching any skill that involves power tools, movement at heights, lifting heavy objects, balance, high heat, deep water, or any other potentially dangerous situation, especially at the beginning of the instructional lesson.

Use Physical Guidance to Initiate Activity Performance or to Encourage Activity Completion. Sometimes learners are able to learn and perform skills for meeting the program objectives, but they are unwilling to do so. Other learners may have limited concentration or have difficulty attending to their performance for any length of time. In such cases, instructors may decide to use physical guidance to prompt the learners to start performing or to encourage them to complete the activity if they stop partway through its performance. In such cases, we recommend using as *little* contact as possible. A nudge, for example, may be entirely sufficient to get performance moving. Later on, the instructor may be able to substitute a gesture or a verbal instruction for the physical contact.

Cautions in the Use of Physical Guidance. Instructors should be cautious and carefully restrained in their use of physical guidance because it too easily can become physical force (or even abuse) if the guidance is too strong or persistent, or if the learner actively resists the guidance. Instructors can avoid crossing the line between physical guidance and physical force by carefully planning instruction ahead of time and being aware of their learners' tolerance for physical contact.

Learner Search

The fifth and last technique for providing information is to make the learners search for the information they need. Instructors use **learner search** when they are confident that the learners can figure out for themselves what information they need to meet the program objectives and that they can obtain and process that information when they interact with the environment. The effectiveness of learner search largely depends on the instructor's ability to structure the environment rather than to interact directly with the learners. Learner search can be a very powerful instructional technique to use with persons with mental retardation because it gives them a large measure of control over their instruction and supports their progress toward independence.

There are three circumstances in which an instructor may find learner search to be an appropriate technique to use (see Table 9.10).

Identify Behavioral Cues

Instructors may be able to teach learners the essential skills for meeting an objective, but the learners still may misinterpret some behavioral cues and exhibit incorrect performance. If instructors give learners opportunities to

TABLE 9.10 Circumstances in Which Learner Search May Be Appropriate

Learner search can be used to
- identify behavior cues,
- practice performance, and
- identify outcomes.

interact with the environment in such a way that they must identify the behavioral cues themselves, the learners may begin to recognize and coordinate their actions with the cues and thus begin to perform the skills correctly. For example, learners who are learning to do the high jump may need to knock the horizontal bar off the standards a number of times before they are ready to begin focusing on where to place their feet before takeoff.

Practice Performance

Learners may identify the cues appropriately but require focused opportunities to refine their actions and coordinate their performance with the cues. For example, a learner may know how to perform all the appropriate parts of a job, but do so too slowly. Such a learner may need to develop more refined movements or learn to make his or her motions more quickly. The instructor could structure opportunities for such a learner to develop more coordinated behavior on his or her own. For example, consider a situation in which learners are learning English sentence patterns in drill activities. Inevitably, these learners will go into environmental settings in which those sentence patterns should be used appropriately. For example, a learner who is learning to ask questions using the modal "can" (as in, "Can I/you *verb?*") may be sent to a cafeteria, at which point he or she must ask for certain kinds of food. The instructor may require the learner to ask, "Can I have some bread?" (Dever, 1978). Similar situations can be developed for almost any applied skill that is taught first in a segregated setting.

Identify Outcomes

A third situation occurs when learners must gain experience with the outcomes of their behavior. It is possible to place learners into settings in which the outcomes become very obvious to them, and in so doing, trigger the motivation to learn certain skills. For example, we know a teacher who obtained jobs for learners with mild retardation in a secondary school. She had tried to teach these learners to memorize their social security numbers with little success. However, the first time they went to pick up their checks, the person who handed out checks asked them to state their social security numbers as identification and did not let them have their paychecks until they could recite them. Needless to say, they memorized their numbers very quickly.

In each of these instances of learner search, the instructor's job is to create the opportunities in the environment for the learners to access the information they need through their own experiences and initiative. Instructors usually will find the greatest number of occasions to use learner search with the following types of learners:

- those with mild retardation;
- those who have more skills on which to draw;
- those who find it easier to pick out important and salient cues in their environment; and
- those who take more initiative in their learning.

This is not to say, however, that learner search cannot be used with learners with severe or profound mental retardation. It can and should be used to provide them with information as often as possible *because* it requires the learners to exhibit a degree of independent learning behavior. Since independence is the ultimate goal of all instruction, learner search is an important instructional technique, even for learners with severe retardation.

Guidelines for Using Learner Search

Learner search can be used for the purposes found in Table 9.11.

Use Learner Search When Learner Comprehends the Outcomes of Performance.   One of the most important factors in deciding whether or not to use learner search to provide information is how much the learner understands about the outcomes of performance. Regardless of the learners' functioning level, learner search should be used only when learners know ahead of time what they are supposed to do. If they do not know what to look for in their environment or what to try to accomplish, they are likely to perform aimlessly or become frustrated in their actions. Therefore, it is important to check the learners' understanding of the program objective beforehand and to communicate the objective's outcome through verbal instructions, demonstration, or whatever other means necessary prior to turning the learners loose to perform the activity.

Use Learner Search When the Learners' Motivational Levels and Interest in the Activity Are High.   Learner search also requires learners to be motivated and aware of what they are doing. The learners must want to try to meet the objective, be alert to sources of information in the environment, and be able to observe the effect of their actions in achieving the objective. But it is important to recognize that all of these factors can be influenced by the performance circumstances and the challenges that learners encounter, especially in community settings. If a group of learners can read and write, they will find that the written directions, signs, and picture displays that are already present in community settings provide very useful guides. For example, if the instructional circumstances for teaching how to order food from a menu are planned properly, learners quickly should learn to focus on the information available to them in the restaurant.

However, learner search does not always require that learners be able to read, write, and explore the community unaided. For example, an instructor could place two or more young children with mental retardation

TABLE 9.11 Guidelines for Using Learner Search to Provide Information

Instructors can use learner search when
- the learner comprehends the outcomes of performance;
- the learner's motivation levels and interest are high;
- the instructor can monitor performance very closely; and
- the instructor wishes to promote an atmosphere of self-direction in the learner's daily routine.

who are blind in confined spaces (e.g., small cribs or beanbag chairs) solely for the purpose of exploring each other's bodies to help them become aware of other children. Similarly, people with moderate and severe retardation who are in supported employment must learn to deal with some of the social demands of the workplace by themselves after the job coach leaves the work setting (Wehman and Hill, 1980).

Use Learner Search When Learner Performance Can Be Monitored Closely. Learner search must always be accompanied by close monitoring to ensure that the learners acquire the necessary and appropriate information. All instructional activities must be planned ahead of time and the learners made aware of the skills they must acquire. Learners with mental retardation very quickly can become confused when left to their own devices. If they do not have appropriate information, they may lose sight of the objectives they are trying to meet, start to act aimlessly, become distracted by extraneous features of the environment, lose confidence in their abilities, and/or become frustrated by minor mistakes and errors. Because of these potential problems, it is very important for instructors to organize the instructional situation in a way that minimizes any sources of confusion that the learners might encounter. The idea is to make sure that their initial attempts at performance go smoothly. Furthermore, instructors must be prepared to stop using learner search and substitute more direct techniques if they find that the learners do not have the proper disposition to learn on their own. Close monitoring of the learners' behavior can prevent problems that can have long-term and severe effects on learner willingness to work on the program objectives in the future.

Use Learner Search to Promote an Atmosphere of Self-Direction in the Daily Routine. To be independent, learners must identify appropriate behaviors and cues by themselves and use learner search on a lifelong basis. It is important to teach and encourage learners to try out new skills, to take some risks in their performance, to use trial and error, and generally to become attentive to the activities taking place around them and to how others perform these activities. Learner search is thus an important and natural part of incidental learning and is a crucial component in everyone's growth and development.

In order to encourage learners with mental retardation to use learner search across instructional settings, they must identify outcomes that they would like to achieve, and take initiative in achieving them. The first step in helping learners begin to use learner search for themselves is to teach them to make choices about what things they would like to do. Then the instructors can begin to place learners in problem-solving situations for which they already have the skills to develop solutions. Once learners have these basic skills, the instructors should actively seek or create situations in which learners must discover for themselves the behaviors, cues, and patterns they need to perform the activity.

Cautions in the Use of Learner Search.   Learner search provides learners with the great dignity of being able to learn for themselves the things that are required for functioning in the community. It also increases their ability to deal with the demands of the community; that is, the old adage "practice makes perfect" applies to the act of finding out what to do for oneself. For these reasons, learner search ultimately may be the most important of the five information-provision instructional techniques.

But the major cautions in using learner search should be obvious:

1. Learner search should never be used to teach behaviors, patterns, cues, and outcomes that presently are beyond the learner's ability to comprehend. If used in such a situation, it would foreordain the learner to failure.
2. Learner search should never be used when a learner engages in activities in which there is potential danger either to the learner or to others.

As long as these constraints are observed, there is every reason for instructors to use learner search to encourage information acquisition.

Selecting Techniques

When selecting information provision techniques, it is necessary to consider both the learning and performance characteristics of learners and the skill requirements for meeting the objectives in the IP. Instructors must ask the following question:

> What technique will work best for this learner, under these circumstances, in teaching this objective?

The answer will vary, even when teaching several learners to achieve the same program objective at the same time. For example, when teaching learners with moderate mental retardation to perform a certain set of skills, it may be necessary to use physical guidance with some, demonstration with others, and a combination of verbal instructions and gestures with still others. Furthermore, it might be better to teach this same set of skills to a group of learners with mild retardation using just verbal instructions or learner search. In other words, the learning and performance characteristics of the learners will affect the ways in which the skills would best be taught.

TABLE 9.12 Guidelines for Selecting Information Provision Techniques

Instructors must consider
- the variables presented by the skills the learners must acquire;
- the variables presented by the learners themselves; and
- the potential speed and effectiveness of the technique in presenting information to the learners.

Guidelines for Selecting Information Provision Techniques

The instructional staff that has selected and analyzed program objectives appropriately usually will be able to select effective instructional techniques without preparing a formal and detailed plan. The reason is that steady learning usually will take place when the instructor knows exactly what the learner is supposed to do and is intent on finding ways to help him or her to do it.

However, we will present some generalized guidelines for selecting information provision techniques to use with learners with mental retardation. The three most important things to consider are found in Table 9.12. In all probability, instructors will employ some combination of information provision techniques, but occasionally, a single technique will emerge as the best choice.

Variables Presented by the Skills. As stated previously, some program objectives *require* the instructor to present information using one or another technique. For example, learning to speak one's native language requires demonstration, and learning to ride a two-wheeled bicycle usually requires physical guidance in the early stages. In addition, activities that present physical danger usually require some physical guidance in order to prevent injury either to the learner or to others. Also, some program objectives *preclude* the use of one or another technique. For example, it is difficult to see how physical guidance can be useful in teaching a learner to sing. The constraints that various skills place on the use of a specific technique are usually fairly obvious or will become clear during the analysis of the program objectives.

Instructors will often discover that two or more techniques can be employed to provide information to the learner and that the need to transmit information effectively may require an instructor to shift techniques during the course of instruction. For example, in teaching janitorial skills, an instructor might use physical guidance and demonstration to teach the actual skills needed to sweep floors, such as how to hold a broom or how to coordinate sweeping movements with the holding of a dustpan. However, when teaching the learner to sweep the floors "clean," verbal instructions might prove far more appropriate for teaching how to look for unswept spots on the floor. In fact, it is difficult to see how physical guidance might be used appropriately to provide this kind of information. Therefore, the techniques an instructor uses to provide information will often shift depending on the type of information the learners need to obtain at any given time.

Variables Presented by the Learner. The physical and learning characteristics of the learner present another factor to consider in deciding which techniques to use. As stated above, there will usually be more than one way to provide information, but one technique might be more appropriate than another for a specific learner because of his or her learning characteristics or physical limitations. For example, it is difficult to use demonstration to teach physical movements to learners with visual disabilities, and physical guidance often will be more productive with this group. On the other hand, physical guidance must be used very carefully with a learner who has spasticity, especially if the spasticity is severe. For such a person, the potential for injury is an important consideration, and it may be more productive to use a combination of demonstration and learner search to allow the learner to find movements that compensate for his or her physical limitations.

Cognitive limitations and/or limitations imposed by a lack of previous learning also place constraints on the possible techniques an instructor can use to provide information to specific learners. For example, it is often ineffective to use verbal instructions to teach learners with severe or profound mental retardation, especially when teaching skills that contain complicated behaviors, cues, patterns, and outcomes. For such learners, combinations of demonstration, gestures, and physical guidance might be more appropriate, especially during the early stages of instruction.

Too often when planning instruction, instructors focus heavily on the learners' limitations and skill deficits. But learners nearly always bring strengths, talents, and areas of competence into the instructional situation, and it is important for instructors to think about how to capitalize on them when choosing instructional techniques. Whenever possible, activities should build on whatever abilities learners have, take advantage of the things they enjoy doing, and employ techniques and methods to which they naturally respond well. Instructors who consider these variables when planning instruction often can give learners a comfortable starting point from which to learn new behavior, can promote better attention to the activities, can extend the learners' confidence level, and can encourage further use and generalization of existing skills.

Potential Speed of a Technique. The instructor's basic job is to get learners to acquire the information they need in the fastest possible way. The more quickly that learners acquire information, the more quickly they will meet the objective. The more objectives they can meet, the closer to independence they will get. Therefore, the speed at which techniques can supply information to the learners must always be one of the major considerations during instruction. Instructors should think of the speed of techniques in terms of both the learners' immediate instructional needs and the long-term effects a particular approach may have on the acquisition of skills.

Some time ago, when applied behavior analysis was a new technique, the idea developed that information provision should be guided by specific rules. For example, it was common to say that instruction should always begin with verbal instructions, and if the learner seems not to be acquiring the information, the instructor should switch to demonstration, and then to physical guidance if the demonstration appears not to be doing the job. At first glance, this approach makes a lot of sense because verbal instructions seem to be the quickest and easiest way to provide information and physical guidance the slowest. However, we believe that such a rigid approach to teaching is actually counterproductive because it overlooks the needs of the learner and the variables presented by the skill and the performance conditions. An instructor often knows before instruction begins that it would not be practical to use specific techniques in some situations. Moreover, most instructors will have a great deal of knowledge about which techniques seem to work best with individual learners. Typically, they start to use a specific technique, and if it does not seem to work, switch to another technique that is also appropriate for the learner. All instructors will find that demonstration, physical guidance, or some combination of techniques sometimes does the job more quickly than verbal instructions, even when the learner has little or no difficulty following the verbal instructions. In addition, in terms of having learners gain information on their own, learner search is often far more appropriate than any of the other techniques because it can produce lasting changes in the learner's behavior. This statement is true even though learner search may work more slowly during the early stages of instruction.

Providing Feedback

In most cases, when learners obtain information for meeting a program objective, they will respond in some manner. Their performance can be "correct" or "incorrect"; that is, they may perform the way they should, or they may not. Whatever they do at this point must be followed by feedback of some kind. If they do what they are supposed to do, their responses must be confirmed to let them know that they performed correctly. If they do something else, their responses must be corrected. There are only a few ways to confirm or correct a response, and we will discuss these methods in this section.

Types of Confirmation

When the learners respond the way they are supposed to respond, the instructor's job is easy: He or she must confirm the response. Any one (or combination) of the three techniques in Table 9.13 can be used to confirm a response.

External Confirmation

One method for informing learners that they did the right thing is to use an external confirmation procedure: Somebody or something that is not inherent in the natural performance of an activity (i.e., something that is "external" to the learners' performance) lets the learners know that their responses were the ones they were supposed to make.

TABLE 9.13 Types of Confirmation

- External confirmation
- Performance confirmation
- No news is good news (NNGN)

When using external feedback, the instructional staff *must* remember that the feedback will not be present when learners perform in the natural setting. Therefore, it will always be necessary to establish procedures for fading this type of confirmation before terminating instruction and to substitute a way for learners to determine for themselves whether or not they are performing correctly.

External confirmation is a very natural thing for instructors to provide, and they can give it in a number of ways. For example, the instructor (or anyone else) can use the following to tell the learners that they did what they were supposed to do:

"Right."
"Good job."
"Nice going."
"You got them all correct."

Or, if the instructor prefers, he or she can use a signal of some sort, such as a "thumbs-up," a pat on the shoulder, or a score on a work sheet. All of these actions will tell the learners that their responses were correct, and these actions can be made by anyone in the environment.

It is not necessary for the instructor directly to tell the learners that they did what they were supposed to do. For example, it is possible to use some sort of mechanical device, such as a flashing light or a ringing bell, to signal the learners that their responses were correct. In school settings it is common to use things like stars, or "happy faces" for confirmation. The advantage of these confirmers is that they can be used in some sort of ratio of confirmer to correct response that indicates a grade for learner performance. The more closely the learners approach the standard for performance, the more stars they receive or the higher their grades will be.

External confirmation procedures are used frequently in most teaching and training settings because they are extremely useful and informative for learners. Unfortunately, external feedback procedures too easily can become simple rewards for participating in the instructional activity rather than techniques for teaching learners to do things. That is, the feedback procedures can become substitutes for the natural outcomes that ultimately must maintain the learners' performance. For this reason, instructors should adhere to the three specific rules for using external confirmation found in Table 9.14.

TABLE 9.14 Rules for Using External Confirmation

When using external confirmation, instructors should
- make the learner acutely aware of what the confirmer means (i.e., that a particular response was correct and that the confirmer is *not* a reward for participating in the instructional activity);
- remove the external confirmer from the instructional interaction as soon as possible and substitute natural confirmers in its place; and
- make the instructional activities focus on getting the learner to understand and respond to the natural outcomes of his or her performance as soon as possible.

Performance Confirmation

After a learner has obtained information about performance, the correct responses themselves will often provide sufficient confirmation for the learner. For example, if the learner understands that he or she must start a machine, correct performance of pressing the "start" button will be confirmed when the machine starts up. It would be unnecessary for the instructor to say or do anything in such a case. Similarly, if the learner knows that correct movement of a key in a lock results in a "click," his or her performance will be confirmed by the click. Likewise, if the learner understands what "clean" means, correct performance in any cleaning activity will be confirmed by the cleanliness evident upon completion of the activity. In each of these cases, the events inherent in correct performance provide the confirmation that the learner's performance is correct.

Performance confirmation requires the learner to become aware of the inherent events that confirm correct performance. Unlike external confirmers, these intrinsic performance events will remain when instruction is complete and the learner performs the activity in its natural setting with no assistance from instructional staff. At that point the learner will have to rely on them because the instructor(s) will not be there to tell the learner whether he or she performed correctly. Therefore, as part of the instruction, the learner must be taught to attend to intrinsic performance events. In most cases, these events will pertain to the standards for the program objective and to the way in which people normally apply them to the learner's behavior.

No News Is Good News (NNGN)

The third confirmation procedure seems first to have been described by Marc Gold (1980b). The way it works is that the instructor does nothing when the learner performs correctly and provides correction only when, and as soon as, the learner makes an error. Thus, as long as the learner is doing exactly what he or she is supposed to do, the very fact that the instructor does nothing tells the learner that he or she is performing correctly. Gold used the phrase "No news is good news" (NNGN) to identify this feedback technique.

NNGN is not the same as simple silence. It requires the instructor to pay close attention to what the learner is doing and to correct learner errors as soon as they occur. If they are not corrected, the learner simply will learn to make errors and thus will acquire incorrect information. Therefore, NNGN is restricted to certain situations and cannot be used whimsically. Instructors can use the technique in the following situations:

- in combination with one or more other correction procedures;
- when the learner is engaged in learner search;
- when the instructor is attending closely to what the learner is doing;
- after the learner begins to grasp much of the information required for performance of the skills inherent in the objective; and
- after the learner fully understands the outcomes of performance.

In any of these situations, NNGN can be highly effective, and we recommend it strongly.

Because the instructor must observe learner behavior very closely, this technique is most useful in one-on-one instructional settings. However, it is possible to use NNGN in group instructional settings under the following conditions:

- when one-on-one instruction occurs within the context of a group setting; and
- when the learners are making choral responses.

Group One-on-One. Instructors often carry out one-on-one instruction in group situations. For example, it often happens in classes for young, moderately, or severely retarded children when they are grouped around semicircular tables, on the floor, or in other small group arrangements to work on performance activities specific to the needs of each child. In such cases, it is possible to use NNGN if the learners perform their activities slowly enough for the instructor to observe *all* errors as they occur and if the instructor is able to correct them immediately. Some other group situations in which NNGN might occur are as follows:

- when several learners are each performing different parts of the same general activity, such as cleaning a room or preparing a meal. If the space is small enough and the number of learners few enough, NNGN could be employed.
- when several learners are each performing the same activity, but doing it at different speeds, such as setting up chairs in an auditorium or learning to assemble parts in a factory setting. Even in relatively large spaces, it may be possible to correct errors as soon as they occur, but there are obvious limitations imposed by the distance the instructor must travel to make a correction.

Choral Responses. NNGN may be used in situations in which learners make responses in unison, as when they engage in drills of various kinds. Instructors can use NNGN under these circumstances because the learner who

TABLE 9.15 Conditions Under Which NNGN Can Be Used

- The focus is only on learner behavior.
- The instructor can correct errors immediately.
- It is used in conjunction with learner search.

makes a response that is different from those of the other learners stands out and will be identified immediately. Such conditions occur during any instruction in which drill is used to teach, such as language pattern drills. In these situations, NNGN is an effective technique to use because the drill proceeds at a set rhythm.

Guidelines for Using NNGN

NNGN will not work in all instructional settings. The guidelines for using NNGN are listed in Table 9.15.

Use NNGN When the Focus Is on Learner Behavior Only. To use NNGN, the instructor must attend closely to the learner's behavior during performance. The learner who knows that the instructor is attending to his or her performance will quickly come to understand that no reaction from the instructor indicates that he or she should continue whatever it is he or she is doing (Gold, 1980b). The instructor's close observation of what the learner is doing makes NNGN an important technique because it generates a businesslike atmosphere that permeates the setting. The fact that it should not be used unless the instructor focuses on the learner's performance requires both learner and instructor to attend to what the learner is doing. Therefore, both become actively engaged in developing the learner's productive and competent performance.

Use NNGN When Errors Can Be Corrected Immediately. Because NNGN requires the instructor to correct errors as soon as they occur, the learner must stop working if the instructor is interrupted (Gold, 1980b). Otherwise, the learner may acquire incorrect information as a result of not having his or her errors corrected.

Use NNGN in Conjunction with Learner Search. NNGN is a very good confirmation technique to use in conjunction with the learner search technique because the combination requires learners to think about what they are doing. For example, when learners make errors and the instructor says:

"No,"
"Try another way,"
"Do it again,"

or simply blocks the learners' responses until they begin to make the correct moves, the learners must think about what they are doing and make the corrections themselves. These acts require learners to make decisions and evaluative judgments about their own performance while they are responding, and these decisions and judgments are often the same ones that everyone must make in order to handle new situations and learn new skills. The more that learners with mental retardation engage in learner search to acquire information, the more confidence they will have in their ability to make decisions, and consequently, the more willing they will become to make decisions.

Correction of Learner Errors

When the learner makes errors or does something wrong, somebody or something must make the learner aware of the mistake and (except for learner search) provide information about what he or she should have done instead. There are three ways to correct performance errors (see Table 9.16).

Provide the Information Again

Sometimes a learner does not comprehend the information the first time someone or something provides it. There are a number of possible reasons for lack of comprehension, examples of which appear in Table 9.17.

If the learner does not understand the information the first time it is provided, the instructor's response is simple: Provide it again. But there are limits to the number of times that information can be given again because the salience of an instruction that is repeated too often can recede and the instruction can become just a part of the background noise. Thus, if an instructor gives the learner the same information in the same way several times in a row, it probably will not penetrate the hundredth time any better than it did the second or third time. Therefore, as a general rule, when the learner does not process the information on the third or fourth attempt, the instructor should provide the information differently.

Change the Form of Information

When simply repeating information is not successful in teaching the learner to make the correct response, the instructor should either change the information provided in the correction or change the technique itself. For example, if on the first time through an activity the learner makes an error, he or she may be told:

> "The red one goes on top."

At this point, it is not unusual for a learner to repeat the error. If he or she does, the correction may be made the second time the same way it was made the first time. After the third consecutive error, it should be changed. For example, the learner may be told:

> "Red one . . . up here."
> "Put the red one there."
> "Do you have the red one in the right place?"
> "Is the red one on top?"
> "Don't forget where the red one goes."

TABLE 9.16 Three Techniques for Correcting Performance Errors

Someone or something can
- provide the information again the way it was provided originally;
- change the information technique and provide the information again in a different way; or
- make the learner search for the correct response.

TABLE 9.17 Reasons Why Learners May Not Comprehend Information

- The learner may have missed or misinterpreted the information because of background noise.
- The instructor may have provided the information before the learner was ready to use it.
- The instructor may have provided the information too rapidly or too slowly.
- The learner may not have been paying attention.
- The learner may have difficulty processing the information.
- The learner may have difficulty understanding how to respond to the information.

The above changes in the way a verbal instruction is provided do not approach the limits of possible variation. The instructor can switch techniques entirely, as from verbal instructions to physical guidance, gestures, or demonstration. For example, in teaching a learner to use a sewing machine, the instructor may use physical guidance to show how to thread the needle the first time through the activity. On the second time through, however, the instructor may remove some of the physical guidance and say to the learner:

"Put the thread through the hole in the needle."

On subsequent attempts to teach, combinations of verbal instructions, physical guidance, and/or demonstration could be used to correct errors.

Planning different ways in which to provide identical information over and over again can be one of the most difficult things to do while teaching, and at times it approaches an art form. But by the same token, the need for frequent repetition of the same information can be a strong indication that there is a problem with the original analysis of the program objective or with the type of teaching activities that are being used. In these cases, rethinking the content of the instruction or the instructional approach might be in order (see Chapter 11).

Make the Learner Search

One of the most effective ways to make a correction is to allow the learners to discover the information on their own. To do this, the somebody or something providing feedback indicates to the learners that the response was not the one they were supposed to make, but allows the learners to discover what to do on their own instead. Instructors will often use this correction technique when they use learner search and NNGN as the information provision technique.

There are many ways in which to make the learner search for the correct response. For example, the learner might be told:

"No."
"Try another way."
"Uh-uh."
"What do you do next?"

Or, rather than saying anything, the instructor simply may block the learner's movements physically until he or she attempts to do something different. In whatever manner it is done, the aim is to require the learner to make a different response. If it is the correct one, NNGN can tell the learner to proceed, but if it is incorrect, the correction must continue.

Guidelines for Making the Learner Search. Learner search is valuable in instructional settings in which the aim is to teach learners to be independent because everyone who lives in the community must be able to get much of the information they need for themselves. The guidelines in Table 9.18 should help instructors decide when and how to use learner search as a correction technique.

Limit response options. A learner who is not used to trying to make different responses may need to be taught *how* to search for the necessary information. The instructor can usually teach the learner this technique by limiting the number of choices available to one or perhaps two possible actions at the time when he or she is first beginning to work on a skill. This approach will eliminate any confusion the learner might experience when there are too many possibilities for making a response. For example, when learners are first learning to store food after shopping for groceries, they often make incorrect moves, such as putting cans of food into the wrong cabinet. In such a case, the instructor simply can block all inappropriate movements until the learner switches to the correct cabinet. As another example, some learners, when first learning how to feed themselves, may insist on grabbing for foods indiscriminately. In such a case, the instructor can place the learner's hands palms down on the table, with the instructor's hands on top of them. Then, the instructor can allow the learner to lift one hand at a time only when the excited movements cease. In both of the above examples, the instructor limits the choices available and blocks the learner's response until he or she begins to perform in a way that meets the demands of the objective.

Confirm correct choices. When using learner search to make corrections, it is necessary to let the learner know when the choice he or she has made is the correct one by using one of the confirmation procedures discussed previously. NNGN (no news is good news) is often appropriate because it forces learners to find the correct way to do something by themselves, and the fact that they can continue whatever they are doing often will provide sufficient confirmation. This is not to say that a learner should not be told, "That's right," or, "Good," when he or she finally does the right thing.

TABLE 9.18 Guidelines for Making a Learner Search to Confirm or Correct
Erroneous Responses

To use learner search to confirm a response,
- limit response options,
- confirm correct choices, and
- time corrections properly.

Such responses are often beneficial because they give encouragement to the learner and help build rapport between the instructor and the learner.

Time corrections appropriately.   The old saying "If it ain't broke, don't fix it" applies to instruction in that it is important for instructors to consider the timing of their corrections. As a general rule when using learner search, response errors should be corrected as soon as possible so that the incorrect behavior does not become part of the learner's performance. Furthermore, it may be possible to correct any learner decisions that result in errors *before* the learner actually makes any overt response (Gold, 1980b). If the instructor can capture the moment, the best time to make a correction is when the learner already has made the decision to produce the wrong performance but has not yet made any overt action. Very close observation of the learner's behavior while engaged in one-on-one instruction is required for the instructor to make corrections in this manner because it is necessary to make the correction *after* the learner decides to make the erroneous response, not before.

Cautions in the Use of Feedback Techniques

Instructors can encounter a problem when providing feedback: They must pay very close attention to learner behavior, but close supervision can distract learners and make them shift their attention away from what they are doing and to the instructor. Close attention to learner behavior is an essential part of instruction, but the instructor must be careful not to interrupt the learners. For example, many instructors believe that eye contact is critical for learning. But this principle does not apply when the learners are engaged in activities to which they themselves must attend closely. More often than not, learners who make eye contact while they are supposed to be attending to their own performance will lose their focus on what they are supposed to be doing. To prevent such a thing from happening, the instructor should position himself or herself behind or beside the learner during instruction if at all possible, and make whatever corrections are necessary from that position. In addition, if a learner attempts to make eye contact when he or she should be focused on performing the activity, the instructor should not respond. In this manner, the learner's attention can remain directed on his or her performance. This principle does not apply when instructors are working with groups, as classroom teachers often do.

Fading

When the learner is able to perform the program objective in an appropriate manner, instruction should stop. Ideally, overt instruction should begin to disappear as soon as the learner starts to perform parts of the objective, and as learning proceeds, all forms of confirmation and correction should progress toward performance confirmation. Ultimately, the learners should receive all their feedback from the natural conditions present in the performance environment. Instructors must firmly keep in mind that the reason they teach is to help the learner be able to perform program objectives *when the instructor is not present.* Eventually, the learner's performance itself should provide all the confirmation and correction he or she needs in order to correct, adjust, and continue the performance of the activity. In order to accomplish this goal, instructors must fade all forms of feedback that are not a normal part of the natural performance conditions. **Fading,** or removing the instructor's presence (or any other external information source), is a crucial part of the instructional process.

Fading can be gradual or abrupt, depending on the learning and performance characteristics of the learner and his or her understanding of the requirements of the program objective. In practice, fading involves having the learner obtain less and less information from external sources, and simultaneously, using more and more learner search and performance confirmation to guide his or her behavior. All corrections should quickly move toward confirmation, and if performance confirmation is not the first confirmation technique employed, further confirmation and correction should move toward performance confirmation as rapidly as possible.

When learners first make errors, they should receive the information they need to correct their responses, but they should obtain the information in increasingly truncated forms as instruction progresses. As soon as the learner begins to comprehend and act correctly on the information, the instructor must focus the fading so that the external confirmation and correction are eliminated altogether. The final fading occurs, of course, when the instructor walks away while the learner performs the activity, confident in the knowledge that he or she does not require someone to give him or her information about how to perform the activity. This independence is the ultimate success in instruction.

Motivation

In this chapter on providing instruction, we have saved the discussion on motivation until the end. One reason for doing so is that much has been written about the importance of motivation in teaching persons with mental retardation and about techniques and methods instructors can use to respond to motivational concerns and issues. Although we realize that motivation is central to the process of learning, we encourage readers to seek out other sources to answer questions about what procedures to use and how to develop interventions with learners who lack motivation, especially when encountering severe, complicated, or long-standing problems in motivation. Space limitations do not allow us to address these issues in the depth required to really assist instructional personnel in this area.

We also believe, however, that motivation should be seen as an issue separate from instruction. While it is true that learners must have enough motivation to participate in the learning activities, it is not always true that instructors must do a lot to provide that motivation. More often than not, learners who enter an instructional setting are perfectly willing to do what the instructor wants them to do, and the instructor's main problems are finding out what the learners must learn to do and how to get them to do it quickly and efficiently. Learners will be especially motivated to do what the instructor wants them to do when they think that an activity is important for them to perform. The supreme example is the fact that driver education instructors almost never have to worry about motivation. If all instruction were as important from the learner's point of view, motivation would not be much of an issue in instruction.

The instructor may never know what makes a learner participate in learning activities willingly. Among other things, a learner may enjoy learning new skills, may want to please the instructor, or may just like to keep busy. Whatever the reason, most learners require few or no additional rewards or aversives to get them to do what an instructor wants them to do, and motivation is usually not a problem. Parenthetically, most instructors try to create an accepting and pleasant learning environment, and many will give periodic rewards to a learner or a group of learners just to keep the relationship pleasant. For example, schoolteachers have placed stars on a chart and have given "free time" for many years, and rehabilitation instructors often take groups on periodic trips to the pizza parlor and engage in other enjoyable activities. Such activities and events are rarely *required* when instruction focuses on matters that are important to learners, but they can help to promote a pleasant, friendly learning environment.

There is no question that learners sometimes do not want to do what their instructors want them to do, and that either they will try to do something else or simply will refuse to perform. It happens mostly when the learners believe that instruction has little relevance for them, but it happens at other times as well for a myriad of reasons. For example, a learner may dislike the instructional activity or may be trying to manipulate the instructor in some way. When learners refuse to participate in the instructional activity, the instructor must figure out how to motivate them. The instructor has only a few choices for motivating a learner to perform. They appear in Table 9.19.

Rewards and Aversives

When instructors use rewards and aversives to motivate learners, the best ones to use are the ones that are most similar to those that operate in the natural setting. For example, the most natural reward for a learner who is learning to cook

TABLE 9.19 Choices for Motivating a Learner to Perform

- Reward the learner for doing what he or she is supposed to do.
- Provide aversives for doing what the learner wants to do instead of what the instructor wants him or her to do.
- Develop a different activity that is more inherently motivating for the learner to teach the same objective.
- Change the objective.
- Forget about teaching until other considerations are addressed, such as health problems, abuse, and development of rapport.

is to be able to eat the food because eating is usually inherent in the performance of the activity; moreover, the absence of food as a result of not cooking is a natural aversive. Both will continue to be present for the learner when instruction is complete and the instructor is no longer available. Such natural rewards and aversives are powerful and instructionally desirable, and should be relied upon whenever possible. Parenthetically, one of the reasons that community-based instruction tends to be so effective is that natural rewards and aversives are present in nearly every activity.

The least desirable rewards and aversives are the ones that have nothing to do with the activity. For example, an instructor might give a learner candy for taking a bus or remove tokens for hitting other learners. One of the problems with such rewards and aversives is that the instructor must be present in order for the learner to get them. As a result, they will not continue to motivate the learner to perform appropriately when instruction is complete, and any performance they generate is not likely to continue when the instructor is not present. Thus, they often promote a dependency relationship that is counter to the goal of independence.

Activity Variables

With a little creativity, instructors can usually change an instructional activity to make it more interesting and palatable to the learner. This is an old trick in instruction, and people have spent a lot of time developing new activities within which to provide the same instruction. It is often possible to find fun ways to teach new skills by couching them in game formats, simulations, service learning, or other activities in which learners like to engage. Whatever the format, activities that learners enjoy performing are inherently motivating. For learners with mental retardation, the more closely a learning activity resembles a community activity, the more likely it will motivate the learner to participate in the instructional activity. For example, academic skills that are taught within the context of either a job or a community service project are more likely to appear relevant and useful to learners with mild mental retardation than are the academic skills taught in traditional classroom settings (Cairn and Kielsmeir, 1995; Hamill and Dunlevy, 1993a; Missouri LINC, 1989–1990).

Sometimes instructors make a mistake and try to teach the wrong thing to a learner. Perhaps the learner is not yet ready to learn the program objective, or perhaps it simply is inappropriate for that learner's program. In such a case, the learner does not have a problem of motivation so much as the instructor has created a problem with inappropriate programming. If the instructor selects a different objective, the problem may be resolved.

Learner Variables

Sometimes learners are unwilling to participate because of a problem that is external to the instruction. A learner who is in pain or who is medicated, for example, may not engage in learning activities wholeheartedly. Similarly, learners who have problems with vision, hearing, seizures, or other physical problems may have difficulty participating in learning activities, and these problems should be addressed as an issue separate from the act of teaching. In Appendix C we present a checklist of potential symptoms of problems that all instructors should look for when experiencing difficulty in getting a learner to participate. If any of these symptoms are found, the instructor should refer the learner for medical evaluation.

In addition to physical problems, however, there are many other factors that may affect a learner's motivation to learn new skills. Learners who are victims of neglect or abuse may have difficulty participating in instructional activities. (Note: In cases of suspected neglect or abuse, many states now have laws that require an instructor to make a report to authorities.) In addition, learners who are experiencing problems such as the breakup of their families may exhibit an unwillingness to participate in instructional activities. Instructors should try to find out whether learners who do not participate willingly in instructional activities have circumstances or events in their lives that are causing them to be preoccupied, and take steps to help correct these problems if they can.

Concluding Statement

In this chapter we discussed the teaching process, which, although complex, can be summarized easily. There is a limited number of techniques for providing information to learners about what they must do to attain the program objective. Despite the many books that have been written on this subject, there are only a few ways in which we actually can provide information to learners: we can tell them what to do; we can point to the features to which they must attend; we can show them what to do; we can move their bodies through the motions; or we can make them find out for themselves.

The information itself is of two kinds. The first is the fundamental information that the learners must have to achieve a program objective. The second is the feedback information the learners need in order to understand whether what they did was appropriate, and if not, what they must do to make it appropriate. If these types of information are provided properly, learning should take place at its optimum rate, whatever that may be for a specific learner.

All the other chapters in the book have dealt with the identification of what the learners must do. This chapter is the first one in the book that focuses directly on what the instructor must do to get the learners to perform. Unbalanced though this ratio may seem, it is the way it must be. The "what" of instruction has not been at the forefront of thinking in special education and rehabilitation, but in order for instruction to be effective, it must become paramount. As this chapter shows, once the instructor knows exactly what the learners are supposed to do, it is easy to find a way to get them to do it. If the instructor does not know what the learners are supposed to do, however, all the techniques in the world will not help them to acquire program objectives, and instruction will be ineffective.

Suggested Resources for Behavior Management Techniques

Alberto, P. A., & Troutman, A. (1990). *Applied behavior analysis for teachers*. Columbus, OH: Merrill/Macmillan.

Bandura, A. (1986). *Social foundations of thought and action*. Englewood Cliffs: Prentice-Hall.

Cooper, J. O., Heron, T. E., & Heward, W. L. (1987). *Applied behavior analysis*. Columbus, OH: Merrill/Macmillan.

Donnellan, A. M., LaVigna, G., Negri-Shoultz, N., & Fassbender, L. (1988). *Progress without punishment: Effective approaches for learners with behavior problems*. New York: Teachers College Press.

Edwards, C. H. (1993). *Classroom discipline and management*. New York: Macmillan.

Kazdin, A. E. (1989). *Behavior modification in applied settings*. Pacific Grove, CA.: Brooks/Cole.

O'Neill, R. E., Horner, R., Albin, R. W., Sorey, K., & Sprague, J. (1990). *Functional analysis of problem behavior*. Sycamore, IL: Sycamore.

Repp, A. C., & Singh, A. A. (1990). *Perspectives on the use of nonaversive and aversive interventions for persons with developmental disabilities*. Sycamore, IL: Sycamore.

Walker, H. M., Colvin, G., & Ramsey, E. (1995). *Antisocial behavior in school: Strategies and best practices*. Pacific Grove, CA: Brooks/Cole.

Wolery, M., Bailey, D., & Sugai, G. (1988). *Effective teaching: Principles and procedures of applied behavior analysis with exceptional students*. Boston: Allyn & Bacon.

Zirpoli, T. J., & Melloy, K. (1993). *Behavior management: Applications for teachers and parents*. New York: Merrill.

CHAPTER 10

Monitoring Instructional Plans

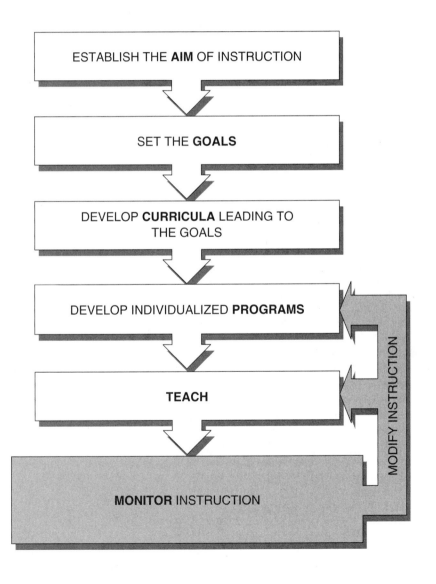

ESTABLISH THE **AIM** OF INSTRUCTION

SET THE **GOALS**

DEVELOP **CURRICULA** LEADING TO THE GOALS

DEVELOP INDIVIDUALIZED **PROGRAMS**

TEACH

MONITOR INSTRUCTION

MODIFY INSTRUCTION

In both education and rehabilitation, the Individual Plan (IP) is designed to specify the instructional services for each learner. An IP has legal status, either because it is mandated by law or because it is required by the regulations that guide community agencies. Because it has a legal underpinning, it is easy to get the impression that once an IP has been written, it is unchangeable. Nothing could be further from the truth: An IP is not a contract, it is a plan for what to do "next," and as a plan, it is always open to change. In fact, it usually is necessary to make the following types of changes after instruction has started:

- regular and systematic changes that keep instruction on course and closely aligned with the learners' newly acquired skills and abilities; and
- deliberate alterations that help instruction address the learners' instructional needs more effectively.

In either case, the changes that instructors make during instruction must be thoughtful, systematic, and based on accurate information about learner behavior.

To understand how and when to make changes after instruction begins, it is necessary to gauge the effects (or lack of effects) that the instructional activities are having on learner behavior. A monitoring system is the tool of choice for evaluating the effectiveness of instruction, and a good one will help instructors pay careful attention to what is happening during the instructional activities. The data derived from the monitoring activities will provide a basis for making decisions about what to do "next" during instruction. As we have stated repeatedly, instructors must always seek to make instruction better than it is, and a good instructional monitoring system provides the means for deciding how to make instruction the best it can be.

In this chapter we will explain the purposes and uses of instructional monitoring and discuss issues and variables that instructors should investigate during the monitoring activities. We will also describe some useful monitoring procedures. The approach we will present focuses mostly on the use of informal observational methods as opposed to formal research-oriented techniques. This informal approach not only will supply instructors with the information they need to evaluate the effectiveness of their lessons and fine-tune their instruction, it also will allow instructors to continue their usual teaching schedules and attend to their normal responsibilities. The approach gives instructional personnel a great deal of flexibility in adapting and changing procedures and allows them to respond to specific concerns and questions they may have at any point during instruction.

We will start our discussion of monitoring by describing its primary functions in instructional programs.

The Concept of Monitoring

Monitoring is not something that just gets tacked on as some kind of after-thought after instruction begins. On the contrary, developing a well-conceived strategy for monitoring instruction is actually the final step in developing a comprehensive instructional plan. A carefully designed monitoring system has two major benefits. It helps ensure that the instructional procedures

1. maintain a consistent focus on the program objectives in the learners' IPs; and
2. keep learners working on a steady course toward the program objectives.

Following up on instruction will keep teaching on track.
Photo courtesy of Jeff Greenberg/Unicorn Stock Photos, Inc.

To carry out an effective program of instruction, instructional staff must find a way to follow closely whatever progress (or lack of progress) learners make during instruction. The monitoring of instruction involves not only the discovery of the successes and failures of the instruction, but also the documentation of the expected and unexpected results of instruction. A thoughtful system of monitoring allows instructors to find out if their procedures adequately address the learners' immediate informational needs and helps instructors tailor their lessons accordingly (Knapczyk and Rodes, 1996). Monitoring also provides a wealth of crucial information about what to do next, which in turn can guide all further work under the IP.

The Link Between Monitoring and Program Objectives

We have indicated previously that instruction should accomplish the following:

- provide learners with the information they need to acquire the skills for attaining program objectives;
- teach the learners to use those skills under natural performance conditions; and
- teach the learners to perform the skills at or above a set of standards.

The first major task in developing a monitoring system is to supply information about whether the learners actually are developing the skills that will allow them to attain the objectives that are listed in their IPs. At this point, the reader may find it useful to review the description of the program objective analysis in Chapter 8 because the work sheet for the analysis of program objectives provides much of the essential information for planning monitoring activities. This information includes

- the *program objectives* that describe overall skills the learners must acquire;
- the *behavioral pattern* that specifies the behaviors and cues they must learn;
- the *situational cues* that indicate the circumstances under which they are to use their skills;
- the *outcomes* that should give purpose to their actions, and thus provide incentive;
- the *standards* that specify the level of behavior they must attain to achieve the objectives; and
- the *level of confidence* that expresses the level of proficiency they need to develop before instruction can end.

Although an analysis of program objectives provides a major link between the instruction carried out under the learner's program plan and the monitoring procedures that keep tabs on the instruction, instructors should bring additional information into play when they decide how to set up their monitoring activities. In the following section we discuss several important issues that instructors must consider in order to develop a comprehensive plan for monitoring a learner's progress. Later in the chapter, we will explain how to obtain information in these areas.

Rationale for Conducting Monitoring Activities

There are probably as many ways to monitor instruction as there are types of instructional activities. However, no matter what approach an instructor might use, the rationale for monitoring is always the same: The instructor has to find out what effect instruction is having on the learner's behavior. Therefore, when setting up monitoring activities, instructors should establish

- which issues are the most important to monitor;
- what kinds of information to obtain from the monitoring activities;
- how much information to gather; and
- what to do with the information after it is obtained.

Table 10.1 provides a list of important reasons for conducting monitoring activities. We will discuss these reasons in this section.

Monitoring Instruction Allows Instructors to Determine the Progress Learners Are Making Toward Achieving Program Objectives

At the most fundamental level, instructors must monitor instruction to find out how much progress learners are making toward achieving their program objectives. This information will allow the instructors to determine whether the learners are acquiring the skills that are the focus of the instruction and to judge whether the instructional activities are having their desired effects. More importantly, even the best planned instruction will require adjustments in procedures as it progresses, and these adjustments can become necessary at any time and for any number of reasons. The information obtained during the monitoring will help the instructors make whatever adjustments are necessary as soon as they are needed and will give instructors a firm basis for planning any further courses of action that might be required. Moreover, the information that is obtained from monitoring will help instructors decide when learners have made enough progress to allow the instructional staff to begin working on more advanced curriculum objectives.

Monitoring Instruction Allows Instructors to Gauge the Initial Effects the Instruction Is Having on Learner Performance

Skill Acquisition Delays. In the early stages of instruction, it is easy to become discouraged if the learners do not acquire new skills immediately, and instructors may be tempted to discard what actually might be very effective instructional procedures. It often takes a couple of days for learners with mental retardation to adapt to new teaching activities, and behavioral

TABLE 10.1 Reasons for Monitoring Instructional Plans

Effective monitoring allows instructors to
- determine the progress learners make toward achieving program objectives;
- gauge the initial effects that instruction has on learner performance;
- bring instructional techniques into line with the learners' progress in achieving program objectives;
- evaluate whether the learners carry their skills over to other situations; and
- obtain additional assessment information about the learners' characteristics and performance.

Knapczyk, D., and Rodes, P. (1996). *Teaching social competence: A practical approach for improving social skills in students at-risk.* Pacific Grove, CA: Brooks/Cole.

changes may not be apparent immediately. During this time, it may be hard to tell whether the learners are making progress toward meeting a program objective.

The instructional staff should observe the learners' behavior closely at the start of instruction because the early instructional procedures may be having more subtle effects than it is possible to observe casually. These subtle changes in learner performance can give instructors some assurance that their procedures are working properly. Monitoring instruction during the initial activities will allow instructors to see what kinds of general effects their teaching is having, to watch how learners react to specific methods and procedures, and to determine whether the particular approach they are using is actually starting to help the learners develop their skills.

For example, it is not unusual during the first days of instruction for a learner to be reticent, apprehensive, or even defensive about participating in new instructional activities. Thus, when instruction first begins, instructors may find that some learners act in an uncooperative manner. But if the instructor looks at these learners' behavior more objectively, he or she may discover that they actually are attending closely to what is going on despite the fact that they may not seem actively engaged in learning. Such observations would encourage the instructor to continue the original instructional plan even if the learners are not progressing as quickly as the instructor had hoped originally.

Comprehension of Purpose. A related issue that instructors may wish to examine at the beginning of instruction is whether the learners actually understand the overall purpose of the instruction and the reasons that the instructors are using a particular approach. Many times an instructor can gain the enthusiastic participation of learners after they understand the purposes of the instructional activities. But it is important to realize that it can take some time for persons with mental retardation to figure out what instruction is all about. Therefore, insofar as possible, learners should be involved in the planning of all instructional activities, so they can begin to focus ahead of time on what they will be working toward. They should not be surprised by sudden changes in their routines, or by any new teaching methods an instructor introduces. Whenever it is feasible, instructors should explain matters such as the following to their learners at the start of instructional activities:

- why they are entering new instructional situations;
- why they are participating in different kinds of activities;
- why they are being asked to change their roles and responsibilities; and/or
- why they are supposed to respond to new and different challenges.

To find out whether learners comprehend the purpose of instruction, the monitoring activities could involve having the learners state what they are trying to do, describe the specific problems they are having in developing the skills, or even explain why they may be apprehensive about behaving in certain ways or under certain conditions.

Comprehension of Outcomes. Monitoring activities also can focus on finding out whether learners understand the outcomes that result from the performance of their new skills. During the initial phase of instruction, the learners may not respond to these new outcomes for any one of a number of reasons. For example, they may not realize that they can attain the outcomes, or they may not view the results as satisfying. Monitoring instruction right from the start can show whether the learners respond favorably to the outcomes for meeting the objectives, or at least, whether they are interested in and attentive to attaining them.

Monitoring Instruction Allows Instructors to Bring Information Provision Techniques into Line with the Learners' Progress Toward the Program Objectives

Instruction is a dynamic process, and its focus can change dramatically across successive time periods. It is quite natural for instructors to alter their teaching approaches substantially during the course of instruction and to acknowledge the progress learners have made by giving them more and more responsibility for their actions. For example, when instruction first begins, an instructor may need to focus on the more conspicuous aspects of a program objective, such as specific behavioral cues or the most fundamental parts of a behavioral pattern. If so, the instructor might begin by using simple verbal instructions, gestures, or physical guidance. As the learner begins to acquire the fundamental aspects of performance, the instructor may begin to concentrate on the more subtle behaviors and cues, and simultaneously, to incorporate demonstration into the lessons. Then, after the learner begins to show greater proficiency and independence in his or her behavior, the instructor may assume a more supervisory role by using learner search and "no news is good news" as the primary instructional techniques, thus allowing the learner to practice and refine his or her skills through interactions with the natural conditions of performance. In order to make changes like these, it is necessary to monitor learner behavior very closely and to determine when the learners have gained enough information from one procedure or activity to allow them to move on to the next approach. Thus, by monitoring instruction, instructors can establish a firm basis for deciding how and when to adjust the procedures to account for the new skills learners have acquired.

Close monitoring of instruction helps instructors react quickly and deliberately to whatever changes are taking place in the learners' behavior and keep instruction in line with the gains learners are making toward meeting the program objectives. Instructors will be able to adapt, adjust, and fine-tune instruction as needed. Instructors will also find that they can advance the learners' skill acquisition more rapidly by making adjustments deliberately and thoughtfully rather than by leaving them to chance. This aspect of monitoring is particularly important when the learners must acquire many component skills or make major advances in their behavior in order to meet the objectives. Thus, as learners become proficient in one part of a behavior pattern, their instructors can begin to concentrate on other parts of the pattern or begin to make salient the situational cues and outcomes found in the natural setting. The monitoring process can clarify when and how to make the adjustments that allow learners to make steady progress toward meeting the program objectives.

Additionally, after learners have become adept in using their skills, instructors should begin to fade direct support and require the learners to take on greater responsibility for their behavior. For example, an instructor may

- start the fading process by having the learners begin to demonstrate how and when to use their skills;
- alter the amount and level of encouragement given; and/or
- have learners themselves begin to identify the outcomes that are associated with the program objective.

To make adjustments such as these at the proper times, instructors must closely observe the effects that instruction is having on the learners' behavior.

Monitoring Allows Instructors to Evaluate Whether the Learners Carry Their Skills Over into Other Situations

Learners often must use their skills under circumstances that are very different from those in which they learn them. Instructors often provide instruction under one or perhaps two clearly defined, but limited, sets of conditions, and the manner in which the learners respond in other situations is never really clear from observing what takes place during the instructional activities. Sometimes learners naturally will carry their skills over to other circumstances in which they should be using them, and sometimes they will not. One focus of monitoring should be to find out whether the learners do, in fact, use their new skills appropriately in all the settings and circumstances in which the program objective applies. If instructors find that learners do not make the necessary transfer and generalizations on their own, instructors will have to expand their teaching to help the learners carry their new skills over to the natural settings.

For example, consider a special education teacher who is teaching personal finance math skills to a group of teenagers with mild mental retardation. This teacher should monitor the students' performance to find out if they are able to perform their skills in real-life situations, such as when budgeting their funds, making purchases, and paying their bills. If the teacher finds that the students do perform their math skills in real settings, he or she will not have to address transfer of skills in the instructional program. On the other hand, if the students do not carry their skills over to other situations, the teacher must expand the instructional activities to ensure that students learn to use the skills under real-life circumstances. The information gathered from the monitoring activities can indicate the extent to which instruction needs to focus on the carryover of skills.

Monitoring Allows Instructors to Obtain Additional Assessment Information About Learner Performance

Careful monitoring can also help instructors obtain important assessment information about learner behavior because the responses that learners make to instruction often provide new insights and perspectives into their abilities, talents, and instructional needs. While carrying out teaching activities, instructors will often uncover new information (or update previously obtained information) on matters such as the following:

- the learners' background knowledge;
- their ability to use prerequisite and lead-in skills;
- their proficiency in certain aspects of a behavior pattern; and/or
- their understanding of situational cues, performance conditions, and outcomes.

In other words, the instructional activities themselves can provide active, ongoing assessment information as the learners develop new skills and abilities. This additional information can be used to update and revise the analysis of program objectives, or it can be incorporated into instruction and increase the effectiveness of subsequent teaching activities.

This source of information is especially beneficial when the instruction does not appear to be having the desired effect, that is, when learners are not making satisfactory progress toward acquiring the skills that are the focus of the instruction. Any time instruction is not going well, it is necessary to determine why the learners are not developing their skills properly. Close observation of the manner in which the learners respond to the teaching activities can provide valuable information about any impediments that affect skill acquisition and can suggest the type of adjustments that instructors would need to make to get instruction back on course.

Many times instructors will find that learners do not make progress in acquiring skills because the instructors did not take certain information into account in the original instructional plan. There are any number of reasons why instructors may overlook important information. For example, during the initial assessment, an instructor may have missed some crucial details about the learner's ability level or performance characteristics. But as instruction proceeds, new information often appears that fills in the gaps, and this information allows the instructor to make the adjustments that will help instruction progress satisfactorily.

Alternately, learners may not make progress because the instructor may have made some incorrect assumptions about the learners' motivation for participating in the teaching activities. In practice, it is very difficult to predict what actually will motivate a learner, and the instructional activities will give the instructor opportunities to try out different types of incentives. Then, as additional information about the learners' motivational needs comes to light, the monitoring procedures can aid in making calculated changes in the instructional procedures.

Consider the instructor who encounters a learner who participates unenthusiastically in the instructional activities. This instructor will have to make some adjustments in the instructional approach used with the learner, but first the instructor must find out what aspects of the procedures need to be changed. One area that the instructor might investigate more closely is that of the learner's prerequisite skills: He or she should check to see whether there are limitations in the learner's motor, sensory, or cognitive skills that may have been missed during the initial assessment. If the learner's skills are not as advanced as the instructor originally thought they were, the instructor may conclude that the learner needs to acquire these skills before working on the originally specified objective. On the other hand, if the instructor sees that the learner has sufficient background knowledge and ability, he or she might make some adjustments that would encourage this learner to participate in the activities more enthusiastically. For instance, the instructor might restructure the activities to make them move at a faster or slower pace in order to maintain the learner's interest, or he or she might modify the setting in some manner to promote greater learner concentration or motivation. The decision on what to do next in circumstances like these will be aided by the specific information gathered during monitoring.

As this discussion suggests, an effective strategy for monitoring instruction can serve a number of very important purposes. These purposes range from the verification of the effectiveness of the instructional plan to making thoughtful adjustments in teaching procedures to account for newly learned skills. In the next section we will discuss how to develop an effective system for monitoring instructional plans.

Developing a Monitoring System

In order to monitor instruction, instructors will need to plan a comprehensive data collection system that will allow them to track the learners' responses to

Overview of the Teaching Process

TABLE 10.2 Steps in Developing a Monitoring System

- Decide on which issues to focus monitoring.
- Select the monitoring procedures.
- Plan to record and summarize results.

the instructional activities. There are three major reasons why it is important to plan such a system:

1. instruction can have many different elements and can get very complicated before the learner achieves all aspects of a program objective;
2. instruction can produce a variety of effects on learner behavior, any of which may suggest a new course of instruction; and
3. instruction can reveal a great deal of surprising information about the learner's skill level that should be documented for later use.

Because instruction is a complex process, it can become very difficult to keep track of what is happening while it is going on. Therefore, before beginning to teach, instructors must make careful plans on how and where to focus their attention so as to get the most useful information possible. Table 10.2 lists the three steps to follow when developing a monitoring system.

The best way for instructors to proceed when planning a monitoring system is to prepare a work sheet for each program objective so they can keep their preparation clearly focused. On each work sheet they should list the issues they plan to address for each objective, describe the procedures they will use, and document the monitoring results. Table 10.3 is an example of a monitoring work sheet for the case of Phil Weatherspoon that we presented in the previous chapters.

This type of work sheet can be attached to the learner's IP and/or to the two-part work sheet used to analyze program objectives (see Table 8.1). If the instructors combine the work sheets, they will have all the information they need to both carry out and monitor instruction in a readily available single set of documents. In addition, instructors can avoid having to repeat much of the basic information about the learner's circumstances, such as background information about the learner and the program area, the statement of the program objective, the standards, and the level of confidence.

Step 1: Decide on Which Issues to Focus Monitoring Activities

The first thing to do when planning a monitoring system is to consider the issues to address during the monitoring activities. This step is especially important when instruction is likely to have several stages because the instructor's concerns will usually change substantially as the teaching progresses. For example, when first beginning to teach, the instructor's primary concerns probably will be issues such as those in the first section of Table 10.4.

TABLE 10.3 Example of a Monitoring Work Sheet

Name: Phil Weatherspoon
Program Objective: Adds/subtracts numbers with decimals
Standard: Obtains 15 of 20 correct in 15 minutes
Location: Classroom
Instructor: Mrs. Franklin

Issues to Monitor	Procedures
Does Phil understand how decimals are used in everyday activities, e.g., handling money?	Talk with Phil about applications
How does Phil react to having Kyle as a tutor during math?	Observation
Does Phil do computations quicker when he works on the computer?	Observation
What types of errors does Phil make in his computations?	Written work; test scores
Does he carry over the computer drills to the written assignments?	Written work; computer readout scores

Daily Results of Monitoring

Days	Results/Comments
November 14	12/20 correct in 14 min. Worked well with Kyle
November 15	16/20 correct in 15 min. Computer drills seemed challenging but kept him on task
November 16	18/20 correct in 13 min. Aligned the numbers better. This eliminated some errors
November 17	17/20 correct in 12 min.
November 21	17/20 correct in 14 min. Still works well with Kyle and computer drills
December 5	19/20 correct in 15 min. Carried over computer drills to written work with more difficult problems. Will work with money next
December 12	18/20 correct in 14 min. on written test

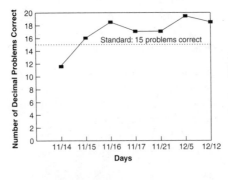

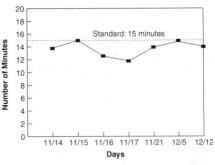

Overview of the Teaching Process

TABLE 10.3 (CONT.)

Name: Phil Weatherspoon
Program Objective: Answers telephone calls and takes messages
Standard: Completes all the steps in the telephone checklist
Location: School office
Instructor: Mrs. Franklin

Issues to Monitor	Procedures
Does Phil talk clearly enough to be heard?	Observation Talk with Mrs. Peters
Can Phil interrupt a conversation to ask someone in the office for additional information about a question someone asked?	Observation Talk with Mrs. Peters
How does Phil react to working with the secretarial staff?	Observation Talk with office staff
How does Phil do in transferring calls? Does he use good phone etiquette?	Talk with school staff
Are the notes and phone messages that Phil writes accurate and legible?	Examine samples of messages and notes

Daily Results of Monitoring

Days	Results/Comments
November 21	Phil was able to repeat the different types of calls on Mrs. Peter's list. He spoke very clearly during the trial
November 22	Reviewed list of calls. Phil was able to explain types of calls. He continues to greet callers clearly
November 23	Phil observed Mrs. Peters in office. He seemed unsure about how to ask the staff for help on calls
December 4	Phil is making progress, but he doesn't ask callers to repeat messages if he doesn't understand them
December 9	Phil does well with transferring calls and enjoys telling teachers that they have someone "on the line"

TABLE 10.3 (CONT.)

Name: Phil Weatherspoon
Program Objective: Answers telephone calls and takes messages
Standard: Completes all the steps in the telephone checklist
Location: School office
Instructor: Mrs. Franklin

Behavior pattern	Trials				
14. Returns receiver to telephone cradle	14	14	14	14	14
13. Gives the caller a salutation (e.g., says, "Thank you for calling Lincoln High School")	13	13	13	13	13
12. Provides additional assistance to caller, if needed	12	12	12	12	12
11. Asks caller if he can be of further assistance	11	11	11	11	11
10. Asks Mrs. Peters to talk to the caller, if needed, and transfers call	10	10	10	10	(10)
9. Asks Mrs. Peters about the questions the callers have	9	9	9	9	9
8. If the request is for information, does one of the following:	8	8	8	8	8
(a) supplies information					
(b) says, "Please wait a minute while I ask Mrs. Peters"					
(c) says, "I will have you talk with Mrs. Peters"					
7. If a request is for a school member, transfers call to that person	7	7	7	(7)	7
6. Listens for a request or question from the caller	6	(6) — (6)	6	6
5. Says, "Can I help you?"	5	5	5	5	5
4. Waits for response to greeting	(4)	4	4	4	4
3. Greets caller without pausing (e.g., says, "Hello, this is Lincoln High School")	3	3	3	3	3
2. Picks up phone receiver	2	2	2	2	2
1. Listens for ringing of telephone	1	1	1	1	1
Probe:	11/21	11/22	11/23	12/4	12/9

As instruction starts to have an effect, the instructor's concerns very well might shift to issues such as those in the center section of the table. And, as instruction approaches a conclusion, the concerns may shift further to those in the last section of the table.

It is easy for instructors to get so engrossed in the act of teaching that they fail to notice such things as whether the learner actually understands the purpose of the instruction or uses skills in situations and settings other than those in which they were taught. Instructors who prepare a written list of issues like these and add them to the work sheet will be able to keep the most immediate concerns in mind and still maintain a focus on the reason for instruction and its overall results. To get the necessary information, it is important for instructors to make provisions for looking at these issues in advance. With a little preparation, it is easy to verify that skill acquisition is (or is not) taking place, and instructors quickly can

TABLE 10.4 Examples to Show How Monitoring Issues Change During Instruction

Early in instruction, the instructor may wish to find out if the learner
- responds favorably to the instructional activities;
- uses previously acquired skills under the new teaching circumstances;
- is sufficiently motivated to participate in the activities and learn the new skills; and/or
- reacts positively to the teaching environment, such as the materials used, the grouping arrangements, and the overall instructional approach.

After instruction is under way, the instructor may wish to find out if the learner
- finds certain types of behavior easier or more difficult to learn and use;
- attends well to certain types of cues;
- forgets certain types of cues quickly;
- has difficulty using certain portions of the behavior pattern proficiently;
- shows continued interest in the instruction; and/or
- comprehends the purpose for learning the skills.

Near the end of instruction, the instructor may wish to find out if the learner
- puts knowledge and skills together to form a complete behavior pattern;
- readily uses skills under natural performance conditions;
- adapts behavior to new and changing circumstances in the environment; and/or
- maintains continuing interest in the outcomes inherent in meeting the program objective.

address any problems the learner has in adapting and refining skills to the changing conditions.

Thus, before beginning instruction, instructors should develop a written list of the questions that they have about the learner's response to the teaching, especially when they have several areas of concern or when these concerns are likely to change during the course of the instruction. They should list these issues in the form of direct, tightly focused statements and base them on what they would like to find out about the learner's behavior or on what they predict will happen to his or her performance.

Table 10.3 provides examples of some concerns that Phil's teacher, Mrs. Franklin, wished to address and shows how they can be entered on a work sheet. Other possible issues for monitoring are listed in Table 10.5. As with all aspects of instruction, instructors should gear their list of issues for monitoring to the characteristics of the particular learners with whom they work.

Step 2: Select the Procedures Used to Monitor Instruction

Once instructors have decided on which issues to concentrate, choosing the procedures for monitoring an instructional plan is a fairly simple and straightforward process. In Chapters 6 and 7, we urged instructors to use as many of their normal teaching and supervisory activities as possible to carry out the assessment. We believe that they should monitor the results of the instruction in a similar manner whenever possible because it will reduce

TABLE 10.5 Questions That Could Be Addressed in Monitoring an Instructional Plan

Does the learner understand the overall purpose or intent of the instruction?
Is the learner willing to put forth the necessary effort to develop the skills?
Does the learner attend to and respond to the instructional procedures?
Is the learner receptive to and cooperative with the instructor's interactions?
Does the learner show interest in the activities and in the people or materials involved in them?
Does the learner focus on certain aspects of the instructional activities more easily or with more difficulty?
Does the learner make progress in achieving the sequence of steps in the analysis of the program objective?
Does the learner progress toward achieving the program objective in a timely manner?
Does the learner consistently get "hung up" on particular steps in the behavior pattern?
Does the learner carry over the skills to the other circumstances in which he or she needs to use them?
Does the instruction have a positive or a negative effect on other areas of the learner's behavior?
Do other people respond differently to the learner as his or her behavior changes?
Are the natural outcomes for using the skills having an effect on learner behavior?
Do the other people who help with instruction carry out the procedures consistently?

their planning and preparation time and help keep the observations unobtrusive and objective.

The following sections provide a brief discussion of monitoring procedures. These procedures are likely to be different depending on whether they are directed toward the first or the second of the following tasks:

1. monitoring the learners' progress toward the program objective, or
2. monitoring the other important issues with which instructors may be concerned.

Procedures for Monitoring Progress Toward the Program Objective

The most basic and certainly the most important reason to monitor instruction is to ascertain whether learners are making progress toward learning the skills being taught. Unfortunately, it is possible for the original purpose of instruction to be obscured during all the planning and preparation for the instructional activities. However, periodic reference to either the learner's IP or the analysis of the program objective will help instructors keep sight of the overall purpose of the instruction.

For example, it is extremely important not to lose sight of the standards for the program objectives because they provide the basis for judging the effectiveness of the instruction. Therefore, as part of the process of referring either to the IP or to the analysis of the objective, instructors should consider what types of measures and what criterion levels will indicate "success" for the program objective. This information will enable the instructors to compare the learner's behavior to the standards that they have established. This act automatically focuses attention on any improvements that may or may not occur in the learner's behavior.

The monitoring of a learner's actual progress toward the program objectives is different from most other types of monitoring in that the procedures should be more formal and data-based. The reason is that instructors need an objective set of standards against which to judge learner progress. In most cases, the procedures they use should be the same or equivalent to those that were used during the initial assessment. The resulting data will give instructors the best and clearest indication of whether the learners are making progress. For example, when conducting the initial assessment, the instructor may have used a tally system to record the results of direct observations of a learner's behavior during specific school, home, or work activities. Now, during instruction, the instructor should use the same tally system to evaluate the learner's progress and conduct the evaluation in the same settings and under the same circumstances. Then, a comparison of the tallies will allow the instructor to determine whether the learner's performance has improved enough to meet the standard for "successful performance." As the teaching progresses, data collection should continue until the learner's performance has reached the confidence level set for the instruction. The level of the learner's behavior observed at each measurement interval will provide a firm basis for deciding what to do "next" in the instructional plan.

For example, Table 10.3 shows results for two program objectives: "adds/subtracts numbers with decimals" and "answers telephone calls." We can see that the learner has met the standard for the first objective, "15 of 20 correct in 15 minutes," but not the second objective, "completes all steps on the telephone checklist."

Procedures for Monitoring Other Questions and Issues

The monitoring procedures instructors use to answer the questions they may have about the instructional procedures, or the broader effects that instruction may have on learner behavior, can be as formal as the ones chosen to assess the learner's progress toward the program objectives; or, they can be very informal, depending upon the depth and scope of the instructor's concerns. For example, to investigate whether an employment trainee carries skills over to a setting other than the one in which he or she was trained, the instructor could use any of the following procedures:

- ask the learner how he or she did in the second setting;
- confer informally with the employment supervisor and ask how the learner performed;
- make videotapes of the learner's behavior; or
- conduct regularly scheduled formal observations at the work site.

The procedures that instructors use to monitor instruction should correspond to how important an issue is to the overall effectiveness of the instructional plan. They should use the most formal and systematic procedures to gather information on the concerns and questions that are the most important for them to investigate and the least formal procedures for the more peripheral concerns.

In most cases, the types of procedures instructors should use will be readily apparent if they have developed sharply focused and clearly stated questions. Furthermore, the initial instructional assessments will have suggested the most effective means for keeping track of what happens during instruction and will help the instructors decide how to monitor learner progress. The main consideration in describing the monitoring procedures on the work sheet is to find a way to match the procedure to the issues and concerns that have been outlined. If an instructor is particularly interested in how the learner reacts to a specific instructional activity or in whether he or she carries over skills to other circumstances, the instructor should probably use direct observation, video, or some other procedure that will provide a close and detailed look at these behaviors. However, when the question focuses on an area of lesser concern, such as whether the learner understands why the instruction is taking place in a particular location, the instructor may simply ask the learner, since a data-based answer may not be as crucial as it would be to another question. Table 10.3 provides examples of how to describe procedures on a monitoring work sheet.

Step 3: Plan to Record and Summarize Results

The last step in preparing to monitor instruction is to establish a format for recording and summarizing the monitoring results, and to set up a daily log of the learners' behavior. In addition to specific information about the learners' progress on the program objective, instructors may need to make provisions for recording results such as the following:

- a record of grades, test scores, and scores on assignments;
- notes from informal observations;
- tallies from formal observations and videos;
- summaries of comments made by other learners;
- accounts of interviews with the learners themselves;
- reports from parents, school or agency personnel, or people from the community; or
- any other information instructors feel is important or interesting to consider as they evaluate the learners' progress.

Table 10.3 shows two different ways to make spaces on a work sheet for documenting the day-by-day results of instruction. These formats are only a few of the possibilities for recording results. The primary aim is to design a format that is easy to use, that is flexible, and that allows plenty of room for making entries on a recording sheet.

As a rule, instructors should use a more formal data-based format to record results about the program objective and other issues identified beforehand as being especially important. More open-ended formats can be used when recording results about less important concerns. Regardless of the format they choose, instructors should realize that they are likely to obtain results that they may not have anticipated, but which may become very helpful in deciding how to adjust instructional procedures. They should document these findings carefully because this information can provide a solid basis for deciding how to alter the teaching procedures. Moreover, the instructor should note any important but informal observations about the instructional activities in the "Comments" section of the work sheet. This action will document results that are not otherwise covered by the more formal record-keeping formats that the instructors may be using.

Format for Charting Progress in Acquiring the Behavior Pattern

Monitoring a learner's progress in meeting a program objective requires a fairly detailed data collection format. We have found a modified version of an instruction-tracking form presented by Gold (1980b) to be an extremely useful recording tool for this purpose. Gold credits Bellamy, Horner, and Inman (1979) with the original idea for this form (see Appendix B). Table 10.6 gives an example of an instruction-tracking form that is partially filled out. It shows that the form has three main sections: (1) the behaviors/behavioral cues column; (2) the standard time column; and (3) the results column.

Behaviors/Behavioral Cues Column.   This column contains either (a) the steps that are listed in an analysis of the program objective; or (b) the list of critical functions, if a detailed analysis was not made. Table 10.6 shows an example of how statements appear on the form. Note that the steps in the analysis appear in order of performance (whenever possible) and are sequenced *from the bottom up.* That is, the first step in the analysis is on the bottom line, the second is on the next line up, and so on until the last step is listed at the top of the column. This format allows an instructor to develop a graph that gives a visual display of the changes that occur in a learner's behavior during instruction. We will explain how to prepare such a graph later in this section.

Standard Time Column.   The first column of the form gives a place to list the amount of time it should take for most people to complete each step under normal circumstances. Instructors can use this information to track the time it takes a learner to complete each step on the chart and to judge whether it is appropriate or too slow.

The standard time for each step is a useful bit of information to have available. For example, sometimes learners with mental retardation can perform all the steps in a skill, but their performance does not look natural because either (a) they take too much time completing one or more steps; or (b) their overall performance exceeds the time limit for the skill, as might happen in competitive employment settings. In cases like these, instructors can use the standard times to determine which particular steps give the learner difficulty. The results would provide information on whether

- to develop more detail in the analysis of the objective;
- to change the behavioral pattern; or

TABLE 10.6 Example of a Skills/Skills Cluster Profile in Use

Skills/Skill Clusters Profile

Scoring Code:

/	=	Step performed correctly w/o prompts
(Blank)	=	Step performed incorrectly
■	=	Not performed during probe
X	=	Step performed correctly during standard time
O	=	Total steps performed correctly in probe

Learner: __Fred Harrison__
Skill: __Cleans up eating areas__
Location: __Mall__
Instructor: _____

Standard Time		Behaviors/Behavioral Cues	Results							
_____	25	_____	25	25	25	25	25	25	25	25
_____	24	_____	24	24	24	24	24	24	24	24
_____	23	_____	23	23	23	23	23	23	23	23
_____	22	_____	22	22	22	22	22	22	22	22
_____	21	_____	21	21	21	21	21	21	21	21
_____	20	_____	20	20	20	20	20	20	20	20
2:30	19	Clock out	19	19	19	19	19	19	19	19
2 min	18	Sign in key	18	18	18	18	18	18	18	18
17 min	17	Clean bathroom	■	■	■	■	■	■	■	■
2 min	16	Wipe high chairs	■	■	16	■	■	16	16	16
_____	15	Mop spills	■	■	■	15	15	15	15	15
As req	14	Wipe tables	14	14	14	14	14	14	14	14
_____	13	Store trays	13	13	13	13	13	13	13	13
_____	12	Collect & wipe trays	12	12	12	12	12	12	12	12
8 min	11	Fill napkins & straws	11	11	11	11	11	11	11	11
17 min	10	Empty & mash trash	10	10	10	10	10	10	10	10
10 min	9	Sweep floor	9	9	9	9	9	9	9	9
_____	8	Pick up debris	8	8	8	8	8	8	8	8
12 min	7	Wipe tables & seats	7	7	7	7	7	7	7	7
9 min	6	Fold towels	6	6	6	6	6	6	6	6
3 min	5	Gather tools & materials	5	5	5	5	5	5	5	5
2 min	4	Get towels	4	4	4	4	4	4	4	4
2 min	3	Get key	3	3	3	3	3	3	3	3
11 a.m.	2	Clock in	2	2	2	2	2	2	2	2
11 a.m.	1	Arrive in clean uniform	1	1	1	1	1	1	1	1

Probe: | 11/2 | 11/3 | 11/4 | 11/5 | 11/6 | 11/9 | 11/12 | 11/15 |

- to institute an instructional approach specifically designed to speed up the learner's actions.

Instructors should be aware that it is not always possible to list an exact time for each step. For example, some factors affecting time may be out of the learner's control, such as when a traffic jam affects travel time or when the learner has to wait for someone else to complete a task before beginning his or hers. Moreover, rather than elapsed time, some steps may be better evaluated in terms of rate of performance, such as "25 pieces/hour," or in terms of duration, such as "35 minutes." Furthermore, there may be situations in which it is not feasible or practical to specify a time standard because no truly accurate measure applies, as would be the case when performing a job "as needed," such as checking diapers on children in a day care center or picking up their toys. The standard time is meant to be an aid to instruction, not an impediment, and instructors should omit the entry when it is too difficult or impossible to estimate.

Results Completed Column.   The largest part of the recording form is devoted to the results column. Each column of numbers represents a single probe (performance opportunity) during which the instructor observes an attempt by the learner to perform the steps in the behavioral pattern. Instructors would make entries on the form as follows:

Learner does not complete the step unassisted.   When a learner needs some kind of assistance in completing a step proficiently, the instructor should not make any mark on the number corresponding to the step. In this case, "assistance" means the learner requires some kind of help, which may range from a simple gesture to a complete instructional intervention using manual guidance or demonstration. Whenever the learner requires some form of instruction, the unmarked number indicates that the instructor has more teaching to do on the corresponding skill.

Learner completes step successfully.   If the learner completes a step successfully, a slash (/) is placed on top of the number corresponding to the step in the behaviors/behavioral cues column. In this case, "success" means that the learner performs the step completely unaided, with no prompts and no errors. A slash mark indicates that the learner has all the information needed to perform the step competently and that the instructor can attend to other aspects of skill performance. The slash should not be given for partial or nearly correct performance, or simply for making an effort. It is reserved for successful, unassisted completion of a step.

Readers will note that the "slash/no mark" recording technique we are suggesting is simpler than many other schemes proposed in texts on teaching. The biggest departure from many other schemes is that we do not suggest that instructors note the type of prompt used, what kind of errors the learner makes, or similar information. This move toward simplicity is deliberate because the instructor's real problem is to determine whether or not the learner can do what he or she is supposed to do. Our aim in suggesting this technique is to give instructors a way to track learner progress without spending too much time collecting information that may have only limited use in planning instruction. The more quickly and efficiently instructors obtain the information they need during monitoring, the more time they can devote to actual teaching.

Learner completes step successfully within the standard time.   The slash on a number indicates that the learner performs a step without prompts or other assistance, but it does not tell whether the learner performs the step in a reasonable amount of time. To provide this information, the instructor would place an X on the number if the learner both (a) performs the step with no prompts and no errors, and (b) does so within the amount of time specified in the "standard time" column. This system allows instructors to see very clearly whether learners perform any or all of the steps in a timely manner.

Steps that are not always required.   Sometimes, learners may have to perform certain steps on some days and not on others. It frequently happens in many school, work, home, and leisure settings, but it may also occur in personal and travel settings as well. To cover these circumstances, instructors could black out the number corresponding to the step for the probe in which it does not have to be performed, and for scoring purposes, count the step the way it was marked during the previous probe: If the learner received a slash or an X on the previous probe, he or she will get the same mark on the current probe; if the learner received a blank on the previous probe, he or she will get a blank on the current probe.

Using the Chart Format to Summarize Performance.   Table 10.6 shows how successive probes of a learner's performance would be entered onto a monitoring work sheet. As shown in the table, this recording format can be used to record the learner's success in performing each of the steps in the analysis of the program objective. We can easily see from the chart that the learner is making steady progress toward achieving the program objective. Note that several instructional sessions may have taken place between each probe.

Format for Graphing Progress Toward the Program Objective

In addition to regular charting of the steps in a behavioral pattern as shown above, instructors might want to prepare a graph to summarize other kinds of monitoring results. For example, graphs can be especially useful in the following circumstances:

- to summarize how a learner participates over successive trials;
- to check performance against the confidence level established for the program objective; or
- to track maintenance of a learner's performance over a given time span.

When the monitoring data are graphed, instructors can easily identify trends, tendencies, or consistencies in the learner's performance. Table 10.6 shows a graphing procedure that focuses on the list of steps developed during the analysis of the program objective. In this case the graph shows the learner's overall progress toward an objective by totaling either the number of slashes or Xs, or the number of slashes and Xs combined, circling the corresponding number in the results column, and drawing a line to connect the circles. If counting either slashes or the combined slashes and Xs, the circled number will indicate the number of steps completed "successfully" by the learner. If counting only the number of Xs, the circled number will indicate the number of steps completed "successfully within the standard time."

The circles from successive probes can be connected to form a graph of skill acquisition, as shown in Table 10.6. The resulting graph thus provides a visual record of both the number of steps completed and the speed with which the learner is acquiring the skill. It is very useful from a record-keeping perspective because instructors can tell at a glance how well instruction is proceeding.

Instructors can develop graphs for some of the other variables they are monitoring as well. The customary way to label a graph is to specify the days or dates on which instructors make recordings along the horizontal axis and to label the units of measure for the behavior in ascending order along the vertical axis. The units of measure can involve duration (e.g., seconds, minutes, or hours), frequency, rate, or any other type of interval measure. Instructors would then make their entries by first writing the date of the observation on the bottom line. Then they would mark the point on the vertical axis that represents the level of the learner's performance as it was observed on that date. Connecting the points across the successive days on which instructors measure the behavior will yield a visual report on how the learner is progressing. Table 10.3 shows two graphs that depict Phil Weatherspoon's performance.

Monitoring gives instructors a systematic and straightforward way to track the progress the learners are making during the teaching activities. The results obtained from monitoring an instructional plan will help instructors make adjustments in the teaching procedures and determine whether learners are meeting, or are making progress in meeting, the program objectives.

Concluding Statement

When instructors carry out an instructional plan, they should think of it as an ongoing process. An important part of this process is monitoring the learners' performance. Monitoring an instructional plan allows instructors to keep a running account of the learners' behavior and the instructional procedures, so they can decide what to do next in the plan. The monitoring activities should enable instructors to verify whether or not learners are making progress toward the program objectives and to obtain new or updated information about learner behavior that will allow adjustments and modifications to be made when they are needed. The results obtained from closely monitoring an instructional plan will help keep the procedures and activities in line with the learners' progress and the new abilities they acquire. The results also will aid in promoting carryover of the skills to other situations and circumstances and in broadening the scope of activities to other high-priority areas.

Like the other activities carried out while preparing an instructional plan, monitoring should be based on careful planning. In addition to information about the analysis of the program objective, an effective monitoring approach involves the following steps:

- considering issues about the learners' performance or instructional activities that are important to document;

- planning procedures for keeping track of these issues; and
- summarizing observations, making charts and graphs, and keeping a record of other results.

During instruction, instructors should keep daily tallies, as well as make notes, comments, and any other records that will aid in evaluating the learners' response to the activities. The information obtained from monitoring will provide the foundation for deciding what to do next with the instructional plan, as there are many options that are available. In Chapter 11 we will discuss courses of action to take while carrying out the instructional plan and monitoring system.

Modifying Instruction

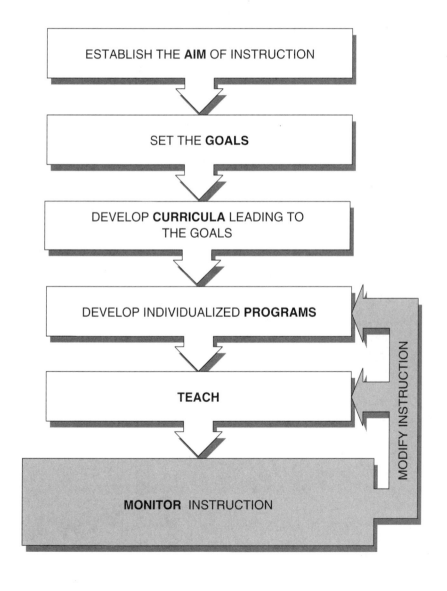

Planning is the heart and soul of instruction, but no matter how carefully instructors make their plans, it is impossible to predict exactly how the learners will respond to the instructional activities once they finally get started. The effectiveness of instruction depends, in large measure, on how well the instructor actually carries out the plan and responds to the effects that instruction has on the learner's behavior. In some cases, the learner's behavior may improve radically in a very short time; in other cases, it may not change at all; and in still other cases, the learner's behavior may become even more problematic than it was before instruction began. Many people will interpret what a learner does during instruction as an indication of the "success" or "failure" of the instructional plan, and indeed, this interpretation is easy to make. However, we believe that the results of instruction, whether "good" or "bad" from the instructor's point of view, usually provide a clear indication of what to do "next" with learners and help the instructor figure out what to do to keep instruction on track.

In this chapter, we will describe several ways in which to modify instructional activities based on the information gained during the monitoring process. We will discuss when to continue, discontinue, or change the instructional plan, and explain how to make these adjustments relative to the amount and kind of progress the learners are making toward achieving the program objectives.

The chapter is divided into two main sections:

1. what to do when learners are progressing satisfactorily toward meeting the program objectives; and
2. what to do when learners are not progressing satisfactorily toward meeting the program objectives.

What to Do When the Learners Are Progressing Satisfactorily Toward Meeting the Program Objectives

It is most gratifying to see learners acquire new skills and make progress toward achieving the objectives in their program plans. All the hard work, attention, and planning that was carried out in preparing for instruction can seem insignificant when we weigh it against the amount of progress that a single learner can make in just a very short time. But even the most successful instruction presents instructors with important decisions on what to do "next" with learners. Some issues instructors should consider are

- how long should the instruction continue?
- should the procedures be altered to account for the skills learners already have acquired?
- should the activities be refocused on other skills? and
- do the new skills still need further refinement?

The procedures that were presented in the discussion of monitoring in the previous chapter will help anticipate many of these questions, but it is

TABLE 11.1 Positive Results of Following an Instructional Plan

The learner makes progress toward meeting the program objective
- and shows signs of applying the new skills to other settings and circumstances
- but does not expand performance beyond the instructional situation
- but remains dependent on the support or encouragement of the instructor
- but remains very far from meeting the standard for performance

likely that there still will be important issues to address and decisions to be made, even when instruction is having very positive results. In the section that follows, we discuss the different results instructors might encounter when instruction is progressing satisfactorily and explain some options for addressing these results. Table 11.1 lists four positive results of instruction that monitoring activities may reveal.

Instructional Result #1: The Learner Makes Progress Toward Meeting the Program Objective and Shows Signs of Applying the New Skills to Other Settings and Circumstances

The easiest result to which instructors can respond is the most desirable one: The learners begin to meet the program objective (or show significant progress toward doing so), and they also begin to apply their new skills in other settings and circumstances. In fact, it is not unusual for instructors to find that the learners make great strides both in acquiring the new skills in the context of the instructional setting and in using these skills in other places and in conjunction with other skills. For example, after learning a set of food preparation skills under one set of circumstances, such as fixing a ham and cheese sandwich for a sack lunch, a learner spontaneously may begin using the same skills in other circumstances, such as when preparing for a picnic or when beginning a new job in a fast-food restaurant. The learner may even use the skills in totally unrelated situations, such as in a job setting in which he or she must bag parts for shipment. Similarly, after learning a set of lawn-care skills under one set of circumstances, a learner spontaneously may begin to use these skills under other circumstances, such as in caring for lawns at other residences or for commercial establishments. Table 11.2 contains two nonexclusive options for following up on results such as these.

Extend the Learner's Instruction

When learners begin to meet the program objective and carry their skills over to other settings or circumstances, the instructors' main focus should be on fading instruction as smoothly and as quickly as possible in order to move on to new curriculum objectives. The best way for instructors to capitalize on a really effective instructional plan is to fade the procedures they are using and let the learners proceed at their own pace and in their own direction. They should remove any aspects of the instruction that are not

TABLE 11.2 Options for When Learners Meet Program Objectives and Apply Skills to Other Circumstances

- Extend the learners' instruction.
- Use the instructional plan with other learners.

found naturally in the performance setting, but for at least a little while, they should also continue to keep a watchful eye on the learners to make sure that they maintain their performance at or above the level of the standards that were established for the objective.

For example, a job coach may find that a learner is developing job skills through natural responses to the different surroundings in which he or she uses the skills. Even so, the instructor should continue to monitor the learner's performance for at least a little while longer just to make sure that the new skills have become an established part of his or her performance routine and that the instructor is available to help the learner make adjustments if the need arises. As we pointed out in the previous chapter, monitoring could mean that the job coach simply checks periodically with the learner's work supervisor to see how much progress is taking place.

Furthermore, if learners are making rapid progress, the instructor should review the program curriculum, choose the next objective in the sequence, and begin to develop plans to address this objective. The insights that the instructor gained from preparing the first instructional plan will often allow him or her to shortcut the process of assessing the learner's behavior and analyzing the new curriculum objective. For example, an instructor could decide that the best way to follow up on a learner's success in learning to mow grass is to teach other yard-care skills, such as using an electric hedge clipper to trim hedges or a power blower to clear sidewalks. Using the information already gathered about the learner, the instructor may be able to develop a new instructional plan that addresses one of these areas and that builds on the learner's previous achievements. Similarly, after successfully teaching a learner to make a sandwich for a sack lunch, the instructor could select program or curriculum objectives that use this skill, such as fixing all the workweek lunches for the other residents of the group home.

Use the Instructional Plan with Other Learners

If instructors find that an instructional approach is very successful, they may be able to use that approach with other learners who have the same objectives in their program plans. Sometimes an instructor can "field-test" some new instructional procedure or activity with an individual learner, and with only minor modifications, be able to use the instructional plan with other learners to accomplish the same curriculum objective.

For example, once an instructor has found that an instructional plan for teaching functional academic skills is successful with one learner, he or she may be able to use the plan with other learners who have the same objectives in their IPs and who could attain them using the same procedures. However, in planning the instruction, the instructor would usually have to make at least some adjustments in the analyses of the program objectives and/or the teaching procedures to accommodate the individual learning and performance characteristics of the new learners.

Instructional Result #2: The Learner Makes Progress Toward Meeting a Program Objective but Does Not Expand Performance Beyond the Instructional Situation

Instruction often can be very successful, yet have effects that are more limited than those described in the previous situation. For example, when working with persons with mental retardation, it is not unusual to find that learners have acquired skills but are able to use them only in the settings and circumstances in which they learned them. In cases in which learners have difficulty applying their skills in a broad array of circumstances, instructors should begin to teach the learners to perform their new skills in these other circumstances. Three options for doing so appear in Table 11.3.

Continue the Instruction but Emphasize Procedures That Promote Carryover of New Skills

Sometimes learners must make significant performance adjustments in order to transfer their skills from one set of circumstances to another. Learners frequently fail to carry over new skills because they do not know how to make such adjustments on their own or because the circumstances in which the instruction takes place are too limited to prepare the learners to make these adaptations. In such cases, the instructors must broaden the instructional plan to include activities that teach the learners how to adjust their behavior. For example, instructors can often teach learners to carry over skills by taking them into a wider array of natural performance environments and showing them how to adjust their behavior.

For example, after teaching basic lawn-mowing techniques, an instructor may find that a learner can mow the lawn he or she was taught to mow but is unable to apply the mowing skills appropriately in other locations that have different mowing conditions, such as lawn configurations (e.g., circular, rectangular, or irregular), obstacles (e.g., trees, shrubs, or rock gardens),

---

TABLE 11.3 Options for Expanding Performance Beyond the Instructional Situation

- Continue the instruction but emphasize procedures that promote carryover of new skills.
- Have others in the learner's environment teach the learner how to use the skills in different settings and activities.
- Check whether the learner needs more incentive to carry over the new skills.

---

or terrains (e.g., hilly or terraced). Therefore, the instructor would have to expand the teaching procedures to address these different types of conditions to help the learner adapt his or her skills to a wider variety of environmental settings and circumstances.

Have Others in the Learners' Environment Teach Learners How to Use the Skills in Different Settings and Activities

Another factor that may affect carryover of skills is that learners may not recognize all the circumstances under which they can use their skills; they simply may not realize that the new skills can (or should) be used in other circumstances as well. For example, a learner may acquire techniques for responding to strangers on the school or agency grounds, but not use the skills in community settings. In order to broaden the scope of instruction and help the learner recognize the situational cues in community settings, the instructor might ask those who have contact with the learner outside the program (such as family members or residential staff) to show the learner how to apply the skills to various types of activities or interactions. In doing so, the instructor should identify the types of situational cues to which the learner would need to respond and help the learner shift his or her attention to them.

Check Whether the Learner Needs More Incentive to Carry Over the New Skills

Sometimes learners do not have sufficient incentive to carry over their skills to other circumstances, either because they are content with their current skill levels or because they do not perceive the benefits of using their skills in the other situations. In such cases, the instructors may have to add procedures that help the learners place more value on the natural outcomes available under these circumstances, or incorporate procedures that use external incentives for participating in the activities of the new setting.

For example, a learner may feel that the success achieved in learning a new recreational activity, such as going to a movie with a friend, is sufficient, and not see the need to use the learned travel skills in other situations. To encourage greater carryover of these travel skills, the instructor might point out the outcomes that would accrue to expanding the skills, such as that the learner could engage in other types of activities or that he or she could use the skills to go places with a wider circle of friends.

In some circumstances, the instructor may feel that a more immediate or concrete incentive is temporarily needed and might introduce a reward system as an incentive to broaden the application of the skills. Then, after the learner begins to see the benefits of expanding the skills and becomes more confident in their use, the instructor will remove the system. The latter procedure will probably not have to be used very often if instruction focuses mostly on skills that are useful in community settings because these skills themselves usually have a very high reward potential for most learners with mental retardation.

Instructional Result #3: The Learner Makes Progress Toward Meeting the Program Objective but Remains Dependent on the Support or Encouragement of the Instructor

A third potential result is that the learners begin to meet the program objective, but do so only when they are closely supervised or when artificial rewards or aversives are present. This situation can arise when the instructor depends too heavily on external incentive procedures to gain the learners' participation in the activities. For example:

- learners may use the artificial outcomes being employed as a sort of crutch for cooperating with the instructor;
- learners may react favorably only to the novelty aspects of the situation; or
- learners may react favorably only to the social aspects of the situation (such as having the instructor's undivided attention).

Under such circumstances, learners may begin to meet the program objective, but do so only because they can earn special privileges, or because the instruction is novel or presents a departure from the normal routine. Under these conditions, the learners' progress may not extend beyond the closely supervised conditions under which the instruction takes place. With results like these, the instructor will need to teach learners to recognize and work for the natural, sustaining outcomes of their skilled behavior. Options for accomplishing this result are outlined in Table 11.4.

Change the Instructional Plan to Emphasize the Natural Outcomes of Behavior

If learners stop using their newly acquired skills when the instructional procedures are removed, it usually indicates either that they do not recognize the natural benefits of skilled behavior, or they do not value these benefits. This problem commonly occurs when instruction depends too heavily on artificial rewards or aversives to increase learner incentive. In such cases, the instructor should adjust instruction to highlight the natural outcomes available to the learners and emphasize those aspects that may be particularly interesting or satisfying to the learners.

TABLE 11.4 Options for Encouraging Greater Independence in Learner Performance

- Change the instructional plan to emphasize the natural outcomes of behavior.
- Fade the instructional procedures more gradually and build the learner's confidence in his or her abilities.
- Integrate clearer outcomes or extra rewards as a permanent part of the overall routine of the setting.

For example, an instructor may have used special rewards or privileges in order to encourage learners to learn to perform some housekeeping chores around their residences, such as making their beds, cleaning their rooms, or washing the dishes. If, after the instruction is completed, the learners' behavior falls below the standards for performance, the instructor would have to place more emphasis on natural outcomes. For example, he or she could show the learners that it is easier to find things when their rooms are neat, that their friends will visit more often if they have places to sit down, or that they can derive personal satisfaction from "keeping their space neat and orderly" or from "doing their share of the work."

Fade the Instructional Procedures More Gradually and Build the Learner's Confidence in His or Her Abilities.

Sometimes instructional activities can work very well, yet learning progresses slowly because the instructional procedures themselves create a "safety net" for learners: Learners depend too heavily on the procedures for support and not on their own abilities and talents. This type of problem often arises when instruction takes place under artificial conditions, such as when instructors work one-on-one with learners in classroom settings, trying to teach skills that the learners typically would perform in community settings.

The conditions for instruction also can provide such a supportive context that the learners may be reluctant to break away from the instructional conditions and use the skills independently. For example, learners who are used to shopping for groceries under very closely supervised conditions may be very hesitant about using their shopping skills unassisted in a crowded supermarket even though they know how to do so independently.

To alleviate problems like these, instructors should concentrate on building the learners' confidence in their ability to use their skills. This goal can be accomplished if the instructors fade the procedures gradually and simultaneously give the learners additional opportunities to practice and refine their skills under increasingly complex and varied circumstances. Thus, rather than placing the learners in the natural context too quickly, the instructional activities slowly could incorporate more and more of the features that characterize the natural conditions until the learners can respond confidently to the performance demands of the setting. This technique is especially useful when instructors are teaching skills that are complex or very difficult for learners to use because it gives them more time to become proficient in the skills, to integrate them into a smooth performance pattern, and to coordinate their performance with ongoing activities and interactions.

For example, in the grocery shopping activity mentioned earlier, an instructor might do several different things depending on the kind of improvements the learners need to make to increase proficiency and confidence level. Some possibilities include

- gradually increase the range of items the learners would have to select without assistance, thus causing them to become more confident in their ability to follow the layout of the store and the manner in which items are displayed;
- schedule the learners' shopping trips so they learn to perform in larger and larger crowds over time; and
- have the learners interact directly with the store's personnel to get them to understand that there are people in the setting who will give them help when they need it.

Along with using each of these approaches, the instructor would also concentrate on fading out of the lessons as the learners' skill and confidence levels improve.

Integrate Clearer Outcomes or Extra Rewards as a Permanent Part of the Overall Routine of the Setting

Practically speaking, some learners require more encouragement, support, or incentive to use their skills than do other learners, and instructors may need to adjust the natural activities in order to ensure that these learners receive the incentives that will maintain their performance levels when instruction is over. In some cases, instructors may be able to incorporate incentives like extra praise or special privileges in the learners' normal routine or to provide them on an intermittent basis when the learners begin to lose interest in using their skills. In other instances, it may be necessary to provide additional incentives indefinitely by doing such things as including novel activities regularly in the learners' routine or giving a learner extra recognition for skilled performance.

For example, the staff in a residential setting may discover that a particular resident does not carry out his or her assigned chores satisfactorily unless he or she gets extra praise and encouragement for doing so. No matter how hard the staff may try to highlight the natural outcomes, they may have to continue to make special provisions to give the resident additional praise and personalized attention for his or her participation. Of course, the staff should give these special rewards as subtly and as infrequently as possible to avoid increasing the learner's dependence even more. But they may find that they have to continue using these procedures indefinitely because of the learner's performance characteristics.

Instructional Result #4: The Learner Makes Progress Toward Meeting the Program Objective but Remains Very Far from Meeting the Standard for Performance

The last thing that can happen when the instructional plan is successful is that the learners show steady progress toward the program objective but still do not reach criterion level performance in a reasonable time. That is, the learners can acquire some of the necessary skills but still need to work on many others. When progress toward a program objective is substantial but not yet complete, it is usually best to leave the instructional plan in place but to be ready to make adjustments that ensure continued progress. Table 11.5 lists possible adjustments.

Continue the Instruction and Recheck the Learner's Performance Later

Learners frequently need to work on their own for a while to develop and refine their actions into smooth and effective behavior patterns. For example, they simply may require time to practice their new skills. For this reason, even when an instructional plan accomplishes its basic purpose in teaching a learner what to do and how and when to do it, the learner still may not meet the curriculum objective because he or she does not perform the skills quickly enough, smoothly enough, or crisply enough. A good approach for the instructor to take under these circumstances is to back away from direct instruction but continue to monitor the learner's behavior closely. In doing so, the instructor should watch for any problems that may arise and for situations that the learner cannot handle by himself or herself. Then, the instructor quickly can provide whatever assistance is required to enhance progress in acquiring the skills.

For example, an instructor may have prepared a comprehensive instructional plan for teaching a learner several basic dressing skills, such as

---

TABLE 11.5 Options for Promoting Greater Progress in Learning Program Objectives

- Continue the instruction and recheck the learner's performance later.
- Continue the instructional plan but shift procedures to keep them aligned with any new areas of behavior the learner needs to develop.

---

putting on pants, a shirt, socks, and shoes. After progressing partially through the plan, such as after teaching the learner to put on a pair of pants, the instructor may find that the learner needs some time to coordinate and refine the newly acquired actions. Rather than introducing a new set of skills at this point, it may be beneficial in the long run to postpone further work on the instructional plan to allow the learner to become proficient in this aspect of dressing. Instruction would begin later on another part of the program plan.

Continue the Instructional Plan but Shift Procedures to Stay Aligned with Any New Areas of Behavior the Learner Needs to Develop

When learners are making progress toward a complex program objective, it is particularly important for the instructional procedures to remain flexible and to stay current with the learners' progress and needs. When an instructional plan is very effective right from the start of the actual instruction, there is a risk of being caught off guard by the gains the learner makes. It is not unusual for learners literally to "take off" and surprise their instructors by the rapidity of their skill acquisition. But such rapid progress can bring learners up against new barriers and performance challenges.

For example, in teaching skills for traveling around the neighborhood and community, an instructor might find that a learner's rapid progress has left him or her eager to go to new places and interact in new situations; but at the same time, this learner may be vulnerable to other types of skill deficits. For example, the learner may lack knowledge about how to interact with strangers and tend to say or do inappropriate things, behavior that can open the learner up to ridicule. Under such circumstances, the instructor would have to adjust the instructional plan to teach the learner to act in ways that would not attract negative attention. Thus, while continuing to follow the original plan, the instructor may have to add new procedures to help the learners improve their behavior in a related skill area as well.

In summary, then, there are many options for how to proceed with instructional plans that are progressing satisfactorily. The direction instruction should take depends largely on how quickly the learners develop and apply their new skills and on what areas might still need improvement. In deciding on the best approach to take, instructors should review the monitoring results carefully, paying particular attention to the program objective and to the issues that were identified on the work sheet.

What to Do When Learners Do Not Progress Satisfactorily

Just as carrying out successful instruction can be one of the most rewarding experiences an instructor can have, following a plan that does not work can be one of the most frustrating. With all the careful thought and systematic preparation that goes into the development of instruction, it can be very discouraging when it fails to produce major changes in learner behavior. When it happens, the instructor's first reaction often is that the learners are un-teachable: "I simply can't get them to understand," or "They just won't co-operate!" But it is important to realize that it is unproductive to blame learners for instruction that fails to work well. In fact, blaming learners for not learning is very likely to lead to inaction rather than to an effective strategy for what to do next.

When instruction does not work, it is important to remember the mindset within which we couched the entire instructional process in Chapter 1: Instead of focusing on the learners' deficits and failures, we need to look at what they must learn to do to achieve the program objectives. Just because a specific instructional plan does not accomplish an objective does not mean that the basic principle is poor; it simply means we need to review the learners' learning and performance characteristics and find another way to do what we set out to do. Perhaps a slight shift in the focus of the plan is all that is required. On the other hand, it may be necessary to start all over with an entirely new and more appropriate set of program objectives.

The most productive way to handle situations when instruction fails to work as planned is to view the results as an opportunity to probe and re-think the learners' needs, rather than as a sign that the learners are unteach-able. Ideally, of course, all the learners' needs should have been identified during the earlier assessment process. But reality dictates that there will be times when instructors miss or misinterpret crucial assessment results, or misjudge the potential effects that the teaching procedures and activities will have on learner behavior. Unfortunately, such problems may not be uncov-ered until after the instructor begins to carry out instruction and finds that the learners do not make progress toward the objectives. When an instructor finds that an instructional activity is not effective, it is necessary to review the monitoring results carefully to determine what has gone wrong and find a way to get the instruction on the right track.

In this part of the chapter, we will describe three types of results that show an instructional plan that is not going well, and we will present some options in each case for modifying or redirecting the instructional plan. Table 11.6 presents three results of unsuccessful instruction that monitoring can reveal.

Instructional Result #1: The Learner Does Not Make Progress Because the Content of the Instruction Is Misdirected

One of the first things instructors should ask in reviewing an instructional plan is, "Is the instruction focused on the right content for the learner?" As we indicated in Chapter 8, the content of an instructional plan is defined by the behaviors, cues, behavior pattern, and outcomes outlined in the analysis of the program objective. Many times, an instructional plan will not be ef-fective because the analysis of the objective does not correspond with the learners' needs and characteristics. If the learners do not make satisfactory progress during instruction, instructors should review the analysis in light of any new information that develops from the monitoring activities. The

TABLE 11.6 Results of an Unsuccessful Instructional Plan

- The learner does not make progress because the content of the instruction is misdirected.
- The learner does not make progress because the instructional procedures and activities are ineffective.
- The learner does not make progress because the instructional plan does not adequately address the learner's need for incentive.

TABLE 11.7 Options for Proceeding with Instruction When the Content of the Instruction Seems to Have Been Misdirected or Misaligned with the Learner's Needs

- Eliminate steps or parts of the analysis that may not be central to meeting the objective, or postpone working on them.
- Shift the emphasis to different aspects of the instructional content.
- Develop more detail for those parts of the analysis in which the learner's progress breaks down.
- Shift the focus of the instruction to a new area or program objective.
- Continue the instructional plan and watch for further effects.

monitoring results should indicate whether the analysis was appropriate and detailed enough for the learners' instruction. Table 11.7 lists the options for proceeding with instruction when the content seems to have been misdirected or misaligned with the learners' needs.

Eliminate Steps or Parts of the Analysis That May Not Be Central to Meeting the Objective, or Postpone Working on Them

When working with people with mental retardation, it is important to concentrate on those aspects of performance that are most closely and directly related to meeting the program objective. Otherwise, the instructors can get sidetracked by other important skills that the learners may need to acquire, but which are not central to the primary purpose of the objective. In the initial planning, it sometimes is difficult to sort out these important but nonessential areas. But when instruction stalls or fails to work, instructors may notice that parts of the instructional procedure actually may distract the learners. By de-emphasizing these distracting parts temporarily, the instructor will be able to concentrate on the skills that are most crucial to meeting the program objective. Thus, the learners' progress often can be hastened by giving the instruction a tighter, sharper, and narrower focus.

For example, in teaching money management skills, an instructor may find that the instructional plan has bogged down completely because the budgetary procedure being taught is overly complicated. In reviewing the analysis of the program objective, the instructor may discover that he or she has built in too many options for spending money or too many contingency plans for handling a shortage of funds, and the range of options is so great that it has caused confusion for the learner. Eliminating the less essential aspects of budgeting, at least for the time being, may help improve the learner's progress in meeting the objective.

Similarly, a review of an analysis for a vocational skill may reveal that too much emphasis is given to the various outcomes of doing a good job or to possible glitches that a learner may encounter only infrequently during the job routine. Temporarily removing these areas from the analysis may help the learner develop the essential work skills as quickly as possible. The important but less immediate aspects of job performance could be incorporated in the learner's instructional program later on.

Change the Emphasis Given to Different Aspects of the Instructional Content

Just as instructors may find that the analysis of a program objective has resulted in instruction that is overly complicated, they may sometimes discover that they have to reorganize the sequence in which they teach various components of the objective to the learner. For example, perhaps a learner needs to obtain information about the outcomes for meeting an objective sooner than originally planned in order to better focus his or her attention on learning the skills. Or, perhaps the instruction needs to be resequenced to allow the learners to acquire some of the simpler, more basic behaviors and cues before moving on to more difficult ones. In such cases, instructors should shift the emphasis and give precedence to areas that need to be addressed first.

It is particularly important to work on the most significant aspects of the instructional content when only a limited number of content areas can be addressed at one time. Some objectives may involve skills that are very difficult to learn or that require a long time to attain. There are times when altering the order in which the content is presented, or limiting the amount of content covered in teaching activities, can have a very strong positive effect on the learners' progress.

For example, an instructor may have started to teach a card game by beginning with the first steps in the activity, such as counting and dealing the cards. After observing a learner's unsuccessful responses to the first lessons, the instructor may realize that the order of instruction should be altered to allow presentation of either the less complicated or the more competitive aspects of playing the game. The first approach may make it easier for the learner to participate in playing the game, whereas the second approach may involve the learner more quickly in the social aspects of the game and thus make it more enjoyable and rewarding. Similarly, when teaching cooking skills, an instructor may need to place more emphasis on the consequences of safe or unsafe use of appliances because a learner's initial reaction to activities turns out to be hazardous to himself or herself and to others. The instructor should then reorganize the content of the instruction to address these more pressing aspects of the program objective before moving on to actual food preparation.

Develop More Detail for Those Parts of the Analysis at Which the Learner's Progress Breaks Down

When learners are not progressing satisfactorily, instructors should check the analysis of the program objective to make sure that it includes all the necessary detail for successful instruction. The problem is to find out whether certain parts of the analysis need to be reanalyzed to develop more detail about the actions the learner must display or the cues that he or she must identify to demonstrate progress in a particular area. Perhaps specific behaviors and cues need to be taught separately from one another, or maybe individual steps in the analysis need to be broken down into more steps and substeps. It is also possible that the behavior pattern needs to be changed to make it easier for the learners to perform the required actions. If changes in the behavior pattern are necessary, the instructor will probably have to revise major parts of the analysis, or even the entire analysis, to make all the component steps correspond to the new pattern.

For example, a vocational instructor who is teaching a learner to follow a fairly involved work routine may discover that some of the individual subtasks are very difficult for the learner to perform. The instructor could reanalyze each of these more complicated subtasks and break them down into several behavioral steps that are more in line with the learner's capability. However, the instructor also could find that the behavior pattern being taught requires the learner to have physical or cognitive attributes that he or she currently does not have. In such cases, the instructor would have to find a different behavior pattern (perhaps even a special behavior pattern: see Chapter 5) that allows the learner to perform the skill without having to use these physical or cognitive abilities. For example, when teaching a learner to make appointments, the instructors may find that the learner's academic skills are not sufficient to allow him or her to learn to use the yellow pages in the telephone directory. In such a case, the instructors may do something like substitute a fixed list of common telephone numbers or get a telephone with a built-in single button dialing system for the learner to use. This and other special behavior patterns are more restrictive than ordinary behavior patterns, but they enable instructors to teach skills that some learners otherwise might not be able to acquire.

Shift the Focus of the Instruction to a New Area or Program Objective

Sometimes, when they review the monitoring results, instructors will find that the reason an instructional plan is not working is because the wrong program objectives were selected. That is, the instructor may have overlooked important objectives in the original analysis that are essential to the learners' progress and that need to be added to the IP. Similarly, the initial instructional activities may bring to light facts that the instructors previously did not identify. For example, it is not uncommon to discover problems with prerequisite skills after learners have begun to make a concerted effort to meet the objective. It may be that the program objective simply is too complicated for a learner or that he or she has other more basic or pressing problems that the instructor must address before concentrating on the initial objective. Instructors should react quickly to this new information and adjust the instructional plan accordingly. Otherwise, continued failure or lack of progress can overwhelm a learner's incentive.

For example, in teaching a learner some sports activities, an instructor may find that a learner's lack of coordination interferes with his or her ability to learn some of the skills. The instructor may need to revise the instructional plan to address the more basic coordination skills first, or alternatively, to shift the instructional focus to an objective that does not require these skills.

The range of situations that could present new information is enormous. For example, an instructor could find that camping in a wooded area sets off previously undiscovered allergic reactions in a learner. This instructor must discontinue instruction in wooded areas until the learner obtains the necessary medical assistance, and should revise the instructional plan accordingly.

Another situation that might require a refocusing of an instructional plan is when instruction results in successes that were never expected, and the learners benefit from the procedures in ways that the instructor had not envisioned. Occasionally, learners may develop skills or overcome problems that are different from those addressed by the instructional plan. In cases like these, instructors should try to understand what the serendipitous results mean and adjust the plan's direction to account for these findings. The instructor may decide that the progress the learners make in this new area represents a more important program objective on which they should continue to work, and would need to adjust the instructional plan accordingly.

For example, instruction in camping may reveal areas of interest or talents a learner has not heretofore shown. Perhaps, when setting up a campsite for the first time, the learner shows a particular aptitude for certain camping activities, such as organizing food supplies and camping equipment, following schematic instructions for pitching a tent, or cooking over a campfire. The instructor may wish to refocus the instructional plan to capitalize on these newly discovered areas of interest or competence.

Continue with the Instructional Plan and Watch for Further Effects

Sometimes, when an instructional plan does not seem to be working, it is best to take a "wait and see" attitude, since the learners may be making important but very subtle responses to the teaching procedures. Before making changes in their behavior, some learners just need time to do things like

- adjust to the new teaching procedures and activities;
- become comfortable with the different ways in which the instructor or people in the environment are responding to them;
- sort through the different aspects of performance they are learning; or
- overcome their initial apprehensions about acquiring the new skills and/or using their new skills under a new set of circumstances.

Even in these cases, the instructor may be able to observe subtle changes in the learners' behavior that will offer some assurance that the plan actually is working. Some things to watch for are the following:

- Do the learners attend closely to what is going on during the instruction? or
- Do they respond more positively to the instructor or to other people during noninstructional times?

When some indirect, but positive, reaction to the instruction is observed, the instructor may wish to continue teaching a little longer, just to see what happens. He or she should also consider whether making minor adjustments in the analysis of the objective or in the procedures might speed up this process. For example, a vocational instructor might notice that a learner on a job site does not progress substantially despite the fact that he or she seems to attend closely to what the instructor or the other workers are doing. At this point, the instructor may not be sure about the effects the instruction is having on the learner, but since the learner shows substantial interest in the procedures, the instructor should continue with instruction awhile longer. For example, he or she might keep it in place for a few more days and watch closely to see how the learner responds. At the same time, however, the instructor should review the analysis of the objective and the teaching procedures to see if he or she can make some minor modifications that could enhance the learner's progress, and should be ready to revise the plan if no further improvements take place.

Instructional Result #2: The Learner Does Not Make Progress Because the Instructional Procedures and Activities Are Ineffective

Another fairly common problem is that the instructional procedures are not effective. The following are examples of problems that might arise during instruction:

- the instructional procedures may be too complicated for learners and confuse them or make them unsure of how to respond;
- the instructional activities may lack creativity or dynamism, be too easy, or be too similar to what learners are used to and thus fail to capture their interest or attention;
- the procedures may be suitable for some learners but fail to teach the intended skills and actions to others; or
- the context in which the activities are presented may be too distracting, confusing, or uninteresting to learners.

In any of these instances, the instructor will need to make changes in the instructional activities. He or she can revise or replace the procedures that are not effective or that fail really to address the goals of the instruction and the learners' characteristics successfully. The options for changing instructional procedures are listed in Table 11.8.

TABLE 11.8 Options for Changing the Instructional Procedures

- Revise or remove instructional activities that are ineffective.
- Readjust the pace of the instructional procedures to match the learner's progress.
- Alter the context in which the instructional procedures are used.
- Develop new procedures to address the program objectives.

Revise or Remove Instructional Activities That Are Ineffective

When an instructional plan is not working well, it is not unusual to find that the activities simply are not effective for one reason or another. The most obvious action to take when instructional activities are not effective is to change or remove them. Whether the problem is one of presentation technique, complexity of the instructions, logistics, or simple miscalculation, sometimes the best solution is for instructors to "cut their losses" and revise the activity, or even replace it completely. In reworking activities that are ineffective, instructors can refocus their efforts on the more important aspects of the instruction or on freeing learners from the distractions or confusion caused by ineffective procedures.

For example, an instructor might decide to stop using a demonstration technique because it fails to direct the learner's attention properly to the required performance cues and actions. By substituting a physical guidance technique, the instructor may be able more precisely to direct the learner's attention to the areas he or she needs to learn. On the other hand, an instructor may have to abandon the use of physical guidance if the learner becomes overly agitated as a result of close proximity or physical contact.

Another issue instructors should consider in reviewing instructional procedures is whether they are aligned properly with the content of the instruction itself. Sometimes procedures can prove ineffective because they were chosen more for their interest or novelty value than for their instructional value in teaching skills to learners. For example, learners may become so immersed in an instructional activity that they are unable to sort out the information they need in order to develop their skills properly. In such cases, it can be very helpful to redirect the procedures so as to concentrate more directly and deliberately on the skills that the learners need to acquire. A classroom teacher, for example, may discover that a teaching game that originally seemed promising fails to work because students are overly distracted by the social or competitive aspects of the activity. Substituting more structured one-on-one activities might refocus the learners' concentration to the more important and relevant aspects of the instruction.

Readjust the Pace of the Instructional Procedures to Match the Learner's Progress

Another impediment to learners' progress is that the instructional activities may move too slowly or too quickly for them. For example, an instructor might find that the learners are capable of learning more rapidly than anticipated and that they become frustrated or impatient when the pace of the instruction is too slow. This problem often becomes an issue when learners are required to engage in activities that focus on skills that they already know how to perform.

On the other hand, it is also important to watch for procedures that progress too quickly for learners or that fail to present the skills in discrete, manageable units. These problems can arise when instructors assume that learners will develop the new skills more quickly than is actually possible, and instruction begins to cause the learners to be frustrated and discouraged. Instructors should suspect difficulties of this nature when learners initially give considerable effort and attention to the instructional procedures but then start to slacken their effort and lose interest. In such cases, it is important to readjust the pacing of the instructional activities to bring it more closely into line with the learners' characteristics and level of interest.

For example, when teaching a learner how to locate items from a shopping list in a grocery store, an instructor may observe that the learner becomes frustrated by the pace of the instruction. After teaching the basic principles of finding grocery items using a technique such as demonstration or verbal instructions, the instructor may find that the learner responds better to a learner search procedure that gives him or her more opportunity to test out his or her own abilities. Another learner may wish to continue locating grocery items even though the original shopping lesson is at an end. When it is practical to do so in situations like these, the instructor should try to adjust or extend the instructional activities in order to capitalize on the interest the learner displays.

Alter the Context in Which the Instructional Procedures Are Used

Another factor that instructors should consider when they review their procedures is whether the activities employ the most effective context for the program objectives. Areas that may deserve consideration include

- the settings in which instruction takes place;
- the situations or the activities in which the procedures are used;
- the materials involved in the procedures; and
- the people who help to carry out the procedures.

In some cases, instructors may discover that factors like these actually present distractions or impediments to skill acquisition because they divert the learners' attention from the instructional content. Some indications that the context of instruction may need to be altered are the following:

- the learners are unable to attend to the particular procedures and techniques being used;
- they show discomfort with working in the particular grouping arrangement (one-on-one, small group, etc.);
- they begin using the materials for purposes other than those defined by the objective;
- they react negatively to the people carrying out the instruction; or

- they get so concerned with earning rewards, or with the other incentive features of the instruction, that they do not concentrate on the instructional activities.

In any of these instances, instructors should change the context of the instruction to encourage the learners to once again give their full attention to the instructional procedures.

For example, a vocational instructor might discover that the problem with a demonstration or role-playing activity is not so much in the actual procedure, but in the fact that the instructor is not the best person to model the job-related behaviors. If he or she changes the context by having a fellow employee model the actions, perhaps the procedure might begin to work very well. Similarly, a classroom teacher might find that the real problem with a learner search procedure is that the learner is overly self-conscious when performing in front of other students. A better approach could be to alter the context to a one-on-one activity, at least until the learner gains some confidence in his or her performance.

Develop New Instructional Procedures to Address the Program Objectives

The last approach to consider when instructional procedures have proven ineffective is simply to develop new ones. Instructors might find, after reviewing the instructional results, that the procedures being used are inadequate for addressing the learners' instructional needs and that the best approach is to devise an entirely new set of activities. However, it is important to avoid discarding procedures in a haphazard fashion because the new approaches may prove no more effective than the old ones. Rather, instructors should evaluate the reasons why the old procedures failed in the first place and try to avoid creating the same problems all over again.

For example, after seeing that the instructional activities have failed to bring about changes in the learner's behavior, an instructor might conclude that he or she needs some fresh ideas for procedures. The instructor might find it helpful to consult with other instructors or with people who are familiar with the learner's circumstances, such as the learner's parents or guardians, previous instructors, or other members of the instructional staff. Discussing the instructional plan and good old-fashioned brainstorming may yield some very useful teaching procedures.

Instructional Result #3: The Learner Does Not Make Progress Because the Instructional Plan Does Not Adequately Address the Learner's Need for Incentive

So far, all the options we have discussed for reworking an instructional plan have assumed that learners are sufficiently motivated to develop the skills for meeting the program objectives. But a slow rate of skill development may also signal a lack of interest or willingness on the learners' part to learn and use new skills. Therefore, when instruction is not working as planned and the instructor has reviewed the program objectives and the instructional procedures, he or she also should reevaluate the incentive features of the instructional plan. It is usually best to review incentive factors last because, more often than not, instructors can overcome incentive problems by redirecting or clarifying the instructional content or by revising instructional procedures. But there still may be occasions when instructors must alter the scope or focus of the incentive that is inherent in an instructional plan.

For example, when an instructor evaluates a learner's behavior, he or she might find that the learner is not showing much enthusiasm for participating in the instructional activities. The learner does not have to be particularly hostile or resistant to the procedures; perhaps the learner just makes too little effort in applying himself or herself or is easily distracted from participating in the activity. The instructor should consider ways to improve the learner's incentive level in order to encourage the learner to concentrate more on improving his or her behavior. Table 11.9 shows the options for revising the incentive features of an instructional plan.

Give More Emphasis to the Natural Outcomes of Performance or Add Extra Incentives for Changing Behavior

Sometimes learners will not make progress in their behavior because they do not fully understand the importance of the skills, or they do not consider the effort required to change their behavior to be worth their while. In these cases the instructor should redesign the instruction so it gives the learners clear, concrete reasons for acquiring the skills and highlights the benefits they can gain from using them. Instructors may need to stress natural outcomes for performance to a greater degree than usual, or if this does not work, they may have to add extra rewards for learning the new skills.

For example, an instructor may discover that a learner is not particularly interested in taking part in an instructional lesson. He or she might not associate the instructional activities with the outcomes of learning new skills or of gaining greater independence in behavior. In this case, the instructor may need to direct instruction toward emphasizing the natural outcomes of improving behavior. The instructor could use demonstration to show how other learners or people in general have benefited from acquiring the skills, or could give the learner opportunities to experience the outcomes firsthand. The instructor could also reward the learner's attention to or participation in activities by using praise, a point system, or some other technique that gives

---

TABLE 11.9 Options for Revising the Incentive Features of an Instructional Plan

- Give more emphasis to the natural outcomes of performance or add extra incentives for changing behavior.
- Change the context of the instruction to help the learners build self-confidence in using the new skills.
- Reduce competing behaviors.

---

him or her a concrete reason for participating. Again, however, we must caution that the use of external incentives must be accompanied by a plan for removing them.

Change the Context of the Instruction to Help the Learners Build Self-Confidence in Using the New Skills

Occasionally, learners may seem particularly resistant to instruction because they lack the confidence they need to learn and use the new skills. They may act in an uncooperative manner in order to cover up their personal discomfort, or they may pretend a lack of interest in the procedures so that they do not have to admit to having a skill deficit. In such cases, the learners actually may want to learn the new skills, but they try hard not to show it by ignoring or openly defying the instructional attempts. Changing the circumstances of the instruction to include more individualized activities or out-of-context situations often can overcome such resistance. These circumstances can alleviate the learners' concerns about failing in front of their peers or about admitting by their cooperation that they lack certain skills. Furthermore, it is usually helpful to build into this new context more opportunities to practice and refine the skills to build greater self-confidence and to reduce the learners' apprehensions about making mistakes under natural performance conditions.

For example, an instructor might notice that a learner is more self-conscious about participating in an instructional lesson than anticipated. The learner might resist participating in the activities because he or she is not confident in his or her ability to try out some new skills "in public." In this case, the instructor might have the learner work in the context of one-on-one lessons or in small, carefully controlled groups before extending the instruction to the more natural performance circumstances. The learner could then develop and practice the necessary skills without the added pressure of trying to overcome his or her self-consciousness.

Reduce Competing Behaviors

Sometimes, learners will not cooperate in instructional activities because they prefer to do something else instead. Thus, an otherwise very good instructional plan may not be effective because the learners are so intent on doing other things that they fail to attend to the content of the instruction. In this case, the instructor may have to adjust the instructional plan by starting with procedures that capture the learners' interest and attention and that stimulate their focus on the instructional activities.

One approach to directing attention away from distracting or competing behavior is to change the circumstances of the instruction so that the learners do not have the same opportunities to engage in the problem behaviors. Without an opportunity to perform these preferred behaviors, the learners instead may attend to the activities that were planned. Another approach is to reprimand the learners or punish the problem behaviors to try to diminish the learners' desire to engage in them. In either case, the learners then may begin to focus their attention on the instructional activities because the problem behaviors are not as rewarding as they were before.

For example, an instructor might find that a learner does not cooperate during instruction because he or she cannot resist a chance to show off in front of other people. The instructor could remove this temptation by having the learner work one-on-one or in a tightly monitored or supervised situation. If the problem persists, the instructor could add an unpleasant outcome by isolating the learner from the other people whenever he or she acts inappropriately. By generating the opposite result (i.e., solitude) from what the learner seeks to achieve (i.e., attention), the instructor may be able to reduce or eliminate the problem behavior. There is a wide variety of very effective techniques for handling problem behavior described in the literature on behavior management (see the suggested readings at the end of Chapter 9).

In summary, when the learners are not making progress in their performance, it is usually because the instructional plan does not address the source of the learners' problems. Instructors should review the analysis of the program objective and reexamine the procedures and activities they are using to determine if changes in the instructional plan are needed. Choosing which options to pursue should be based on careful consideration of the monitoring results that were obtained during instruction. These results, and further consideration of the instructional plan, will help to get instruction back on track.

Concluding Statement

Instructors should think of instruction as an ongoing process that shifts and changes as it progresses. Instructors can interpret the results of instruction in terms of the different ways in which to proceed next with the IP and can group the results into two broad categories: 1) the instructional plan is working satisfactorily, and 2) the instructional plan is not working satisfactorily.

When instructional plans are working well, the results are likely to be broad and generalized improvements in learner behavior. Sometimes the learners not only will meet the program objectives but will expand their progress to other areas as well. At other times, instructors will observe more narrow progress: The learners may show some improvement in their skills but may not meet the program objective. In between these two extremes, learners might begin meeting the objective without carrying their skills over to other situations, or they might begin meeting the objective only under circumstances in which they receive artificial rewards for participating in the instructional activity. For each of these possibilities there are a variety of options for what to do next. These options range from fading the intervention and moving on to other objectives, to keeping the plan in place and adding new features to enhance the learners' progress.

When instructional plans are not working, instructors should review the monitoring results carefully to determine the source or sources of the problem. They might find that the content of the program objectives is misdirected and fails to address the learners' needs. Or they could discover that the procedures being used are ineffective or misaligned with the objectives. Finally, they might find that the plan has insufficiently addressed the learners' need for incentive. Each of these possibilities has several options for revising and reapplying the instructional plan. These options include changing the instructional content or shifting the emphasis given to different aspects of the content, revising the procedures used or the way they are applied, or adding more emphasis on building the learners' incentive. The purpose in following any of these options is to get the learners' instruction back on a productive course.

APPENDIX A
LIST OF TERMINAL GOALS

Domain P: Personal Maintenance and Development

P/I: Goals Related to Routine Body Maintenance

P/I A: The Learner Will Maintain Personal Cleanliness and Grooming
1. Clean body parts
   a. Identify need to clean body (e.g., hands, face, teeth, entire body, etc.)
   b. Go to appropriate location
   c. Obtain appropriate provisions (soap, water, toothbrush, shampoo, sink, tub, shower, deodorant, etc.)
   d. Clean body parts as necessary (wash, bathe, shower, shampoo, brush teeth, floss teeth, apply deodorant, etc.)
2. Care for skin
   a. Identify need for skin care
   b. Go to appropriate location (bathroom, beauty parlor, etc.)
   c. Obtain required materials (soap, lotions, medicines, etc.)
   d. Apply provisions
3. Care for hair
   a. Identify need for hair care (length, style, neatness, shape, etc.)
   b. Obtain necessary provisions (money, comb, brush, etc.), or go to appropriate services (beauty shop, barber, etc.)
   c. Obtain appropriate service (barber, beauty shop) or go to appropriate location (rest room, etc.)
   d. Care for hair (comb, brush, get haircut, get hair styled, etc.)
4. Apply makeup (females)
   a. Identify need/time to apply makeup (morning, when wearing off, etc.)
   b. Go to appropriate location (rest room, bedroom, private space, etc.)
   c. Apply makeup
5. Care for nails (fingers, toes)
   a. Identify need for nail care (nails too long, broken, ragged, dirty, etc.)
   b. Obtain required equipment (nail trimmer, file, etc.)
   c. Clean/trim nails
6. Clean nose
   a. Identify need to clean nose (cold, allergy, normal mucus buildup)
   b. Obtain required equipment (handkerchief, tissue, etc.)
   c. Store/dispose of equipment (purse, pocket, trash, etc.)

7. Eliminate waste
    a. Identify need to eliminate waste (urinate, move bowels)
    b. Go to appropriate location (bathroom, public rest room, etc.)
    c. Eliminate waste
    d. Wipe body parts if appropriate
    e. Flush
8. Care for menses (females)
    a. Identify need for menses care (begin period, full pad/tampon, etc.)
    b. Obtain required equipment (pad, tampon, etc.)
    c. Go to appropriate location (bathroom, public rest room, etc.)
    d. Remove soiled pad/tampon
    e. Attach/insert clean pad/tampon
    f. Dispose of soiled pad/tampon

P/I B: The Learner Will Dress Appropriately
1. Maintain neatness in clothing being worn
    a. Identify need for adjustments (while dressing, after dressing)
    b. Make adjustments (tucking, straightening, shoes tied and on correct feet, etc.)
2. Maintain clothing cleanliness
    a. Identify unclean clothing (dirt, dust, stains, sweat, etc.)
    b. Clean dirty clothing (launder, dry-clean)
3. Wear appropriate clothing
    a. Identify activity (work, leisure, sports, etc.)
    b. Identify location (indoors, outdoors, special location, etc.)
    c. Identify weather conditions (rain, snow, clear, hot, cold, etc.)
    d. Identify level of formality (formal, semiformal, informal)
    e. Select clothing appropriate to activity, location, weather conditions, and level of formality
    f. Put on clothing appropriate for activity, location, weather conditions, and level of formality
4. Maintain neatness in clothing while storing
    a. Identify need to store clothing (clean/dirty, end of season, etc.)
    b. Store in appropriate clothing container (closet, chest, box, etc.)
    c. Store container in appropriate location (closet, basement, etc.)
5. Maintain shoes
    a. Identify need for maintenance procedure (worn, dirty, wet, etc.)
    b. Obtain needed equipment (shoe trees, brush, rag, polish, etc.), or go to appropriate service (e.g., shoe store, cobbler)
    c. Follow maintenance procedure (clean, polish, store), or obtain necessary services
6. Care for wet clothing
    a. Identify wet clothing (clothes, shoes)
    b. Go to appropriate location (home, dry location)
    c. Care for wet clothing (change clothes, dry clothes, block shoes, etc.)

P/I C: The Learner Will Follow Illness Prevention Procedures
1. Follow sleep patterns
    a. Identify required sleep patterns (learner sleep needs, demands of work/chores/engagement schedule, etc.)
    b. Establish appropriate sleep pattern (length, specific times)
    c. Obtain necessary equipment (bed, alarm, etc.)
    d. Follow sleep pattern (sleep time, rising time)
2. Maintain nutrition
    a. Identify nutritional needs (food types, nutritional balance, quantities, food patterns, weight control needs, etc.)
    b. Establish food intake pattern (menus, times to eat, snacks, etc.)
    c. Follow established patterns

3. Exercise
   a. Obtain physician's clearance for exercise
   b. Set personal fitness goals (cardiovascular, skeletal-muscle conditioning, etc.)
   c. Establish fitness program (type, length, and location of exercise)
   d. Obtain necessary equipment (clothing, shoes, exercise equipment, etc.)
   e. Follow fitness program
4. Maintain substance control
   a. Identify substances (drugs, tobacco, alcohol, caffeine, over-the-counter medicines, etc.)
   b. Determine use (abstain, appropriate limits, etc.)
   c. Abstain or observe limits
5. Obtain routine medical checkups
   a. Identify routine medical checkups (physical examinations, dental checkups, eyeglasses or prostheses checks, etc.)
   b. Identify appropriate medical personnel (physician, dentist, etc.)
   c. Make appointments
   d. Keep appointments
   e. Follow orders/suggestions of medical personnel

P/II: Goals Related to Illness Treatment

P/II A: The Learner Will Use First Aid and Illness Treatment Procedures
1. Treat illnesses and injuries requiring first aid
   a. Identify illness/injury requiring first aid (colds, flu, minor cuts, scrapes, splinters, sprains, burns, minor illnesses, occasional headaches, etc.)
   b. Obtain necessary supplies (bandages, tape, antibacterial ointment, aspirin, tweezers, antihistamine, etc.)
   c. Replace supplies when low or depleted
   d. Treat illness/injury appropriately

P/II B: The Learner Will Obtain Medical Advice and/or Treatment When Necessary
1. Seek treatment for injury or illness requiring medical intervention
   a. Identify symptom (bleeding, pain, vomiting, cuts, burns, sprains, broken bones, illness, etc.)
   b. Relate symptom to need for treatment (emergency room, physician, optometrist, chiropractor, dentist, etc.)
   c. Locate medical personnel geographically
   d. Make appointment
   e. Obtain treatment
2. Follow prescribed medication procedures
   a. Obtain prescribed medication
   b. Follow prescribed course of medication

P/III: Goals Related to Establishing and Maintaining Personal Relationships

P/III A: The Learner Will Interact with Family
1. Perform acceptable interactions with family members
   a. Identify family members (parents, siblings, spouse, children, other close relatives)
   b. Identify acceptable interactions (conversation topics, activities, touches, discipline, acquiescence, etc.)
   c. Perform acceptable interactions
2. Refrain from inappropriate interactions with family members
   a. Identify inappropriate interactions (quarrels, fights, abuse, neglect, touches, disrespect, etc.)
   b. Refrain from inappropriate interactions

3. Observe demeanor requirements with family members
   a. Identify acceptable demeanor (language usage, assertiveness, deference, familiarity, etc.)
   b. Exhibit acceptable demeanor
4. Exhibit appropriate body language with family members
   a. Identify acceptable body language (posture, facial expressions, gestures, movements, etc.)
   b. Exhibit acceptable body language
5. Respond to inappropriate conduct of family
   a. Identify inappropriate conduct (incest/abuse, aggression, neglect, etc.)
   b. Respond to inappropriate conduct (seek assistance from friends/neighbors/officials, etc.)

P/III B: The Learner Will Make Friends
1. Interact with potential friends
   a. Identify places to meet potential friends (church, dances, job site, clubs, activity locations, etc.)
   b. Go to places
   c. Interact with other people
2. Make friends
   a. Identify potential friends (same sex, opposite sex)
   b. Make appropriate overtures
   c. Make friends

P/III C: The Learner Will Interact with Friends
1. Observe required interactions with friends
   a. Identify appropriate interactions (conversation topics, activities, touches, emotional responses, etc.) for friends of same sex/opposite sex
   b. Perform appropriate interactions
2. Refrain from inappropriate interactions with friends
   a. Identify inappropriate interactions (aggression, quarrels, fights, abuse, touches, etc.) for friends of same sex/opposite sex
   b. Refrain from inappropriate interactions
3. Observe demeanor requirements with friends
   a. Identify appropriate demeanor for friends (language, assertiveness, familiarity, etc.) of same sex/opposite sex
   b. Exhibit appropriate demeanor
4. Exhibit appropriate body language with friends
   a. Identify appropriate body language (posture, facial expressions, gestures, movements, etc.) for friends of same sex/opposite sex
   b. Exhibit appropriate body language
5. Respond to inappropriate conduct of friends
   a. Identify inappropriate conduct (exploitation, manipulation, harassment, teasing, incest/abuse, aggression, neglect, etc.)
   b. Respond to inappropriate conduct (leave area, seek assistance from friends/neighbors/officials, defend self, etc.)

P/III D: The Learner Will Maintain Relationships with Family and Friends
1. Respond to problems in personal relationships
   a. Identify problems in personal relationships (strained relations/lost relations)
   b. Identify source of strained/ended relations (quarrels, death, divorce, divided loyalties, inappropriate conduct of self/others, etc.)
   c. Cope with problems in personal relationships (seek assistance from professionals/family/friends, solve problem, adjust to lack of solution, etc.)
2. Respond acceptably to sexual needs
   a. Identify sexual needs

b. Identify social constraints to sexual responses (approval/disapproval, public acts, legal constraints, etc.)

c. Respond to sexual needs within social constraints (sex partners, masturbation, birth control, etc.)

P/IV: Goals Related to Coping with Personal Glitches

P/IV A: The Learner Will Cope with Changes in Daily Schedule
1. Cope with the result of sleep pattern disruptions
   a. Identify sleep pattern disruptions (insomnia, schedule changes, emergencies, etc.)
   b. Identify effect of sleep pattern disruption (fatigue, irritability, poor task performance next day, etc.)
   c. Adjust to sleep pattern disruption (change schedule, take naps, obtain medical assistance, etc.)
2. Cope with changes in daily routine
   a. Identify changes in daily routine (holidays, weather related, emergencies, etc.)
   b. Adjust to changes in daily routine (stay home from work/school/normal activity, engage in leisure activities, etc.)
3. Cope with changes in other routines
   a. Identify changes in routines (canceled appointments, leaving job, etc.)
   b. Adjust to changes in routine (make new appointments, find alternate service, find new job, etc.)

P/IV B: The Learner Will Cope with Equipment Breakdowns or Material Depletions
1. Cope with broken equipment
   a. Identify broken equipment (broken shoelaces, torn clothing, electric razor, etc.)
   b. Repair or replace broken equipment
   c. Adjust to resulting disruptions in routine (cancel activity, perform alternate activity, etc.)
2. Cope with material depletion
   a. Identify depleted material (shampoo, medications, clean handkerchiefs, etc.)
   b. Replace depleted material
   c. Adjust to resulting disruptions in routine (cancel activity, perform alternate activity, etc.)

Domain H: Homemaking and Community Life

H/I: Goals Related to Obtaining Living Quarters

H/I A: The Learner Will Find Living Quarters
1. Locate potential living quarters
   a. Identify geographical area in which to live
   b. Decide on type of living quarters (apartment, house, sleeping room, etc.)
   c. Use formal (newspaper ads, real estate agents, etc.) and informal (family, friends, acquaintances, etc.) resources to identify potential living quarters
   d. Locate potential living quarters geographically (section of town, physical plant)
2. Assess acceptability/desirability of potential living quarters
   a. Assess quality of neighborhood (income level, crime rate, upkeep, etc.)
   b. Assess location of neighborhood (availability of stores, medical services, transportation, recreation facilities, access to work, etc.)
   c. Assess physical aspects of living quarters (physical aids, physical barriers, equipment, furnishings, conveniences, upkeep, etc.)
   d. Assess compatibility of roommates/housemates
3. Assess ability to pay costs
   a. Assess budget for funds available relative to costs
   b. Assess potential for roommates/housemates to share costs
4. Rent/buy living quarters
   a. Decide to rent/buy quarters
   b. Agree on price with owner/landlord
   c. Seek mortgage, if appropriate
   d. Sign agreements (owner/landlord, roommates, bank, etc.)
   e. Make deposit(s)

H/I B: The Learner Will Set Up Living Quarters
1. Move into living quarters
   a. Obtain equipment (furniture, tools, materials, food, etc.)
   b. Pack personal items (clothing, linens, etc.)
   c. Move into living quarters
2. Set up living quarters
   a. Assemble/arrange furniture
   b. Unpack personal items
   c. Store tools, materials, food, etc.

H/II: Goals Related to Community Life Routines

H/II A: The Learner Will Keep Living Quarters Neat and Clean
1. Remove dirt and dust to meet or exceed neighborhood standards
   a. Establish cleaning schedule (daily, weekly, monthly, seasonally, yearly)
   b. Vacuum dust/dirt (floors, baseboards, walls, ceilings, etc.)
   c. Dust surfaces (furniture, corners, appliances, etc.)
   d. Wash surfaces (floors, fixtures, interior windows, tiles, porcelain, formica, etc.)
   e. Damp-wipe surfaces (appliances, fixtures, countertops, metal furniture, etc.)
   f. Clean/polish wood surfaces (furniture, cabinets, wall paneling, floors, etc.)
   g. Tidy rooms (beds, clutter, accumulation, spills, etc.)
   h. Tidy storage areas (closets, cabinets, dressers, kitchen drawers, etc.)
   i. Defrost/clean refrigerator
   j. Remove waste
   k. Store cleaning supplies after use (empty/full/partially full)

H/II B: The Learner Will Clean/Repair/Replace Fabric Items
1. Keep fabrics clean
   a. Establish cleaning schedule (daily, weekly, monthly, seasonally, yearly)

    b. Wash dirty fabrics (clothing, linens, towels, carpets, furniture, etc.)
    c. Dry-clean dirty fabrics (clothing, curtains, etc.)
2. Store fabrics
    a. Establish storage schedule (daily, weekly, monthly, seasonally, yearly, etc.)
    b. Store dirty fabrics (laundry, rags, etc.)
    c. Store clean fabrics (laundry, linens, towels, etc.)
3. Replace/repair/mend fabrics as necessary
    a. Identify fabrics needing and capable of repair/mending
    b. Identify fabrics requiring replacement
    c. Replace/repair/mend fabrics

H/II C: The Learner Will Maintain the Interior of Living Quarters

1. Repair or replace household equipment
    a. Identify household equipment needing repair (electric cords, lightbulbs, fuses, faucets, locks, windowpanes, etc.)
    b. Identify household equipment needing replacement (worn/broken appliances, tools, fixtures, etc.)
    c. Repair or replace household equipment as necessary
2. Replenish maintenance supplies
    a. Inventory supplies (soap, cleaning fluid, toilet paper, scrub pads, etc.)
    b. Replenish low supplies
    c. Discard used/empty supply containers
3. Refinish surfaces
    a. Identify surfaces requiring refinishing (furniture, floors, walls, molding, doors, etc.)
    b. Purchase finish (paint, varnish, thinners, etc.)
    c. Purchase application equipment (sandpaper, scrapers, brushes, rollers, pads, etc.)
    d. Refinish surfaces

H/II D: The Learner Will Maintain the Exterior of Living Quarters

1. Keep exterior neat and clean
    a. Pick up debris from exterior
    b. Store accumulating trash/garbage in appropriate containers
    c. Follow disposal procedures for trash/garbage (municipal procedures, rural procedures, etc.)
    d. Recycle recyclables (paper, plastics, glass, etc.)
2. Perform seasonal chores
    a. Clean outdoor equipment (furniture, grill, etc.)
    b. Repair/replace outdoor equipment as needed
    c. Store/retrieve outdoor equipment
3. Maintain exterior of building
    a. Identify building exterior requiring maintenance (walls, roof, gutters, windows, storm fixtures, yard, flower boxes, etc.)
    b. Repair/replace as needed

H/II E: The Learner Will Respond to Seasonal Changes

1. Respond to seasonal changes
    a. Schedule chores by seasons (winter, spring, summer, fall chores)
    b. Perform routine interior seasonal building maintenance (clean furnace, empty ashes from fireplace drop, etc.)
    c. Perform routine exterior seasonal building maintenance (clean gutters, store/retrieve outdoor furniture, change storm doors/windows, blacktop drive, etc.)
    d. Perform routine yard maintenance (mow, rake, seed, fertilize, etc.)
    e. Tend plants (flowers, vegetable garden, shrubs, etc.)
    f. Clear walks/drive of ice and snow

H/II F: The Learner Will Follow Home Safety Procedures

1. Prevent household fire/accident
   a. Identify safe use of equipment (safe/unsafe movements, handling, etc.)
   b. Observe procedures relative to safe use of materials (chemicals use, timing, movements, handling, etc.)
   c. Identify fire/accident hazards (material use, material storage, tool use, tool storage, slippery surfaces, heights, flammable materials, etc.)
   d. Identify material/equipment hazards (broken tools, broken equipment, exposed wiring, exposed heat sources, etc.)
   e. Identify weather hazards (storms, heat, cold, etc.)
   f. Use recommended/required protective gear for activities (eye, hand, feet, skin, etc.)
   g. Remove/neutralize hazards
   h. Avoid hazardous areas (heights, unrepaired locations, etc.)

H/II G: The Learner Will Follow Home Accident/Emergency Procedures

1. Respond to accident/emergency
   a. Determine when/if external assistance is required (accident/emergency personnel, repair personnel, etc.)
   b. Inform accident/emergency personnel (911, police, fire department, repair personnel, etc.)
   c. Follow standard home emergency procedures (fight fire, disconnect electricity, evacuate, provide first aid, etc.)

H/II H: The Learner Will Maintain Food Stock

1. Inventory food stock
   a. Check menus for foods to prepare
   b. Assess current food stock for quantity of menu foods (vegetables, meat, fruits, bread, milk, etc.)
   c. Make grocery list of required foods
   d. Check store ads and coupon sources for potential savings
2. Purchase required foods
   a. Obtain required quantities of food
   b. Store purchased foods (dry food, frozen food, refrigerated food, etc.)
   c. Dispose of empty bags/containers (discard, recycle, etc.)

H/II I: The Learner Will Prepare Meals

1. Prepare meals
   a. Establish menus (balanced nutrition, variety, taste, etc.)
   b. Prepare meals (appropriate quantities, appearance, timing, etc.)
   c. Serve meals
2. Clean up after meals
   a. Clean up (wash dishes, clean table and eating area, etc.)
   b. Preserve and store leftovers (dry foods, refrigerated foods, liquids, etc.)
   c. Sort discards for trash/garbage/recycling

H/II J: The Learner Will Budget Money

1. Obtain income (work, SSI, pension, etc.)
2. Allocate funds
   a. Determine expenses (rent/mortgage, utilities, food, transportation, personal care, clothing, supplies, equipment, taxes, savings, emergency fund, leisure activities, etc.)
   b. Allocate existing funds
3. Use banking services
   a. Identify needed services (savings, checking, charge card, personal loans, equipment loans, mortgage, etc.)
   b. Apply for services
   c. Use services as required

H/II K: The Learner Will Pay Bills

1. Pay bills
   a. Pay fixed bills (food, rent/mortgage, utilities, transportation, taxes, etc.)
   b. Pay occasional bills (repairs, vacations, leisure, personal equipment, supplies, etc.)

H/III: Goals Related to Coexisting with Others in a Neighborhood and Community

H/III A: The Learner Will Interact with Others in the Community

1. Perform appropriate interactions with others in the community (neighbors, merchants, service personnel, officials, etc.)
   a. Identify appropriate interactions (conversation topics, activities, touches, helping, etc.)
   b. Perform appropriate interactions
2. Refrain from inappropriate interactions with others in the community
   a. Identify inappropriate interactions (conversation topics, quarrels, fights, familiarity, etc.)
   b. Refrain from inappropriate interactions
3. Observe demeanor requirements with others in the community
   a. Identify acceptable demeanor (language use, assertiveness, deference, familiarity, etc.)
   b. Exhibit appropriate demeanor
4. Exhibit appropriate body language while interacting with others in the community
   a. Identify appropriate body language (posture, facial expressions, gestures, movements, etc.)
   b. Exhibit appropriate body language

H/III B: The Learner Will Observe the Requirements of the Law

1. Observe the requirements of the law
   a. Observe traffic laws (pedestrian, vehicle, etc.)
   b. Observe nuisance laws (noise, alcohol, loitering, etc.)
   c. Observe laws governing the use of public facilities (rest rooms, parks, streets, buildings, etc.)
   d. Observe property laws (purchase, ownership, use, etc.)
   e. Observe contract laws (purchases, payments, etc.)
2. Refrain from illegal acts
   a. Identify illegal acts (stealing, drunkenness, sexual acts, vehicle usage, disturbing the peace, etc.)
   b. Refrain from illegal acts
3. Exercise rights if arrested
   a. Identify rights if arrested (telephone call, representation, silence, etc.)
   b. Exercise rights when appropriate

H/III C: The Learner Will Respond to the Inappropriate Conduct of Others in the Community

1. Respond to the inappropriate conduct of others
   a. Identify the inappropriate physical conduct of others (fighting, aggression, etc.)
   b. Identify the inappropriate social conduct of others (harassment, manipulation, exploitation, victimization, etc.)
   c. Identify the inappropriate legal conduct of others (cheating, false arrest, etc.)
   d. Respond to inappropriate physical conduct of others (avoid contact, seek assistance from law enforcement personnel, etc.)
   e. Respond to inappropriate social conduct of others (avoid contact, seek assistance from friends/legal system, etc.)
   f. Respond to inappropriate legal conduct of others (seek assistance from the legal system)

H/III D: The Learner Will Carry Out Civic Duties

1. Register for duties
   a. Identify required registrations (voting, draft, etc.)
   b. Register for duties

2. Carry out civic responsibilities
   a. Identify civic duties (attend civic meetings, vote, fulfill jury duty, etc.)
   b. Carry out civic responsibilities
3. Perform volunteer service work
   a. Identify appropriate volunteer service work (public service, charity, political, etc.)
   b. Perform volunteer service work

H/IV: Goals Related to Handling Community-Related Glitches

H/IV A: The Learner Will Cope with Community Schedule Disruptions
1. Cope with changes in daily routine (holidays, weather related, emergencies, etc.)
   a. Identify changes in the daily routine (home during work hours, arrival of visitors, etc.)
   b. Adjust schedule (postpone tasks, perform alternate tasks, etc.)
2. Cope with changes in other routines (chores, shopping trips, etc.)
   a. Identify changes in routines (early completion of chores, broken equipment, stores closed, etc.)
   b. Adjust schedule (postpone tasks, perform alternate tasks, etc.)

H/IV B: The Learner Will Cope with Equipment Breakdowns or Material Depletions
1. Cope with broken equipment
   a. Identify broken equipment (broken appliances, tools, vehicles, etc.)
   b. Repair or replace broken equipment
2. Cope with material depletion
   a. Identify depleted material (cleaning fluid, toilet paper, etc.)
   b. Replace depleted material
   c. Reschedule activities

H/IV C: The Learner Will Cope with Sudden Changes in the Weather
1. Cope with weather changes
   a. Identify unexpected changes in the weather (storms, temperature climbs/drops, wind, etc.)
   b. Adjust to weather changes (close/open doors and windows, adjust heat, etc.)

Domain V: Vocational

V/I: Goals Related to Obtaining Employment

V/I A: The Learner Will Seek Employment
1. Find new employment
   a. Use formal vocational resources to identify new employment possibilities (advertisements, agencies, etc.)
   b. Use informal vocational resources to identify new employment possibilities (family, friends, etc.)
   c. Decide which new employment possibilities are appropriate (personal interests, prior experience, etc.)
   d. Select job(s) for which to apply
2. Apply for employment
   a. Obtain and complete job application
   b. Interview
   c. Take required competency tests
   d. Obtain information relative to job requirements (hours, physical requirements, academic requirements, etc.)
   e. Obtain information relative to job benefits (salary, bonuses, insurance, retirement, etc.)
   f. Obtain job offer
3. Assess suitability of potential job
   a. Assess physical demands of job (strength, endurance, agility, etc.)
   b. Assess academic requirements of job (reading, writing, arithmetic, information, etc.)
   c. Assess problem-solving requirements of job (complex/simple, etc.)
   d. Assess financial needs relative to compensation
4. Assess work environment of potential job
   a. Assess work climate (friendly/unfriendly, relaxed/tense, high/low pace, etc.)
   b. Assess safety features (safe/unsafe)
   c. Assess employee facilities (break areas, rest rooms, etc.)
   d. Assess barriers (physical, attitudinal, emotional, etc.)
   e. Assess location (transportation availability, commuting time, neighborhood quality, potential dangers, etc.)

V/I B: The Learner Will Accept Employment
1. Indicate acceptance of job
   a. Decide to accept job
   b. Indicate acceptance (letter, telephone, personal communication, etc.)
2. Fill out papers
   a. Obtain relevant papers (W-4, employee forms, etc.)
   b. Fill out papers
3. Submit to required physical exam(s)
   a. Identify exam requirements (personnel, location, etc.)
   b. Get exam(s)
4. Report to work
   a. Identify variables related to beginning work (time, place, contact person, etc.)
   b. Report for work

V/I C: The Learner Will Use Unemployment Services
1. Identify when to apply for unemployment benefits
   a. Locate Employment Security Office
   b. File for unemployment
2. Request job search assistance
   a. Locate assistance agency (Employment Security Division, Vocational Rehabilitation, Goodwill, etc.)
   b. File for assistance

V/II: Goals Related to Performing Work Routines

V/II A: The Learner Will Perform the Job Routine
1. Perform job routine
   a. Identify required activities (regular, occasional, etc.)
   b. Identify required/optional sequence of activities
   c. Identify substitute activities (early completion of assigned tasks, fill-ins, pullouts, etc.)
   d. Identify clothing/equipment requirements (uniforms, work clothes, tools, protective equipment, etc.)
   e. Perform work activities as required
2. Use work site facilities
   a. Identify facilities (rest rooms, eating/break space(s), lockers, etc.)
   b. Identify times for facility use (breaks, eating times, before/after work, etc.)
   c. Use facilities
3. Observe acceptable production rate (upper/lower limits)
   a. Identify upper/lower limits of production (employer requirements, union/customary limits)
   b. Observe limits
4. Meet work quality standards
   a. Identify work quality standards
   b. Meet work quality standards

V/II B: The Learner Will Follow Work-Related Daily Schedule
1. Follow daily schedule
   a. Identify attendance requirements (arrival, departure, absence notification, etc.)
   b. Identify work schedule (starting/quitting times, split shifts, breaks, etc.)
   c. Follow daily schedule
2. Follow nonwork schedule
   a. Identify nonwork schedule (days off, holidays, vacations, etc.)
   b. Follow nonwork schedule

V/II C: The Learner Will Follow Employer Rules and Regulations
1. Follow employer rules and regulations
   a. Identify employer rules and regulations (attendance, facilities use, permissions, controlled substance use, theft, chain of command, unpaid leave, reporting absences, reporting problems, etc.)
   b. Identify unwritten rules (customs, employee constructs, etc.)
   c. Follow all rules and regulations on job site

V/II D: The Learner Will Maintain the Workstation
1. Observe work environment maintenance standards
   a. Identify work environment maintenance schedules (cleanliness, clutter, machine/tool maintenance, etc.)
   b. Identify maintenance tools/materials
   c. Identify clothing maintenance/storage standards (dirty/clean standards, repairs, laundry schedule, etc.)
   d. Follow work environment maintenance schedules (tool/material/clothing storage, use, etc.)
   e. Observe work environment maintenance standards (cleanliness, clutter, etc.)

V/II E: The Learner Will Follow Safety Procedures on the Job
1. Follow standard safety procedures for use of tools and materials
   a. Identify tool and materials safety procedures (handling, storage, etc.)
   b. Identify use of safety equipment (clothing, ear/eye protection, head protection, foot protection, etc.)
   c. Identify procedures governing job station safety hazards (clutter, nearby equipment, unsafe areas, etc.)
   d. Observe all safety procedures while on work site

V/II F: The Learner Will Follow Standard Accident and Emergency Procedures on the Work Site
1. Follow standard accident and emergency work site procedures
   a. Identify standard accident procedures (injury, equipment malfunctions, material mishaps, etc.)
   b. Identify standard emergency work site procedures (supervisor/staff notification, first aid, fire alarms, emergency alarms, return to work, etc.)
   c. Follow all standard accident/emergency procedures

V/III: Goals Related to Coexisting with Others on the Job

V/III A: The Learner Will Interact with Others on the Job
1. Perform appropriate interactions with others on the job site (supervisor(s), fellow employees, public, subordinates, etc.)
   a. Identify appropriate interactions (conversation topics, activities, assistance, etc.)
   b. Perform appropriate interactions
2. Refrain from inappropriate interactions with others on the job site
   a. Identify inappropriate interactions (insubordination, rudeness, quarrels, fights, teasing, etc.)
   b. Refrain from inappropriate interactions
3. Exhibit acceptable demeanor on the job site
   a. Identify acceptable demeanor (language vocabulary and usage, assertiveness, deference, familiarity, etc.)
   b. Exhibit acceptable demeanor
4. Exhibit acceptable body language while interacting with others on the job site
   a. Identify acceptable body language (posture, facial expressions, gestures, movements)
   b. Exhibit acceptable body language

V/III B: The Learner Will Respond to the Inappropriate Conduct of Others on the Job
1. Identify the inappropriate conduct of others on the job site (aggression, manipulation, setups, excessive demands, rudeness, lollygagging, insubordination, harassment, etc.)
2. Respond to the inappropriate conduct of others
   a. Follow company procedures (incident reports, supervisor notification, etc.)
   b. Obtain assistance (avoidance, enlist support of family, friends, etc.)

V/IV: Goals Related to Handling Work-Related Glitches

V/IV A: The Learner Will Cope with Changes in the Work Routine
1. Cope with changes in work routine
   a. Identify unexpected changes in the work routine (schedule change, transportation problem, illness, downtime, strike, temporary layoff, etc.)
   b. Follow procedures for unexpected absences (telephone call, documentation, enforced leisure, job change, etc.)
   c. Adjust to externally caused changes (change schedule, make work, observe strike, etc.)
2. Cope with equipment/tool breakdowns
   a. Identify equipment/tool breakdowns (reportable, nonreportable)
   b. Notify appropriate personnel (supervisor, repair personnel, etc.)
   c. Repair or replace equipment/tool or wait for assistance as appropriate
3. Cope with material depletion
   a. Identify unexpected material depletion (reportable/nonreportable)
   b. Notify appropriate personnel (supervisor, material expeditor, etc.)
   c. Replenish/replace material or wait for assistance as appropriate

Domain L: Leisure

L/I: Goals Related to Developing Leisure Activities

L/I A: The Learner Will Find New Leisure Activities
1. Find new leisure activity
   a. Use formal resources to identify potential new leisure activities (advertisements, leisure agencies, etc.)
   b. Use informal resources to identify potential new leisure activities (family, friends, etc.)
   c. Assess projected benefits of potential new activities (interest value, social value, physical value, etc.)
   d. Assess personal abilities/disabilities (physical, intellectual, etc.)
   e. Assess accessibility of new activity (availability, costs, etc.)
   f. Decide if pursuit of activity is appropriate
2. Acquire skills for new leisure activity
   a. Identify required/optional equipment
   b. Identify required activities
   c. Learn skills (formal lessons, informal lessons, observation, printed materials, video, etc.)
   d. Practice skills

L/II: Goals Related to Performing Leisure Activities

L/II A: The Learner Will Perform Leisure Activities
1. Establish activity schedule
   a. Select leisure activities
   b. Ascertain available leisure time (schedule work, chores, sleep, etc.)
   c. Schedule leisure activities (available personal time, available facility time, available fellow participant time, etc.)
   d. Acquire tools and materials for leisure activity (buy, borrow, rent, etc.)
2. Perform leisure activity
   a. Pay required fees
   b. Identify facility rules and routines (usage times/periods, waiting times, usage sequences, signed permissions, equipment rental/checkouts, activity patterns, use of facility equipment, etc.)
   c. Perform activities

L/II B: The Learner Will Maintain Personal Leisure Equipment
1. Maintain leisure equipment and clothing
   a. Identify problems in equipment/clothing (worn/broken/defective, required adjustments)
   b. Fix problems in equipment/clothing (clean, repair, replace, adjust)
   c. Follow equipment/clothing storage and retrieval procedures (racks, hangers, holders, bags, etc.)
2. Replace depleted leisure activity supplies
   a. Identify low supplies
   b. Replenish supplies prior to engaging in activity

L/II C: The Learner Will Follow Leisure Activity Safety Procedures
1. Identify leisure activity safety rules/procedures
   a. Identify safe use of equipment (protective gear, safe/unsafe movements, etc.)
   b. Identify unsafe/restricted areas in leisure facility
   c. Identify activity hazards (cleanliness, required equipment discards, etc.)
   d. Identify officials in leisure activity location (uniforms, badges, locations, etc.)
   e. Identify roles officials play in leisure facility (ticket takers, information givers, movement facilitators, activity schedulers, order keepers, equipment managers, etc.)
2. Follow all leisure activity safety rules/procedures
   a. Use recommended/required protective gear for activity
   b. Observe procedures relative to safe use of equipment (movements, handling, etc.)

    c. Refrain from entering unsafe/restricted areas in facility

    d. Remove hazards or avoid hazardous spots/areas

    e. Follow directions of officials

    f. Observe moderation in use of substances during leisure activity (tobacco, alcohol, etc.)

L/II D: The Learner Will Follow Accident and Emergency Procedures for Leisure Activities

1. Respond to accident/emergency

    a. Identify accident/emergency (injury, illness, fire, sudden hazard, etc.)

    b. Follow standard accident/emergency reporting procedures (inform facility officials, call 911, etc.)

    c. Follow standard emergency/accident action procedures (provide first aid, direct traffic, follow directions of officials, etc.)

L/III: Goals Related to Coexisting with Others During Leisure Activities

L/III A: The Learner Will Interact with Others During Leisure Time

1. Perform acceptable interactions

    a. Identify acceptable interactions with fellow participants, spectators, officials, bystanders (rules, customs, routines, etc.)

    b. Perform acceptable interactions

2. Refrain from inappropriate interactions

    a. Identify inappropriate interactions (quarrels, fights, not following directions of officials, not observing rules/customs of activity, etc.)

    b. Refrain from inappropriate interactions

3. Exhibit acceptable demeanor during leisure activity

    a. Identify acceptable demeanor (language vocabulary and usage, assertiveness, deference, familiarity, etc.)

    b. Exhibit acceptable demeanor

4. Exhibit acceptable body language during leisure activity

    a. Identify acceptable body language (posture, facial expressions, gestures, movements, etc.)

    b. Exhibit acceptable body language

L/III B: The Learner Will Respond to the Inappropriate Conduct of Others During Leisure Activity

1. Respond to the inappropriate conduct of others during leisure activity

    a. Identify inappropriate conduct (not following rules/customs, exploitation, manipulation, harassment, teasing, aggression, etc.)

    b. Respond to inappropriate conduct (leave area, seek assistance from officials, defend self, etc.)

L/IV: Goals Related to Handling Leisure-Related Glitches

L/IV A: The Learner Will Respond to Changes in Leisure Routine

1. Cope with schedule/routine changes

    a. Identify leisure schedule/routine changes (weather, illness, accidents, schedule changes by fellow participants, etc.)

    b. Adjust to schedule changes (reschedule, cancel, perform alternate activity, etc.)

L/IV B: The Learner Will Respond to Equipment Breakdowns and Material Depletions

1. Cope with equipment breakdowns

    a. Identify equipment breakdowns

    b. Adjust to equipment breakdowns (repair, replace, reschedule/cancel/perform alternate activity)

2. Cope with material depletions

    a. Identify material depletions

    b. Adjust to material depletions (replenish, reschedule/cancel/perform alternate activity)

Domain T: Travel

T/I: Goals Related to Routine Travel in the Community

T/I A: The Learner Will Develop Mental Maps of Frequented Buildings
1. Travel to locations in frequented buildings
    a. Travel to locations in living quarters (kitchen, living room, den, bedroom, bath, etc.)
    b. Travel to locations at school/job site (classroom/workstation, cafeteria/eating area, rest rooms, outdoor areas, etc.)
    c. Travel to locations in various community buildings (mall/shopping areas, stores, services, rest rooms, public areas, etc.)
    d. Travel to locations in leisure activity sites (ticket booths, equipment rooms, rest areas, rest rooms, showers, etc.)
2. Travel to various community locations
    a. Travel to commercial locations (grocery stores, fast-food restaurants, sit-down restaurants, discount and department stores, shoe stores, clothing stores, hardware stores, shopping centers, banks, etc.)
    b. Travel to medical assistance locations (physician, dentist, chiropractor, hospital, emergency treatment, etc.)
    c. Travel to church
    d. Travel to leisure locations (parks, entertainment facilities, movies, music facilities, theaters, athletic facilities, public gathering spots, etc.)
    e. Travel to city center
    f. Travel to local shopping malls
    g. Travel between above locations

T/II: Goals Related to the Use of Conveyances

T/II A: The Learner Will Follow Usage Procedures for Conveyances
1. Follow usage procedures for private conveyances
    a. Identify private conveyance (bicycle, car, van, etc.)
    b. Identify procedures for private conveyance use (boarding/entering, seat belts, balance, etc.)
    c. Follow procedures for private conveyance use
    d. Observe laws for private conveyance operation (bicycle, motor vehicle, traffic, etc.)
2. Follow usage procedures for public conveyances
    a. Identify public conveyance (taxi, bus/trolley, subway/elevated/passenger train, airline, etc.)
    b. Identify procedures for use of public conveyances (fares, boarding, departure, etc.)
    c. Follow procedures for public conveyance use

T/II B: The Learner Will Make Decisions Prior to Travel
1. Select destination
    a. Decide to travel
    b. Select transportation (private, public, etc.)
2. Select departure time
    a. Identify arrival time
    b. Identify travel time
    c. Identify departure time
3. Select appropriate clothing
    a. Identify reason for going to destination (activity, etc.)
    b. Identify external variables (weather, level of formality, etc.)
    c. Select clothing
4. Obtain funds when necessary
    a. Identify amount of funds required
    b. Obtain required funds

T/II C: The Learner Will Follow Travel Safety Procedures
1. Follow travel safety procedures
   a. Identify pedestrian safety procedures (sidewalks/no sidewalks, streets, crossings, signals, etc.)
   b. Identify private conveyance safety procedures (bicycle, automobile, van, etc.)
   c. Identify public conveyance safety procedures (bus/trolley, taxi, elevated/subway/passenger train, airline, etc.)
   d. Observe all travel safety procedures

T/II D: The Learner Will Follow Accident/Emergency Procedures While Traveling
1. Follow accident/emergency reporting procedures
   a. Identify accidents (vehicle related, pedestrian related, etc.)
   b. Identify emergencies (injuries, illnesses, etc.)
   c. Make report (911, police report, insurance report, witness report, etc.)
2. Follow accident/emergency action procedures
   a. Identify responsible person (police official, fire official, etc.)
   b. Follow directions of official (stand clear, direct traffic, provide information, etc.)
   c. Provide first aid where appropriate

T/III: Goals Related to Coexisting with Others During Travel

T/III A: The Learner Will Interact with Others During Travel
1. Perform acceptable interactions
   a. Identify acceptable interactions (drivers, information personnel, ticket sellers, fellow passengers, pedestrians, etc.)
   b. Perform acceptable interactions
2. Refrain from inappropriate interactions
   a. Identify inappropriate interactions (seating, familiarity, not following directions of officials, not observing rules/customs of activity, etc.)
   b. Refrain from inappropriate interactions
3. Exhibit acceptable demeanor for leisure activity
   a. Identify acceptable demeanor (language use, assertiveness, deference, familiarity, etc.)
   b. Exhibit acceptable demeanor
4. Exhibit acceptable body language during leisure activity
   a. Identify acceptable body language (posture, facial expressions, gestures, movements, etc.)
   b. Exhibit acceptable body language

T/III B: The Learner Will Respond to the Inappropriate Conduct of Others During Travel
1. Respond to inappropriate conduct of others during leisure activity
   a. Identify inappropriate conduct (aggression, harassment, teasing, etc.)
   b. Respond to inappropriate conduct (leave area, seek assistance from officials, defend self, etc.)

T/IV: Goals Related to Handling Travel-Related Glitches

T/IV A: The Learner Will Cope with Glitches While Traveling
1. Cope with conveyance schedule change
   a. Identify schedule change (missed conveyance, weather problem, equipment malfunction, etc.)
   b. Inform others affected by change (work, leisure, home, etc.)
   c. Adjust schedule (next bus, arrive late, cancel trip, etc.)
2. Cope with personal error
   a. Identify personal error (alarm not set, dawdling, etc.)
   b. Inform others affected by schedule change (work, leisure, home, etc.)
   c. Adjust schedule (arrive late, cancel trip, etc.)

3. Cope with equipment breakdowns and material depletions while traveling
    a. Identify equipment breakdown (accident, flat tire, etc.)
    b. Identify material depletions during travel (gasoline, etc.)
    c. Locate/inform responsible person (repair person, towing service, police, fire officials, etc.)
    d. Repair/replace broken equipment if appropriate
    e. Replenish depleted material
    f. Adjust schedule
4. Cope with being lost
    a. Identify when lost (unrecognized landmarks, inappropriate direction, etc.)
    b. Approach other person for assistance (official, private person, etc.)
    c. Follow directions to intended destination

APPENDIX B
WORK SHEETS

Work Sheet for Specifying a Curriculum Aim and Goals

Name of School or Agency: _____

School/Agency
Mission: _____
_____
_____
_____
_____
_____

Name of the
Instructional Unit: _____

Program Thrusts: _____
_____
_____
_____

Aim of the
Curriculum: _____
_____
_____
_____
_____
_____

Considerations/Assumptions:
Learner
Characteristics: _____
_____
_____
_____

Talents of Staff: _____
_____
_____
_____
_____
_____
_____
_____

Limitations of the
Physical Plant: _____
_____
_____
_____

Community
Resources: _____
_____
_____
_____
_____
_____
_____
_____

Location of the
Instructional Unit: _____
_____
_____

Program Times: _____
_____

Limiting Policies: _____
_____
_____
_____
_____
_____
_____
_____

Work Sheet for Formulating Curriculum Goals

GOALS:

Goal 1: _____

_____

_____

Skill Cluster: _____

_____

_____

_____

_____

_____

_____

Goal 2: _____

_____

Skill Cluster: _____

_____

_____

_____

_____

_____

Format for a Curriculum Document

Curriculum Area: _____

Goal 1: _____

Curriculum Objectives
The learner will:

1.1 _____
1.2 _____
1.3 _____
1.4 _____
1.5 _____
1.6 _____
1.7 _____
1.8 _____
1.9 _____
1.10 _____
1.11 _____
1.12 _____
1.13 _____
1.14 _____
1.15 _____
1.16 _____
•
•
•
1.n _____

Work Sheet for Developing a Behavior Pattern

Step One: State the goal:

The learners will: _____

_____

Step Two: List the conditions:

Location(s): _____

_____

Time(s): _____

_____

Persons present: _____

_____

Tools and materials: _____

_____

_____

_____

Step Three: List the critical functions:

_____

_____

_____

_____

_____

_____

_____

_____

Step Four: State the behavior pattern:

To show that the learner has attained this objective, the learner will:

_____

_____

_____

_____

_____

_____

_____

_____

_____

_____

_____

_____

_____

_____

_____

_____

_____

_____

_____

Assessment Work Sheet

Name of Learner: _____   **Age:** _____

Dates of Assessment: _____

Grade/Program Area: _____

Name of Instructor/Assessor: _____

Location of Assessment: _____

Assessment Setting/Situation:

Curriculum Objectives	*Standards*	*Procedures*	*Results*

COMMENTS:

Assessment Schedule Work Sheet

Name of Learner: _____ **Age:** _____

Dates of Assessment: _____

Assessment Setting/Situation:

Days/Times	Activities	Procedures	Personnel/Materials Needed

OBJECTIVE ANALYSIS WORK SHEET
COVER SHEET

Unit: _____   Date: _____

Learners: _____

Objective: _____
_____
_____
_____

Learner Characteristics: _____
_____
_____

Critical Functions:

_____ 1. _____
_____ 2. _____
_____ 3. _____
_____ 4. _____
_____ 5. _____
_____ 6. _____
_____ 7. _____
_____ 8. _____
_____ 9. _____
_____ 10. _____

Outcomes: _____
_____
_____
_____
_____
_____
_____
_____

Mastery Criteria: _____
_____
_____
_____

Settings and Circumstances: _____
_____

Tools and Materials: _____
_____
_____
_____

Instructors: _____

Date Completed: _____

Completion Certified by: _____

List of Skills

1. _____
2. _____
3. _____
4. _____
5. _____
6. _____
7. _____
8. _____
9. _____
10. _____
11. _____
12. _____
13. _____
14. _____
15. _____
16. _____
17. _____
18. _____
19. _____
20. _____
21. _____
22. _____
23. _____
24. _____
25. _____
26. _____
27. _____
28. _____
29. _____
30. _____
31. _____
32. _____
33. _____
34. _____
35. _____
36. _____
37. _____
38. _____
39. _____
40. _____
41. _____
42. _____
43. _____
44. _____
45. _____
46. _____
47. _____
48. _____
49. _____
50. _____

Monitoring Work Sheet

Name: _____

Program Objective: _____

Standard: _____

Location: _____

Instructor: _____

Issues to Monitor	Procedures
_____	_____
_____	_____
_____	_____
_____	_____
_____	_____
_____	_____
_____	_____
_____	_____
_____	_____
_____	_____
_____	_____
_____	_____
_____	_____
_____	_____
_____	_____
_____	_____
_____	_____
_____	_____
_____	_____
_____	_____
_____	_____
_____	_____
_____	_____

Daily Results of Monitoring

Days	Results/Comments

Skills/Skill Clusters Profile

Scoring Code:

/	=	Step performed correctly w/o prompts
(Blank)	=	Step performed incorrectly
■	=	Not performed during probe
X	=	Step performed correctly during standard time
O	=	Total steps performed correctly in probe

Learner: _____

Skill: _____

Location: _____

Instructor: _____

Standard Time:	*Behaviors/Behavioral Cues*	*Results*							
_____ 25	_____	25	25	25	25	25	25	25	25
_____ 24	_____	24	24	24	24	24	24	24	24
_____ 23	_____	23	23	23	23	23	23	23	23
_____ 22	_____	22	22	22	22	22	22	22	22
_____ 21	_____	21	21	21	21	21	21	21	21
_____ 20	_____	20	20	20	20	20	20	20	20
_____ 19	_____	19	19	19	19	19	19	19	19
_____ 18	_____	18	18	18	18	18	18	18	18
_____ 17	_____	17	17	17	17	17	17	17	17
_____ 16	_____	16	16	16	16	16	16	16	16
_____ 15	_____	15	15	15	15	15	15	15	15
_____ 14	_____	14	14	14	14	14	14	14	14
_____ 13	_____	13	13	13	13	13	13	13	13
_____ 12	_____	12	12	12	12	12	12	12	12
_____ 11	_____	11	11	11	11	11	11	11	11
_____ 10	_____	10	10	10	10	10	10	10	10
_____ 9	_____	9	9	9	9	9	9	9	9
_____ 8	_____	8	8	8	8	8	8	8	8
_____ 7	_____	7	7	7	7	7	7	7	7
_____ 6	_____	6	6	6	6	6	6	6	6
_____ 5	_____	5	5	5	5	5	5	5	5
_____ 4	_____	4	4	4	4	4	4	4	4
_____ 3	_____	3	3	3	3	3	3	3	3
_____ 2	_____	2	2	2	2	2	2	2	2
_____ 1	_____	1	1	1	1	1	1	1	1

Probe: ☐ ☐ ☐ ☐ ☐ ☐ ☐ ☐

APPENDIX C
CHECKLIST FOR POTENTIAL
PHYSICAL PROBLEMS

Instructors often find that their learners have undetected physical problems that can prevent or slow skill acquisition. It is a sad fact that the instructional staff members often are the only people in a position to detect the presence of one of these problems.

The symptoms that are listed on the following pages indicate the potential for problems that may or may not exist. For example, if a learner who has red, runny eyes may have an eye problem or allergies, he or she may have had a fight, or his or her parents may have separated the night before (among other things). Since instructional personnel are in no position to make a medical judgment, a referral to a physician is probably the best course. Instructional personnel usually are not trained to make medical diagnoses and cannot prescribe medical treatment. However, they can make referrals for suspected problems, and the instructor who suspects that a learner has an undiagnosed physical or sensory problem is under a moral obligation to find someone who can make a diagnosis, and if necessary, provide treatment.

The instructor's responsibility is to ensure that learning takes place in a smooth manner. Factors that get in the way of skill acquisition should be attended to. The checklist on the following pages is a simple inventory that was designed to help identify the possibility that a learner requires medical assistance, and the checklist should not be viewed in any other light.

I. Vision

Learners with visual problems may want to attend to what is happening around them. Because they are unable to do so, they miss information, tire easily, or they may experience pain as a result of their efforts. Potential

Adapted from: Dever, R. & Knapczyk, D. (1980). Screening for physical problems in classrooms for severely handicapped students. *JASH*, 5 (2), 194–204.

problems fall into a number of categories, including (but not limited to) acuity, eye musculature, visual field, and diseases of the eye. Learners with suspected problems should be referred to a qualified ophthalmologist or optometrist.

Learners may have visual problems if they exhibit the following symptoms:

_____ 1. Have watering or discharge from the eyes

_____ 2. Have frequent sties

_____ 3. Have redness, encrustation, or swelling around the eyes

_____ 4. Have frequent headaches

_____ 5. Have pupils with cloudy spots

_____ 6. Hold objects or materials close to eyes or hold head close to objects or materials while working with them

_____ 7. Hold head to one side while working

_____ 8. Frown, squint, or close one eye while working

_____ 9. Frequently change distance of head from task while working

_____ 10. Lack persistence at task or tire easily

_____ 11. Show excessive activity while working at tasks requiring visual attention

_____ 12. Are easily distracted to irrelevant parts of task

_____ 13. Rub or poke at eyes frequently or try to brush away an imaginary shield

_____ 14. Blink frequently

_____ 15. Exhibit inattention to near or far objects

_____ 16. Have difficulty following moving objects

_____ 17. Have eyes that tremble or vibrate, or have one eye that "wanders"

_____ 18. Have one pupil noticeably larger than the other

_____ 19. Frequently get sick, dizzy, or tired while reading or watching movies

_____ 20. Appear not to discriminate between two or more colors

_____ 21. Have pupils that do not constrict or dilate in response to light and/or darkness

_____ 22. Move hand in front of face while gazing at light source

_____ 23. Cover one eye with hand while working

_____ 24. Work easily at chalkboard but not on paper, or vice versa

_____ 25. Hold books, papers, etc. at arm's length while working

_____ 26. Consistently fail to get information from one side of paper or chalkboard

_____ 27. Hold onto railings, walls, or other objects when descending stairs

_____ 28. Stop to feel the floor or ground when the surface color changes or consistently miss the first step when ascending stairs

If you suspect that a learner has previously undetected visual problems, make sure that his or her eyes are examined by a qualified optometrist or ophthalmologist. If you know that a learner has visual problems, do the following:

1. See that the learner wears prescribed glasses at all appropriate times and in the appropriate manner.
2. Have eyeglass prescriptions checked every year.
3. Keep eyeglasses clean; even better, teach the learner to clean his or her own eyeglasses frequently and appropriately.
4. A learner who requires frequent periods of eye rest should learn to schedule them appropriately.
5. When necessary, limit "close" work to short periods and alternate it with "far" work.
6. Have a learner whose eyes tire easily bathe his or her eyes at regular intervals with cloths soaked in cool water.
7. The direction of incoming light makes a difference for people with visual problems. Arrange the learner's seat so that light falls on the work, not on the learner's face. Consult an optometrist or ophthalmologist for correct positioning of either work or student so as to make the most efficient use of light.
8. Do not force a color-blind learner to name colors.

II. Auditory Problems

Learners who do not hear well may not understand all or part of any information that must be obtained auditorily. In addition, it is possible for an instructor to misinterpret behaviors that stem from having a hearing problem: The instructor may think that the learner is acting defiantly or trying to manipulate when the learner simply may not get the information he or she needs to comply with the teacher's directions or requests. Hearing problems have many possible sources ranging from wax buildup in the ears to central nervous system dysfunction, and they may be long-standing or have a sudden onset.

Learners may have hearing problems if they exhibit the following symptoms:

1. Have chronic respiratory infections, runny ears, or earaches
2. Breathe through the mouth
3. Pull, rub, or poke their ears excessively
4. Consistently omit specific sounds, especially *f, s, sh,* and final consonants
5. Have abnormally high, soft, loud, monotonous, or raspy voices
6. Turn head or strain to hear, or watch the lips of the speaker instead of the face
7. Do not attend when spoken to by name, especially when not looking at the speaker
8. Appear to lack confidence, to be nervous about minor details, or to be introverted
9. Appear defensive or antisocial
10. Lose balance for no apparent reason
11. Lack "startle" response
12. Have difficulty localizing sounds
13. Exhibit inconsistent responses to sounds
14. Exhibit delayed speech or produce few or no sounds
15. Consistently mispronounce common words

If you suspect hearing problems, you should refer the learner to a qualified audiologist or ear, nose, and throat physician as soon as possible. If learners have known auditory problems, do the following:

1. Make sure all hearing aids are in good working order at all times. Routine daily checks should include the following:
   a. condition of the batteries;
   b. cleanliness of the ear mold;
   c. position of the volume control;
   d. status of the "on/off" switch; and
   e. integrity of any wires, such as between the body of the aid and the ear mold.
2. Teach the learner to wear his or her hearing aid properly.

3. Seat the learner with his or her back toward the light sources so that the light will fall on the speaker's face, not the learner's.
4. Make sure the learner is attending before giving directions or instruction.
5. Do not exaggerate speech movements; speak in a normal voice, but be sure to speak clearly.
6. Rephrase or rework statements the learner does not understand easily.
7. Use Total Communication (combined speech, sign, gestures, writing, pictures, or anything else that may assist the communicative act when learners have difficulty acquiring information through sound).
8. If any learner tends to have wax buildup in his or her ears, a nurse or physician should clean the ears periodically. Instructors should put nothing in a learner's ear but his or her own personal ear mold.
9. Ensure that all learners with hearing problems are examined by a specialist at least once each year.

III. Seizures

It is easy to tell when a learner has a grand mal seizure, but other types of seizures may be difficult to detect. Petit mal seizures, hallucinatory seizures, myoclonic jerks, and psychomotor seizures may go completely undetected or be misinterpreted as behavioral problems. In addition, because a seizure tends to block incoming stimuli, learners who have seizures may miss a great deal of information and appear less capable than they actually are. Fortunately, many seizures can be controlled through medication, and any learner who is suspected of having seizures should be referred to a neurologist or other qualified physician for diagnosis, referral, and possible treatment.

Learners may experience seizures if they exhibit the following symptoms:

1. Go "blank" for short periods of time, during which their eyes may be unfocused, or blink frequently
2. Miss bits of information during the normal flow of events
3. Hear, see, taste, or feel things that others do not experience
4. Complain of occasional or repeated numbness or pain in specific parts of the body
5. Occasionally exhibit strange or bizarre behaviors, especially if they seem to have no memory of the behavior afterward or pay no attention to environmental stimuli while engaging in the behaviors
6. Drop objects for no apparent reason
7. Exhibit tics, trembling, or rhythmic movements, especially around the eyes or mouth but in other parts of the body as well

If you suspect that a learner may be having seizures, refer him or her to a competent neurologist. If learners are known to have seizures, do the following:

1. During a grand mal seizure, make sure the learner is lying on his or her side to prevent saliva from accumulating in the throat; move any objects on which the learner could hit his or her head out of the vicinity; do *not* place anything in the learner's mouth; and when the seizure has run its course, allow the learner to rest for a while. Rapid or loud speech following a seizure will probably confuse the learner, and it is best to speak calmly and softly until you are sure the learner understands what you are saying.
2. If a learner shows signs of a lack of oxygen following a seizure, begin artificial respiration (because it is difficult to tell when a seizure ends, mouth-to-mouth resuscitation may *not* be appropriate). When instructors do not have the necessary training, get medical help immediately.
3. If the learner defecates or urinates during a seizure, make sure he or she is cleaned up afterwards to avoid embarrassment.

4. Do not give any medication that is not authorized in writing by a physician, but make sure that *all* authorized medication is taken on schedule.
5. Keep accurate records of all medication given, including name of the medication and time, date, and dosage given.
6. Keep records of the dates, times, number, severity, length, and type of seizure for physician's reference.
7. Make sure all medications are rechecked at least once a year by the attending physician. During puberty and other times when seizures may vary in duration or intensity, medication levels should be checked more often.
8. A learner who takes medication to control seizures may experience the world in slow motion, especially if he or she must take a lot of the medication. Do not confuse such a person by speaking too rapidly or by trying to say a lot in a short period of time.
9. If a learner seems to miss information, repeat it.

IV. Orthopedic Problems and Cerebral Palsy

Learners may be born with cerebral palsy or other orthopedic problems, or they may develop them. There are many sources for these problems, including accidents, developmental problems, and degenerative diseases. Once orthopedic problems or cerebral palsy are present, they may trigger or exacerbate other problems. For example, a learner who is paralyzed may develop spinal problems from sitting in one position for too long, especially if the sitting position is improper, and a learner with cerebral palsy may develop other orthopedic problems. Learners who have orthopedic problems of any kind are usually subject to pain from muscle spasms, contractures, pressure sores, and/or nerve stimulation. Instructors who have learners with known orthopedic problems or cerebral palsy must obtain medical advice on matters such as positioning, moving, and lifting, and must do everything possible to keep the problems from becoming worse.

Learners may have orthopedic problems or cerebral palsy if they exhibit the following symptoms:

_____	1. Tend to sit slumped, on one foot, or to one side
_____	2. Stand with weight on one foot, leaning to one side, or with one shoulder noticeably lower than the other
_____	3. Have a noticeable *S* or *C* curve in the back when viewed from the rear or the side
_____	4. Stand stooped or with an exaggerated backward ("drum major") stance
_____	5. Walk or handle objects with a jerky motion
_____	6. Appear very stiff or very limp in one or more limbs
_____	7. Do not sit still and exhibit continuous wormlike movements in any part of the body
_____	8. Drool or have a slack jaw
_____	9. Have difficulty controlling tongue, jaw, or breathing during speaking or eating
_____	10. Hold onto objects while walking
_____	11. Have difficulty holding or picking up objects
_____	12. Have feet that point noticeably in or out while walking
_____	13. Have ankles or knees that are not vertically in line with their feet
_____	14. Have difficulty walking in a straight line
_____	15. Exhibit delayed motor development
_____	16. Have difficulty maintaining balance with their heads, neck, or trunk
_____	17. Experience sudden weight gain or growth spurt
_____	18. Constantly walk on toes
_____	19. Have a noticeably different gait
_____	20. Appear inordinately weak in one or more limbs
_____	21. Wear a prosthesis

If you suspect orthopedic problems, refer the learner to a qualified orthopedic specialist; if you suspect cerebral palsy, refer the learner to a neurologist or other qualified physician. If a learner has known orthopedic problems or cerebral palsy, do the following:

1. Follow all directions from physicians, physical therapists (PTs), or occupational therapists (OTs) regarding sitting, standing, walking, and other positioning or movements.
2. Check frequently for blisters, sores, and calluses on the learner's body and for wear spots, broken straps, and so forth on prostheses or other special equipment that indicate problems in fit. Refer learners to PT or OT as soon as changes are necessary.
3. Check frequently for signs of the learner's body growing out of prostheses or special equipment, such as increased difficulty attaching prosthesis. Refer learner to PT or OT when necessary.
4. Wheelchair-bound learners should not lean in a single position for any length of time. Shift position of wheelchair-bound learners frequently.
5. If possible, take a wheelchair-bound learner out of his or her chair periodically (two hours in a chair is a long time). Follow directions of PT or OT in this matter.
6. Make sure that a learner's hands, feet, and articles of clothing are clear of the wheelchair's wheels before starting to move it.
7. Check for pressure sores daily when a learner is in a wheelchair or prosthesis.
8. Follow PT/OT directions regarding periodic removal of prostheses.
9. Do not cause the limbs of a learner with spasticity to move suddenly or to change direction quickly.
10. Follow the direction of a physician, PT, or OT with regard to support of learner's body when at rest.

V. Pain

Learners who experience pain may have difficulty cooperating in learning activities. There are innumerable sources of pain ranging from headaches to arthritis, allergies, and ill-fitting shoes. Some sources of pain are easy to alleviate, but others may prove to be very difficult. Any of the previously listed problems may be accompanied by pain, but there are many other sources as well.

Learners may be experiencing pain if they exhibit the following symptoms:

_____   1. Have recent burns, animal or insect bites, cuts, bruises, or any other identifiable condition that may cause pain
_____   2. Have clothing or shoes that do not fit properly
_____   3. Have a current illness
_____   4. Rub, pat, hold, poke, or bang a spot on the body, including the head
_____   5. Are in wheelchairs, wear prosthetic devices, have had surgery, or wear a hearing aid
_____   6. Have recently been subject to physical stress, such as automobile accidents or falls
_____   7. Have recently been subject to mental stress, such as parental divorce
_____   8. Begin to cry for no apparent reason
_____   9. Suddenly begin to sit, stand, or walk strangely
_____   10. Have runny, red, or swollen eyes or nose
_____   11. Begin to breathe as if "all stuffed up" or are short of breath
_____   12. Wheeze, cough, or rattle when they breathe
_____   13. Sweat excessively
_____   14. Have very frequent bowel movements
_____   15. Are sluggish or do not respond to external stimuli
_____   16. Exhibit unexplained behavior problems, especially aggressiveness or self-injury

If you suspect a learner is in pain, do the following:

1. Try to remove any external source of pain (tight shoes, etc.).
2. Refer learner to a qualified physician or dentist where applicable.
3. Remember that pain is a distraction to the learner, and any frustration you may feel because you cannot "get through" may be magnified in the learner's own frustration.
4. Remember that certain seasons of the year mean trouble for learners with allergies. Check with a local allergist to find out which times of the year may be "problem seasons."
5. Obtain and follow all directions from physicians, PTs, OTs, and dentists for making physical responses to a learner.
6. Record all medications given to a learner, that is, medication, time, date, and amount.
7. If a learner has had recent physical or mental trauma, be alert for responses that indicate the learner needs medical or psychological assistance.

REFERENCES

Afflek, J., Edgar, E., Levine, P., & Kortering, L. (1990). Postschool status of students classified as mildly mentally retarded, learning disabled, or nonhandicapped: Does it get better with time? *Education and Training of the Mentally Retarded, 25,* 315–324.

Alberto, P., & Troutman, A. (1986). *Applied behavior analysis for teachers.* Columbus, OH: Merrill.

Asher, A. S., & Hymel, S. (1981). Children's social competence in peer relations: Sociometric and behavioral assessment. In J. D. Wine & M. D. Syme (Eds.), *Social competence.* New York: Guilford.

Baker, M., & Salon, R. (1986). Setting free the captives: The power of community integration in liberating institutionalized adults from the bonds of their past. *Journal of the Association for Persons with Severe Handicaps, 11,* 176–181.

Bandura, A. (1986). *Social foundations and thought and action: A social cognitive theory.* Englewood Cliffs, NJ: Prentice Hall.

Barker, R. (1968). *Ecological psychology: Concepts and methods for studying the environment of human behavior.* Stanford, CA: Stanford University Press.

Beebe, P., & Karan, O. (1986). A methodology for a community-based vocational program for adults. In R. Horner, L. Meyer, & H. Fredericks (Eds.), *Education of learners with severe handicaps: Exemplary service strategies.* Baltimore: Brookes.

Bellack, A. (1979). Behavioral assessment of social skills. In A. S. Bellack & M. Hersen (Eds.), *Research and practice in social skills training.* New York: Plenum.

Bellamy, G., Horner, R., & Inman, D. (1979). *Project skills.* Washington, D.C.: National Children's Center.

Bercovici, S. (1981). Qualitative methods and cultural perspectives in the study of deinstitutionalization. In R. Bruninks, C. Meyers, B. Sigford, & C. Lakin (Eds.), *Deinstitutionalization and community adjustment of mentally retarded people* (American Association on Mental Deficiency Monograph No. 4). Washington, D.C.: American Association on Mental Deficiency.

Berkman, K., & Meyer, L. (1988). Alternative strategies and multiple outcomes in the remediation of severe self-injury: Going "all-out" nonaversively. *Journal of the Association for Persons with Severe Handicaps, 13,* 76–86.

Bigge, J. (1988). *Curriculum-based instruction for special education students.* Mountain View, CA: Mayfield.

Bloom, B. (Ed.). (1956). *Taxonomy of educational objectives.* New York: Longman.

Borich, G. (1988). *Active teaching methods.* Columbus, OH: Merrill.

Brickey, M., Campbell, K., & Browning, L. (1985). A five-year follow-up of sheltered workshop employees placed in competitive jobs. *Mental Retardation, 23,* 67–73.

Brolin, D. (1993). *Life centered career education: A competency-based approach* (4th ed.). Reston, VA: Council for Exceptional Children.

Brolin, D. (1995). *Career education: A functional life skills approach.* Englewood Cliffs, NJ: Merrill.

Browder, D., & Snell, M. (1983). Daily living skills. In M. Snell (Ed.), *Systematic instruction of the moderately and severely handicapped* (2nd ed.). Columbus, OH: Merrill.

Brown, L., Branston, M., Hamre-Nietupski, S., Johnson, F., Wilcox, B., & Gruenewald, L. (1979). A rationale for comprehensive longitudinal interactions between severely handicapped students and other handicapped citizens. *AAESPH Review, 4,* 3–14.

Brown, L., Branston, M., Hamre-Nietupski, S., Pumpian, I., Certo, N., & Gruenewald, L. (1979). A strategy for developing a chronological age appropriate and functional curriculum content for severely handicapped adolescents and adults. *Journal of Special Education, 13,* 81–90.

Brown, L., Falvey, M., Vincent, L., Kay, N., Johnson, F., Ferrara-Parrish, P., & Gruenewald, L. (1980). Strategies for generating comprehensive longitudinal and chronological age appropriate plans for adolescent and young adult severely handicapped students. In L. Brown, M. Falvey, D. Baumgart, I. Pumpian, J. Schroeder, & L. Gruenewald (Eds.), *Strategies for teaching chronological age appropriate functional skills to adolescent and young adult severely handicapped students* (Vol. IX, Part I). Madison, WI: Madison Public Schools.

Brown, L., Ford, A., Nisbet, J., Sweet, M., Donellan, A., & Gruenewald, L. (1983). Opportunities available when severely handicapped students attend chronological age appropriate regular schools. *Journal of the Association for Persons with Severe Handicaps, 8,* 16–23.

Brown, L., Nisbet, J., Ford, A., Sweet, M., Shiraga, B., York, J., & Loomis, R. (1983). The critical need for non-school instruction in educational programs for severely handicapped students. *Journal of the Association for Persons with Severe Handicaps, 8,* 71–77.

Brown, L., & York, R. (1974). Developing programs for severely handicapped students: Teacher training and classroom instruction. In L. Brown, W. Williams, & and T. Crowner (Eds.), *A collection of papers and programs related to public school services for severely handicapped students.* Madison, WI: Madison Public Schools.

Burden, P., & Byrd, D. (1994). *Methods for effective teaching.* Boston: Allyn & Bacon.

Bursick, W., & Epstein, M. (1986). A survey of training programs for teachers of mildly handicapped adolescents. *Teacher Education and Special Education, 9* (1), 3–8.

Cairn, R., & Kielsmeir, J. (1995). *Growing hope: A source book on integrating youth service into the school curriculum.* St. Paul, MN: National Youth Leadership Council.

Cartledge, G., & Milburn, J. F. (1986). *Teaching social skills to children: Innovative approaches.* Elmsford, NY: Pergamon.

Cartwright, C., & Cartwright, G. (1984). *Developing observation skills.* New York: McGraw-Hill.

CEC. (1993). CEC policy on inclusive schools and community settings. *Teaching Exceptional Children Supplement, 25* (4).

CEC News. (1991). *Exceptional Children, 57* (3), 282.

Cegelka, P., & Prehm, H. (1982). *Mental retardation: From categories to people.* Columbus, OH: Merrill.

Certo, N. (1983). Characteristics of educational services. In M. Snell (Ed.), *Systematic instruction of the moderately and severely handicapped.* Columbus, OH: Merrill.

Chalfant, J., & Silikovitz, R. (1972). *Systematic instruction for retarded children: The Illinois program* (Parts I–IV). Springfield, IL: The Office of the Superintendent of Public Instruction, State of Illinois.

Charters, W. (1923). *Curriculum construction.* New York: McMillan.

Choate, J., Enright, B., Miller, L., Poteet, J., & Rakes, T. (1995). *Curriculum-based assessment and programming* (3rd. ed.). Boston: Allyn & Bacon.

Clark, G. (1984). Issues in teacher education for secondary education. *Teacher Education and Special Education, 7* (3), 170–177.

Cone, J., & Hawkins, R. (1977). *Behavioral assessment: New directions in clinical psychology.* New York: Bruner/Mazel.

Contrucci, V. (1976). *Basic life functions instructional program model: Curriculum guide for children with exceptional educational needs.* Madison, WI: Wisconsin Bureau for Handicapped Children.

Cullen, B., & Pratt, T. (1992). Measuring and reporting student progress. In S. Stainback & W. Stainback (Eds.), *Curriculum considerations in inclusive classrooms: Facilitating learning for all students.* Baltimore: Brookes.

Day, M., & Horner, R. (1989). Building response classes: A comparison of two procedures for teaching generalized pouring to learners with severe disabilities. *Journal of Applied Behavior Analysis, 22,* 223–229.

Dever, R. (1978). *TALK (teaching the American language to kids).* Columbus, OH: Merrill.

Dever, R. (1988). *Community living skills: A taxonomy* (Monograph of the American Association on Mental Retardation). Washington, D.C.: American Association on Mental Retardation.

Dever, R. (1989). A taxonomy of community living skills. *Exceptional Children, 55,* 395–404.

Dever, R. (1990). Defining mental retardation from an instructional perspective. *Mental Retardation, 28,* 147–153.

Dever, R., & Knapczyk, D. (1980). Screening for physical problems in classrooms for severely handicapped students. *Journal of the Association for Persons with Severe Handicaps, 5,* 194–204.

Dewey, J. (1902). *The child and the curriculum.* Chicago: University of Chicago Press.

Disability Research Systems, Inc. (1991). *Addressing unique needs of individuals with disabilities: SMI outcome indicators.* East Lansing, MI: Disability Research Systems.

Disability Research Systems, Inc. (1992a). *Addressing unique needs of individuals with disabilities: EMI outcome indicators.* Lansing, MI: Disability Research Systems.

Disability Research Systems, Inc. (1992b). *Addressing unique needs of individuals with disabilities: LD outcome indicators.* East Lansing, MI: Disability Research Systems.

Dowrick, P. W. (1986). *Social survival for children.* New York: Brunner/Mazel.

Easterday, J., & Sitlington, P. (1985). *Conducting an analysis of community work environments relative to the employment of the severely handicapped* (COMPETE Working Paper #85-4). Bloomington, IN: Center for Innovation in Teaching the Handicapped.

Edgar, E. (1987). Secondary programs in special education: Are many of them justifiable? *Exceptional Children, 53* (6), 555–561.

Edgerton, R. (1967). *The cloak of competence: Stigma in the lives of the mentally retarded.* Berkeley, CA: University of California Press.

Edgerton, R. (1975). Issues relating to the quality of life among mentally retarded persons. In M. Begab & S. Richardson (Eds.), *The mentally retarded and society: A social science perspective.* Baltimore: University Park Press.

Eisler, R., & Frederiksen, L. (1980). *Perfecting social skills.* New York: Plenum.

Falvey, M. (1986). *Community based instruction: Instructional strategies for students with severe handicaps.* Baltimore: Brookes.

Ford, A., Brown, L., Pumpian, I., Baumgart, D., Nisbet, J., Schroeder, J., & Loomis, R. (1984). Strategies for developing individualized recreation and leisure programs for severely handicapped students. In N. Certo, N. Haring, & R. York (Eds.), *Public school integration of severely handicapped students.* Baltimore: Brookes.

Frank, A., Sitlington, P., Cooper, L., & Cool, V. (1990). Adult adjustment of recent graduates of Iowa mental disabilities program. *Education and Training of the Mentally Retarded, 25* (1), 62–75.

Franklin, B. (1994). *From backwardness to at-risk: Childhood learning difficulties and contradictions of school reform.* Albany, NY: SUNY Press.

Frey, W., Burke, D., & Lynch, L. (1990). *Outcome indicators for special education: A model for studying the expected outcomes of special education.* East Lansing, MI: Disability Research Systems.

Fuchs, D., & Fuchs, L. (1994). Inclusive schools movement and radicalization of special education. *Exceptional Children, 60* (4), 294–309.

Gajar, A., Goodman, L., & McAfee, J. (1993). *Secondary schools and beyond: Transition of individuals with disabilities.* New York: Merrill.

Gallahue, D., Werner, P., & Luedke, G. (1975). *A conceptual approach to moving and learning.* New York: John Wiley.

Gaylord-Ross, R., Forte, J., Storey, K., Gaylord-Ross, C., Siegel, S., Jameson, D., & Pomies, J. (1985). *Community vocational training for handicapped youth.* San Francisco: San Francisco State University.

Gaylord-Ross, R., Haring, T., Breen, C., Lee, M., Pitts-Conway, V., & Roger, B. (1984). *The social development of handicapped students.* San Francisco: San Francisco State University.

Gaylord-Ross, R. J., & Holvoet, J. F. (1985). *Strategies for educating students with severe handicaps.* Boston: Little, Brown.

Geiger, W. (1974). *A catalog of instructional objectives for trainable mentally retarded students.* Jacksonville, FL: Duval County School Board.

Gold, M. (1980a). *Did I say that?* Champaign, IL: Research Press.

Gold, M. (1980b). *Try another way training manual.* Champaign, IL: Research Press.

Goldstein, A. (1988). Prepare: A prosocial curriculum for aggressive youth. In R. Rutherford, C. Nelson, & S. Forness (Eds.), *Bases of severe behavior disorders in children and youth.* Boston: College-Hill.

Greenwood, C., & Carta, J. (1987). An ecobehavioral interaction analysis within special education. *Focus on Exceptional Children, 19,* 1–11.

Gresham, F., & Elliot, S. (1984). Assessment and classification of children's social skills: A review of methods and issues. *School Psychology Review, 13,* 292–301.

Grossman, H. (1973). *Manual on terminology and classification in mental retardation.* Washington, D.C.: American Association on Mental Deficiency.

Grossman, H. (1983). *Classification in mental retardation.* Washington, D.C.: American Association on Mental Deficiency.

Guess, D., Horner, R., Utley, B., Holvoet, J., Maxon, D., Tucker, D., & Warren, S. (1978). A functional curriculum sequencing model for teaching the severely handicapped. *AAESPH Review, 3,* 202–215.

Halpern, A. (1985). Transition: A look at the foundations. *Exceptional Children, 51,* 479–486.

Halpern, A. (1992). Transition: New wine in old bottles. *Exceptional Children, 59,* 202–211.

Halpern, A., & Benz, M. (1987). A statewide examination of secondary special education for students with mild disabilities: Implications for the high school curriculum. *Exceptional Children, 54* (2), 122–129.

Hamill, L., & Dunlevy, A. (1993a). *GAIN (group activities for individual needs): Book 1. Work boxes.* Oxford, OH: J. Weston Walsh.

Hamill, L., & Dunlevy, A. (1993b). *GAIN (group activities for individual needs): Book 2. A restaurant.* Oxford, OH: J. Weston Walsh.

Hamilton, S. (1980). Experiential learning programs for youth. *American Journal of Education,* 179–215.

Harris, W., & Schutz, P. (1986). *The special education resource room.* Prospect Heights, IL: Waveland.

Hasazi, S., Gordon, L., & Roe, C. (1985). Factors associated with the employment status of handicapped youth exiting from high school from 1979 to 1983. *Exceptional Children, 51* (6), 455–469.

Hasazi, S., Gordon, L., Roe, C., Hull, M., Finck, K., & Salembier, G. (1985). A statewide follow-up in post high school employment and residential status of students labelled "mentally retarded." *Education and Training of the Mentally Retarded, 20* (4), 222–234.

Heber, R. (1959). *A manual on terminology and classification in mental retardation.* Washington, D.C.: American Association on Mental Deficiency.

Heber, R. (1962). *A manual on terminology and classification in mental retardation.* Washington, D.C.: American Association on Mental Deficiency.

Henderson, S., & MacDonald, M. (1973). *Step-by-step dressing.* Champaign, IL: Suburban Publications.

Hockett, C. (1958). *A course in modern linguistics.* New York: MacMillan.

Howell, K., Fox, S., & Morehead, M. (1993). *Curriculum-based evaluation: Teaching and decision making.* Pacific Grove, CA.: Brooks/Cole.

Howell, K., & Morehead, M. (1987). *Curriculum-based evaluation for special and remedial education.* Columbus: Merrill.

Hughes, C., & Rusch, F. (1989). Teaching supported employees with severe mental retardation to solve problems. *Journal of Applied Behavior Analysis, 22,* 365–372.

Jacobs, J. (1978). Gleaning: Sheltered employment for retarded adults in rural areas. *Mental Retardation, 16,* 118–122.

Johnson, D., & Johnson, R. (1990). Cooperative learning and achievement. In S. Sharan (Ed.), *Cooperative learning: Theory and practice.* New York: Praeger.

Kaufman, J. (1993). How we might achieve the radical reform of special education. *Exceptional Children, 60,* 6–16.

Keogh, B. (1988). Improving services for problem learners: Rethinking and restructuring. *Journal of Learning Disabilities, 21,* 19–28.

Kerr, M., & Nelson, C. (1989). *Strategies for managing behavior problems in the classroom* (2nd ed.). Columbus, OH: Merrill.

Klein, N., Pasch, M., & Frew, T. (1979). *Curriculum analysis and design for retarded learners.* Columbus, OH: Merrill.

Knapczyk, D. (1975). Task analytic assessment of severe learning problems. *Education and Training of the Mentally Retarded, 10,* 74–77.

Knapczyk, D. (1988). Constructing an agency curriculum. In R. Dever (Ed.), *Community living skills: A taxonomy* (Monograph of the American Association on Mental Retardation). Washington, D.C.: American Association on Mental Retardation.

Knapczyk, D. (1989). Peer-mediated training and cooperative play between special and regular class students in integrated play settings. *Education and Training of the Mentally Retarded, 24,* 255–264.

Knapczyk, D. (1992). Effects of developing alternative responses on the aggressive behavior of adolescents. *Behavioral Disorders, 17,* 247–263.

Knapczyk, D., & Rodes, P. (1996). *Teaching social competence: A practical approach for improving social skills in students at-risk.* Pacific Grove, CA: Brooks/Cole.

Kokaska, C., & Brolin, D. (1985). *Career education for handicapped individuals.* Columbus, OH: Merrill.

Kruger, L. (1990). Classroom-based approaches to promoting school success. In L. Kruger (Ed.), *Promoting success with at-risk students: Emerging perspectives and practical approaches.* New York: Haworth.

Lakin, K. C., Bruininks, R., & Sigford, B. (1981). Early perspectives on community adjustment of mentally retarded people. In R. Bruininks, C. Meyers, B. Sigford, & K. C. Lakin (Eds.), *Deinstitutionalization and community adjustment of mentally retarded people* (American Association on Mental Deficiency Monograph No. 4). Washington, D.C.: American Association on Mental Deficiency.

Langone, J. (1990). *Teaching students with mild and moderate learning problems.* Boston: Allyn & Bacon.

Lehr, J., & Harris, H. (1988). *At-risk, low-achieving students in the classroom.* Washington: National Education Association.

Luckasson, R. (1992). *Mental retardation: definition, classification, and systems of supports* (9th ed.). Washington, D.C.: American Association on Mental Retardation.

MacMillan, D. L., Siperstein, G. N., & Gresham, F. M. (1996). A challenge to the validity of mild mental retardation as a diagnostic category. *Exceptional Children, 62,* 356–371.

McDonnell, J., Wilcox, B., & Hardman, M. (1991). *Secondary programs for students with developmental disabilities.* Boston: Allyn & Bacon.

McFall, R. (1982). A review and reformulation of the concept of social skills. *Behavioral Assessment, 4,* 1–33.

McGee, J., Menoloscino, F., Hobbs, D., & Menousek, P. (1987). *Gentle teaching.* New York: Human Sciences Press.

McLaughlin, M. (1993). Including special education in the school community. *NICHCY News Digest, 2* (2). Washington, D.C.: National Information Center for Children and Youth with Disabilities.

Menoloscino, F., & McGee, J. (1981). The new institutions: Last ditch arguments. *Mental Retardation, 19,* 215–220.

Merrell, K. (1994). *Assessment of behavioral, social, and emotional problems: Direct and objective methods for use with children and adolescents.* New York: Longman.

Miller, N., & Harrington, H. (1990). A situational identify perspective on cultural diversity and teamwork in the classroom. In S. Sharan (Ed.), *Cooperative learning: Theory and practice.* New York: Praeger.

Missouri LINC (1989–90). *Designing a functional curriculum for students with disabilities.* Columbia, MO: University of Missouri.

Moon, S., Goodall, P., Barcus, M., & Brooke, V. (1985). *The supported work model of competitive employment for citizens with severe handicaps.* Richmond, VA: Virginia Commonwealth University.

Neel, R., & Billingsley, F. (1989). *Impact.* Baltimore: Brookes.

Nirje, B. (1969). The normalization principle and its human management implications. In R. Kugel & W. Wolfensberger (Eds.), *Changing patterns in residential services for the mentally retarded.* Washington, D.C.: President's Committee on Mental Retardation.

Orelove, F., & Sobsey, D. (1987). *Educating children with multiple disabilities: A transdisciplinary approach.* Baltimore: Brookes.

Park, H., & Gaylord-Ross, R. (1989). A problem-solving approach to social skills training in employment settings with mentally retarded youth. *Journal of Applied Behavior Analysis, 22,* 373–380.

Patton, J., Cronin, M., Polloway, E., Hutchinson, D., & Robinson, G. (1989). Curricular considerations: A life skills orientation. In G. Robinson, J. Patton, E. Polloway, & L. Sargent (Eds.), *Best practices in mild mental retardation.* Reston, VA: Council for Exceptional Children, Division on Mental Retardation.

Peterson, D., & Miller, J. (1990). Providing opportunities for student success through cooperative training and peer tutoring. In L. J. Kruger (Ed.), *Promoting success with at-risk students.* New York: Haworth.

Pike, K. (1967). *Language in relation to a unified theory of the structure of human behavior.* The Hague: Mouton.

Polloway, E., & Epstein, M. (1985). Current research issues in mild mental retardation: A survey of the field. *Education & Training of the Mentally Retarded, 20,* 171–174.

Polloway, E., Patton, J., Smith, J., & Roderique, T. (1991). Issues in program design for students with mild retardation: Emphasis on curriculum development. *Education & Training of the Mentally Retarded, 26,* 142–150.

Popham, W., & Baker, E. (1970). *Systematic instruction.* Englewood Cliffs, NJ: Prentice-Hall.

Powell, T., Pancsofar, E., Steere, D., Butterworth, J., Itzkowitz, J., & Rainforth, B. (1991). *Supported employment: Providing integrated opportunities for persons with disabilities.* New York: Longman.

Powers, W. (1973). *Behavior: The control of perceptions.* Chicago: Aldine.

Provus, M. (1971). *Discrepancy evaluation.* Berkeley, CA: McCutchan.

Pugach, M. (1992). Uncharted territory: Research on the socialization of special education teachers. *Exceptional Children, 15,* 133–147.

Renshaw, P., & Asher, S. (1982). Social competence and peer status. In K. H. Rubin and H. S. Ross (Eds.), *Peer relationships and social skills in childhood.* New York: Springer-Verlag.

Retish, P., Hitchings, W., Horvath, M., & Schmalle, B. (1991). *Students with mild disabilities in the public school.* New York: Longman.

Reynolds, M., Wang, M., & Walberg, H. (1987). The necessary restructuring of special and regular education. *Exceptional Children, 53,* 391–398.

Rhodes, L., & Valenta, L. (1985). *Journal of the Association for Persons with Severe Handicaps, 10,* 12–20.

Rotatori, A., Banbury, M., & Fox, R. (1987). *Issues in special education.* Mountain View, CA: Mayfield.

Rusch, F. (1983). Competitive vocational training. In M. Snell (Ed.), *Systematic instruction of the moderately and severely handicapped* (2nd ed.). Columbus: Merrill.

Rusch, F., & Hughes, C. (1989). Overview of supported employment. *Journal of Applied Behavior Analysis, 22,* 351–364.

Rusch, F., & Mithaug, D. (1980). *Vocational training for mentally retarded adults: A behavior analytic approach.* Champaign, IL: Research Press.

Rusch, F., & Mithaug, D. (1986). Competitive employment education: A systems-analytic approach to transitional programming of the student with severe handicaps. In C. Lakin & R. Bruninks (Eds.), *Strategies for achieving community integration of developmentally disabled adults.* Baltimore: Brookes.

Rusch, F., Sowers, J., Connis, R., & Thompson, L. (1977). *Developing vocational training programs for mentally retarded young adults* (The Food Service Vocational Training Program, Rep. No. 5). Seattle: The University of Washington Child Development and Training Center.

Sailor, W., & Guess, D. (1983). *Severely handicapped students: An instructional design.* Boston: Houghton Mifflin.

Salvia, J., & Hughes, C. (1990). *Curriculum-based assessment.* New York: Macmillan.

Salvia, J., & Ysseldyke, J. (1995). *Assessment* (6th ed.). Boston: Houghton Mifflin.

Scheerenberger, R. (1981). Deinstitutionalization: Trends and difficulties. In R. Bruninks, C. Meyers, B. Sigford, & K. Lakin (Eds.), *Deinstitutionalization and community adjustment of mentally retarded people* (American Association on Mental Deficiency Monograph No. 4). Washington, D.C.: American Association on Mental Deficiency.

Sharan, S. (1980). Cooperative learning in small groups: Recent methods and effects on achievement, attitudes and ethnic relations. *Review of Educational Research, 50* (2), 241–271.

Sinclair, M., Christianson, S., Thurlow, M., & Evelo, D. (1994). *Are we pushing students in special education to drop out of school?* (Policy Research Brief No. 6, Vol 1). University of Minnesota: Center on Residential Services and Community Integration.

Skrtic, T. (1986). The crisis in special education knowledge: A perspective on perspective. *Focus on Exceptional Children, 18,* 11–16.

Slavin, R., Karweit, N., & Madden, N. (1989). *Effective programs for students at risk.* Boston: Allyn & Bacon.

Sloan, W., & Birch, J. (1955). A rationale for degrees of retardation. *American Journal of Mental Deficiency, 60,* 258–264.

Smith, B., Stanley, W., & Shores, B. (1957). *Fundamentals of curriculum development.* Yonkers, NY: World Books.

Smith, D. (1989). *Teaching students with learning and behavior problems.* Englewood Cliffs, NJ: Prentice Hall.

Snell, M. (1983). Developing the IEP: Selecting and assessing skills. In M. Snell (Ed.), *Systematic instruction of the moderately and severely handicapped* (2nd ed.). Columbus, OH: Merrill.

Snell, M. (1987). *Systematic instruction of persons with severe handicaps* (3rd ed.). Columbus, OH: Merrill.

Snell, M., & Browder, D. (1986). Community-referenced instruction: Research issues. *Journal of the Association for Persons with Severe Handicaps, 11,* 1–11.

Solity, J., & Bull, S. (1987). *Special needs: Bridging the curriculum gap.* Philadelphia: Open University Press.

Stevens, T., Blackhurst, A., & Magliocca, L. (1988). *Teaching mainstreamed students.* New York: Pergamon.

Taba, H. (1962). *Curriculum development: Theory and practice.* New York: Harcourt, Brace, & Jovanovich.

Tanner, D., & Tanner, L. (1995). *Curriculum development: Theory into practice* (3rd ed.). New York: Macmillan.

Tarver, S. (1992). Direct instruction. In W. Stainback & S. Stainback (Eds.), *Controversial issues confronting special education: Divergent perspectives.* Boston: Allyn & Bacon.

Tyler, R. (1949). *Principles of instruction.* Chicago: University of Chicago Press.

Villa, R., Thousand, J., Stainback, W., & Stainback, S. (1992). *Restructuring for caring and effective education.* Baltimore: Brookes.

Vincent, L., Salisbury, C., Walter, G., Brown, P., Gruenewald, L., Powers, M. (1980). Program evaluation and curriculum development in early childhood: Criteria of the next environment. In W. Sailor, B. Wilcox, & L. Brown (Eds.), *Methods of instruction for severely handicapped students.* Baltimore: Brookes.

Voeltz, L., & Evans, I. (1983). Educational validity: Procedures to evaluate outcomes in programs for severely handicapped students. *Journal for the Association for the Severely Handicapped, 8,* 3–15.

Wambold, C., & Salisbury, C. (1978). The development and implementation of self-care programs with severely and profoundly retarded children. *AAESPH Review, 3* (3), 178–184.

Wasik, B. (1990). Issues in identification and assessment. In L. Kruger (Ed.), *Promoting success with at-risk students: Emerging perspectives and practical approaches*. New York: Haworth.

Wehman, P., & Hill, M. (1980). *Vocational training and placement of severely disabled persons* (Vol. 2). Richmond, VA: Virginia Commonwealth University.

Wehman, P., Hill, M., Hill, J., Brooke, J., Pendleton, P., & Britt, C. (1986). Competitive employment for persons with mental retardation: A follow-up six years later. *Mental Retardation, 23*, 274–281.

Wehman, P., Hill, J., Wood, W., & Parent, W. (1987). A report on competitive employment histories of persons labelled severely mentally retarded. *Journal of the Association for Persons with Severe Handicaps, 12*, 11–17.

Wehman, P., & Kregel, J. (1985). A supported work approach to competitive employment of individuals with moderate and severe handicaps. *Journal of the Association for Persons with Severe Handicaps, 10*, 3–11.

Wehman, P., Kregel, J., Barcus, J., & Schalock, R. (1986). Vocational transition for students with developmental disabilities. In W. Kiernan & J. Stark (Eds.), *Pathways to employment for adults with developmental disabilities*. Baltimore: Brookes.

Wehman, P., & McGlaughlin, P. (1981). *Program development in special education*. New York: McGraw-Hill.

Wehman, P., Moon, S., Everson, J., Wood, W., & Barcus, J. (1988). *Transition from school to work: New challenges for youth with severe disabilities*. Baltimore: Brookes.

White, O. (1980). Adaptive performance objectives: Form vs. function. In W. Sailor, B. Wilcox, & L. Brown (Eds.), *Methods of instruction for severely handicapped students*. Baltimore, MD: Brookes.

Why disabled students left school. (1990, August 2). *Education Daily*, p. 4.

Wilcox, B., & Bellamy, T. (1987). *The activities catalog: An alternative curriculum for youth and adults with severe disabilities*. Baltimore: Brookes.

Will, M. (1984). *OSERS programming for the transition of youth with disabilities: Bridges from school to working life*. Washington, D.C.: Office of Special Education and Rehabilitative Services.

Will, M. (1986). Educating children with learning problems: A shared responsibility. *Exceptional Children, 5*, 411–416.

Wolery, M., Bailey, D. B., & Sugai, G. M. (1988). *Effective teaching: Principles of behavior analysis with exceptional students*. Boston: Allyn & Bacon.

Wolf, M. M. (1978). Social validity: The case for subjective measurement or how applied behavior analysis is finding a heart. *Journal of Applied Behavior Analysis, 11*, 204–214.

Wolfensberger, W. (1972) *Normalization: The principle of normalization in human services*. Toronto, Canada: Leonard Crainford.

Wolfensberger, W. (1983). Social role valorization: A proposed new term for normalization. *Mental Retardation, 21*, 234–239.

NAME INDEX

Afflek, J., 1, 10, 16, 17, 42
Alberto, P., 282
Albin, R. W., 282
Asher, A. S., 168
Asher, S., 204

Bailey, D. B., 202, 203, 205, 282
Baker, E., 20, 63
Baker, M., 17, 19, 145
Banbury, M., 20
Bandura, A., 253, 258, 282
Barcus, J., 3, 11, 77
Barcus, M., 125
Barker, R., 37, 127
Baumgart, D., 57, 58, 92, 124
Beebe, P., 80
Bellack, A., 168, 179
Bellamy, G., 301
Bellamy, T., 2, 11, 12, 47, 78, 124
Benz, M., 2, 11
Bercovici, S., 19, 36
Berkman, K., 19, 27, 145
Billingsley, F., 15, 47, 48, 59
Birch, J., 28, 29
Blackhurst, A., 20
Bloom, B., 12, 63
Borich, G., 167, 184
Branston, M., 2, 36, 48, 125
Breen, C., 92
Brickey, M., 17, 27
Britt, C., 27, 38
Brolin, D., 3, 8, 20, 59, 92, 94, 97
Brooke, J., 27, 38

Brooke, V., 125
Browder, D., 15, 17, 27, 56
Brown, L., 2, 16, 17, 18, 19, 36, 48, 57, 58, 92, 124, 125
Brown, P., 48
Browning, L., 17, 27
Bull, S., 202
Burden, P., 170
Bursick, W., 2, 10
Butterworth, J., 11, 17, 37, 38
Byrd, D., 170

Cairn, R., 205, 280
Campbell, K., 17, 27
Carta, J., 167, 208
Cartledge, G., 206
Cartwright, C., 154, 173, 179, 183
Cartwright, G., 154, 173, 179, 183
CEC, 16
CEC News, 95
Certo, N., 2, 15, 17, 36, 48
Chalfant, J., 92
Charters, W., 14, 20, 32, 61
Choate, 157
Christianson, S., 1, 2, 10
Clark, G., 2, 10, 11
Colvin, G., 282
Cone, J., 153
Connis, R., 11
Contrucci, V., 92
Cool, V., 1, 10, 16, 42
Cooper, J. O., 282
Cooper, L., 1, 10, 16, 42

Cronin, M., 1, 10, 42, 92

Day, M., 18
Dever, R., 3, 6, 26, 33, 34, 41, 49, 87, 249, 263, 361
Dewey, J., 14, 20, 22, 31, 65
Disability Research Systems, Inc., 3, 43, 94, 99, 100, 101, 102, 103
Donellan, A., 16, 17, 18, 19, 36
Donnellan, A. M., 282
Dowrick, P. W., 180, 254
Dunlevy, A., 11, 19, 94, 95, 255, 280

Easterday, J., 125
Edgar, E., 1, 2, 10, 11, 16, 17, 42
Edgerton, R., 38
Education Daily, 1, 10
Edwards, C. H., 282
Eisler, R., 167
Elliot, S., 153, 206
Enright, B., 157
Epstein, M., 2, 10
Evans, I., 56
Evelo, D., 1, 2, 10
Everson, J., 11

Falvey, M., 2, 11, 15, 16, 17, 18, 58, 78, 124
Fassbender, L., 282
Ferrara-Parrish, P., 17
Finck, K., 1, 16

Ford, A., 16, 17, 18, 19, 36, 57, 58, 92, 124
Fox, R., 20
Fox, S., 144, 157
Frank, A., 1, 10, 16, 42
Franklin, B., 14
Frederiksen, L., 167
Frew, T., 48
Frey, W., 43, 59, 60, 63
Fuchs, D., 1
Fuchs, L., 1

Gajar, A., 2
Gallahue, D., 56
Gaylord-Ross, R., 18, 47, 92
Geiger, W., 92
Gold, M., 8, 11, 24, 27, 134, 204, 218, 233, 240, 259, 271, 273, 277, 301
Goldstein, A., 258
Goodall, P., 125
Goodman, L., 2
Gordon, L., 1, 10, 16
Greenwood, C., 167, 208
Gresham, F., 153, 206
Gresham, F. M., 28, 30, 42, 63
Grossman, H., 26
Gruenewald, L., 2, 17, 36, 48, 125
Grunewald, L., 2, 16, 17, 18, 19, 36, 48
Guess, D., 2, 15, 17, 47, 48

Halpern, A., 2, 11, 16, 17, 41
Hamill, L., 11, 19, 94, 95, 255, 280
Hamilton, S., 19, 205
Hamre-Nietupski, S., 2, 36, 48, 125
Hardman, M., 36
Haring, T., 92
Harrington, H., 205
Harris, H., 205
Harris, W., 15, 20, 209, 213
Hasazi, S., 1, 10, 16
Hawkins, R., 153
Heber, R., 26
Heckman, D., 137, 152
Henderson, S., 92
Heron, T. E., 282
Heward, W. K., 282
Hill, J., 17, 27, 37, 38
Hill, M., 11, 27, 38, 265
Hobbs, D., 8, 28, 38
Hockett, C., 248
Holvoet, J. F., 2, 47, 48
Horner, R., 2, 18, 48, 282, 301
Howell, K., 144, 154, 157, 186
Hubbard, B. J., 117
Hughes, C., 18, 37, 154, 167, 208, 213

Hull, M., 1, 16
Hutchinson, D., 1, 10, 42, 92
Hymel, S., 168

Inman, D., 301
Itzkowitz, J., 11, 17, 37, 38

Jacobs, J., 17, 27
Johnson, D., 204
Johnson, F., 2, 17, 36, 125
Johnson, R., 204

Karan, O., 80
Karweit, N., 204
Kaufman, J., 1
Kay, N., 17
Kazdin, A. E., 282
Keogh, B., 36
Kerr, M., 173, 203
Kielsmeir, J., 205, 280
Klein, N., 48
Knapczyk, D., 3, 18, 20, 31, 37, 38, 39, 40, 56, 57, 58, 59, 60, 61, 66, 78, 82, 123, 153, 159, 160, 166, 170, 173, 179, 180, 181, 191, 202, 218, 223, 229, 254, 258, 286, 288, 361
Kokaska, C., 92
Kortering, L., 1, 10, 16, 17, 42
Kregel, J., 3, 17, 77
Kruger, L., 173

Langone, J., 48
LaVinga, G., 282
Lee, M., 92
Lehr, J., 205
Levine, P., 1, 10, 16, 17, 42
Loomis, R., 18, 57, 58, 92, 124
Luckasson, R., 8, 26
Luedke, G., 56
Lynch, L., 43, 59, 63

MacDonald, M., 92
MacMillan, D. L., 28, 30, 42, 63
Madden, N., 204
Magliocca, L., 20
Maxon, D., 2, 48
McAfee, J., 2
McDonnell, J., 36
McFall, R., 39, 154
McGee, J., 8, 28, 38
McGlaughlin, P., 48
McLaughlin, M., 126
Melloy, K., 282
Menoloscino, F., 8, 28, 38

Menousek, P., 8, 28, 38
Merrell, K., 180
Meyer, L., 19, 27, 145
Milburn, J. F., 206
Miller, J., 205
Miller, L., 157
Miller, N., 205
Missouri LINC, 19, 95, 280
Mithaug, D., 17
Moon, S., 11, 125
Morehead, M., 144, 154, 157, 186

Neel, R., 15, 47, 48, 59
Negri-Shoultz, N., 282
Nelson, C., 173, 203
Nirje, B., 8
Nisbet, J., 16, 17, 18, 19, 36, 57, 58, 92, 124

O'Neill, R. E., 282
Orelove, F., 2

Pancsofar, E., 11, 17, 37, 38
Parent, W., 17, 27, 37
Park, H., 18
Pasch, M., 48
Patton, J., 1, 10, 11, 42, 92
Pendleton, P., 27, 38
Peterson, D., 205
Pike, K., 230
Pitts-Conway, V., 92
Polloway, E., 1, 10, 11, 42, 92
Popham, W., 20, 63
Poteet, J., 157
Powell, T., 11, 17, 37, 38
Powers, M., 48
Powers, W., 8
Provus, M., 48, 59
Pugach, M., 16
Pumpian, I., 2, 36, 48, 57, 58, 92, 124

Rainforth, B., 11, 17, 37, 38
Rakes, T., 157
Ramsey, E., 282
Renshaw, P., 204
Repp, A. C., 282
Reynolds, M., 36
Rhodes, L., 17, 27
Robinson, G., 1, 10, 42, 92
Roderique, T., 11, 42
Rodes, P., 37, 38, 39, 40, 56, 57, 66, 123, 153, 159, 160, 166, 170, 173, 179, 181, 191, 202, 218, 223, 258, 286, 288

Roe, C., 1, 10, 16
Roger, G., 92
Rotatori, A., 20
Rusch, F., 11, 17, 18, 27, 37

Sailor, W., 2, 15, 17, 47
Salembier, G., 1, 16
Salisbury, C., 48
Salon, R., 17, 19, 145
Salvia, J., 154, 157, 167, 180, 194, 208, 213
Schalock, R., 3, 77
Scheerenberger, R., 12
Schroeder, J., 57, 58, 92, 124
Schutz, P., 15, 20, 209, 213
Sharan, S., 258
Shiraga, B., 18
Shores, B., 20
Silikovitz, R., 92
Sinclair, M., 1, 2, 10
Singh, A. A., 282
Siperstein, G. N., 28, 30, 42, 63
Sitlington, P., 1, 10, 16, 42, 125
Skrtic, T., 36
Slavin, R., 204
Sloan, W., 28, 29
Smith, B., 20
Smith, D., 208
Smith, J., 11, 42

Snell, M., 2, 15, 17, 27, 47, 56, 125
Sobsey, D., 2
Solity, J., 202
Somers, J., 11
Sorey, K., 282
Sprague, J., 282
Stainback, S., 15
Stainback, W., 15
Stanley, W., 20
Steere, D., 11, 17, 37, 38
Stevens, T., 20
Sugai, G. M., 202, 203, 205, 282
Sweet, M., 16, 17, 18, 19, 36

Taba, H., 20
Tanner, D., 14, 20
Tanner, L., 14, 20
Tarver, S., 63
Thompson, L., 11
Thousand, J., 15
Thurlow, M., 1, 2, 10
Troutman, A., 282
Tucker, D., 2, 48
Tyler, R., 20

Utley, B., 2, 48

Valenta, L., 17, 27
Villa, R., 15

Vincent, L., 17, 48
Voeltz, L., 56

Walberg, H., 36
Walker, H. M., 282
Walter, G., 48
Wambold, C., 48
Wang, M., 36
Warren, S., 2, 48
Wasik, B., 202
Wehman, P., 3, 11, 17, 27, 37, 38, 48, 77, 265
Werner, P., 56
White, O., 58, 131
Wilcox, B., 2, 11, 12, 36, 47, 78, 124, 125
Will, M., 1, 16, 41
Wolery, M., 202, 203, 205, 282
Wolf, M. M., 206
Wolfensberger, W., 8, 17, 37
Wood, W., 11, 17, 27, 37

York, J., 18
York, R., 48
Ysseldyke, J., 157, 180, 194

Zabel, L., 137, 152
Zirpoli, T. J., 282

SUBJECT INDEX

work sheet for development of, 122

written behavior patterns, 134

Career, definition of, 94

Choral responses, as feedback on learning, 272–273

Circumstances of performance adjustments to, 127

and behavior patterns, 125–126

and program objectives, 226–227

Community

active living in and label of mentally retarded, 30

educational resources of, 80–81

independent use by mentally retarded, 35–37

Community-based instruction

advantages of, 18

areas of instruction, 41

and skill analysis, 143

Community life, domains, 88, 91

Community Living Skills: A Taxonomy, 87

Comprehensive curriculum, 119

characteristics of instructional units, 119

in general education, 119

nature of, 54

Content

of functional instruction, 17

in general education programs, 13–14

and lack of learner progress, 318–323

and special education programs, 14–15

Correction of learner errors, 274–277

changing form of instruction, 274–275

by learner search, 275–277

reteaching, 274

Cues, 236–239

behavioral cues, 237–238

meaning of, 236

situational cues, 238–239

teacher gestures to focus student attention, 252

teaching with physical guidance, 259–261

Curriculum

comprehensive curriculum, 54, 119

continuity of, 60–61

curriculum-based instruction, 49–50

curriculum objectives, 53–54

definition of, 47, 49

and environmental demands, 58

factors affecting scope of, 76

group focus in, 50–51

versus individualized instruction, 48–49

integration in, 56–57

as local responsibility, 59–60

long-term focus, 51–52

and monitoring of instruction, 59

pathways of objectives, 47–48, 58–59

restricted curriculum, 54–55, 118–119

sequencing in development of, 49

social validity of, 56

variables in changes of, 51

Curriculum development, 56–61

behavior pattern, analysis of skills required in, 134–143

behavior pattern, establishment of, 120–134

curriculum pathway, formulation of, 146, 148–152

example situations, 114–115

impediments to, 15–16

instructional model, 22–23

prerequisite and lead-in skills, 144–146

principles of, 56–61

steps in, 120–152

Curriculum format, 115–117

development of, 115, 117

illustration of, 116–117

Curriculum goals

behavioral goals, 63, 64

and building of instruction, 66–67

content of, 64

and curriculum objectives, 66

to delimit instruction, 108–109

and direction of instruction, 65–66 ·

formulation of, 62, 105–112

functions of, 65–68

information sources on, 94

and instructional consistency, 67–68

intermediate goals, 69, 70–73, 93–95

nature of, 47

nonbehavioral goals, 63, 64

organization of, 111

for preschools/elementary schools, 106–107

purposes of, 61

for secondary schools/adult rehabilitation settings, 107

and skill clusters, 108–111

structure of, 63

terminal goals, 69–70, 86–93

Curriculum objectives

and assessment, 157–158, 165–166, 190–191, 199, 202–207

and curriculum goals, 66

for individualized instructional plan, 209, 212

Curriculum variables, 118–120

scope of curriculum, 118–119

specificity of curriculum, 120

Dangerous skills, teaching of, 226

Demonstration, 252–258

of discrete actions, 255–256

models for, 254–255

phases of, 253

range of uses of, 252–253

Documentation

of assessment results, 182–183, 195–200

of major skill clusters, 129

Domains

community life, 88, 91

homemaking, 88, 91, 336–340

leisure, 89, 91, 344–348

personal maintenance and development, 88, 91, 331–335

for terminal curriculum goals, 87–91

travel, 90, 91

vocational, 89, 91, 341–343

Dressing

clothing selection chart, 117

skill cluster analysis, 234–236

skill clusters for appropriate clothing, 110

Dropouts, mildly retarded as, 10

Duration standards, 176

Educable mental impairment, outcome indicators for, 99–104

Elementary schools

curriculum goals, 106–107

priority skills, 203

Equipment, and teaching behavior patterns, 126

and dependency of learner, 313–316
and extending instruction, 309–310
promotion of carryover of skills, 311–312
in some not all skill areas, 316–317
Learner search, 262–266
for error correction, 275–277
and learner motivation, 264–265
and self-direction, 265–266
situations for use, 262–264
Leisure, domains, 89, 91, 344–348
Life Centered Career Education Curriculum (LCCE), 94–95
basic premise of, 95
curriculum areas in, 96–99
information source for, 94
nature of curriculum, 94–95
organization of, 94

Major skill clusters, 127–129
analysis of, 127–129
definition of, 127
documentation of, 129
example of, 129–130
program objective analysis, 222
Mastery criteria, 223–226
and amount of practice, 226
and complexity of skills, 225
and dangerous skills, 226
and level of functioning, 225–226
statement, purposes of, 224
Materials
meaning of, 227
and program objectives, 227–228
Meal preparation
inventory of food stock, 122
major skill clusters, 130
pathways of objectives for, 149
performance pattern in, 135–136, 141
prerequisite/lead-in skills, 147
seven day repeating menu, 133
terminal goals for, 104
Mental retardation
corollaries to definition of, 27–32
definition of, 26–27
learning capability, 27–28
societal perception of, 8
Middle school, priority skills, 203
Mission statement, 76–77
development of, 76–77
examples of, 78

Models, 254–255
animate models, 254
cautions in use of, 258
and functional instruction, 18–19
guidelines for use, 255–258
and imitation, 256–258
inanimate models, 254–255
Monitoring of instruction
for assessment information, 291–292
benefits of, 285
for comprehension of outcomes, 289–291
for comprehension of purpose, 288–289
with curriculum, 59
to determine learner progress, 287
for generalization of learning, 290–291
in instructional model, 24
and program objectives, 286–287, 289–290
rationale for, 287–292
for skill acquisition delays, 287–288
system for. *See* Monitoring system
Monitoring system
importance of, 293
issues to be addressed, 293, 296–297
procedure selection in, 297–300
recording results, 300–305
work sheet, 294–296
Motivation, 278–281
and aversives, 279–280
and instructional activity, 280–281
and learner search method, 264–265
learner variables, 281
and rewards, 279–280
Movie date, skill cluster analysis, 242

Natural conditions, assessment in, 159–160, 179–180
No news is good news (NNGN) as feedback on learning, 271–274
guidelines for use, 273–274

Objectives, program objectives, 209
Observation, assessment by, 179, 181–182, 192–193
Occurrence standards, 173, 175

Orthopedic problems/cerebral palsy, 368–369
signs of, 368
steps to take, 369
Outcome indicators, 95–105
as behavioral statements, 101
educable mental impairment example, 99–104
and grade groups, 104–105
importance of, 103–104
information source on, 94
outcome sequences, 100, 102
performance expectations, 99–101
for telephone book use, 103
for travel, 102, 107
use of, 100–101, 103–104
Outcome sequences, 100, 102

Pain, 370
signs of, 370
steps to take, 370
Pathways of objectives
assignment to instructional units, 148–149, 151–152
community referents, 148
examples of, 149–151
for financial management, 150–152
for meal preparation, 149
nature of, 47–48, 58–59
preparation of, 148
sequence variation, 148
sequencing of objectives, 146, 148
Performance confirmation, of learning, 271
Performance expectations, 99–101
for ability to travel, 101
and outcome indicators, 99–101
Performance standards and models, 257
in program objective analysis, 223
Personal maintenance, domains, 88, 91, 331–335
Physical guidance, 258–262
cautions in use of, 262
guidelines for use of, 259–262
to initiate activity performance, 262
for injury prevention, 261–262
for strategic physical support, 261
to teach behaviors, 259
for teaching cues, 259–261
Physical problems
auditory problems, 364–365
orthopedic problems/cerebral palsy, 368–369